Small Things in the Eighteenth Century

Offering an intimate history of how small things were used, handled, and worn, this collection shows how objects such as mugs and handkerchiefs were entangled with quotidian practices and rituals of bodily care. Small things, from tiny books to ceramic trinkets and toothpick cases, could delight and entertain, generating tactile pleasures for users while at the same time signaling the limits of the body's adeptness or the hand's dexterity. Simultaneously, the volume explores the striking mobility of small things: how fans, coins, rings, and pottery could, for instance, carry political, philosophical, and cultural concepts into circumscribed spaces. From the decorative and playful to the useful and performative, such small things as tea caddies, wampum beads, and drawings of ants negotiated larger political, cultural, and scientific shifts as they transported aesthetic and cultural practices across borders, via nationalist imagery, gift exchange, and the movement of global goods.

CHLOE WIGSTON SMITH is the author of *Women, Work, and Clothes in the Eighteenth-Century Novel* (2013) and editor, with Serena Dyer, of *Material Literacy in Eighteenth-Century Britain: A Nation of Makers* (2020). Her current research, supported by a British Academy fellowship, centers on material culture and the Atlantic world.

BETH FOWKES TOBIN, a recipient of National Endowment for the Humanities (NEH) and National Science Foundation (NSF) fellowships, is the author of *The Duchess's Shells: Natural History Collecting in the Age of Cook's Voyages* (2014), *Colonizing Nature: The Tropics in British Arts and Letters, 1760–1830* (2005), and *Picturing Imperial Power: Colonial Subjects in Eighteenth-Century British Painting* (1999).

Small Things in the Eighteenth Century

The Political and Personal Value of the Miniature

―――

Edited by

CHLOE WIGSTON SMITH
University of York

BETH FOWKES TOBIN
Arizona State University

Shaftesbury Road, Cambridge CB2 8EA, United Kingdom

One Liberty Plaza, 20th Floor, New York, NY 10006, USA

477 Williamstown Road, Port Melbourne, VIC 3207, Australia

314–321, 3rd Floor, Plot 3, Splendor Forum, Jasola District Centre, New Delhi – 110025, India

103 Penang Road, #05–06/07, Visioncrest Commercial, Singapore 238467

Cambridge University Press is part of Cambridge University Press & Assessment, a department of the University of Cambridge.

We share the University's mission to contribute to society through the pursuit of education, learning and research at the highest international levels of excellence.

www.cambridge.org
Information on this title: www.cambridge.org/9781108995078

DOI: 10.1017/9781108993296

© Cambridge University Press & Assessment 2022

This publication is in copyright. Subject to statutory exception and to the provisions of relevant collective licensing agreements, no reproduction of any part may take place without the written permission of Cambridge University Press & Assessment.

First published 2022
First paperback edition 2025

A catalogue record for this publication is available from the British Library

Library of Congress Cataloging-in-Publication data
Names: Smith, Chloe Wigston, editor. | Tobin, Beth Fowkes, editor.
Title: Small things in the eighteenth century : the political and personal value of the miniature / edited by Chloe Wigston Smith, University of York; Beth Fowkes Tobin, Arizona State University.
Description: Cambridge ; New York, NY : Cambridge University Press, 2022. | Includes bibliographical references and index.
Identifiers: LCCN 2022004100 | ISBN 9781108834452 (hardback) | ISBN 9781108993296 (ebook)
Subjects: LCSH: Miniature objects – Social aspects. | Material culture – Social aspects.
Classification: LCC NK8470 .S63 2022 | DDC 306.4/6–dc23/eng/20220611
LC record available at https://lccn.loc.gov/2022004100

ISBN   978-1-108-83445-2   Hardback
ISBN   978-1-108-99507-8   Paperback

Cambridge University Press & Assessment has no responsibility for the persistence or accuracy of URLs for external or third-party internet websites referred to in this publication and does not guarantee that any content on such websites is, or will remain, accurate or appropriate.

Contents

List of Figures   [*page* viii]
Notes on Contributors   [xii]
Acknowledgments   [xv]

Introduction: The Scale and Sense of Small Things   [1]
CHLOE WIGSTON SMITH AND BETH FOWKES TOBIN

PART I   READING SMALL THINGS

1 "The Sum of All in All": The Miniature Book and the Nature of Legibility   [15]
   ABIGAIL WILLIAMS

2 Nuts, Flies, Thimbles, and Thumbs: Eighteenth-Century Children's Literature and Scale   [31]
   KATHERINE WAKELY-MULRONEY

3 Gothic Syntax   [47]
   CYNTHIA WALL

4 Small, Familiar Things on Trial and on Stage   [64]
   CHLOE WIGSTON SMITH

PART II   SMALL THINGS IN TIME AND SPACE

5 On the Smallness of Numismatic Objects   [79]
   CRYSTAL B. LAKE

6 Crinoidal Limestone and Staffordshire Teapots: Material and Temporal Scales in Eighteenth-Century Britain   [95]
   KATE SMITH

7 "Joineriana": The Small Fragments and Parts of Eighteenth-Century Assemblages   [109]
   FREYA GOWRLEY

8 "Pray What a Pox Are Those Damned Strings
of Wampum?": British Understandings of Wampum
in the Eighteenth Century [125]
ROBBIE RICHARDSON

PART III   SMALL THINGS AT HAND

9 "We Bought a Guillotine Neatly Done in Bone":
Illicit Industries on Board British Prison Hulks,
1775–1815 [143]
ANNA MCKAY

10 "What Number?": Reform, Authority, and Identity in Late
Eighteenth-Century Military Buttons [158]
MATTHEW KEAGLE

11 Two Men's Leather Letter Cases: Mercantile Pride
and Hierarchies of Display [172]
PAULINE RUSHTON

12 The Aesthetic of Smallness: Chelsea Porcelain Seal Trinkets
and Britain's Global Gaze, 1750–1775 [187]
PATRICIA F. FERGUSON

13 "Small Gifts Foster Friendship": Hortense de Beauharnais,
Amateur Art, and the Politics of Exchange
in Postrevolutionary France [204]
MARINA KLIGER

PART IV   SMALL THINGS ON THE MOVE

14 Hooke's Ant [225]
TITA CHICO

15 Portable Patriotism: Britannia and Material Nationhood
in Miniature [240]
SERENA DYER

16 Revolutionary Histories in Small Things: Louis XVI
and Marie Antoinette on Printed Ceramics,
c. 1793–1796 [257]
CAROLINE MCCAFFREY-HOWARTH

17   A Box of Tea and the British Empire   [274]
ROMITA RAY

Afterword: A Thing's Perspective   [291]
HANNEKE GROOTENBOER

Select Bibliography   [295]
Index   [309]

Figures

1.1 William Moodie, *Old English, Scots and Irish Songs with Music* (Glasgow, 1890), The Bodleian Libraries, University of Oxford, Johnson g.315, 104 × 54 mm   [*page* 18]

1.2 Anacreon, Sappho, and Erinna, *Hai Tou Anakreontos Odai, Kai Ta Sapphous, Kai Erinnas Leipsana* (Edinburgh, 1766), The Bodleian Libraries, University of Oxford, Morton 120, H: 88 mm; W: 62 mm; D: 13 mm   [25]

1.3 Jeremiah Rich, *The Whole Book of Psalms in Meter. According to the Art of Short-Writing written by Jeremiah Rich, Author and Teacher of the Said Art* (London, 1659), The Bodleian Libraries, University of Oxford, Arch. A g.19 (1), 60 × 40 mm   [26]

3.1 Horace Walpole, *The Castle of Otranto: A Gothic Story*, 2nd ed. (London, 1765), 35. Albert and Shirley Small Special Collections Library, University of Virginia   [56]

6.1 Side view of white stoneware teapot and cover with enamel and salt glaze, Staffordshire, c. 1760. H.: 10.8 cm; Diam. (body): 10.5 cm; Diam. (handle-spout): 17.5 cm. Photo credit: Gavin Ashworth. © The Chipstone Foundation, Milwaukee, 1997.19.a–b   [97]

6.2 Teapot and cover, c. 1785. Creamware: 13 × 20 (with handle and spout) × 10 cm (diam). Photo credit: Gavin Ashworth. © The Chipstone Foundation, Milwaukee, 1995.1.a–b   [101]

6.3 View of base of white stoneware teapot with enamel and salt glaze, Staffordshire, c. 1760. H.: 10.8 cm; Diam. (body): 10.5 cm; Diam. (handle-spout): 17.5 cm. Photo credit: Gavin Ashworth. © The Chipstone Foundation, Milwaukee, 1997.19.a–b   [105]

7.1 View of the library window, Plas Newydd, Llangollen. Photograph, the author   [115]

7.2 Jane and Mary Parminter, Specimen table, Exmouth, Devon, 1790s. Glass, mineral, shell, paint, paper, and wood. 1312249, National Trust Collections, A la Ronde, Devon. © National Trust Images/James Dobson   [118]

7.3 Patchwork needle case, made from printed and woven fabrics, embroidered with a heart and the initials SC, and cut in half, made in c. 1767. Foundling 16516. © Coram   [123]

List of Figures

8.1 The Indians Giving a Talk to Colonel Bouquet in a conference at a Council Fire Near his Camp on the Banks of Muskingum in America, Benjamin West, c. 1765. Yale Center for British Art, Paul Mellon Collection, B1975.4.798   [134]

8.2 Tee Yee Neen Ho Ga Row, Emperour of the Six Nations, mezzotint by John Simon c. 1755, after Johannes Verelst, 1710. Yale Center for British Art, Paul Mellon Collection, B2001.2.1509   [136]

9.1 Domino box, watch stand, and straw work casket, AAA0002, AAA0004, AAA0005. © National Maritime Museum, Greenwich, London. Sutcliffe-Smith Collection   [147]

9.2 Convict-made objects recovered from the *Dromedary* hulk in Bermuda, 1824–1863. Photograph courtesy of the National Museum of Bermuda   [154]

10.1 British military buttons recovered at Fort Ticonderoga in the United States, 1768–1781. Fort Ticonderoga Museum Collection. Photo: Gavin Ashworth   [165]

11.1 Letter cases of John Bridge, 1750 (top), and Harold Hillam, 1767 (bottom). Photograph courtesy of National Museums Liverpool   [175]

11.2 Letter case of Hesketh Yarburgh, Bristol, 1738. Photograph courtesy of the Borthwick Institute for Archives, University of York   [184]

12.1 Two seal-trinkets of a dalmation and a cupid with dalmation, soft-paste porcelain, St. James's factory, c. 1751–1759, suspended from an équipage made by Daniel Marchand and Company, Hanau, Germany, c. 1762–1764, with a pocket watch by Jean Baptiste Baillon, c. 1755. Length 4.5 cm. BK-NM-11238. © Rijksmuseum, Amsterdam   [191]

12.2 Gilbert Ernest Bryant (1878–1965), watercolor, depicting twenty-four seal trinkets, reproduced in *The Chelsea Porcelain Toys* (London: Medici Society, 1925), Plate 38, 31 × 25 cm. Photograph, the author   [195]

12.3 Three seal trinkets, "Indian boy with handscreen," "Grotesque Punch," "Cupid disguised as an Eunuch," soft-paste porcelain, Charles Gouyn, proprietor, St. James's factory, London, c. 1751–1760. Height 3.75 cm and smaller [1887,0307,II.209 at 3.75 cm; 1887,0307,II.229 at 3 cm; 1887,0307,II.198 at 3.10 cm]. © Trustees of the British Museum, London   [199]

13.1 Hortense de Beauharnais, after Fleury Richard, *Madame de La Vallière Carmélite*, c. 1813–1824. Miniature mounted on a leather toothpick case. 3 × 2.5 cm (miniature), 9 × 3.8 cm (case). The collections of H.M. the King of Sweden, Stockholm. Inv. no. MR 526. © The Royal Court, Sweden, photo Lisa Raihle Rehbäck   [206]

List of Figures

13.2 Jean Urbain Guerin, *Portrait of Queen Hortense*, c. 1804–1814. Miniature on ivory mounted in a silver pendant framed with diamonds and backed with an arrangement of hair. 3.5 × 2.5 cm. Musée du Louvre, Paris. RF 30721. © RMN-Grand Palais / Art Resource, NY   [216]

13.3 Hortense de Beauharnais, *View of Lake Geneva at Prégny*, 1815. Watercolor and graphite on paper. 50 × 68 cm. Musée national des châteaux de Malmaison et Bois-Préau, Rueil-Malmaison. M.M.47.7060. © RMN-Grand Palais / Art Resource, NY   [218]

15.1 Enameled box depicting Britannia, 1789, Metropolitan Museum of Art, 26.33.4   [246]

15.2 Unmounted fan leaf depicting The United Sisters, 1801, 1891,0713.391. © The Trustees of the British Museum   [250]

15.3 Unmounted fan leaf mourning the death of Admiral Rodney, 1792, 1891,0713.386. © The Trustees of the British Museum   [253]

16.1 Mug with *The Last Interview*, c. 1793–1795, perhaps Liverpool, creamware, transfer printed in black, h. 14.9 cm. © British Museum   [263]

16.2 Mug with a guillotine scene, c. 1793–1795, John Aynsley, Lane End, Staffordshire, creamware, transfer printed in black, h. 12 cm. © British Museum   [265]

16.3 Mug with a guillotine scene, c. 1793–1796, previously thought to be Cambrian pottery, Swansea, but probably Staffordshire, transfer printed in black underglaze, h. 8.7 cm. © British Museum   [268]

16.4 Jug with a guillotine scene, c. 1793–1795, perhaps Liverpool, transfer printed in red, Henry Willett esq. Collection, Royal Pavilion & Museums, Brighton & Hove   [270]

17.1 Unknown maker, Tea Caddy, wood with tortoiseshell and mother-of-pearl knobs, 1800–1840, gift of Dr. and Mrs. Eugene R. Smith, Syracuse University Art Museum, 1969.1651   [275]

17.2 Unknown Chinese artist, *Tea Production in China*, 1790–1820, oil on canvas, H: 143 cm, W: 205 cm, Peabody Essex Museum, M25794, Museum purchase with funds donated anonymously, 1993   [280]

17.3 Trade card, "Arnaud & Green Late Blakistons, Grocers & Tea Dealers No. 29. Strand," etching, 1792–1799. © The Trustees of the British Museum, Heal, 68.4   [283]

17.4 Frontispiece, John Ellis, *Directions for Bringing over Seeds and Plants, from the East-Indies and Other Distant Countries, in A State of Vegetation: Together with a Catalogue of Such Foreign Plants as are Worthy of being Encouraged in our American Colonies, for the Purposes of Medicine, Agriculture, and Commerce, to Which is Added the Figure and Botanical Description of a New Sensitive Plant, called Dionæa Muscipula: or, Venus's Fly-Trap* (London, 1770). © Dumbarton Oaks Research Library and Collection, Rare Book Collection, Trustees for Harvard University, Washington, DC   [287]

Notes on Contributors

TITA CHICO is Professor of English at the University of Maryland. She is the author of *The Experimental Imagination: Literary Knowledge and Science in the British Enlightenment* and *Designing Women: The Dressing Room in Eighteenth-Century English Literature and Culture*, and co-editor of *Atlantic Worlds in the Long Eighteenth Century: Seduction and Sentiment*. Her next book, *Wonder: Literature and Science in the Long Eighteenth Century*, is forthcoming from Cambridge University Press.

SERENA DYER is Lecturer in History of Design and Material Culture at De Montfort University. She is the author of *Material Lives: Women Makers and Consumer Culture in the Eighteenth Century* and co-editor of *Material Literacy in Eighteenth-Century Britain: A Nation of Makers*.

PATRICIA F. FERGUSON, Hon. Adviser on Ceramics to the National Trust, has worked as a curator at the British Museum and the Victoria and Albert Museum. She is the author of *Ceramics: 400 Years of British Collecting in 100 Masterpieces* and editor of *Pots, Prints and Politics: Ceramics with an Agenda, from the 14th to the 20th Century*.

FREYA GOWRLEY is Lecturer in History of Art and Liberal Arts at the University of Bristol. She is the author of *Domestic Space in Britain, 1750–1840: Materiality, Sociability and Emotion*.

HANNEKE GROOTENBOER is Professor of History of Art at Radboud University. She is the author of *Rhetoric of Perspective: Realism and Illusionism in Seventeenth-Century Dutch Still Life Painting*; *Treasuring the Gaze: Intimacy and Extremity of Vision Eye Miniature Portraits*; and *The Pensive Image: Art as a Form of Thinking*, as well as co-author of *Conchophilia: Shells, Art, and Curiosity in Early Modern Europe*.

MATTHEW KEAGLE is Curator of Collections at Fort Ticonderoga and completed his PhD at the Bard Graduate Center. He has researched and spoken widely on both sides of the Atlantic on early modern military material culture with a focus on military dress.

MARINA KLIGER is the Eugene V. Thaw Fellow for Collections Cataloguing at the Metropolitan Museum of Art. She completed her PhD at the Institute of Fine Arts, New York University.

CRYSTAL B. LAKE is Professor of English at Wright State University and a co-editor of the-rambling.com. She is the author of *Artifacts: How We Think and Write about Found Objects* and co-leader of the NEH-funded *Vetusta Monumenta* digital project.

CAROLINE MCCAFFREY-HOWARTH is an art and design historian specializing in decorative arts, material culture, and the history of collecting. She is Lecturer in 18th and 19th Century Visual and Material Culture at the University of Edinburgh and Visiting Research Fellow at the University of Leeds. She was previously Curator of Ceramics 1600–1800 at the V&A Museum.

ANNA MCKAY is a Government of Ireland Postdoctoral Fellow at University College Cork. She completed her PhD at the University of Leicester and the National Maritime Museum, Greenwich. Her research focuses on confinement and the British maritime world.

ROMITA RAY is Associate Professor of Art History at Syracuse University. She is the author of *Under the Banyan Tree: Relocating the Picturesque in British India* and co-editor of the forthcoming four-volume collection *Empire and Cultural Change: Visual Arts, Film, and Architecture*. She is currently working on a book on tea, tentatively titled *Leafy Wonders: Art, Aesthetics, and the Science of Tea in India*.

ROBBIE RICHARDSON is Assistant Professor of English at Princeton University and previously Senior Lecturer at the University of Kent. He is the author of *The Savage and Modern Self: North American Indians in Eighteenth-Century Literature and Culture*. He is a member of Pabineau First Nation in New Brunswick, Canada.

PAULINE RUSHTON is Head of Decorative Arts and Sudley House, the former home of merchant family the Holts, at National Museums Liverpool. Since 2012, she has been on the board of Eighteenth-Century Worlds, an interdisciplinary research center at the University of Liverpool, and contributes to their undergraduate teaching.

CHLOE WIGSTON SMITH is Senior Lecturer in the Department of English and Related Literature and the Centre for Eighteenth Century Studies at the University of York. She is the author of *Women, Work, and Clothes in the Eighteenth-Century Novel* and co-editor of *Material Literacy in Eighteenth-Century Britain: A Nation of Makers*.

KATE SMITH is Associate Professor in Eighteenth-Century History at the University of Birmingham. She is the author of *Material Goods, Moving Hands: Perceiving Production in England, 1700–1830* and co-editor of *British Women and Cultural Practices of Empire, 1770–1940*; *The East India Company at Home, 1757–1857*; and *New Paths to Public Histories: Collaborative Strategies for Uncovering Britain's Colonial Past*.

BETH FOWKES TOBIN, Professor Emerita, Department of English, Arizona State University, is the author of four monographs, most recently *The Duchess's Shells: Natural History Collecting in the Age of Cook's Voyages*. She is also co-editor of four books on material culture, including *Women and Things, 1750–1950: Gendered Material Strategies*; *Women and the Material Culture of Needlework and Textiles, 1750–1950*; and *Material Women, 1750–1950: Consuming Desires and Collecting Practices*.

KATHERINE WAKELY-MULRONEY is Assistant Professor of English at Nanyang Technological University. She is the author of several articles and chapters on children's literature in the eighteenth century and co-editor of *The Aesthetics of Children's Poetry: A Study of Children's Verse in English*.

CYNTHIA WALL is the William R. Kenan, Jr. Professor of English at the University of Virginia. She is the author of *Grammars of Approach: Landscape, Narrative, and the Linguistic Picturesque*; *The Prose of Things: Transformations of Description in the Eighteenth Century*; and *The Literary and Cultural Spaces of Restoration London*. She also co-edited *The Eighteenth Centuries: Global Networks of Enlightenment* and *Eighteenth-Century Genre and Culture: Serious Reflections on Occasional Forms*.

ABIGAIL WILLIAMS is Professor of English Literature and Lord White Tutorial Fellow, St. Peter's College, University of Oxford. She is the author of *The Social Life of Books: Reading Together in the Eighteenth-Century Home* and *Poetry and the Creation of a Whig Literary Culture 1681–1714*. She has also edited Jonathan Swift's *Journal to Stella* and led the *Digital Miscellanies Index* project. She is currently completing *Reading it Wrong*, a study of misreading in eighteenth-century literature.

Acknowledgments

Together we wish to acknowledge the support of the British Academy and the Centre for Eighteenth Century Studies and Department of English and Related Literature at the University of York, which each provided vital funding for a June 2019 conference on the theme of "Small Things in the Eighteenth Century." We thank the speakers, keynotes, and delegates who made that conference a joy to organize and host, and we remember, with fondness, the event as modeling the best of academic exchange and the possibilities of generosity and reciprocity between generations and disciplines. Since that conference, our plans for this volume have grown and shifted in response to those conversations, and we thank the hard work (and good cheer) of our contributors for making the collection what it is today. We are grateful for their time, thoughts, and reflections over the past two years in which big things disturbed, distressed, and distanced us in unrelenting ways. Hanneke Grootenboer offered her meaningful and well-timed support of the project. We were fortunate to receive additional funds from the Department of English and Related Literature at York and its F. R. Leavis Fund for the final preparation of the manuscript. We thank Puck Fletcher for the keenest editorial eye.

We remain enormously grateful to Bethany Thomas at Cambridge University Press for her curiosity about small things from the very start and also to our anonymous readers for their enthusiasm for our topic and their careful and attentive feedback. At Cambridge University Press, we are also grateful for the help of George Paul Laver and Bethany Johnson. We thank each other and our families, for the countless, small ways in which they helped (in both deliberate and inadvertent ways) to make a large volume like this a reality.

Introduction

The Scale and Sense of Small Things

CHLOE WIGSTON SMITH AND BETH FOWKES TOBIN

Look around you. You may be seated at a desk or in a comfortable reading chair. No matter your position, there is bound to be something small in view or at hand. A paperclip. A reminder on a scrap of paper. The watch on your wrist. A pencil. A rubber band. A stray thread, a coin, or wisp of lint sheltered in your pocket. A piece of Lego underfoot, a USB key, or smartphone. This preliminary list of the small things that linger and lurk in our surroundings will inevitably remain incomplete and so we invite you to note the small things within your grasp and within sight. Now as in the eighteenth century, small things were here, there, and everywhere, from the pins that fell between wooden floorboards to the clumps of sugar spooned into tea. Small things were displayed on dressing tables and in curio cabinets, tucked in pockets, nestled in palms, and talked about. It's our contention in this collection that small things are all too frequently overlooked but that they were ubiquitous features of eighteenth-century life, significant enough to the authors, artisans, merchants, settlers, printers, and thieves who made them, sought them out, and debated their meanings.

This collection brings together a multidisciplinary group of scholars to think through the relations between scale and material culture in the eighteenth century in a collective effort to make small things appear not merely as self-evident artifacts of daily life but to grapple with the full contours of their intimate and political complexities. Our contributors attend to an expansive range of diminutive items that circulated in the period, some miniature versions of larger things and others merely small. In chapters that examine the range of social and material functions of small things, from the decorative and playful to the useful and performative, our collection illuminates the variety of purposes, from the personal to the political, and beyond, that small things fulfilled in eighteenth-century life. Some small things were designed to facilitate conversation and sociability and to perform as objects of inquiry and discussion. Other small things were created for private use, to be held and cherished by individuals, away from the public eye. Our contributors consider how small things helped individuals negotiate larger political, cultural, and scientific shifts.

Small things, we contend, came in many forms and shapes, but their small scale frequently demanded additional scrutiny, nimbleness, and concentration to apprehend and handle. Throughout, our collection pays close attention to the rich interaction between scale and the body. Small things could delight and entertain, but they could equally signal the limits of the body's adeptness or the hand's dexterity. Some small things were sources of tactile pleasure, while others skewed towards haptic frustration. Tiny books challenge fingers with pages too small to be turned with ease, with print too minute to read without difficulty. Some small things were used to achieve mundane and familiar goals, from drinking tea to securing the closure of a coat, all the while providing haptic and visual pleasure if designed well and frustration if not. Our contributors return to how small things made sensory claims on their users, concentrating visual perception on the details of their surfaces and intricacies of construction, or obliging fingers and hands to proceed with deliberate care.[1] Not all small things were expensive or even cherished in the eighteenth century, but many of them survive in museum collections thanks to their ubiquity, their durability, or the endearing qualities that ensured their preservation.

We have chosen to use the word "thing" instead of object in keeping with Jane Bennett's and Bruno Latour's formulations that stress the liveliness of things and the agency of nonhuman subjects. Because things possess the capacity for forming assemblages with each other and with humans, the resultant entanglements, Latour contends, cannot be explained effectively with "those obsolete figures of object and subject."[2] Likewise, Bennett argues that the term thing "has advantages over 'object,' in its refusal of Western philosophy's subject/object divide," or, in her words, "active (American, manly) subjects and passive objects." The world, she argues, is not filled with passive objects; it is "populated by materially diverse, lively

---

[1] Our interest in the links between small things and the body contrasts, for instance, with the approach of Peter Stallybrass and Ann Rosalind Jones to the movement of "detachable parts—rings, jewels, gloves, for instance" in the early modern period, in "Fetishizing the Glove in Renaissance Europe," *Critical Inquiry*, 28.1 (2001), 114–132 (116).

[2] Bruno Latour, "Factures/Fractures: From the Concept of Network to the Concept of Attachment," *Res: Anthropology and Aesthetics*, 36 (1999), 20–32 (22). See also Bill Brown's differentiation between things and objects: "We begin to confront the thingness of objects when they stop working for us": "Thing Theory," *Critical Inquiry*, 28.1 (2001), 1–22 (4). Brown's insight here owes something to Latour's "Mixing Humans and Nonhumans Together: The Sociology of a Door-Closer," *Social Problems*, 35.3 (1988), 298–310, an article Latour published under the pseudonym Jim Johnson, and Latour's "The Berlin Key or How to Do Words with Things" in P. M. Graves-Brown (ed.), *Matter, Materiality, and Modern Culture* (London: Routledge, 2000), 10–21.

bodies," such as an electrical grid, rotting garbage and dead rats, the minerals that reside in our bones and move when we do – things she ponders in her book *Vibrant Matter*. Because we humans live in a material world, "things—what is special about them given their sensuous specificity, their particular material configuration and their distinctive, idiosyncratic history—matter a lot."[3] Clearly, we agree that things matter a lot, and our contributors pay close attention to the sensuous specificity, material configuration, and idiosyncratic history of a few of the millions of small things that made up eighteenth-century material culture.

Our approach to studying things is to focus on "relationality," Bennett's word for the "complex system of relations" that structure our interactions with things. Unlike the object-oriented ontology espoused by Graham Harman and Timothy Morton, we are interested in how people interact with things, in particular how their thoughts and actions are shaped by the small things that surround them.[4] To achieve this goal, what our contributors have done is "to put the things in the foreground and the people in the background," a method that Bennett says is "really hard to do."[5] Our approach to small things attends to how scale demands our attention and time: many small items test our abilities to handle, see, and spot them. To explore how we relate to the material world, we think that description is our best tool. Description, too often modified with the word "mere," may seem toothless and naive, but to describe well, according to Latour, is extremely challenging. In a playful Platonic dialogue, he defends the rigors of description: "To describe: to be attentive to the concrete states of affairs, to find the uniquely adequate account of a given situation, I have, myself, always found this incredibly demanding."[6] Rather than generating ideas a priori about the things under our investigation, we embrace curatorial protocols and other empiricist practices, such as going into the archives to be in the presence of the fans, leather wallets, and miniature bibles under discussion, so that we may experience them and their affordances and constraints. In sum, small things assert their thingness by demanding our time and attention.

---

[3] Jane Bennett, "Systems and Things: A Response to Graham Harman and Timothy Morton," *New Literary History*, 43.2 (2012), 225–233 (231).
[4] Ibid., 226.
[5] Jane Bennett, "Power of the Hoard: Artistry and Agency in a World of Vibrant Matter" (lecture, The New School, New York, September 27, 2011, www.youtube.com/watch?v=q607Ni23QjA, accessed April 5, 2021).
[6] Bruno Latour, "On Using ANT for Studying Information Systems: A Somewhat (Socratic) Dialogue" in Chrisanthi Avgerou, Claudio Ciborra, and Frank Land (eds.), *The Social Study of Information and Communication Technology: Innovation, Actors, and Contexts* (Oxford: Oxford University Press, 2004), 62–76 (64–65).

Of course, this is not the first book to call attention to the significance, and palpable presence, of the small in scale: our contributors draw on the influential work of James Deetz, Susan Stewart, and Melinda Alliker Rabb to frame and understand the familiarity, craftsmanship, and imaginative worlds of small things, or what Rabb evocatively describes as a collective "fascination with downsizing" in the period.[7] Our attention to scale makes additional room for the diminutive, from the miniature to the simply small. Miniatures, of course, have drawn their fair share of attention (for good reason), but many of our small things were tiny in and of themselves and designed for utilitarian purposes, as opposed to the scaled-down miniatures that captivate Susan Stewart as "emblematic of craft and discipline." Stewart goes on to identify "the essential *theatricality* of all miniatures" that resides in their "representative quality."[8] Our authors take up small things that perform narratives of nationhood, empire, and political and personal drama, but they also engage with commonplace and practical items, where small size was essential to their use and circulation. In this, several chapters defy some scholarly attempts to equate the small scale with the beautiful.[9] Our collection, as a result, celebrates unassuming small things such as plain leather cases, mended patchwork, and buttons, alongside finely decorated toothpick cases, rings, and teapots.

Several contributors underscore the fact that the small things they study have been ignored by curators and researchers in museums and in the academy, for a range of reasons. The functions some of these objects performed were viewed as too ordinary or vulgar to merit sustained study. The very ubiquity, and presumed insignificance, of buttons, for instance, has lessened their appeal for critical analysis and historical recovery. Other

---

[7] James Deetz, *Small Things Forgotten: An Archaeology of Early American Life* (1977; New York: Doubleday, 1996); Susan Stewart, *On Longing: Narratives of the Miniature, the Gigantic, the Souvenir, the Collection* (Durham, NC: Duke University Press, 1993); Melinda Alliker Rabb, *Miniature and the English Imagination: Literature, Cognition, and Small-Scale Culture, 1650–1765* (Cambridge: Cambridge University Press, 2019), 2. See also Sara Pennell, "Mundane Materiality, or Should Small Things Still Be Forgotten? Material Culture, Micro-Histories and the Problem of Scale" in Karen Harvey (ed.), *History and Material Culture: A Student's Guide to Approaching Alternative Sources* (London: Routledge, 2009), 173–191; Chloe Wigston Smith, "Bodkin Aesthetics: Small Things in the Eighteenth Century," *Eighteenth-Century Fiction*, 31.2 (2019), 271–294; James Walvin, *Slavery in Small Things: Slavery and Modern Cultural Habits* (Chichester: Wiley Blackwell, 2017).

[8] Stewart, *On Longing*, 38, 54.

[9] See, for instance, Sidney R. Nagel, who in contemplating the views offered by the telescope, finds himself "seduced by the shape of objects on small scale," stating that "these smaller objects [are] of an equal if a more delicate beauty," in "Shadows and Ephemera," *Critical Inquiry*, 28.1 (2001), 23–39 (29).

things may have seemed unworthy because their materials were deemed inferior. The absence of leather cases from museum displays, for instance, can be explained by leather ranking low on the hierarchy of materials for the decorative arts, in contrast to gold, silver, gems, and other precious materials. Smallness itself can lead to being overlooked: small things slip through our hands too quickly and land out of sight and out of mind. They bear the signs of rough handling, their torn, broken, and worn surfaces disclosing the challenges they present to human dexterity.

The small things under consideration in this volume were products of eighteenth-century Europe's burgeoning manufacturing sector and the rise of consumer culture. In their engagements with material culture studies, our contributors describe the production, distribution, and consumption of objects as well as explore their social and cultural significance. Combining the attention that Jules David Prown pays to ordinary objects, and how they were made and used, with more recent approaches to materiality, such as those employed by Lynn Festa, Pamela H. Smith, and Michael Yonan, our contributors examine the agentic capacities of small things.[10] While the study of material culture has long been the purview of anthropology, archeology, and museum studies, the past fifteen years have seen interest in materiality permeate the fields of art history, literary studies, history of science, feminist studies, and social, cultural, and economic history, as made evident by the increase in studies that focus on objects and their biographies, trajectories, affects, and impacts.[11] At the same time, several major historical object studies have focused on the global scale of the production, exchange, and consumption of particular objects in a subset of

---

[10] Jules David Prown, "The Truth of Material Culture: History or Fiction?" in Jules David Prown and Kenneth Haltman (eds.), *American Artifacts: Essays in Material Culture* (East Lansing: Michigan State University Press, 2000), 11–29; Lynn Festa, *Fiction without Humanity: Person, Animal, Thing in Early Enlightenment Literature and Culture* (Philadelphia: University of Pennsylvania Press, 2019) and "Personal Effects: Wigs and Possessive Individualism in the Long Eighteenth Century," *Eighteenth-Century Life*, 29.2 (2005), 47–90; Pamela H. Smith, Amy R. W. Meyers, and Harold J. Cook (eds.), *Ways of Making and Knowing: The Material Culture of Empirical Knowledge* (New York and Ann Arbor: Bard Graduate Center/University of Michigan Press, 2014); Pamela H. Smith, *From Lived Experience to the Written Word: Reconstructing Practical Knowledge in Early Modern Europe* (Chicago, IL: University of Chicago Press, forthcoming); Michael Yonan, "Toward a Fusion of Art History and Material Culture Studies," *West 86th: A Journal of Decorative Arts, Design History, and Material Culture*, 18.2 (2011), 232–248. See also the double special issue, "Material Fictions," ed. Michael Yonan and Eugenia Zuroski, *Eighteenth-Century Fiction*, 31/32 (2018/2019).

[11] See, for instance, Fiona Candlin and Raiford Guins (eds.), *The Object Reader* (New York: Routledge, 2009); and Chris Tilly (ed.), *The Handbook of Material Culture* (London: Sage, 2006); Ileana Baird and Christina Ionescu, *Eighteenth-Century Thing Theory in a Global Context: From Consumerism to Celebrity Culture* (Farnham: Ashgate, 2013).

histories of single commodities, such as salt, silk, sugar, tea, and cotton.[12] In contrast to these histories of commodity production and consumption, our collection offers a more intimate history of how small things were used, handled, and worn: how they were entangled with quotidian practices and rituals of bodily care; how they produced meaning within circumscribed spheres of social exchange, carrying into these spaces political, philosophical, and cultural concepts on their surfaces; and how they were shaped by and contributed to empire and Enlightenment systems of knowledge production. Our contributors demonstrate how small things of seeming unimportance were embedded in daily life and, as such, formed meaningful alliances with those who possessed them. At the same time, as our contributors show, small things were frequently on the move, transporting aesthetics, ideas, and knowledge across geographic borders. Small things slid into domestic and private spaces with ease, carrying with them messages from the world beyond. The imagery displayed on the surfaces of small domestic ceramics designed for use in ordinary daily life could reference substantial, political events at home and abroad. Our contributors cover not only the compression of information and the portability of aesthetics but also how small things were connected with vast geographic distance and embedded in the trade routes of saltwater slavery and empire building. While our collection mostly focuses on eighteenth-century Europe, our chapters show the geographic reach and global circulation of small things.

We have organized our seventeen chapters into four parts that together address the size, composition, handling, and circulation of small things. The first part, "Reading Small Things," focuses attention on how individuals read and interpreted small things, and how scale facilitated and, sometimes, impeded access to the small scaled, such as books, typographical marks, and personal possessions. Tiny books, some meant for children and others exquisitely crafted as precious objects, compelled fingers to adjust to their small pages and demanded a range of viewing habits. As Abigail

---

[12] Mark Kurlansky, *Salt: A World History* (London: Vintage, 2003); Ben Marsh, *Unravelled Dreams: Silk and the Atlantic World, 1500–1840* (Cambridge: Cambridge University Press, 2020); Sidney W. Mintz, *Sweetness and Power: The Place of Sugar in Modern History* (New York: Penguin, 1985); Markman Ellis, Richard Coulton, and Matthew Mauger, *Empire of Tea: The Asian Leaf That Conquered the World* (London: Reaktion, 2015); Giorgio Riello, *Cotton: The Fabric That Made the Modern World* (Cambridge: Cambridge University Press, 2013). See also Frank Trentmann, *Empire of Things: How We Became a World of Consumers, from the Fifteenth Century to the Twenty-First* (New York: Harper, 2016); and Anne Gerritsen and Giorgio Riello (eds.), *The Global Lives of Things: The Material Culture of Connections in the Early Modern World* (New York: Routledge, 2016).

Williams discusses in "'The Sum of All in All': The Miniature Book and the Nature of Legibility" (Chapter 1) many small books challenge dexterity and impede legibility. Studying the tensions that emerge between scale and ease of use, Williams concludes that these eighteenth-century miniature books are full of paradoxes that render them both legible and illegible. On the other hand, small children's books, which Katherine Wakely-Mulroney examines in "Nuts, Flies, Thimbles, and Thumbs: Eighteenth-Century Children's Literature and Scale" (Chapter 2), lay the foundations for literacy. Wakely-Mulroney studies how the linguistic simplicity of small books for children coincided with their thematic complexity and formal intricacy. Examining the relations between legibility and visual typography in "Gothic Syntax" (Chapter 3), Cynthia Wall explores the effects of small changes in punctuation in *The Castle of Otranto*'s various editions to trace how the tiny marks of syntax shape what readers see and comprehend. In her chapter, "Small, Familiar Things on Trial and on Stage" (Chapter 4), Chloe Wigston Smith turns to the visible affordances that made small possessions remarkable to their owners, by looking at descriptions of marks, mending, initials, and other memorable details in the Old Bailey Trials and John Gay's *The Beggar's Opera* (1728). Stolen items, such as buttons, thimbles, coins, and innumerable other small things, were familiar but loved, and efforts to recoup them – or to strip them of identifying marks – evoke the ways in which Georgian Britons paid careful attention to the personal markers that differentiated one small thing from another. These chapters together address both the challenges and rewards of using, seeing, and reading small things, conjuring the complex imaginative and haptic interplay between scale and understanding.

Our second part, "Small Things in Time and Space," gathers chapters that explore the relations between time and the material composition of small things in order to uncover how these items reach backwards and forwards to national histories, geological time, personal memories, and political negotiations. In "On the Smallness of Numismatic Objects" (Chapter 5), Crystal B. Lake traces the celebration of the smallness of old coins and medals in numismatic writing that sought to draw the connections between metal things and the distant past as well as the memories and imaginations of their collectors. Yet antiquarians and collectors simultaneously worried about the material decay of numismatic things, even as they prized their durability and littleness. As Lake shows, for antiquarians the small scale of coins and medals remained key to their proliferation and variety, and to their deep embeddedness in history. The distant past is also visualized in the bits and pieces of fossils painted onto the surfaces of the teapots that form the focus of Kate Smith's "Crinoidal Limestone and Staffordshire Teapots: Material and Temporal Scales in Eighteenth-Century Britain" (Chapter 6). These fossil fragments, as she shows, unsettled commonly accepted notions about biblical time and the age of the Earth, extending geological time well beyond the human as the subject of history. Assemblages of small fragments, both textual and material, can also carry histories that are private and personal: the subject of Freya Gowrley's "'Joineriana': The Small Fragments and Parts of Eighteenth-Century Assemblages" (Chapter 7). For Gowrley, these material assemblages, whether botanical collages, decorative tables, or textile patchworks, record personal histories of emotion and loss, calling attention to the intersections between scale and ephemerality. Moving from the personal to the political, Robbie Richardson's "'Pray What a Pox Are Those Damned *Strings of Wampum*?': British Understandings of Wampum in the Eighteenth Century" (Chapter 8) looks at wampum belts crafted of tiny shell beads by Indigenous peoples of northeastern North America as "an important form of literacy and cultural memory." Richardson traces how wampum performed a complex range of political and personal functions, its patterns of tiny beads serving diverse uses in treaty negotiations, cultural and ceremonial records, memory keeping, and personal ornamentation. British collectors of wampum, however, frequently struggled to understand how these tiny beads could perform such complex functions. As the chapters in this section address, the practice of collecting or assembling small things – coins, shells, fossils, and wampum – to form larger wholes could yield both comprehension and misunderstanding, raising nagging questions about the unstable materials and meanings of small things.

The third part, "Small Things at Hand," focuses on how the hand encounters and manipulates the materiality of minute things: buttons, wallets, ceramic toys, trinkets, all items handheld or worn on the body. In addition to attending to the manipulation of materials – metal, leather, ceramic, paper, or bone – as well as to the interactive nature of small things, this section traces how these items carried with them and on their surfaces images, numbers, and words that spoke of political conflict. Anna McKay's "'We Bought a Guillotine Neatly Done in Bone': Illicit Industries on Board British Prison Hulks, 1775–1815" (Chapter 9) addresses the small crafts made by British convicts and French prisoners of war, held on British hulk ships in locations such as Portsmouth and Bermuda. Prisoners scavenged or bartered for bone, straw, copper sheathing, and wood chips to make crafts to trade and sell, finding in this process a modicum of meaning. Small things, despite their diminutive size and quotidian nature, were laden with imagery that referenced conflict within nations and beyond, a theme also evoked by Matthew Keagle in "'What Number?': Reform, Authority, and Identity in Late Eighteenth-Century Military Buttons" (Chapter 10). Bearing regimental numbers, buttons worn by soldiers register the nearly constant warfare between Britain and France as these two nations strove for global dominance. In changes to the designs and markings of these small buttons, Keagle finds evidence of the attempts of state bureaucracies to rationalize their militaries in their efforts to modernize their armies. The following three chapters each connect the material composition of small things to their owners' personal and social relations, starting with Pauline Rushton in "Two Men's Leather Letter Cases: Mercantile Pride and Hierarchies of Display" (Chapter 11). Rushton studies the leather wallets that Liverpool merchants carried on their person to signal their prosperity, the origins of which she traces to the direct and indirect involvement of these merchants in the enslavement of Africans and Caribbean plantation economies. In a similar vein, Patricia F. Ferguson, in "The Aesthetic of Smallness: Chelsea Porcelain Seal Trinkets and Britain's Global Gaze, 1750–1775" (Chapter 12), turns to porcelain seal trinkets, designed to be worn or carried around the body on fobs and chains, which reference the exotic and global trade in human bodies. These pocket-sized ceramic toys, as Ferguson notes, were manufactured for personal amusement and made for novel gifts, but these handheld figurines also turned imagery of global commerce, empire, and slavery into a disquieting form of tactile entertainment for consumers. In her "'Small Gifts Foster Friendship': Hortense de Beauharnais, Amateur Art, and the Politics of Exchange in Postrevolutionary France" (Chapter 13), Marina Kliger studies the elegant and carefully wrought gifts sent by Napoleon's sister-in-law to her confidantes. Kliger zeroes in on a toothpick case Queen Hortense made for her brother to show how a careful study of its materials and design yields insights into the strategic social practice of elaborate gift exchanges that relied on elite networks to negotiate dwindling power and declining status.

Our fourth part, "Small Things on the Move," concerns the multiple forms of aesthetic and physical movement that potentially adhere to small things. Their small scale meant they could be easily carried from room to room, on the person and in pockets, and also across borders. In "Hooke's Ant" (Chapter 14), Tita Chico opens this section by drawing attention to how one tiny insect resisted the microscope's scrutiny as it crawled about on the slide, refusing the coherence of scientific clarity. Chico explains how Hooke associated the unruly ant with the colonial economy of enslaved Africans in Barbados by alluding to Richard Ligon's

A True and Exact History of the Island of Barbadoes (1657). For Chico, the small ant contains multitudes, pointing to Britain's global reach and the enforced movement of persons within its empire. Serena Dyer, in "Portable Patriotism: Britannia and Material Nationhood in Miniature" (Chapter 15), attends also to the large-scale national ambitions embedded in small, portable things. Political work around questions of nationhood and patriotism was carried out by seemingly frivolous accessories – rings, fans, and snuffboxes – decorated with images of Britannia. For Dyer, these small Britannias performed patriotism through designs that responded to political events and helped to negotiate national feeling. Caroline McCaffrey-Howarth, in "Revolutionary Histories in Small Things: Louis XVI and Marie Antoinette on Printed Ceramics, c. 1793–1796" (Chapter 16), turns to the geographic and aesthetic movement of political imagery, by looking at small, creamware ale mugs and jugs that scaled down engraved prints of the most infamous events of the French Revolution for British consumers. Decorated with political imagery – including scenes of execution, of guillotines and their victims – these ceramics, McCaffrey-Howarth uncovers, brought controversial conversations about the monarchy and nation-state into the home and tavern. In this part's final chapter, Romita Ray illuminates in "A Box of Tea and the British Empire" (Chapter 17) how tea and its paraphernalia were among the most mobile of small things that circulated within the British imperial economy. Ray surveys the porcelain teapots, cups, and sugar bowls, the silver trays and teaspoons, the delicate mahogany tea tables, and the sturdy wooden tea caddies that protected the precious cargo as it travelled across the globe. Tracing the movement of tea caddies and the boxes that brought Britons and others their tea, Ray argues that tea things are paradigmatic of the mobility and movement of bodies and things across maritime spaces. Finally, in Hanneke Grootenboer's Afterword, small, unassuming things, such as a hazelnut strung on a necklace, show how ordinary and ubiquitous things embed themselves in our lives, entangling their materiality with ours in powerful but largely unrecognized ways.

Together, our contributors have assembled a series of intricate snapshots of the variety of small things that populated domestic and political life and were circulated through vast trade routes. While Parts I–IV group together similar items or the shared usages of small things, several themes recur across chapters: the ubiquity of small things to both ordinary life and extraordinary events; their presence in domestic settings and political spaces; their commemorative and emotional resonances; the way that their scale marries up with their movements between people and geographies. Despite the variety of possessions and products documented here, no single collection could comprehend the full range of small things to be handled, purchased, traded, stolen, described, and read about in the eighteenth century. We anticipate that some small things from the period will curb our attempts at comprehensiveness, just as our starting point from your surroundings will both meet and miss small things particular to you, but these inevitable gaps lead us toward a world of small things in eighteenth-century print, material, and visual culture, bringing these things closer to our intellectual and imaginative reach.

PART I

Reading Small Things

1   "The Sum of All in All"

The Miniature Book and the Nature of Legibility

ABIGAIL WILLIAMS

"Though the Volume and the Work be smal, / Yet it containes the sum of All in All." So runs the preface to a mid-seventeenth century edition of *Verbum Sempiternum*, a miniaturized devotional work.[1] In these lines, the size of the book frames a tension between human and divine scale. Smallness is made to articulate ontological implications, showing how a human form might attempt to comprehend a limitless divine reality. And in doing so, the book demonstrates the way in which miniature texts of the eighteenth century played with the idea of a large subject in small form. Like many other works in this format, it also tests its own utility: it is a book that is both essential yet almost impossible to use. In its tininess, it challenges readerly dexterity, foregrounding an out-of-scale clumsiness. We only have to look at the giant marginalia stumbling across the pages of other surviving miniature books to see how a reduction in size affected the reader's haptic encounter with the text. In this chapter, I will use examples of a series of miniature books published across the late seventeenth and eighteenth centuries to explore questions of materiality, utility, scale, and legibility. I will argue that these objects worked on the premise of totality made accessible through compression.

Such books could operate as metaphors for human accession to the divine, and for the individual apprehension of global and transhistorical knowledge. They could be a kind of epistemological comfort blanket, the promise of a world of knowledge and information that their readers could own, wear, or display. In the virtuosity of their execution, their acts of precision engraving, typesetting, and binding, they offered fine examples of human ingenuity. But at the same time, in reducing the most important documents of Western faith and civilization into compact form, they also raised questions about their own credibility. The compression of a large subject into a tiny work was at once miraculous and disquieting. How could readers be sure that the minute

---

[1] John Taylor, *Verbum Sempiternum* (London, 1693), 2 ⅛ × 1 ½ inches binding, cited in Laura Forsberg, "Multum in Parvo: The Nineteenth-Century Miniature Book," *Papers of the Bibliographic Society of America*, 110 (2016), 403–432, 421.

representations of knowledge, of revelation, of piety promised in these works were reliable? If a thumb bible contained less than 1 percent of the original, what had been left out? Did *A Concise Epitome of the History of England* (1799) really capture the most notable events on its single page per reign? And what, then, was the role of readerly trust in the history of the miniature book?

The Definition and Development of the Miniature Book

The standard definition of a miniature book is that it must measure less than 3 inches in all directions.[2] According to Anne Bromer and Julian Edison's *Miniature Books*, with the exception of microminiatures, most miniature books can be read without a magnifying glass, in a type whose size is similar to that of newspapers.[3] The secondary literature on miniature books of the eighteenth century is not extensive.[4] Many miniature books rest in private collections and their study has often been led by an engaged community of learned amateur enthusiasts. This close relationship between private collection and the culture of connoisseurship can be seen in the scholarship in this field, where there is an emphasis on cataloguing and description rather than theoretical or literary-critical analysis.[5] The rise of the miniature book as commodity has been linked to consumer culture and rising affluence, but it has also been described in ways that can be problematic for eighteenth-century scholars.[6]

Some critics have advanced more theoretical considerations of the form. Susan Stewart writes provocatively in *On Longing* about the miniature book in relation to interiority and the nature of the sign, but this

---

[2] Forsberg, "Multum in Parvo," 407.
[3] Anne Bromer and Julian Edison, *Miniature Books: 4,000 Years of Tiny Treasures* (New York: Grolier Club, 2007), 11. H. T. Sheringham asserts that "a miniature volume is not really a book if it is not both readable and read" ("A Library in Miniature. Part I. Books of the Sixteenth and Seventeenth Centuries," *The Connoisseur*, 3 [1902], 223).
[4] Examples to describe the history of the form include Louis W. Bondy, *Miniature Books: Their History from the Beginnings to the Present Day* (London: Richard Joseph, 1981); Robert F. Hanson (ed.) "Remembrance of the Miniature Book Society Conclave III," *Microbibliophile*, 1.1 (1997), 1–10; Doris V. Welsh, *The History of Miniature Books* (Albany, NY: Fort Orange Press, 1987); Doris V. Welsh, *A Bibliography of Miniature Books, 1470–1965*, ed. Francis J. Weber (Cobleskill, NY: K. I. Rickard, 1989).
[5] Comprehensive bibliographies include Ruth Adomeit, *Three Centuries of Thumb Bibles: A Checklist* (New York: Garland, 1980); and Welsh, *Bibliography of Miniature Books*.
[6] For an example of this, see Louis W. Bondy's discussion of "feminine" culture and children's books, *Miniature Books*, 21.

is a largely abstract argument.[7] Perhaps one of the reasons why there is not an extensive body of critical engagement with the material culture of these tiny forms is that miniature books present practical challenges for the researcher. Unlike many rare books, the particularities of their size do not easily translate in digital remediation because of the lack of scale in a digital medium. Both individual works or collections can be hard to find within a library collection because their dominant feature, their size, is not the primary way in which rare book archives are organized. They cannot be kept on shelves and browsed, instead remaining hidden away within envelopes and bespoke storage boxes. In some settings, the books are stored with other miniaturized objects. The Bodleian Library's Morton collection of miniature books is housed in a large cardboard box, within which is also a book-shaped case called "Letter Writer," which contains sealing wax, a seal, wafers, and a tiny inkpot.[8] This collection is less a bibliographical group than a world of ingenious library-related tininess. As the current volume of essays demonstrates, it is productive to think about miniature texts in a culture of small objects – but we also need to think about how they operate as books.

It is clear from a survey of even a few exemplars that there is much variation in the compressed formats of miniature books, and in the size of letters on small pages. Some works show only a few words of huge type on a page, whilst others cannot be read without a magnifying glass. So, for example, *A Box of Spikenard: or a little Manual of sacramental instruction and devotion especially helpful to the people of God, at and about the time of receiving the Lords Supper* (1660) is a tiny book measuring only 104 × 54 mm.[9] The type is disproportionately large, particularly in the dedication, which has a much bigger font. It is not a book that is big enough to include much content, and the relative size of the materials within it suggests some priorities. The shift in scale for the dedicatory material is significant and tells us something about the relative importance of legibility across the whole volume. It seems to have been more important to enable the patron to read the dedication than the user to access the devotional instruction within. As this suggests, whilst miniature books presented

---

[7] Susan Stewart, *On Longing: Narratives of the Miniature, the Gigantic, the Souvenir, the Collection* (London: Duke University Press, 1993), 37–69.

[8] Writing set housed in a book-like case, including inkwell, wax, wafers, and a seal, c. 1800, Bodleian Library, Morton 112.

[9] Thomas Warmstry, *A Box of Spikenard: or a little manual of sacramental instruction and devotion especially helpful to the people of God, at and about the time of receiving the Lords Supper*, 3rd ed. (London, 1660), Bodleian Library, Morton 11.

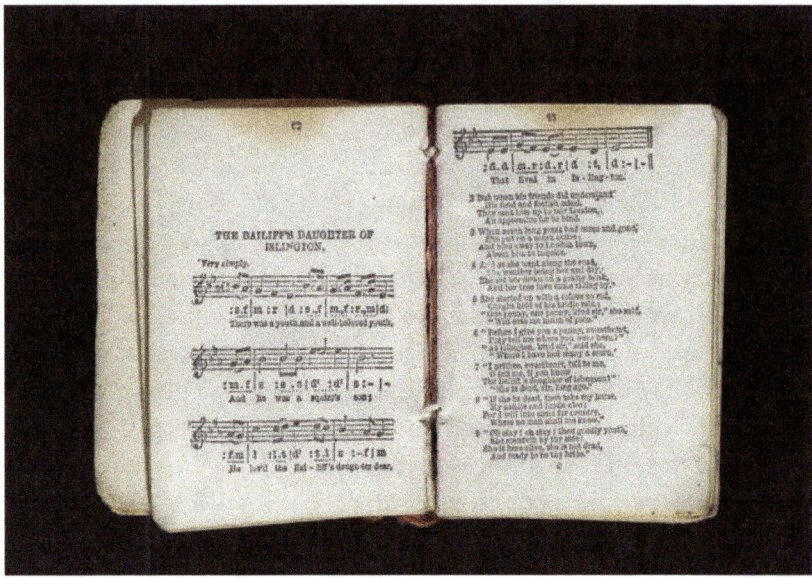

Figure 1.1 William Moodie, *Old English, Scots and Irish Songs with Music* (Glasgow, 1890), The Bodleian Libraries, University of Oxford, Johnson g.315, 104 × 54 mm.

remarkable feats of textual compression, a reduction in size was not always consistently applied.

The relationship between page size, type size, and utility also varied from one book to another. William Moodie's miniature edition of *Old English, Scots and Irish Songs with Music* measures only 27 × 20 mm (Figure 1.1). It is not a usable collection of music scores: the pages are too small to turn easily and the notation and words require a degree of close inspection incompatible with performance. In this case, there is a double haptic challenge: the voice is unable to express the notes, while the hands are unable to turn the pages. As these examples suggest, the question of scale impacts in different ways in the miniature book. In the case of *Old English Scots and Irish Songs* it is scarcely possible to use the book at all: how can you sing from notation too tiny to tell the notes apart? In such cases, miniaturization offers a form of ingenious mimicry of the original object. The totemic significance of the book in hand is more important than its utility.

The evolution of the miniature book is a story of secularization. The majority of catalogued seventeenth-century examples are religious, offering in small form the works of daily devotion found elsewhere in homes of the period. There are collections of psalms and miniature bibles, and the Book of Common Prayer. In the late seventeenth and eighteenth centuries, more titles and different kinds of works began to appear, although the output of miniature books did not rise exponentially until the nineteenth century.[10] One of the significant developments in the period was the rise of editions offering greatly compacted versions of informational material, along with books for children. It was an era of miniaturized almanacs, histories, gazetteers, dictionaries, and grammars, such as *The Little Gazetteer or Universal Geographical Dictionary in Miniature*, *The Little Linguist; or, A Complete Guide to English Philology*, and *A Concise Epitome of the History of England, on 36 Plates*.[11] It is not until the early nineteenth century that we start to see the miniaturization of literary works. The first version of *Gulliver's Travels* in miniature form was published in New York in 1793; *Paradise Lost* appears in 1823.[12] As this summary suggests, the secularization of the miniature book over the course of the eighteenth and nineteenth centuries realized first the appeal of a miniaturized world of fact, and then of fiction.

Materiality

In many ways miniature books create a perfect opportunity for thinking about the history of the book because they are works whose significance lies almost entirely in their form rather than their content. The small book is not remarkable for what it contains within it; it is remarkable because of the form into which it has compressed that content. This realignment of the dynamic between form and content inevitably changes the status of reading in relation to the miniature book. The act of reading is less significant than the act of making, or, further down the line, the act of owning. As a form of craftsmanship, the miniature book makes the ordinary extraordinary: it defamiliarizes the basic content of the printed book by foregrounding the remarkable acts of abridgement, typesetting, engraving, and binding that we take for granted in a standard-size book. Commonplace paratextual features such as dates, places of publication, indexes, page numbers, and illustrations become exotic and virtuoso when miniaturized. The bibliographical self-consciousness shown here is also evident

---

[10] According to one study, the publication rate rose from 400 in the seventeenth century to 650 in the eighteenth century and 3,000 in the nineteenth century. Welsh, *History of Miniature Books*, 35, 40, 44.

[11] See Forsberg, "Multum in Parvo," 410–412.

[12] See The Celebrated Dean Swift, *Adventures of Captain Gulliver in a voyage to the Islands of Lilliput and Brobdingnag* (New York: W. Durell, c. 1793); John Milton, *Paradise Lost: A Poem in Twelve Books* (London: Jones & Company, 1823), Bodleian Library, Morton 64.

in the kinds of works that are published in miniature form in the eighteenth century. *A Short Account of the First Rise and Progress of Printing* is a work published only in miniature-book form, 60 mm high, produced in London in 1763.[13] The volume traces the history of woodblock printing in Asia to metal type in England in the 1450s. Running at 123 pages, it covers Caxton, Wynken de Worde, and the first London printer, Richard Pynson. At the end there is a bibliography of each printer, including references to the universities and churches where their work can be found. What is the point of this book? It seems less useful as a reference tool than as a remarkable act of self-consciousness around the making of books, the trade they are a part of, and the skill and ingenuity that goes into the making of them. Also in this volume is a complete list of first books printed. Surely a miniature book is entirely the wrong place for a bibliography, a genre of text more usually associated with length and copious textual detail than brevity and beauty. But the purpose of *A Short Account*, as with so many miniature books, is not to use the form to encase appropriate material – it is worth noting that there are few collections of epigrams or aphorisms in miniature. Rather, the small book is repeatedly used to represent inappropriate material; in this case, the whole history of all printing, centuries of technical knowledge, beauty, skill, and progress – all compressed into a book 60 mm high. While Stewart has emphasized miniaturization as a response to the labor "of the hand, of the body, of the product" inherent in manuscript writing, and no longer present in print, here the process of miniaturization is a celebration of the often-unacknowledged labor and craft that go into making a full-size printed book.[14]

Scale

One of the things that becomes apparent from looking at the examples discussed so far is that their content is informed by questions of proportion – juxtapositions of large and small. The enfolding of centuries of achievement and expertise into a product smaller than the palm of a small hand represents a reduction in scale of content and history. At other times the juxtaposition is more literal – tiny books about huge people. Some of the most remarkable miniature books of the century were the *Gigantick*

---

[13] *A Short Account of the First Rise and Progress of Printing* (London, 1763), Bodleian Library Arch. A g.19 (10).
[14] Stewart, *On Longing*, 39.

Histories children's books published by Thomas Boreman in London in the early 1740s.¹⁵ These *Gigantick Histories* were called so because Boreman's bookshop was situated "near the two Giants in Guildhall," the famous Gog and Magog. The books were 63 mm high and 47 mm wide. They contained lists of child subscribers, and they covered subjects of hugeness: the history of the two famous giants; pictures of St. Paul's Cathedral, Westminster Abbey; or the history of Cajanus, the Swedish giant.

A mismatch of scale is also evident at the level of knowledge. Miniature books are used to suggest the possibility of access to a vast body of knowledge or information within an accessible span, as with the *Short Account of Printing*. Almanacs, small but compendious annual information planners, were so popular that they sold in a quantity only second to the bible in the seventeenth century, and they were also an ideal genre for miniaturization. The almanac promised a world at the reader's fingertips: weather forecasts, tides, lists of kings and queens, planting schedules – the natural and human world of pattern all set down in the form of a small book. The miniaturized almanacs of the eighteenth century replicated this sense of worldly knowledge on an even smaller physical scale. *The London Almanack for 1788* measures 25 × 50 mm. Again, we find within it a work purporting to contain the world in a tiny compass.¹⁶ The frontispiece offers a portrait of the king of Prussia, followed by portraits of the prince of Orange, duke of Brunswick, duke of York, and an engraving of St. Paul's – emblems of grandeur fit for a corner of the pocket. The miniature *London Almanack* for 1775 is tiny, 50 × 31 mm, and contains a range of useful information with dates of festivals, lunar cycles, table of kings and queens' reigns, all the lord mayors and sheriffs, lists of holidays, and weights of current coins, alongside engravings of some London buildings.¹⁷

Historical books operated on a similar basis. *A Concise Epitome of the History of England, on 36 Plates* offered a series of fine engravings of busts of leaders, accompanied by "a succinct account of the principal Occurrences that took Place during each Reign."¹⁸ The miniature history offered virtuoso compression of both time and space. Each image of a ruler, and their consort,

---

[15] See Bondy, *Miniature Books*, 21–23.
[16] *London Almanack for 1778* (London, 1778), Bodleian Arch. A g.19 (7).
[17] *London Almanack for the year of Christ 1775* (London, 1774), Bodleian Library, Morton 96.
[18] Jean Dassier, *A Concise Epitome of the History of England, on 36 Plates: Being a Representation of Dassier's Medals of the Sovereigns of England, with the Addition of Their Present Majesties. To Which Is Annexed, a Succinct Account of the Principal Occurrences That Took Place during Each Reign, Selected Chiefly from Sandford's Genealogical History* (London, 1799), Bodleian Library, Morton 270.

was given two columns of text that offered a very abbreviated account of the events of their reign, with what appears to be an emphasis on ghoulish detail. Despite the physical constraints, readers are informed that an enemy of Richard the Lionheart was seized and "his skin flayed over his ears, and then hanged [...] on a gibbet," that Richard II was "murdered by running a hot iron up his fundament," and that the garrison at Derry (Londonderry) in 1688 survived by "eating horses, dogs, cats, and even dried and salted hides." As we shall see, in many of these abridged works, the act of epitomizing in itself brought the nature of the knowledge within into question.

The works discussed earlier enabled the user to "own" a totality of information and to keep it about their person in ways that may reflect a broader early modern anxiety around the proliferation of books and information. Ann Blair has shown the ways in which different kinds of books emerge as responses to early modern information overload.[19] We might see miniature books, and particularly the kinds of miniature reference books published within this period, as part of that picture. They offer beautifully crafted, elite companions to the digests, primers, epitomes, and indexes that proliferate over the course of the seventeenth and eighteenth centuries. Like those works, miniature books of knowledge could operate as a form of information management, their portability and wearability offering a form of control and ownership of the ever-expanding world of human intellectual endeavor.[20]

Multum in Parvo

Although the eighteenth century saw an increase in secular miniature books, the most common troping of the large subject in small form idea lay in the publication of religious texts. This is particularly evident in works that use the compacted form as a metaphor for divine revelation. A miniature book could become an emblem of man's ability to apprehend the unknowability of godly creation within a small canvas. The best-selling miniature devotional work of this period is John Taylor's *Verbum Sempiternum and Salvator Mundi*. The preface to one seventeenth-century *Verbum Sempiternum* reads:

---

[19] Ann Blair, *Too Much to Know: Managing Scholarly Information before the Modern Age* (New Haven, CT: Yale University Press, 2010).
[20] On the wearing of miniature books, see Stewart, *On Longing*, 41–42.

> Dread Soveraign, I with pains and care have took
> From out the greatest Book this little Book.
> And with great reverence I have cul'd from thence,
> All things that are of greatest consequence.
> And though the Volume and the Work be smal,
> Yet it containes the sum of All in All.[21]

Here we start to see the religious or ontological implications of smallness, the role of the miniature book in encompassing something beyond comprehension, being "all in all" despite its diminutive nature. But what were the consequences of that reduction in size? The "thumb bible," which evolved over the course of the seventeenth and eighteenth centuries, offered a miniaturized version of the scriptures, aimed at children.[22] One eighteenth-century example introduced its contents with the observation that "It is a melancholy reflection that in a country where all have the BIBLE in their hands, so many should be ignorant of the first principles of the oracles of God."[23] So the thumb bible put first principles into every hand. Or did it? An average thumb bible contains, according to one bibliographer's estimates, about seven thousand words in total.[24] As a result, only a tiny fraction of the bible's content is included. The scale of reduction is evident in almost every example. The Bodleian copy of the 1795 *Bible in Miniature* referred to earlier was clearly a treasured item, with multiple ownership inscriptions dated from the 1790s through to 1867. The annotations suggest that it was gifted at least once: "Edward Eaton, given to him by his respected friend, Miss Richmond, May 2nd 1867."[25] But what was the value of its content? The book covers the whole of the Old and New Testaments in 200 tiny pages, each one containing between twenty-five and thirty words. This entire bible is considerably less than 6,000 words: the King James Bible has over 780,000 in total. This thumb bible covers less than 1 percent of the original, which holds implications for the presentation of the content. The first section is entitled "Treating of God," where the whole debate over the nature and existence of the divine creator is reduced to just three pages and fifty

---

[21] Taylor, *Verbum Sempiternum*, cited in Forsberg, "Multum in Parvo," 421.
[22] The earliest thumb bible known today is John Weever's *An Agnus Dei* (London, 1601). For a fuller account, see Adomeit, *Three Centuries of Thumb Bibles*.
[23] *The Bible in Miniature; Or, a Concise History of the Old & New Testaments* (London, 1795), Bodleian Library, Johnson g.302, a2r.
[24] H. T. Sheringham, "A Library in Miniature. Part II. Books of the Eighteenth and Nineteenth Centuries," *The Connoisseur*, 3 (1902), 167.
[25] *The Bible in Miniature*, Bodleian Library, Johnson g.302.

words. The second book, "Treating of the Creation of the Visible World, &c," is dispatched within five pages. There is an inevitable bathos to a work such as this. The gap between the vast aspiration of the original work and the realities of its shrunken textual forms are made evident on closer inspection. Biblical miniaturization alluringly promised to contain and to transmit complete biblical understanding to a child reader. Its appeal endured despite both the impossibility of the goal and the imperfection of its realization in individual examples. We are reminded of the curious status of text within the miniaturized book – the words are often the least important thing about a miniature book. They come to stand as placeholders for all the words, sentences, paragraphs, and chapters that cannot be present, less important for what they actually say than what they stand in for.

The Miniature and the Haptic Challenge

Thumb bibles were intended for children, often passed down from one generation to another, and commonly bear ownership inscriptions. One of the things we see looking at this evidence of reading and ownership is the haptics of miniaturization – the physical difficulties presented by human encounters with tiny objects. Miniature books challenge a reader's nimbleness, foregrounding clumsy fingers and awkward hands. The ungainly marginalia scattered across many copies of thumb bibles shows the evidence of this readerly interaction, its revelations of human limitation. Despite attempts by publishers to establish a link in the minds of potential purchasers between small books and small readers, miniature books are, in fact, disproportionately small in comparison to child readers.[26] Miniature volumes also posed special challenges for children; their small pages and thin paper meant that they required a manual dexterity that children often lack. Within the Bodleian 1795 thumb bible, annotations on the pages of the book illustrate the tension between the precision crafting of the object and the lack of manual dexterity of the child.

The haptic challenges of miniature books are not confined to thumb bibles. A tiny edition of odes by Anacreon and Sappho (Figure 1.2) contains nicely printed verses in Greek, with marginalia that dwarfs the text. Across the delicate pages gallop the inelegant jottings of a reader. As these

---

[26] Forsberg, "Multum in Parvo," 417.

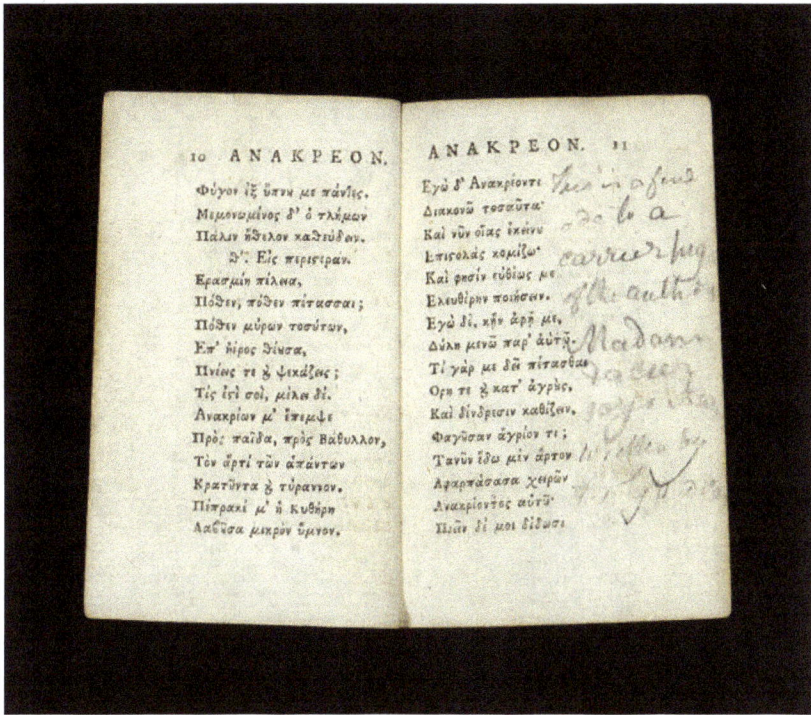

Figure 1.2 Anacreon, Sappho, and Erinna, *Hai Tou Anakreontos Odai, Kai Ta Sapphous, Kai Erinnas Leipsana* (Edinburgh, 1766), The Bodleian Libraries, University of Oxford, Morton 120, H: 88 mm; W: 62 mm; D: 13 mm.

examples show, there is a futility and impracticality at the heart of the miniature book, a lack of utility. The individual cannot interact easily with the vastness of subject promised by the ingenious format, and is only able to appear clumsy in comparison with the expanse of knowledge compressed within the pages.

Legibility

I have argued in this chapter that miniature books can be seen as offering a kind of epistemological balm, the promise of a world of knowledge that was ownable, wearable, possessable. Such a claim for the miniature book rests on the notion that these objects do in fact make the world more legible, and that they are legible in themselves. This question of readability, in both a practical and epistemological sense, is at the heart of our encounters

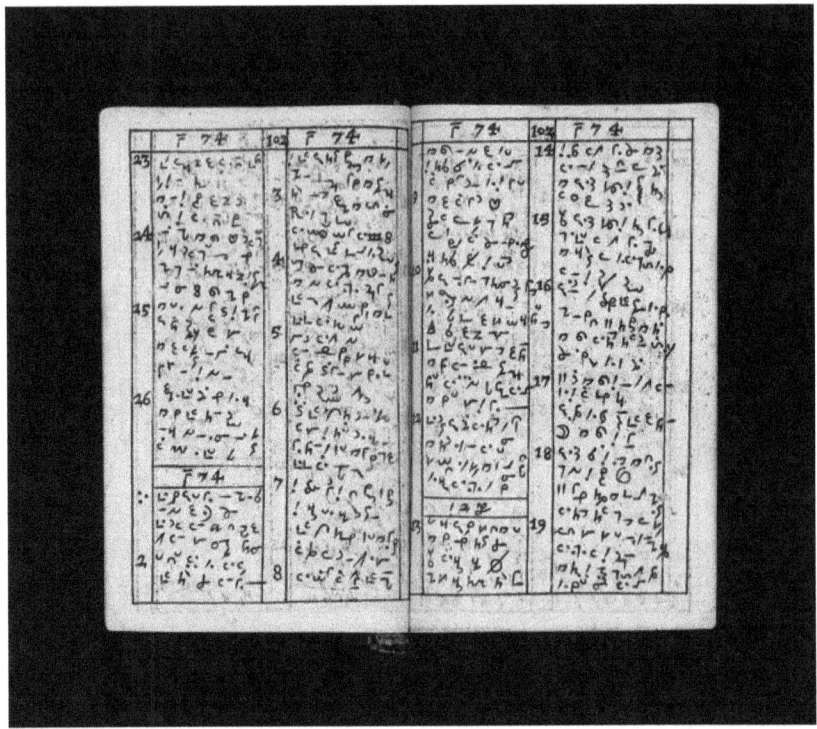

Figure 1.3 Jeremiah Rich, *The Whole Book of Psalms in Meter. According to the Art of Short-Writing written by Jeremiah Rich, Author and Teacher of the Said Art* (London, 1659), The Bodleian Libraries, University of Oxford, Arch. A g.19 (1), 60 × 40 mm.

with the miniature book, which seems so often to play with what we can see – and what we can't. Do miniature books make the world more visible or less?

Many examples of the form make a claim to represent sizable entities: they boast of their ability to contain the whole of a national history, God, a universal geography, a complete dictionary. We might understand them as in some ways offering an Enlightenment fiction of knowledge made available through accessible totality. Yet these same forms also specialized in rendering knowledge less readable. One of the most virtuoso exercises in this vein is *The Whole Book of Psalms in Meter* by Jeremiah Rich (Figure 1.3). Produced in 1660, it is the earliest English text of any size printed entirely from engravings. Rich's book is ingenious in many different ways. It is extremely small, measuring only 60 × 40 mm. It is based on the considerable formal challenge of reproducing the Psalms all in meter. And the whole book, apart from the preface and dedication, is written in a particular form of shorthand that had been invented by Rich's uncle,

William Cartwright.[27] The work thus multiplies the number of kinds of difficulty and effort that can be put into making and reading a book. *The Whole Books of Psalms* was said to have taken a year to produce, and only twenty copies were issued, most of which are beautifully bound in contemporary black morocco and finely gilt-tooled leather.[28] As with other miniature books, readerly access was restricted at the point of sale – as well as in content – in works that were often produced at high cost and in limited quantities. *The Whole Books of Psalms* is a treasure both because of its jewel-like miniature precision and its limited print run. This miniature book frames a paradox of accessibility. In the prefatory pages, Rich makes claims for the particular utility of the work: "in other parts of ye World where the Bible is not suffered" the book will be especially valuable, because "here the gospel is plaine to the Christian: but lockt up the secrets of a Character, from ye inquisition of a pagan."[29] The *Psalms* were both easier to use, Rich suggests, because of their potential for concealment and portability in non-Christian cultures, and at the same time restricted in their use, through practicality and price.[30]

The Whole Book of Psalms in Meter also foregrounds the question of textual legibility. It is a book that is already fairly difficult to read because of its size. This difficulty is compounded by the fact that it is also written in shorthand, one of the aspects of its virtuosity, which makes the work a different kind of unreadable. The preface demonstrates that Rich sees this difficulty of access as intrinsically linked to its subject matter, to the revelatory nature of God's word and the nature of Christian devotion: "a Lanthorn of light to the eyes of a virtuous recreation for the minde wherein the soule may find a treasury of wisdom and knowledge […] the paines it self is both profit and pleasure and the very work is wages."[31]

---

[27] See Bondy, *Miniature Books*, 18.
[28] Ibid., 19–20.
[29] Jeremiah Rich, *The Whole Book of Psalms in Meter. According to the Art of Short-Writing written by Jeremiah Rich, Author and Teacher of the Said Art* (London, 1659), Bodleian Library, Arch. A g.19 (1), 3.
[30] We find similar emphasis on limited circulation in other expensive publications. Dassier's *Concise Epitome of the History of England* is priced at 7s. 6d. – expensive for an abridgement, which was commonly a cheaper way of acquiring knowledge. The Advertisement reads "many abridgements have been made, but none exactly similar to this. The delicacy of the Engravings will not admit of numerous impressions being taken, therefore an experiment is made on a small scale, and now introduced for the approbation of those who have the care or instruction of youth. The Medals were engraved on six Plates, six Medals on each; only 100 Impressions were taken before this was adopted; and they are now selling, printed on Imperial Quarto, at the original Price of One Guinea."
[31] Rich, *Whole Book of Psalms*, 4.

He also links the idea of effort, in both creating and reading the book, to the work of the Christian life: "If any should ask why I writ them it was because I would not my self be idle; if why I printed them because I would have others well imployed. Wee cannot without industry have the reward of ingenuity no learneing is got without labour."[32] Labor and pain, work as wages: these are key to Rich's vision of spiritual growth. And the author's and the reader's labor and pain, the extent they both have to work to create and access the meaning within the text, is intrinsically connected to the material and textual form of the book. In this case, miniaturization makes religious understanding both easier and harder to access, which makes it perfectly emblematic of the bigger Christian journey.

The idea that a reduction in scale can come to operate as a metaphor for divine presence is at the heart of other kinds of seventeenth-century virtuosity. The majority of the books discussed so far are printed, but there is also a strong tradition of micrography in this period, the practice and art of impossibly small calligraphy, in which virtuoso writing masters copied out seminal texts within a tiny area. For instance, Robert Spofforth's engraving of the Lord's Prayer, produced in Oxford in 1700, offers the whole of the prayer, written out in a circle less than 10 mm in diameter.[33] The piece is a celebration of human virtuosity, the craftsmanship, control, and skill that can be linked to other aspects of virtuoso print culture in this period, such as the engraving of trompe l'oeil print medleys that create impossibly precise fictions of material presence with which to tease the viewer.[34] Yet we might also see such works as the embodiment of a conviction that the wonders of the world are as impressive at a micro level as they are at the macro. Robert Hooke's *Micrographia* (1665) had offered a celebrated description of Adam, in which he described the patterns of nature newly visible under the microscope as a form of divine language.[35] He argued that the miniature detail of divine creation could show us mysterious

---

[32] Ibid., 5.
[33] Robert Spofforth, *The Lord's Prayer, Engr. within a Circle 8mm. in Diameter, by R. Spofforth* (Oxford, 1700), Bodleian Library, Arch. A g.19 (2).
[34] On the medley tradition and trompe l'oeil engraving, see Dror Wahrman, *Mr. Collier's Letter Racks: A Tale of Art & Illusion at the Threshold of the Modern Information Age* (Oxford: Oxford University Press, 2012); Tim Somers, "Micrography in Later Stuart Britain: Curious Spectacles and Political Emblems" in Rosamund Oates and Jessica Purdy (eds.), *Communities of Print: Readers and Their Books in Early Modern Europe* (Leiden: Brill, 2021), 215–217.
[35] Robert Hooke, "Of the Seeds of Tyme" in *Micrographia, or, some physiological descriptions of minute bodies made by magnifying glasses with observations and inquiries thereupon* (London, 1665), 153–154 (154).

designs that with industry we might be able to read and understand. Yet Hooke's emphasis was on the way the *natural* world shows us remarkable structures and complexity when we look at it under a microscope. He has a rather different perspective on human attempts at miniature creation. Here Hooke describes what happens when he looks at some micrographic writing under his microscope:

Nay, having view'd certain pieces of exceeding curious writing of the kind (one of which in the bredth of a *two-pence* compris'd *the Lords prayer, the Apostles Creed, the ten Commandments, and about half a dozen verses besides of the Bible*), whose *lines* were *so small* and *near together*, that I was unable to *number* them with my *naked eye*, a very ordinary *Microscope*, I had then about me, inabled me to see that what the Writer of it had asserted was *true*, but withall discover'd of what pitifull *bungling scribbles* and *scrawls* it was compos'd, *Arabian* and *China* characters being almost as well shap'd, yet thus much I must say for the Man, that it was for the most part *legible* enough, though in some places there wanted a good *fantsy* well *preposest* to help one through.[36]

Hooke casts doubt here on the accuracy and skill that were seen to be at the heart of the claims for miniature text, and also suggests that the labor inherent in micrography might be as much of a task for the reader as for the writer. He raises a question mark over the reliability of miniaturization.

Nearly all the items discussed in this essay use the rhetoric of a large world compressed to a small form to reinforce their claims for knowledge or divine revelation. The conceit of *multum in parvo* is made to do substantial intellectual and theological heavy lifting. But as we have seen, there were many ways in which the promise of accessibility was unfulfilled: in works that omitted the majority of a sacred text, that were too small to use, or that used forms of writing that were partially illegible. They force the question of readerly trust in the history of the miniature book. The tiny forms of knowledge, of revelation, of piety promised were not necessarily reliable. The bible might not have been abridged in the right way, given how much was necessarily left out in order to fit the format. Perhaps not all the kings made it into the history of England. The tiny squiggles of miniature writing might not actually say what they claimed to say.

Miniature books work on the premise of accessible totality through compression. They can be metaphors for human accession to the divine and individual apprehension of global and transhistorical knowledge.

---

[36] Hooke, "Of the Point of a Small Sharp Needle" in *Micrographia*, 3.

They are full of paradoxes: they make their content both accessible and inaccessible; legible and illegible. They expose both human precision and clumsiness. In their compression of huge works into tiny forms they at once claim to make vast subjects newly accessible and undermine that accessibility through the haptic challenges of their minute material forms. But in doing all this, they rely on the reader or user's trust in ways that make them profoundly vulnerable, and that vulnerability, the fact that they both are and are not what they say they are, is a key part of their history – and their beauty.

2 Nuts, Flies, Thimbles, and Thumbs

Eighteenth-Century Children's Literature and Scale

KATHERINE WAKELY-MULRONEY

In 1751, John Newbery, among the most influential figures in the history of children's literature, published *The Lilliputian Magazine*, a serial for young readers that comprised rhymes, fables, riddles, hymns, and other materials calculated to amuse and instruct. In its opening piece, "A Dialogue Between a Gentleman and the Author," the latter defends the lofty ambitions of his project, which sought, at a price of threepence monthly, to "sow in [children's] minds the seeds of polite literature, and to teach them the *great grammar of the universe*." His interlocutor remains skeptical, however, questioning whether "such a trifling affair will ever engage the attention of people of consequence." This remark refers primarily to the *Magazine*'s subscription cost, a "trifle" insufficient, in the Gentleman's view, to fund a work of "great" scope and import. But the Author receives it as an attack on his project as a whole, and its efforts to supply as much information as possible within a series of small, and consequently affordable, volumes. "A trifling affair, sir, do you call it!" he responds in disbelief. "If education is a trifling affair; I profess to you I don't know what is momentous ... You'll please to consider sir, that the largest book is not always the best."[1]

In the space of a few short lines, we encounter the underlying philosophy not only of Newbery's *Magazine* but also of children's literature as an emerging enterprise. Over the course of the eighteenth century, publishers and authors began to recognize that short, simple books for little readers were big business. Their task as a result was to invest apparently trifling works with enough intellectual and moral significance to justify their position in the increasingly crowded children's literature marketplace. In the eighteenth century (as in the twenty-first), the suspicion that "anyone" could write a children's book led writers, critics, and consumers to assign the greatest value to works where linguistic simplicity and material slightness coincided with a kind of conceptual heft, emotional depth, or imaginative scope. Newbery's defensive stance is therefore typical of the children's literature preface genre of the period, where authors perpetually defended the decision to "lower" themselves to the level of a child's understanding

---

[1] *The Lilliputian Magazine: or, the Young Gentleman & Lady's Golden Library* (London, 1752), 3.

on the grounds that early education was of the highest consequence. "Who but stoops with satisfaction to lead an infant by the hand?" asks Ellenor Fenn in the preface to *Fables in Monosyllables* (1783). "Who but delights to adapt her steps to its short and unequal paces? … No office is *mean* which concerns the health (*corporeal* or *mental*) of the rising generation."[2]

As Fenn's title suggests, children's books tend to comprise bounded forms, such as fables, and short, often monosyllabic words; but they also direct our attention to that which is little, and seemingly inconsequential. The very titles of books for young readers reveal a metaphorical alignment between children's literature and small things: the eighteenth-century child was offered a *Sugar-Plum* (1771), *A Bag of Nuts Ready Cracked* (1774), or a *Silver Thimble* (1799). In Fenn's *Cobwebs to Catch Flies* (1783), instruction proceeds along an entomological scale; the work itself is divided into short chapters on various small objects, among them a rat, a fan, and a doll's house. To venture within such volumes is to enter a microcosm where ontological profusion is contrasted with stylistic spareness. In Anna Letitia Barbauld's *Lessons for Children* (1778–1779), snail shells, gemstones, and raisins are examined on pages containing very few words, a typographic decision designed to facilitate reading comprehension. The intimate scope of Barbauld's text targeted a reading audience with very little life experience to draw on. By way of contrast, many religious books for children addressed themselves to readers with potentially very little time left, their sense of urgency shaped by spiritual anxieties regarding the child's soul as well as the high child mortality rates of the late seventeenth and early to mid-eighteenth centuries.[3] The smallness of eighteenth-century children's books may therefore be understood in terms of their thematic preoccupations, linguistic register, and typographic presentation.

This chapter examines the shifting significations of smallness in early children's literature along these lines. How, I ask, might the contents of individual volumes reflect the intersection of children's print culture with contemporaneous pedagogical theory, which began to view children's minds in explicitly spatial terms, capable of receiving information little by little? In what ways did this graduated approach intersect with a different notion of books for young readers founded on encapsulation? The latter concept is at the heart of Newbery's and Fenn's claims that their works communicate something momentous within the restricted parameters

---

[2] Ellenor Fenn, *Fables in Monosyllables by Mrs. Teachwell* (London, 1783), xi–xii.
[3] Peter Razzell and Christine Spence, "The History of Infant, Child and Adult Mortality in London, 1550–1850," *The London Journal*, 23.2 (2007), 271–292.

(stylistic, linguistic, conceptual) of children's literature. These contrasting positions – that books for young readers should contain only very small amounts of information, or else model themselves on Fortunatus's magic purse, full beyond all imagining – coincided with a more dynamic conception of scale in which the dimensions of children's books and bodies were shown to be in a continual state of flux, informed as much by physical as by temporal scale. With these variations in mind, I conclude by peering into *Tom Thumb's Folio* (1768), a volume that draws together different notions of littleness, conceptual and stylistic, within its small confines.

Little Books, Little Lives

In considering children's books as "small things," it is perhaps most useful to begin with their physical dimensions. After all, partially literate and preliterate children experience books as tactile objects before understanding them as written texts. Gillian Brown has shown that the pleasing smallness of volumes produced by figures such as Newbery signaled a new attention to "the physicality of reading" and the "touchability ... of books" – one that anticipates the now received understanding that multisensory learning is critical to cognitive development.[4] But just how small were children's books during this period? For much of the eighteenth century, works produced for children were merely little, rather than truly miniature. As Laura Forsberg observes, notions of what constitutes "miniature" vary among bibliographers and collectors; in general, however, a miniature book should be less than 3 inches in both height and width.[5] While most eighteenth-century children's books were somewhat larger than this, Thomas Boreman's *Gigantick Histories* (1740) is a true miniature, its title a comic reference to the fact that volumes in the series measure just 2 ½ inches high. While Boreman uses this format to relate the mighty deeds of London's Guildhall giants, Gogmagog and

---

[4] Gillian Brown, "The Metamorphic Book: Children's Print Culture in the Eighteenth Century," *Eighteenth-Century Studies*, 39.3 (2006), 357. M. O. Grenby has suggested that "'book use' ... [is] a more inclusive, and frequently more accurate, term than 'reading'" where children are concerned (*The Child Reader, 1700–1840* [Cambridge: Cambridge University Press, 2011], 194). On the tactility of eighteenth-century children's books, see Heather Klemann, "The Matter of Moral Education: Locke, Newbery, and the Didactic Book-Toy Hybrid," *Eighteenth-Century Studies*, 44.2 (2011), 223–244.

[5] Laura Forsberg, "Multum in Parvo: The Nineteenth-Century Miniature Book," *Papers of the Bibliographic Society of America*, 110.4 (2016), 403–432.

Corineus, his work folds not only giants but also young readers themselves into its tiny compass. Boreman's *Histories* were the first books for children to include subscribers' lists among their contents; as a result, patrons such as Master Tommy Allen and Miss Jenny Austin were able to trace their names in the volumes' pages.[6] But any feeling of being bound up within the text would have been directly contrasted by the sense of enormousness produced by handling it: Boreman's microscopic volumes magnify their reader, a transformation of scale that was, as we shall see, central to early children's books that engaged with smallness in its many forms.

Over the course of the eighteenth century, advances in print technology meant that it became easier and cheaper to produce high-quality miniature books designed specifically for children.[7] This resulted in a trend for miniature libraries. These collections of simple, elegant books tended to follow the format of a conventional primer, pairing attractive engravings with short captions. The sixteen volumes of John Marshall's *The Infant's Library* (1800–1816), each measuring just over 2 inches long and less than 2 inches wide, are housed within a small cabinet designed to resemble a bookcase. Most items in the series have a single, easily identifiable theme: the first book is an abecedary, the second a syllabary; book seven catalogues different types of flowers; book nine is dedicated to games. But certain volumes in Marshall's *Library* are more ambiguous in terms of their theme, presenting young readers with a disparate series of vignettes: ships coming into harbor, boys walking to school, tents on a battlefield. Here, captions seem designed to attract the reader's close attention, whether to count the number of tents or speculate on the nature of a particular scene ("I suppose he is lame," "perhaps little Mary is going to have her supper").[8] Looking into such pages feels like peering through a small window to glimpse a wider world, producing a feeling of depth entirely disproportionate to the volumes' slightness. While this phenomenon is typical of the miniature book format, where material reduction heightens the reader's sensation of intricacy, complexity, even mystery, it catches one by surprise in the case of Marshall's *Library*, given the text's uncomplicated register and spare format.

---

[6] Thomas Boreman, *The Gigantick History*, 2nd vol. (London, 1741), v.
[7] On the cost and profitability of children's books, see Andrew O' Malley, *The Making of the Modern Child: Children's Literature and Childhood in the Late Eighteenth Century* (New York: Routledge, 2003), 21; Grenby, *Child Reader*, 70–85; Lissa Paul, *The Children's Book Business: Lessons from the Long Eighteenth Century* (New York: Routledge, 2011), *passim*.
[8] John Marshall, *The Infant's Library*, 16 vols. (London, c. 1801), vol. 3, 11; vol. 4, 18.

The very slightness of *The Infant's Library* calls into question its status as children's literature, its child-friendly language and design notwithstanding. Though ostensibly contrived to teach young readers their letters, or train them in subjects such as botany and the history of the English monarchy (the subject of the final book in the series), these volumes, John Mack suggests, were "just as likely … [to] have ended up as additions to a doll's house."⁹ Forsberg likewise concludes that works such as Marshall's *Library* were scaled to the dimensions not of a child but of a child's plaything.¹⁰ While the relationship between book and toy is central to the history of children's literature, with many eighteenth-century volumes featuring moveable flaps and other tactile elements, doll-sized books invite a different, less boisterous kind of play.¹¹ To toy with Marshall's *Library* is to risk its destruction. For this reason, most children's books of the period adhered to a slightly larger format. At 3 by 4 inches, Newbery's *A Little Pretty Pocket-Book* (1744) was designed to be carried about on the child's person rather than safeguarded in an ornamental cabinet, displacing the act of play onto the ball or pincushion with which it was sold. This vision of children's reading – the book held firmly in hand rather than between the fingertips – would determine the material format of volumes across the eighteenth century more broadly. Despite the popularity of miniature libraries at the turn of the century, the notion that books for young readers should be sized with children's habits of use and manual dexterity in view resulted in a comparatively enduring trend for larger, more robust volumes (as the dimensions of many nineteenth-century texts bear witness).

If the physical size of children's books fluctuated over the course of the eighteenth century, their typographic dimensions followed a more coherent trajectory. The slightness of Marshall's *Library* is formal as well as material: individual pages are minimal in their design, featuring a single sentence printed in large type, or even (in the case of the abecedarian volume) a single letter. We might contrast this spareness with the layout of works published earlier in the history of children's literature, such as *A Little Book for Little Children* (1660) by Puritan divine Thomas White. As I have argued elsewhere, the typographic density of White's volume reflects the spiritual urgency of its premise; this *Little Book* was designed to convey a sense of the reader's Christian obligations as early and intensively as

---

⁹ John Mack, *The Art of Small Things* (London: British Museum, 2007), 146.
¹⁰ Forsberg, "Multum in Parvo," 48.
¹¹ For more on the interactive nature of eighteenth-century children's books and the intersection between play and print culture, see Brown, "Metamorphic Book," and Klemann, "Matter of Moral Education."

possible.¹² The same is true of James Janeway's *Token for Children* (1671), packed with examples of boys and girls prepared to meet their maker, and the *New-England Primer* (1727), which repeatedly reminds readers that no sin is too trifling, and no person too small to escape death or judgment, for every "child is old in the sin of the world."¹³ What we see developing over the course of the eighteenth century, however, is an alternative conception of childhood shaped by a different temporal framework, one that would dramatically reconfigure the smallness of children's books.

Graduated texts by figures such as Anna Letitia Barbauld, who began writing for children in the late 1770s, envisioned youth as a comparatively prolonged experience, with readers progressing through volumes of increasing difficulty over the course of their early lives. Where earlier works such as *A Little Book for Little Children* and the *New-England Primer* dwelt on the prospect of child mortality, Barbauld's four-volume *Lessons for Children* prioritized the child's ongoing growth. The text, which consists primarily of conversations between a mother and son, delineates four specific stages of development between the ages of two and four. Volumes become more syntactically complex and conceptually demanding over the course of the series, in keeping with the child's progressing literacy. While the prospect of early death remains present in Barbauld's *Lessons*, it is portrayed as a somewhat unlikely, even avoidable event. In the first book in the series, Mamma reminds Charles that he cannot swim, and "will be drowned" if he enters the water. However, she reassures him that he will eventually be as capable as another, older boy: "You shall learn to swim when you are as big as Billy."¹⁴ The threat of Charles's hypothetical drowning is immediately effaced by the promise that he will live to grow big, a development that will allow him to participate in activities from which little children are barred (such as swimming), and also to access subsequent volumes in Barbauld's series. When young people have the leisure to learn things little by little over the course of their early lives, individual books are released from the burden of compendiousness.

The cumulative nature of *Lessons for Children* becomes apparent when we consider how the same subject is handled across different stages of

---

[12] For more on the form of White's *Little Book* and its significance to the history of children's literature, see Katherine Wakely-Mulroney, "Riddling the Catechism in Early Children's Literature," *The Review of English Studies*, 70.294 (2018), 272–290 (272–275).

[13] Elisa New, "'Both Great and Small': Adult Proportion and Divine Scale in Edward Taylor's 'Preface' and The New-England Primer," *Early American Literature*, 28.2 (1993), 120–132 (121).

[14] Anna Letitia Barbauld, *Lessons for Children from Two to Three Years Old* (London, 1787), 38–39.

Barbauld's program. When snow appears in the first volume, it is presented as an object of play ("Let us make snow-balls") as well as a substance whose physical properties are worthy of closer investigation ("Bring the snow to the fire. / See, see how it melts. It is all gone, there is nothing but water").[15] We learn just a fraction more in the second book, *Lessons for Children of Three Years Old, Part I*, where winter's climate is deemed ideal for other forms of play, such as sliding and skating, and water is shown to freeze in the same manner as other liquids ("The oil is frozen, and the milk is frozen, and the river is frozen, and every thing").[16] Though the sensation of moving between the two volumes is one of minute progression, the child's conceptual and experiential frames of reference are becoming progressively larger.

As one might expect, the pages of Barbauld's *Lessons* become more typographically dense as the implied reader advances in age and size, with short sentences and paragraphs giving way to longer blocks of text. Nevertheless, the consistent use of a large typeface and liberal amounts of white space mean that even the most advanced book in the series contains very little information relative to its size. Among Barbauld's chief contributions to the field of early children's literature was her sense, articulated in the advertisement to Book I, that young readers require "clear and large type, *and* large spaces" for "*The eye of a child and of a learner cannot catch, as ours can, a small, obscure, ill-formed word, amidst a number of others all unknown to him.*"[17] In this case, the word "small" designates that which is ill-suited to young readers and their limited capacities: little books for little children, Barbauld argues, require big writing and large margins. She was not the first to draw this conclusion; in the preface to *A Play-Book for Children* (1694), author J. G. complained that the layout of available books for the young, with their "close Stuft" pages and heavy "black Print," seemed "design[ed] … to frighten from, rather than allure to, learning."[18] Yet it was *Lessons for Children* almost a century later that popularized the style of formatting now ubiquitous in children's publishing.

Ellenor Fenn and Dorothy Kilner were among the first writers to respond to Barbauld's directives concerning the scale of children's print. Featuring large type and wide spacing, Fenn's *Fables in Monosyllables* and *Cobwebs to Catch-Flies* comprise words that are little in terms of their syllabic

---

[15] Ibid., 34–35.
[16] Anna Letitia Barbauld, *Lessons for Children of Three Years Old, Part I* (London, 1788), 9. *Lessons for Children* was first published in 1778–1779.
[17] Barbauld, *Lessons for Children from Two to Three*, n.p, emphasis original.
[18] J. G., *A Play-book for Children*, quoted in William Sloane, *Children's Books in England and America in the Seventeenth Century* (New York: King's Crown Press, 1955), 211.

length, yet large in the space they occupy on the page. Sentences are likewise short in the number of words they contain, yet long in terms of their extension (Fenn stretches the phrase "I like to feed the poor duck" beyond the width of a single line, for example).[19] The title of Kilner's *Little Stories for Little Folks, in Easy Lessons of One, Two, and Three Syllables* (c. 1785) not only figures the process of acquiring literacy in explicitly progressive terms but also provides yet another conflation between the smallness of a text (measured by the length of its words and stories) and that of young readers themselves, a correspondence that became increasingly fine-tuned as understandings of child cognition developed over time. Works by Barbauld, Fenn, and Kilner indicate that modern attitudes towards children's ability to process information in the earliest stages of literacy appear in the changing face of children's print well before the emergence of developmental psychology as a specialist field in the nineteenth century.

Growing in the Great Big World

Having examined the smallness of early children's books in terms of their material, typographic, and syntactic features, I would like to consider how scale informs not only the design but also the content of *Lessons for Children*. The world of Barbauld's text is one of minute observation: Mamma encourages Charles to examine insects, pins, bird's eggs, coins, currants, and myriad other small items that fit in the palm of his hand. Naturally, these object lessons are often conducted in relation to the child's own body, which may seem large, even powerful, by comparison.[20] Charles is cautioned not to handle his father's pocket-watch too roughly, for example, lest he break its delicate glass. He learns that his "little finger" is large enough to frighten a "little snail" into its shell, and that he is big enough to crush his mother's work basket by sitting on it.[21] At the same time, he receives repeated, and increasingly frequent, reminders of his own smallness in the grander scheme of things. In a passage from Book II, Mamma invites her son to gather strawberries: "Here is a very large one," she says,

---

[19] Ellenor Fenn, *Cobwebs to Catch Flies* (London, 1783), vol. 1, 57. The first volume of Fenn's work is for children aged three to five; the second (with slightly longer words) for those aged five to eight.

[20] On Barbauld's use of sensory objects in the cultivation of mental images and patterns of association during childhood, see Joanna Wharton, *Material Enlightenment: Women Writers and the Science of the Mind, 1770–1830* (Woodbridge: Boydell, 2018), 43–47.

[21] Barbauld, *Lessons for Children from Two to Three*, 17, 19–20, 33.

"It is almost too big to go into your mouth."[22] Though Charles (like the implied child reader) grows bigger as the series progresses, he must learn to adjust his egotistical sense of his own significance as he moves out of the small-scale domestic sphere that is the young child's whole universe into the wider world.

In the final volume of *Lessons for Children*, Charles and his mother travel to France, a journey intended not simply to expose the child to a different culture but to remove him from the familiar microcosm where he occupies a disproportionately large role. When Charles lands on the other side of the Channel, his limited French prevents him from performing the most simple transactions, leading everyone, his mother included, to belittle him: "Ha, ha, ha! He, he, he! Ho, ho, ho! Here is a foolish little boy come a great way over the sea, and does not know that every body speaks French in France."[23] But this experience of being brought down to size, so to speak, is merely the culmination of a series of lessons on the mutability of scale. Charles has been encouraged to mark other curious inversions of big and small over the course of his journey. He finds, for instance, that the tiny land masses and bodies of water represented on his map at home are in actual fact vast, and seemingly unfathomable. "Well, this is very strange!" Mamma exclaims upon arriving at the Channel: "we are come to the sea that is in our map. But it is very little in the map. I can lay my finger over it. Yes; it is little in the map, because everything is little in the map: the towns are little, and the rivers are little."[24] Charles decreases in significance as the landscape increases in scale; no longer able to obliterate the sea with a single finger, he finds himself in danger of being swallowed up instead. Mamma tells him "not [to] be afraid" even though there is "water every where around us!" She likewise draws attention to the fact that large objects appear small when viewed from afar: "I see some things in the sea at a great distance. Those are more ships and boats. How very small they are! they look like nut shells in a great pond."[25] Large vessels, and by extension the grand pursuits of trade and military conquest, shrink to mere trifles through a trick of perspective (one Barbauld would later exploit in "Washing Day," a poem that composes into a single frame the Montgolfier hot-air balloon and soap bubbles blown by children). Charles may well

---

[22] Barbauld, *Lessons for Children of Three*, 22–23.
[23] Anna Letitia Barbauld, *Lessons for Children from Three to Four Years Old* (London, 1788), 69–70.
[24] Ibid., 50–51.
[25] Ibid., 60–61.

consider that in boarding his own ship he enters a space no larger than a nutshell from the viewpoint of some distant figure. These inversions of size are found everywhere in Barbauld's series, presented as the natural food for thought of growing children – readers whose own scales remain in a continual state of flux.

Many young readers of the period would have gleaned similar lessons on scale from *Gulliver's Travels* (1726).[26] With its elements of fantasy and bawdy humor, Swift's satirical novel was embraced by children almost immediately following its publication, particularly when made available in abridged formats. As the titles of children's books such as Newbery's *Lilliputian Magazine*, Richard Johnson's *Lilliputian Library* (c. 1780), and Fenn's *Lilliputian Spectacle de la Nature* (1790) attest, "Lilliputian" became marketing shorthand for "child" or "child-sized" over the course of the eighteenth century. But Brobdingnag has its own children. While Gulliver becomes a kind of doll or baby for nine-year-old Glumdalclitch during his second voyage, he trembles before her older brother, recalling how "mischievous all Children ... naturally are" to creatures smaller than themselves, "Sparrows, Rabbits, young Kittens, and Puppy Dogs."[27] Swift, like Barbauld, constructs a world where smallness and largeness (and therefore vulnerability and authority) must be understood as relative, continually shifting qualities. Mark McGurl suggests that the popularity of the first two voyages of *Gulliver's Travels* as children's literature "makes sense if we consider the various ways they [young readers] are learning to scale the world through which they move, associating the physical scale of things with various scales of value." There is something inherently satisfying in these ongoing acts of calibration (McGurl describes this as "the *pleasure of measure*"); nonetheless, he reminds us that Gulliver's fluctuations in size prove disorientating, even frightening, and that this too is part of the child's experience.[28]

Jane and Ann Taylor warn young readers against the dangers of growing too big, too quickly in "The Boy Turned Giant" (1810), where a child regrets his wish to grow taller almost as soon as it is granted. His newfound height – all 30 feet of it – is both uncomfortable and impractical, not least because he has outgrown his home. Lines describing this

---

[26] For more on smallness in *Gulliver's Travels*, see Melinda Alliker Rabb, *Miniature and the English Imagination: Literature, Cognition, and Small-Scale Culture, 1650–1765* (Cambridge: Cambridge University Press, 2019), 41–70.

[27] Jonathan Swift, *Gulliver's Travels*, ed. Albert J. Rivero (New York: Norton, 2002), 75.

[28] Mark McGurl, "Gigantic Realism: The Rise of the Novel and the Comedy of Scale," *Critical Inquiry*, 43.2 (2017), 403–430 (414–415).

predicament anticipate Alice's plight in the White Rabbit's house by almost six decades:

> Return'd,—it was in vain he tried
> Beneath his native roof to hide;
> His knee was at the second floor!
> His foot alone block'd up the door![29]

The boy is restored to his original size only after realizing how foolish he has been in seeking to change his usual state for something supposedly better. The poem's moral asks children to "be content" with their status in life, as well as their stature, as though young people are any more capable of containing their desires than policing the boundaries of their unruly, expanding bodies.[30] But this trite conclusion is perhaps no more than we expect from a didactic fable, a form that requires authors to package the contents of their narrative, no matter how fantastic, within the bounded form of a lesson by the story's end. The boy's height is therefore not the only thing to fluctuate over the course of the poem – its imaginative scope expands and contracts in kind.

At the end of "The Boy Turned Giant," the protagonist comes to accept that youth and small size are commensurate: he will gradually grow bigger as he grows older. But his experience in the middle of the story, in which he finds himself suddenly out of proportion to his environment, echoes the relationship of eighteenth-century children to their books. As we have seen, the material and typographic dimensions and the thematic scope of these volumes were subject to tremendous variation, their pages shaped by different notions of how children learn to read as well as what they read *for* – whether preparing themselves for an early death or facilitating the gradual process of growing up. The child's own experience of size would have varied dramatically in kind, towering over Boreman's and Marshall's minuscule volumes one moment and shrinking within the expanding world of Barbauld's *Lessons* the next. By way of conclusion, I turn to a work that proclaims not only that size is a relative concept, subject to perpetual change, but presents alternative possibilities through which smallness might coincide with greatness – a lesson as significant for child readers as for critics of children's literature.

---

[29] Jane and Ann Taylor, *Signor Topsy Turvy's Wonderful Magic Lantern; or, The World Turned Upside Down* (London: Tabart, 1810), 55–56.
[30] Ibid., 51–56.

The Little Great Man

Tom Thumb's Folio; or, A New Penny Play-Thing for Little Giants was originally published by Newberry in 1767. The earliest extant edition (1768) measures just 3 ½ by 2 ⅜ inches. Bound up within this tiny vessel are a short history of Tom Thumb's life, literacy aids, religious lessons, moral tales, and abridged versions of Aesop's fables. Where Marshall relegates different subjects to their respective volumes of *The Infant's Library* and Barbauld spaces her *Lessons* out over the course of several years, Newbery crowds the *Folio*'s contents as closely as possible, allowing readers to travel from fantasy to piety with the turn of a page. While Brian Alderson and Felix de Marez Oyens characterize the *Folio*'s confection of different forms and genres as "rather random" in nature, I argue that the work's heterogeneity reflects a particularly eighteenth-century ideal of the children's book as compendium.[31] Other works that epitomize this aim include Boreman's *A Description of Three Hundred Animals* (1730), a natural history that draws together the magical and mundane in the style of a medieval bestiary, and Newbery's *Nurse Truelove's New-Year's Gift* (1750), subtitled "the Book of Books for Children," where "The House that Jack Built" runs directly into a catechism. One might argue that such texts display an utter disregard for thematic consistency, with different components brought together primarily to pad out and sell volumes. But we might also accept that eighteenth-century notions of what a single children's book may contain between its covers were broader than our own.

In terms of its design, the *Folio* channels seventeenth- and early eighteenth-century notions of how works for young readers ought to be formatted: pages are dense with small, fully justified type and minimal white space. But this feeling of compactness is part of the volume's charm, signaling, together with its diverse contents, an ability to supply *multum in parvo* – much in little.[32] While this motto frequently appeared on the frontispieces of eighteenth-century miscellanies and abridgements for adult readers, it has a special resonance where children's literature, a genre that seeks to be profound yet accessible, is concerned. The *multum in parvo*

---

[31] Brian Alderson and Felix de Marez Oyens, *Be Merry and Wise: Origins of Children's Book Publishing in England, 1650–1850* (New Castle, DL: Oak Knoll and British Library, 2006), 29.

[32] Lynne Vallone identifies the *multum in parvo* trope as central to comprehending "the powerful nature of the miniature." While Vallone considers the bawdy implications of Tom Thumb's small person, my work highlights the complexity of what she terms "the child's Tom Thumb" (see *Big & Small: A Cultural History of Extraordinary Bodies* [New Haven, CT: Yale University Press, 2017], 33, 47).

trope is underscored by the *Folio*'s playful conceptualization of child readers as "little giants," reminding us that small people, like small texts, may possess a hidden magnitude – a quality epitomized by Tom Thumb.

Originally a hero of the chapbook tradition, Tom Thumb migrated from the realm of folklore and adult popular culture to children's literature over the course of the eighteenth century, his name becoming as significant as "Lilliput" or "Lilliputian" in the marketing of books for young readers.[33] Tom's smallness symbolically mirrors the child's own stature; his comic misadventures parallel the child's experience of navigating a world scaled for adults. But Tom is also suitable for children by the logic that aligns early life with all things small: pocket-watches, pincushions, doll houses. With this in mind, the child reader is invited not only to sympathize with Tom's littleness but also to feel amplified by it. But how small was Tom, exactly? His dimensions fluctuate not only over the course of his textual history but within the *Folio* itself. As a result, the work has more in common with *Lessons for Children* than one might anticipate, offering child readers yet another lens through which to examine scale in relation to their own experience.

The first thing we learn about Tom, for instance, is that he is not necessarily thumb-sized at all. He is instead the son of Mr. Theophilus Thumb of Thumb Hall, in Northumberland, so that any parallel between his surname and stature is a matter of coincidence. Tom is typically depicted in the *Folio* as roughly 3 or 4 inches high, small enough to use a needle as a sword and a hazelnut shell as a helmet. But at times it seems as though he must be larger than this, as when he carries off a raven's egg in his pocket, or else smaller, as when the narrator suggests that he make a living as a physician rather than a soldier, "as his diminutive Size might permit him to slide down a Patient's Throat, and see what was the Matter within."[34] Tom's most significant transformation of scale appears as a matter of perspective rather than physical dimension, however.

The opening chapter of his history reveals that Tom was so small at birth as to be "almost invisible." His parents are "disconcerted at having such a little tiney [sic] Toy of a child" and take "little Notice of him" at first, associating smallness with triviality and dispensability. But their outlook changes when "a very learned Gentleman" examines Tom "through a great

---

[33] Andrea Immel and Brian Anderson, *Tommy Thumb's Pretty Song-Book: The First Collection of English Nursery Rhymes. A Facsimile Edition with a History and Annotations* (Los Angeles, CA: Cotsen Occasional Press, 2013).

[34] *Tom Thumb's Folio; or, a New Penny Play-Thing for Little Giants* (London, 1768), 6. Hereafter cited in text.

Pair of Spectacles," declaring that "he would be a very little Man, and a very great Man; which is a Paradox, or Riddle, we are to solve by-and-by" (4). True to the condensed scale of the volume, "by-and-by" comes sooner rather than later. The riddle's solution is given on the following page: "what makes a great Man[?] Is it a great Head? No. Is it a long Arm? No. Is it a big Body? No. Is it a large Leg? No.... It is a wise Head and a good Heart that constitutes a great Man" (5). By presenting greatness as an internal quality rather than a question of physical proportion, the gentleman recalibrates Tom's parents' perception of their near-invisible infant. On discovering that greatness may reside within littleness, Tom's father "took him up upon his little Finger, and chirped to him as a Boy does to a Bird; and his mother wrapped him up in a Piece of Cotton, put him into a Thimble instead of a Cradle, and carried him about in her warm Pocket" (4). The Thumbs' earlier sense of Tom's insignificance has been replaced by a new conceptualization that regards small things as worthy of the utmost care and attention; the tiny toy has become a treasure. A similar adjustment is necessary when critically evaluating "minor" works of children's literature – important texts that may at first appear insubstantial, even trifling in terms of their contents, eliciting greater interest from bibliographers and cultural historians than literary critics. *Tom Thumb's Folio* is precisely such a work, with seemingly little to recommend it from an aesthetic standpoint.

On closer inspection, however, we find that the *Folio* encompasses two key concepts of littleness relevant to eighteenth-century children and their books – those of compression and gradation. Regarding the former, both Tom Thumb and the volume containing his history are condensed versions of larger things. The *Folio* is not only a miniature book but also contains a succession of miniaturized literary forms. Though Tom's history extends over the course of several chapters, some occupy a single page, giving his biography an appropriately compressed aspect. Towards the end of the volume, we find Aesop's already brief fable of the fox and the crow retold in six lines of iambic pentameter. This abridgement is followed by an even shorter moral summarizing the fable's lesson in six words: "The Flatterer's art / Betrays the Heart" (27). In negotiating such materials, children learn that the same lesson may be conveyed in increasingly abbreviated forms: where the human body is measured against a thumb, a story may be told in the space of a couplet.

But *Tom Thumb's Folio* also embraces a graduated approach to growth and learning in which little things lead to big things, or else get bigger themselves. Though Tom remains small, his implied child reader is perpetually growing, verging towards a greatness that is literal rather than figurative (measured in long arms, big bodies, and large legs). The soubriquet "little giants" implies as much, positioning children on one end of a developmental trajectory that culminates in full-scale adulthood. Similarly, while the *Folio* functions as a compendium (much in little), its contents nonetheless gesture towards the importance of graduated instruction. For example, Tom's own path to maturity is paved by a succession of different volumes in a mode of reading reminiscent of Barbauld's *Lessons*. When Mr. Thumb learns that greatness is the product of intelligence and virtue:

[H]e immediately bought for his Son all Mr. *Newbery*'s little Books, he having been informed, that they were published with no other View, but to make People wise and good; and *Tom* read from the Beginning to the End, first one Volume, and then another, till he had made himself Master of the whole (5).

While this passage is blatant self-promotion on Newbery's part, it also serves as a reminder that no single book is sufficient in a child's education, with the activity of reading framed in progressive terms: "first one Volume, and then another."

This graduated approach is further reflected in the *Folio*'s literacy aids, which appear after Tom Thumb's history. We begin with different methods for representing and categorizing individual letters of the alphabet ("The Great Letter Lesson," "The Little Letter Lesson," "The Vowel Lesson") before discovering how these small units may be joined to form longer, semantically meaningful sequences ("The Syllable Lesson," "The Word Lesson," "The Sentence Lesson"). But even here, readers encounter the possibility that categories such as little and big, short and long may be deceiving, for "*I* is a Word, as well as *Strength*, though the first contains but one Letter, and the last eight," and individual sentences may "contain a greater or less Number of Words" (22). Following close on the heels of Tom's history, these lessons cannot help but reinforce the text's dual thematic elements: small things may possess a hidden magnitude, or else they may be valuable in their ability to contribute towards greatness, even by a very little.

This chapter has considered the smallness of eighteenth-century children and their books through different lenses, considering its material, bodily, textual, and temporal implications. As we have seen, ideas of what constituted a "little book" were as changeable as attitudes towards the littleness of children themselves, whose bodies threatened to be either too small or too big, their lives perilously short or blissfully long, depending on the angle of approach. The greatness or littleness of children's literature as a genre is likewise variable, contingent on our willingness as critics to subject minor works to close scrutiny. Modern critics have insisted on the aesthetic value of *Lessons for Children*, a deceptively simple text of "intricate craftsmanship directed at complex purposes."[35] But far from all works for young readers possess the stylistic or conceptual richness that tends to be associated with literary greatness. The eighteenth-century child's reading experience included books that were formulaic, simplistic, or seemingly random in their composition. And although texts of this type are often overlooked by modern scholars, a closer engagement with their contents promises to produce a more comprehensive understanding of early children's literature as a genre, in all its variations of size, scope, and significance.

---

[35] Isobel Grundy, "'Slip-Shod Measure' and 'Language of Gods': Barbauld's Stylistic Range" in William McCarthy and Olivia Murphy (eds.), *Anna Letitia Barbauld: New Perspectives* (Lewisburg, PA: Bucknell University Press, 2014), 23–36 (27).

3 Gothic Syntax

CYNTHIA WALL

> I waked one morning in the beginning of last June from a dream, of which all I could recover was, that I had thought myself in an ancient castle (a very natural dream for a head filled like mine with Gothic story) and that on the uppermost bannister of a great staircase I saw a gigantic hand in armour. In the evening I sat down and began to write, without knowing in the least what I intended to say or relate. The work grew on my hands, and I grew fond of it—add that I was very glad to think of anything rather than politics[.][1]

So Horace Walpole narrates the genesis of that cornerstone of British gothic, *The Castle of Otranto*, to his friend William Cole on March 9, 1765, just over two months after the first edition of five hundred copies was published on December 24, 1764. He tells a story of a dream, of an impulse without direction, of a political distraction. It was a spontaneous effusion, taking less than two months to write, and as E. J. Clery has outlined, "the dream-origin" has operated more as "an explanation for its short-comings, than as a cause for enthusiasm."[2] The great Walpole biographer and collector W. S. Lewis himself confesses: "I marvel how such a lucid and entertaining writer as Horace Walpole could have written so confused and clumsy a book."[3] Yet it ignited a slow fuse in the 1760s that would explode into the "Gothic" of the 1790s and stoke the conflagration of subgenres in the following centuries, including horror fiction, historical romance, science fiction, and the mystery novel. "The slender tale of *Otranto*," Clery aptly observes, "might well appear as insubstantial as poor Conrad beneath the weight of such a legacy. That it is still read [there have been close to a hundred editions, it has been translated into a number of languages, and there are umpteen paperbacks available], and read with interest, is something of

---

[1] Horace Walpole, *The Yale Edition of Horace Walpole's Correspondence*, ed. W. S. Lewis, 48 vols. (New Haven, CT: Yale University Press, 1937–83), vol. 1, 88. Hereafter references are given parenthetically in the text.

[2] Austin Dobson, *Horace Walpole: A Memoir* (London, 1890), 195 (quoting the same letter to William Cole); E. J. Clery, introduction to *The Castle of Otranto*, by Horace Walpole, ed. W. S. Lewis (Oxford: Oxford University Press, 1996), ix.

[3] W. S. Lewis, *Rescuing Horace Walpole* (New Haven, CT: Yale University Press, 1978), 188.

a tribute to Walpole's foresight, as well as to his imaginative powers."[4] This chapter argues that the minute levels of syntax and typography reveal consistent patterns of a textual architecture that is itself a *performance* of gothic architecture, hollowing out subterranean passages, carving out unexpected corners, deliberately designing for the reader the kind of epistemological darkness and confusion confronting the characters, forcing us to grope around those corners and long for the overhead lights of typographical modernity.

I am speaking primarily, of course, about quotation marks, or lack thereof. Neither the first nor the second edition of *Otranto* employs quotation marks to distinguish dialogue. Of course, in a period where quotation marks enclosing dialogue were still tiny pioneers, it is not entirely surprising that *Otranto* has none. Yet Henry Fielding was already using inverted commas in *Joseph Andrews* (1742) and *Tom Jones* (1749). And Walpole makes no use of Defovian tactics such as new lines or italicized directions, nor of Bunyan's (and Defoe's) dramatic speech-prefixes, nor of Richardsonian dashes and paragraphs to clarify its speakers. Or rather, it uses such small typographical markers more often as *miscues*, bleeding one voice into another: "cried *Matilda* sinking ; good heaven, receive my soul ! Savage inhuman monster ! what hast thou done ! cried *Theodore*."[5] When I ask students to read this and related passages, on first try the person voicing the gentle, dutiful, soft-spoken Matilda always finds herself surprised to continue: "'Savage inhuman … monster'? *Oops!*" The person voicing Theodore never speaks up in time. I want to suggest that the print product of a man who describes his own character as satirical, who is utterly devoted to detail in every other aspect of his life and art, and who was himself a printer, is more likely to be the product of design than confusion or clumsiness.

Walpole finishes his account of the writing of *Otranto* with a wry look at its syntactics:

—In short I was so engrossed with my tale, which I completed in less than two months, that one evening I wrote from the time I had drunk my tea, about six o'clock till half an hour after one in the morning, when my hand and fingers were so weary, that I could not hold the pen to finish the sentence, but left Matilda and Isabella talking, in the middle of a paragraph. (Correspondence, I:88)

---

[4] Clery, Introduction, ix.
[5] Horace Walpole, *The Castle of Otranto: A Gothic Story*, 2nd ed. (London: Printed for William Bathoe, 1765), 187. Hereafter references are given parenthetically in the text.

In the middle of a paragraph. It turns out that in much Gothic fiction, the middle of the paragraph operates syntactically like an underground labyrinth. The Gothic turn of a sentence is a Gothic turn of the screw.

A Brief History of Quotation Marks

Perhaps the briefest of brief histories of the quotation mark appears in a witty exhibition catalogue:

> THERE WAS NO CONSISTENT MARK FOR QUOTATIONS BEFORE THE SEVENTEENTH CENTURY. ANCIENT GREEK TEXTS USED THE PARAGRAPHOS TO SHOW CHANGES IN DIALOGUE. DIRECT SPEECH WAS USUALLY CONSIDERED TO BE ANNOUNCED SUFFICIENTLY BY PHRASES LIKE HE SAID. „THE DOUBLE COMMA WAS INITIALLY USED TO POINT OUT IMPORTANT SENTENCES AND WAS " LATER USED TO ENCLOSE QUOTATIONS. ELIZABETHAN PRINTERS OFTEN EDGED BOTH MARGINS " " OF A QUOTED TEXT WITH DOUBLE COMMAS. THIS CONVENTION TREATED TEXT AS A SPATIAL " " PLANE RATHER THAN A TEMPORAL LINE, FRAMING THE QUOTED PASSAGE LIKE A PICTURE.   "[6]

In the seventeenth century, the diple (initially > or ») was the "note or mark in the Margent, to signifie that there is somewhat to be amended," and was beginning to be used in some cases to mark instances of direct speech (instead of a quotation from another author), though it tended only to point towards that speech occurring somewhere in the line; italicized quotations were more common and more accurate.[7] By the late seventeenth century, the diple curled and rose into an inverted comma – the first "modern" quotation mark.

Through much of the eighteenth century, inverted commas were still used primarily to identify quotations by another author:

Comma's are used to distinguish quoted Matter from the mean Text : for which purpose two inverted Comma's are put at the beginning of such Matter, and continued before each line of the quotation, till the close thereof is signified by two Apostrophus' ; which by some is called, the *Mark for Silence* ; intimating thereby, that the borrowed or quoted passage from another Author ceases with that mark. But the rule for double-comma's is sometimes confounded, when they are put before matter which is only an Extract[.][8]

---

[6] [Ellen Lupton], *Period Styles: A Punctuated History* (New York: Herb Lubalin Study Center of Design and Typography, 1988), exhibition catalogue, 3.

[7] Thomas Blount, *Glossographia, or, a Dictionary Interpreting the Hard Words of Whatsoever Language Now in Our Refined English Tongue [...]*, 5th ed. (1656; London, 1681), 199; on the diple, see M. B. Parkes, *Pause and Effect: An Introduction to the History of Punctuation in the West* (Aldershot: Scolar Press, 1992), 59.

[8] John Smith, *The Printer's Grammar* (London, 1755), 89.

In 1785, Joseph Robertson, in his *Essay on Punctuation*, defines the "characters" proper for

A Quotation " ". Two inverted commas are generally placed at the beginning of a phrase or a passage, which is quoted or transcribed from some author, in his own words; and two commas, in their direct position, are placed at the conclusion : as,
> An excellent poet says :
> "The proper study of mankind is man."[9]

Even in the early nineteenth century, the most common function of quotation marks was to "denote extracts or quotations from other works"; "dialogue matter, or any passages or expressions not original"[10] still trail behind – though by the time of Jane Austen, quotation marks (single or double) were more frequently used for either direct or indirect speech, or even "a conflation of several utterances."[11]

John Lennard has lamented that punctuation for the modern reader is "too readily invisible."[12] This is partly the work of editors, who want punctuation to function invisibly so that the reading process is as accessible as possible: "According to the *Chicago Manual of Style* (§ 5.5), dash-hybrids are currently illegal in the U.S."[13] On the other hand, Nicholson Baker, a man after my own heart (or perhaps it's the other way around), sees the beginning of a beautiful friendship in the relationship of punctuation to its text: "Punctuation, like marginal and interlinear commentary, seems at times to have been a ritual of reciprocation, a way of returning something to the text in grateful tribute after it had released its meaning in the reader's mind."[14]

Walpole's Typographical Contexts

Direct speech in earlier fiction was represented in a number of ways, some influenced by dramatic conventions. In *The Pilgrim's Progress* (1678), the non-theatergoing Dissenter John Bunyan intermingled in-text and parenthetical indicators with the speech-prefixes familiar from plays:

---

[9] Joseph Robertson, *An Essay on Punctuation* (London, 1785), 147.
[10] Caleb Stower, *The Printer's Grammar; or, Introduction to the Art of Printing* (London, 1808), 82.
[11] Bronwen Thomas, "Dialogue" in Peter Melville Logan (gen. ed.), *The Encyclopedia of the Novel*, 2 vols. (Oxford: Blackwell, 2012), vol. 1, 250–254 (250).
[12] John Lennard, "In/visible Punctuation," *Visible Language*, 45.1/2 (2011), 121–138 (123).
[13] Nicholson Baker, "The History of Punctuation" in *The Size of Thoughts* (1982; New York: Vintage Books, 1997), 87.
[14] Ibid., 77.

Then said the Man, Neighbours, *Wherefore are you come*? They said To perswade you to go back with us, but he said, That can by no means be: you dwell, said he, in the City of Destruction (the place also where I was born,) [...] Be content good Neighbours, and go along with me.

    What! said *Obstinate, and leave our Friends, and our comforts behind us!*   *Obstinate*.
    *Yes, said *Christian*, (for that was his name) [...]   *Christian*.
    Chr. I seek an *Inheritance, incorruptible, undefiled and that fadeth not away*; and it is laid up in Heaven [...] Read it so, if you will, in my Book.
Ob. *Tush* said *Obstinate*, away with your Book; will you go back with us, or no?[15]

The reader has no trouble distinguishing the speakers, as Bunyan employs at least four techniques throughout the story: italics; parentheticals; speech-prefixes; and a liberal scattering of he said, she said.

Daniel Defoe, another Dissenter, sets up extra obstacles for himself in that so many of his characters remain nameless: even the narrators' nearest and dearest (husbands, children, that sort of thing) tend to disappear behind common nouns. One exception is the younger brother Robin in *Moll Flanders* (1722), whom Moll eventually, reluctantly marries, much preferring his Elder Brother. When Elder Brother reports to Moll (not yet her assigned name) about Robin's honorable devotion, she "interrupted him in his Story thus" – and thus begins a complicated but completely navigable dialogue:

AY! *said I*, does he think I can not deny him? but he shall find I can Deny him, for all that. [...]

    THEN he went on and *told me*, that he reply'd thus: But Brother, you know She has nothing, and you may have several Ladies with good Fortunes: 'Tis no matter for that, *said* Robin, I Love the Girl; and I will never please my Pocket in Marrying, and not please my Fancy; and so my Dear *adds he*, there is no Opposing him.

    YES, yes, *says I*, you shall see I can Oppose him, I have learnt to say NO now[.][16]

The speakers commandeer their own paragraphs; within those paragraphs, italics quickly alert the reader to shifts, which themselves take over after the fairly heavy-duty punctuation mark of the colon.

Eliza Haywood, another nonuser of quotation marks, is equally adept with Bunyan and Defoe at mapping out discourse. Mistress-of-disguise Fantomina, her games of seducing Beauplaisir brought to an abrupt end by the coincidental arrivals of her mother and then her baby, is ordered to name her seducer, and a complicated triangle of dialogue and silence ensues:

---

[15] John Bunyan, *The Pilgrim's Progress*, ed. Cynthia Wall (New York: W. W. Norton, 2009), 13.
[16] Daniel Defoe, *Moll Flanders*, ed. G. A. Starr and Linda Bree (Oxford: Oxford University Press, 2011), 31. Although we do not have direct evidence of Defoe's directions to the printers or corrections to proofs, Defoe's typographical patterns are largely consistent throughout the lifetime editions of his works.

> [*Fantomina*,] covering herself with the [bed] Cloaths, and ready to die a second Time with the inward Agitations of her Soul, shriek'd out, Oh, I am undone — I cannot live, and bear this Shame ! ---- But the old Lady believing that now or never was the Time to dive into the Bottom of this Mystery, forcing her to rear her Head, told her, she should not hope to escape the Scrutiny of a parent she had dishonour'd in such a Manner, and pointing to *Beauplaisir*, Is this the Gentleman, (*said she,*) to whom you owe your Ruin ? or have you deceiv'd me by a fictitious Tale ? Oh! no, (*resum'd the trembling Creature,*) he is, indeed, the innocent Cause of my Undoing :--- Promise me your Pardon, (*continued she,*) and I will relate the Means. Here she ceas'd, expecting what she would reply, which, on hearing *Beauplaisir* cry out, What mean you, Madam? I your Undoing, who never harbour'd the least Design on you in my Life, she did in these Words, Though the Injury you have done your Family, (*said she*) is of a Nature, which cannot justly hope Forgiveness, yet be assur'd, I shall much sooner excuse you when satisfied of the Truth, than while I am kept in a Suspence[.][17]

In the more or less microscopic world of punctuation, the plentiful exclamation points followed by long dashes (one of what Baker calls "the great dash-hybrids" – presumably an "exclamash") are large gestures, visually amplifying Fantomina's shrieks.[18] The "said shes", on the other hand, are doubly quieted, their incurling italics encased in parentheses. Yet both typographical gestures, obtrusive and unobtrusive, complement the straightforward verb phrases ("Here she ceas'd"), the strategically placed pronouns ("in my Life, she did in these Words"), and the clear green traffic lights ("on hearing Beauplaisir cry out, What mean you, Madam?") to send even the modern student skimming over the narrative without losing her way. The tiny marks lay the tracks for a linear reading.

The early users of those amphibious diple-commas – the emerging quotation marks – were grappling for an even more immediate, more efficient signage for direct discourse. D. F. McKenzie has tracked their uses in the early editions of William Congreve's prose fiction.[19] M. B. Parkes notes that the "use of single marks for raised and inverted commas at this date is peculiar to the English speaking world," as part of a project by novelists

---

[17] Eliza Haywood, *Fantomina: or, Love in a Maze. Being a Secret History of an Amour Between Two Persons of Condition*, in *Secret Histories, Novels and Poems*, vol. 3 (London, 1725), 289–290.
[18] Baker, "History of Punctuation," 82.
[19] D. F. McKenzie, "Note on This Edition" in *The Works of William Congreve*, ed. D. F. McKenzie, 3 vols. (Oxford: Oxford University Press, 2011), vol. 1, xl. See also McKenzie, "Typography and Meaning: The Case of William Congreve" in Giles Barber and Bernhard Fabian (eds.), *The Book and the Book Trade in Eighteenth-Century Europe* (Hamburg: Ernst Hauswedell, 1977), 81–123.

to develop "special conventions involving choice of vocabulary and syntactical features [… as well as] new conventions of layout and punctuation […] to make it as clear to the reader as possible that the representation of spoken language was intended."[20] The diple was typically *supplemented* by the parenthetical reminders about the direct speech, but its agency is immediately clear: "Here comes a Voice!" it cries.

Henry Fielding wielded the inverted comma for his characters' direct speech, and in *Joseph Andrews* (1742) he (or at least his printer, Andrew Millar) signified the close thereof by one "Apostrophus," which (paraphrasing John Smith) is called "the *Mark for Silence* ; intimating thereby, that the borrowed or quoted passage from another [Character] ceases with that mark."[21] After a little reported discourse instigated by the landlady Mrs. Tow-wowse spotting a gold coin in the pocket of the poor itinerant servant Joseph Andrews (beleaguered brother to Samuel Richardson's virtuous maid Pamela), Mrs. Tow-wowse bursts into dipled speech that marks the closing of her mouth and the opening of Joseph's:

> [Mrs. *Tow-wouse*] told *Joseph*, she did not conceive a
> Man could want Money whilst he had Gold in his
> Pocket. *Joseph* answered, he had such a Value
> for that little Piece of Gold, that he would not
> part with it for a hundred times the riches which
> the greatest Esquire in the County was worth. ' A
> ' pretty Way indeed,' said Mrs. *Tow-wouse,* ' to
> ' run in debt, and then refuse to part with your
> ' Money, because you have a Value for it. I ne-
> ' ver knew any Piece of Gold of more Value than
> ' as many Shillings as it would change for.' ' Not
> ' to preserve my Life from starving, nor to re-
> ' deem it from a Robber, would I part with this
> ' dear Piece,' answered *Joseph*.[22]

The inverted commas at the beginnings of lines are matched within the line by end marks (the "dear Piece" is a memento from his beloved Fanny). The parenthetical speech reminders still play a part: "What (says Mrs. *Tow-wowse*) I suppose'" (I:102). But then Mr. Tow-wowse jumps in without hesitation (or readerly ambiguity) on Mrs. Tow-wowse's cue:

---

[20] Parkes, *Pause and Effect*, 228, 92.
[21] Smith, *Printer's Grammar*, 89.
[22] Henry Fielding, *The History of the Adventures of Joseph Andrews, And his Friend Mr. Abraham Adams*, 2 vols., 3rd ed. (London, 1743), vol. 1, 101–102. Hereafter references are given parenthetically in the text.

"[']My / 'Husband is a Fool if he parts with the Horse / ' without being paid for him.' 'No, no, I can't / 'part with the Horse indeed till I have the Mo- / ' ney,' cry'd *Tow-wowse*" (I:102). The speech-boundaries are as clear as chapter headings – and in their own tiny way, they function like "Those little Spaces between our Chapters," as a kind of "Inn or Resting-Place" (I:95) where the reader instantly recognizes the "mark of silence," the pause of voice, the change in identity.

In *Clarissa* (1747–1748), Richardson does not make use of inverted commas, but his paragraphing and punctuation easily do the heavy lifting of discourse direction. Clarissa's mother urges her to obey her father and be nice to her suitor, the icky Mr. Solmes:

> But, Clary, this one further opportunity I give you— Go in again to Mr Solmes, and behave discreetly to him ; and let your papa find you together, upon *civil* terms at least.
>
> My feet moved (of themselves, I think), farther from the parlour where he was, and towards the stairs ; and there I stopp'd and paused. […]
>
> I was moving to go up—
>
> And *will* you go up, Clary ? […]
>
> What can I do, Madam ?—What *can* I do ?—
>
> Go in again, my child—Go in again, my *dear* child !—repeated she ; and let your papa find you together !—[23]

Richardson makes full use not just of the colon and semicolon but also of dramatic dashes and paragraphical indentations to give the rhythmic soundscape of deliberation, pause, expectation, hesitation, division – and vocal identity. We know who is speaking by the look of the page. The small things of typography disambiguate identity.

Free-Range Voices in *The Castle of Otranto*

Paragraphs; parentheticals; italics; she-saids; (*he saids*); dashes; diples; diples-and-dashes – the various seventeenth- and eighteenth-century apparatuses for clearly marking characters' speech – were thus all available to the well-read Walpole (himself an artisanal printer) in 1764, when he was writing *The Castle of Otranto*. In fact, the text of the Oxford World's Classics edition (edited by W. S. Lewis in 1969 and Nick Groom in 2014) is based on "that in the *Works of Horatio Walpole, Earl of Orford*

---

[23] Samuel Richardson, *Clarissa. Or, The History of a Young Lady* […], 7 vols. (London: Printed for S. Richardson, 1747–48), vol. 1, 145.

Gothic Syntax 55

(London, 1798), ii. 1–90,"[24] and by 1798, inverted commas, both single *and* double, were quite common in marking dialogue.[25] And yet one of the most exasperating experiences of first reading *Otranto* is discovering how utterly *confusing* the dialogues are. Walpole makes little use of these techniques; or if he does, the markers seem to be in the wrong place at the wrong time – miscues rather than cues.

Nick Groom has admirably addressed this (alas, Lewis did not): he notes that the seventh edition, published in 1793, modernized Walpole's punctuation (including inserting quotation marks), "but this innovation was evidently felt to be misguided and was not adopted in subsequent lifetime editions."[26] One argument for the lack of quotation marks could be implied in the preface to the first edition, which claims that the "work was found in the library of an ancient Catholic family in the north of *England*. It was printed at *Naples*, in the black letter, in the year 1529."[27] In 1529, quotation marks didn't exist and diples (>) were just beginning to be replaced by commas. But a more interesting (gothic) reading of the omission of quotation marks is raised by Groom: "the claustrophobic atmosphere of *The Castle of Otranto* is deepened by the headlong rapidity of dialogue, creating a clamour of voices that overlap and run into the narrative itself." He says that the "faithfully produced" long dashes "(— and -----) are used to herald direct speech, mark breaks and pauses, and distinguish parenthetical clauses or distinct phrases."[28] Here, I want to push the effect of Walpole's choice of speech representation even further. There is not only a lack of quotation marks; there is a sense in which even the dashes presumably meant to distinguish voices actually collapse them, posing obstacles just as much for the readers of 1765 and 1798 as for those in a classroom today. The syntax creates epistemological corners, where things go bump in the night.

One literal "clamour of voices" occurs in Chapter 1 (Figure 3.1) when the excitable domestics Diego and Jaquez see a giant foot and part of a leg in the gallery of Otranto and rush to tell Prince Manfred about it (although it takes them from page 34 to page 39 in the second edition to get it out):

---

[24] W. S. Lewis, "A Note on the Text" in *The Castle of Otranto*, by Horace Walpole, ed. Lewis, intro. E. J. Clery (Oxford: Oxford University Press, 1996), xxxiv.
[25] The 2001 Penguin edition, edited by Michael Gamer, uses the same 1798 text and also "preserve[s] Walpole's spelling and punctuation" ("A Note on the Text," xlii).
[26] Nick Groom, "A Note on the Text" in *The Castle of Otranto*, by Horace Walpole, ed. Groom (Oxford: Oxford University Press, 2014), xxxix.
[27] Horace Walpole, *The Castle of Otranto, A Story. Translated by William Marshal, Gent. From the Original Italian of Onuphrio Muralto, Canon of the Church of St. Nicholas at Otranto* (London: Printed for Thomas Lownds, 1764), A2.
[28] Groom, "Note on the Text," xxxix.

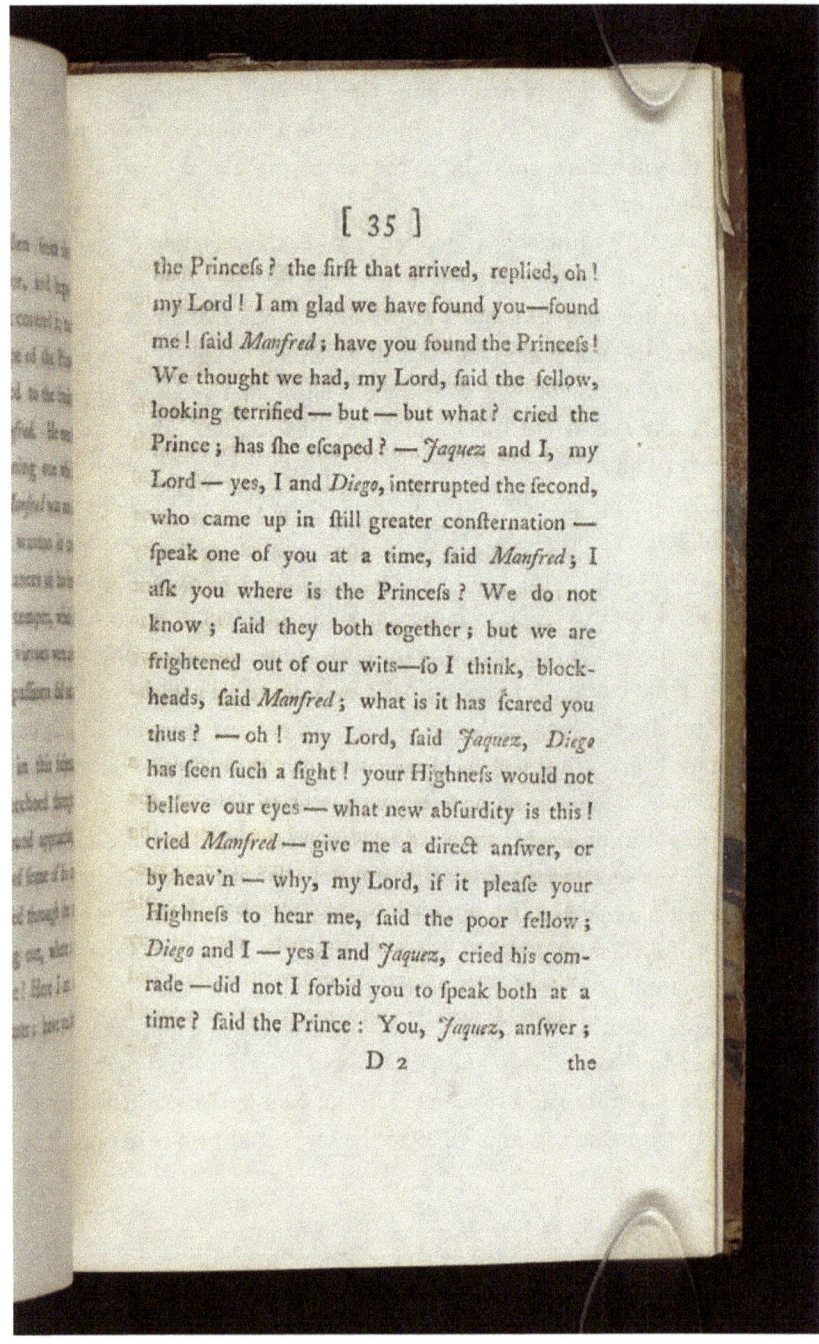

Figure 3.1 Horace Walpole, *The Castle of Otranto: A Gothic Story*, 2nd ed. (London, 1765), 35. Albert and Shirley Small Special Collections Library, University of Virginia.

In a way, this page replicates the use of dashes and "said-he"s employed by Fielding and Richardson, but a little reading aloud, especially by two or more persons new to the tale, results in an off-page clamor of voices. "I am glad we have found you—found me ! said *Manfred* ; I ask you where is the princess ?" But the servants' response is not signaled by a dash, and Manfred interrupts his own speech with a dash in line 17. "*Jaquez, Diego*" in line 14 doesn't help matters; nor does "*Diego* and I — yes I" in line 20. And at least we have italicized proper names to alert us to some sort of linguistic handoff; the "faithfully produced" Oxford has eliminated even that slim purchase.

The "New Edition" of 1792 brings on quotation marks *and* paragraphing to help the dashes sort out the mess:

" Here I am," said Manfred as they came nearer : " have you found the Princess?"

The first that arrived replied, "Oh ! my Lord ! " I am glad we have found you."

" Found me !" said Manfred ; " have you " found the Princess ?"

" We thought we had, my Lord," said the fellow, looking terrified—" but " —

" But what?" cried the Prince ; " has she " escaped ?"

" Jaquez and I, my Lord" —

" Yes, I and Diego," interrupted the second, who came up in still greater consternation—

" Speak one of you at a time," said Manfred ; " I ask you where is the Princess ?"

" We do not know," said they both together ; " but we are frightened out of our wits." ——

" So I think, blockhead," said Manfred ; " what is it has feared you thus ?"

" Oh! my Lord," said Jaquez, " Diego has " seen such a sight ! Your Highness would not " believe our eyes – – !"

" What new absurdity is this !" cried Man- fred : —" give me a direct answer, or, by hea- " ven" —

" Why, my Lord, if it please your Highness " to hear me," said the poor fellow, " Diego " and I" —

" Yes, I and Jaquez," cried his comrade—

" Did not I forbid you to speak both at a
" time?" said the Prince : "You, Jacques, an-
" swer ; for the other fool seems more distracted
" than thou art : what is the matter ?"
" My gracious Lord," said Jaquez, " if it
" please your Highness to hear me, Diego and I, [...]²⁹

The Cassell's National Library edition of 1886 follows this text (it has no "Note on the Text," merely a biographical introduction by Henry Morley).³⁰ E. F. Bleiler, in *Three Gothic Novels* (1966), employs quotation marks but not paragraphs.³¹

Thus the literal clamor of voices prompted an editorial clamor of "improvements," but a closer look at the syntactical possibilities of removing linguistic border markers opens up even more gothic sensibilities than the rush of claustrophobia noted by Groom. When Diego and Jaquez declare they will not go back to the gallery with Manfred "for all your Highness's revenue," the "young peasant,"

who had stood silent, now spoke. Will your Highness, said he, permit me to try this adventure? my life is of consequence to nobody : I fear no bad angel, and have offended no good one. Your behaviour is above your seeming ; said *Manfred*, viewing him with surprise and admiration ---- hereafter I will reward your bravery[.] (2nd ed., 41)

"Your behaviour" could still be something the young peasant might be observing (if a bit cheekily, pronominally speaking), though "above your seeming," certainly not; "said *Manfred*" straightens out our surprise as it denotes his.

Later, in Chapter 2, when the "hermit" sees the birthmark of a bloody arrow on "young peasant" Theodore's shoulder and recognizes that "it is my child ! my *Theodore* !" the emotions slosh around the page:

The passions that ensued, must be conceived ; they cannot be painted. The tears of the assistants were suspended by wonder, rather than stopped by joy. They seemed to enquire in the eyes of their Lord what they ought to feel. Surprise, doubt, tenderness, respect, succeeded each other in the countenance of the youth. (2nd ed., 83–84)

---

²⁹ Horace Walpole, *The Castle of Otranto, A Gothic Story [. . .]*, A New Edition (London: Wenman and Hodgson, 1792), 41.

³⁰ Horace Walpole, *The Castle of Otranto* (London, Paris, New York, and Melbourne: Cassell, 1886), 44. The long ʃ is modernized in this edition.

³¹ Horace Walpole, *The Castle of Otranto*, in *Three Gothic Novels*, ed. E. F. Bleiler (Toronto: Dover Publications, 1966), 40–41. There is no note on the text; the copyright page announces that "This Dover edition, first published in 1966, is an unabridged republication of the following editions of these works: *The Castle of Otranto*, Second Edition." There is no mention of its modernizations.

"Surprise" and "doubt," possibly "tenderness" and "respect" as well, seem to be answers to what the assistants "ought to feel." But at the end of the sentence, up looms "the youth," who himself makes a surprising syntactical leap in front of their Lord Manfred.

In Chapter 3, Matilda and Theodore have a contest of wills replayed in a contest of vocal identities. When Matilda takes several pages urging the "virtuous youth" to "fly [...] while it is in [her] power to save [him]," she repeats herself once again:

—I run no risk, said *Matilda*, but by thy delay. Depart ; it cannot be known that I assisted thy flight. Swear by the saints above, said *Theodore*, that thou canst not be suspected ; else here I vow to await whatever can befal me. Oh ! thou art too generous ; said *Matilda* ; but rest assured that no suspicion can alight on me. Give me thy beauteous hand ... (2nd ed., 114)

A modern Matilda reading this aloud for the first time almost always slides into "Swear by" (unless they've read closely enough to know that Matilda would never swear, even by the saints – any more than she would growl "Savage inhuman monster !"); a classroom Theodore would quite naturally assume that he would go on to praise Matilda's generosity; and the classroom generally erupts in laughter when Matilda then orders Theodore to give her his beauteous hand.

When Theodore declares his undying loyalty to the prince (emotions aren't particularly logical in this work), his impassioned rhetoric spills into the narrative; I have bolded the moments where the voice of one character slides over the implied but invisible boundary into another's, and then the moment where we slam into the corner: "There is not a sentiment engraven on my heart, that does not **venerate you and yours. The grace and fervour with which *Theodore*** uttered these words, interested every person present in his favour" (2nd ed., 137). "The grace and fervour with which" you served the helmeted knights at dinner, *or* you spoke of Isabella, *or* you once defended us from robber-barons – only the italicized *Theodore* stops Theodore in his uttered tracks. Manfred's wife, the princess Hippolita, objects to their ward Isabella accusing Manfred of "wicked purposes" (he had, after all, chased her into the subterranean vaults, intending to capture and marry her after divorcing his wife): "Your feeling, *Isabella*, is warm ; but until this hour I never knew it betray you into intemperance. What deed of *Manfred* authorizes you to treat him as a murderer, an assassin ? **Thou virtuous, and too credulous** Princess ! replied *Isabella*" (2nd ed., 149–150). Hippolita certainly knows Isabella to be virtuous, and perhaps too credulous in believing ill of Himself?

I will close the examples of diple-less syntax with the tangled death scene towards the end. As Manfred glides "softly between the isles" of the church of St. Nicholas, "guided by an imperfect gleam of moonshine that shone faintly through the illuminated windows, he stole towards the tomb of Alfonso, to which he was directed by indistinct whispers of the persons he sought":

> The first sounds he could distinguish were-----Does it alas ! depend on me ? *Manfred* will never permit our union-----No, this shall prevent it ! cried the tyrant, drawing his dagger, and plunging it over her shoulder into the bosom of the person that spoke-----ah ! me, I am slain ! cried *Matilda* sinking ; good heaven, receive my soul ! (2nd ed., 187)

Manfred is not the only one groping through a moonlit gloom; the reader finds herself struggling to see clearly as well. How could he plunge his dagger over Matilda's shoulder into her bosom? Matilda is speaking to Theodore (who will next roar, "Savage inhuman monster !" in the same breath as Matilda's sinking); if she has her back to Manfred, why not stab the speaking person's back? If facing him, why not just stab the speaking person in the heart? The slash of separation between "our union" and "No" is also murky; the syntactical corner could turn the other way: "*Manfred* will never permit our union-----No, this shall save us ! cried *Theodore*," or even, "No, O thou of the Beauteous Hand, I shall take care of everything!" Even knowing that Manfred thinks it is Isabella speaking to Theodore, surely the gloom is not so gloomy that he mistakes the back of a man for that of a woman?

Bronwen Thomas has argued that the Victorian novel codified the conventions of the quotation mark, "helping to perpetuate a notion of the speech of an individual as his or her private property."[32] One of the commonplaces about the gothic is that it exaggerates the kinds of concerns, fears, or preoccupations of more mainstream or "ordinary" genres. David Oakleaf, in his note on the text to the Broadview edition of Eliza Haywood's *Love in Excess* (1719), admits that, although he adds quotation marks to clarify discourse, the convention of "shift[ing] from one character's speech to another's within a single sentence" is something that "suit[s] Haywood's intersubjectivity and deliberate blurring of boundaries."[33] Eve Kosofsky Sedgwick argues that personal identity in the gothic is "at no moment inherent in one but is applicable—is applied—only from outside, *après-coup*, and by a process of visual assimilation or 'seeing as.'"[34] The omission

---

[32] Thomas, "Dialogue," vol. 1, 250.
[33] David Oakleaf, "A Note on the Text" in *Love in Excess; Or, The Fatal Enquiry*, by Eliza Haywood (Peterborough, ON: Broadview Press, 1994), 25–26.
[34] Eve Kosofsky Sedgwick, "The Character in the Veil: Imagery of the Surface in the Gothic Novel," *PMLA*, 96.2 (1981), 255–270 (262).

of clear discourse signaling in *The Castle of Otranto* muddles voices, bodies, identities. As Walpole had "left Matilda and Isabella talking, in the middle of a paragraph" (*Correspondence*, I:88) when writing the manuscript, so "*Isabella*" and "dear *Matilda*" are bundled up together in the middle of the last paragraph (*Otranto*, 2nd ed., 187). Later editions of *Otranto*, inserting quotation marks, would light up the syntactic interior. But what Walpole initiates for the gothic – on the level of typography and syntax as well as of atmosphere and plot – is precisely the uneasiness of boundaries obscured and identities blurred.

Syntactical Gothic Architecture

Quotation marks are not the only small things affecting the gothic atmosphere of structure on the syntactic as well as architectural levels. A closer look at the beginnings, middles, and ends of paragraphs and chapters as well as sentences in *Otranto* reveals further subterranean passages and obscure corners.

It is worth paying attention to the ends of sentences, for example. The punctuation of the very first sentence of *The Castle of Otranto* imparts more than first it seems:

> **M**ANFRED, Prince of Otranto, had one son and one daughter: The latter a most beautiful virgin, aged eighteen, was called *Matilda*. *Conrad*, the son, was three years younger, a homely youth, sickly, and of no promising disposition ; yet he was the darling of his father, who never showed any symptoms of affection to *Matilda*. (2nd ed., 1–2)

The eighteenth-century typography, with the bolded, oversize initial and italicized large capitals, emphatically proclaims Manfred's power and position; expectedly, the son appears before the daughter. But after the colon, Matilda is described first, and she ends the sentence. As James Buchanan defined it in 1767, "A Colon, marked thus (:) is the greatest Portion or Member of a Period or full Sentence, and marks a perfect Sense ; yet, so as to leave the Mind in Suspense and Expectation of what is to follow."[35] Conrad is separated from her by a full stop (not to mention the happy

---

[35] James Buchanan, *A Regular English Syntax* (London, 1767), 184.

happenstance of an extra wide space in the line), and it's already implied that we need to be reminded about him ("the son"); where Matilda's mini-portrait is ushered in by the majesty of a colon, Conrad's depressing vital statistics are followed by a semi-colon that attaches him to his father. "A Semicolon," says Buchanan, "marked thus (;) is a greater Portion of a Sentence than a Comma" but it "carries in it an incomplete Sense."[36] He of no promising disposition will remain incomplete – until he comes to a full stop very shortly, crushed to death under a giant helmet. Matilda will complete the second sentence as well as the first. This syntactical prominence prefigures other notable gender subversions in the upper galleries of plot, as when Matilda leads Theodore to safety and (after four pages or so of reminding him that *she* runs no risk but by *his* delay [2nd ed., 114]), finally "command[ing] the youth to be gone with an air that would not be disobeyed," closing the gate on him to "put an end to [the] interview" (2nd ed., 118).

The ends of paragraphs also offer gothic opportunities. Walpole introduces an early cliffhanger when Isabella, fleeing Manfred in the secret passage in the lower part of the castle (which "was hollowed into several intricate cloysters" [2nd ed., 22]), thinks she hears someone following her. Just as she "fortif[ies] herself" with some common-sense reflections, "a sudden gust of wind that met her at the door, extinguished her lamp, and left her in total darkness." "Darkness" ends the paragraph; the new line of the next paragraph underscores the abyss of that textual silence: "Words cannot paint the horror" (2nd ed., 25). And we mustn't forget the "happy ending," where *after* Theodore has "frequent discourses with *Isabella* of his dear *Matilda*," he realizes "he could know no happiness but in the society of one with whom he could for ever indulge the melancholy that had taken possession of his soul" (2nd ed., 187). Lucky, lucky Isabella.

¶

Walpole's epigraph to *The Castle of Otranto* is from Horace's *Ars Poetica*:

> ------- *Vanæ*
> *Fingentur species, tamen ut Pes, & Caput uni*
> *Reddantur formæ.* -------
>   H O R.

Clery's note translates the Latin as: "'(idle fancies shall be shaped [like a sick man's dream] so that neither foot nor head can be assigned to a

---

[36] Ibid., 183.

single shape').")[37] She argues that "Walpole reverses the meaning to say that 'nevertheless head and foot are assigned to a single shape.'" I have argued here that even Walpole's sentence structure can be assigned to that single shape, joining the very small things of punctuation and syntax with the forces of gigantic helmets, feet, and feathers. *The Castle of Otranto* uncovers a template of gothic syntactical structures that *enact* gothic architectural structures.

---

[37] E. J. Clery, "Explanatory Notes" in *The Castle of Otranto*, by Horace Walpole, ed. W. S. Lewis, with a new introduction and notes by E. J. Clery (Oxford: Oxford University Press, 1996), 116.

4 | Small, Familiar Things on Trial and on Stage

CHLOE WIGSTON SMITH

Some small things were neither expensive nor finely crafted but were nevertheless cherished by their owners, as affirmed by their attempts to retrieve them. Items such as buttons, thimbles, needles, and handkerchiefs were easily pilfered by thieves, and appear frequently as stolen goods that women and men sought to recover through the courts. In inventories of stolen goods and catalogues of lost property, no item is too small to mark as missing. True, some small things did hold sizable value, depending on their materials of composition and the quality of their craftmanship; we see this documented in the silver spoons, coins, fine jewelry, and ivory keepsakes that eighteenth-century Britons inscribed with their initials, passed between generations, and sought to repossess. My discussion focuses on how women and men described their stolen small things, differentiating ways to see and spot items cherished for either their sentimental value or rarity. In these cases, as we shall see, owners of stolen small things make the claim that their rights to possession rest in even smaller signs and details known to them, an intimate relationship built on repeated handling and viewing over time.

In his study of small things, the anthropologist James Deetz defends the value of overlooked material objects, but his case studies often understand "small" as the familiar and commonplace as opposed to the small-scaled.[1] My chapter, by contrast, examines small things whose size made them highly portable and, in many ways, commonplace, in their ubiquity in the pockets and on the persons of victims of theft. Yet their commonplaceness within the world of eighteenth-century goods did not render them interchangeable to their owners. Many small things, as I hope to show, remained deeply familiar to those who had lost them and, most important, distinct from other similar items. Often such distinctions remained discernible only to the persons who first purchased the items: owners identify unusual

---

[1] James Deetz, for instance, studies houses; see *In Small Things Forgotten: An Archaeology of Early American Life* (1977; New York: Knopf Doubleday, 2010), 4. See also Sara Pennell, "Mundane Materiality, or, Should Small Things Still Be Forgotten?: Material Culture, Micro-Histories and the Problem of Scale" in Karen Harvey (ed.), *History and Material Culture: A Student's Guide to Approaching Alternative Sources* (London: Routledge, 2009), 173–191.

qualities; wear and tear from their possession; and, in some cases, marks added with their own hands. In this way, these lost goods offer alternative ways to comprehend the affordance of things in the eighteenth century.

Affordance is often understood through our physical interaction with objects; our hands touch, turn, grasp, and hold objects, their materials, designs, and structures shaping our use and handling of spoons, thimbles, watches, and patch boxes.[2] For instance, Samuel Richardson made the use and handling of affordances a notable feature of fiction when he launched Pamela Andrews through an open sash window – in 1740, a relatively recent technology in domestic architecture – to escape Lady Davers's inquisition. Pamela recounts that she first "lifted up the sash" to communicate her entrapment and then she "saw it was no hard matter to get out of the Window into the Front-yard."[3] Blessed with a sash rather than a casement window, Pamela repurposes the window's sliding sash, which affords an opening through which her body might pass. Pamela spies the sash window with her eyes, but it's the manual lifting of it, by her hands and arms, that allows her to create an opening through which to leap.

In this chapter, I want to offer a different route through affordance that refocuses our attention on sight. As Donald A. Norman has succinctly summarized, the perceptual psychologist James J. Gibson "believed that the combined information picked up by all our sensory apparatus—sight, sound, smell, touch, balance, kinesthetic, acceleration, body position—determines our perceptions without the need for internal recognition or cognition."[4] Sight, however, has often been underplayed within this constellation of sensory interactions, and, in this chapter, I study how tiny marks visible on small things enabled their return to the hands of their original owners. Such visible marks made lost possessions uniquely recognizable to

---

[2] The term "affordance" is closely associated with James J. Gibson, especially his full-length study *The Ecological Approach to Visual Perception* (Boston, MA: Houghton Mifflin, 1979). For a consideration of affordance in relation to eighteenth-century material culture, see Crystal B. Lake, *Artifacts: How We Think and Write about Found Objects* (Baltimore, MD: Johns Hopkins University Press, 2020), 68–69. On affordance and making, see Ariane Fennetaux, "'Work'd pocketts to my intire sattisfaction': Women and the Multiple Literacies of Making" in Serena Dyer and Chloe Wigston Smith (eds.), *Material Literacy in Eighteenth-Century Britain: A Nation of Makers* (London: Bloomsbury, 2020), 18–34 (26–27).

[3] Samuel Richardson, *Pamela, or Virtue Rewarded*, ed. Thomas Keymer and Alice Wakely (1740; Oxford: Oxford University Press, 2001), 398, 397. See Cynthia Sundberg Wall's reading of Pamela's use of the sash-window, in which she concludes, "Sash windows, after all, were not constructed for ladies to leap out of" (*The Prose of Things: Transformations of Descriptions in the Eighteenth Century* [Chicago: University of Chicago Press, 2006], 141).

[4] Donald Norman, *The Design of Everyday Things*, rev. ed. (1990; Cambridge, MA: MIT Press, 2013), 12.

their rightful owners. Smallness, on the one hand, made things moveable; in this way, size rendered small things more susceptible to theft. On the other hand, small marks on lost things countered such circulation by enabling lost possessions to be seen and recognized anew.

In the first section of this chapter, I discuss trials for theft at the Old Bailey, at which individuals insisted that they could recognize their lost possessions through visible marks that distinguished them from other similar objects. Court trials show how women and men strove to describe the small signs that marked their ownership of lost property and that made their lost objects different from others in the same category. The owners of lost things frequently relied on the descriptor "remarkable" to persuade the court that their item remained known to them through tiny visible marks. In my second section, I turn to *The Beggar's Opera* (1728) to consider how these very same personal marks prove troublesome to the theatrical thieves of John Gay's ballad opera, and how they ultimately interrupt the circulation of some stolen goods. At both the courthouse and the playhouse, thieves and victims agreed that small, familiar things could be recognized and identified, and could be made distinct from the host of other small things that eighteenth-century Britons observed, touched, shared, and took from each other.

Seeing Small Things in Court

The records of the Old Bailey contain an abundance of information about the possessions of eighteenth-century Londoners and, as I've discussed elsewhere, the overwhelming majority of trials for pickpockets involved goods small enough to pass easily from owner to thief, frequently textiles, garments, and accessories.[5] References to small things recur across the testimonies of prosecutors, witnesses, and defendants; as John Coleby recounted of a house burglary in which he participated, "we took away a pair of stone shoe buckles, a pair of knee buckles, and a mourning ring; there were several small things."[6] As John Styles has shown, court proceedings from the Old Bailey in London and assize courts in the North yield insights into the possessions, small and large, missed by plebeian owners

---

[5] Chloe Wigston Smith, *Women, Work, and Clothes in the Eighteenth-Century Novel* (Cambridge: Cambridge University Press, 2013), 94–99.

[6] *Old Bailey Proceedings Online* (www.oldbaileyonline.org), version 8.0, March 2018, hereafter *OBP*), September 1773, trial of Samuel Marriot and Emanuel Peal (t17730908-28).

in particular.⁷ Here I return to the trials to consider how, in select cases, witness testimony affirmed the importance of the visible details of small things. Women, men, and children insist on their abilities to recall small, significant features in ways that evoke Gibson's visual theory of "information pickup," in which perception involves the "experiencing of things rather than a having of experiences."⁸ The trials I discuss here sit comfortably within Enlightenment philosophy's epistemological commitments to sight, scrutiny, and close observation, which Tita Chico's contribution to this collection (Chapter 14) studies in depth.⁹ Yet, as I hope to show, they make room for a form of looking that deviates from empiricist study, by turning attention to what is visible and, to use an oft repeated term from the trials, "remarkable" to a single person. "Remarkable," in court testimony, differs from this descriptor's application to wondrous occurrences or to the challenges and dangers in tales of adventure.¹⁰ In these trials, the act of looking carefully leads neither to the universal spread of knowledge; nor to ever more complex ideas; or the ordering of the natural world (or even the improved understanding of what is only perceptible under the microscope), but rather it makes visible the scant detail recognizable to the small thing's owner, gesturing to commonplace strategies for regulating domestic items.

At proceedings from the Old Bailey, victims of theft made repeated claims of ownership for the smallest of things. For instance, Catherine Smith catalogued a long list that included substantial items, such as a gown, shift, and hood, but also smaller ones, such as a thimble and shoe buckle.

---

[7] John Styles uses court trials as evidence across *The Dress of the People: Everyday Fashion in Eighteenth-Century England* (New Haven, CT: Yale University Press, 2007); see also his analysis of these kinds of records (327–334). In some ways, these trials evoke the small fabric swatches and metal tokens left by mothers at the Foundling Hospital, as touched on by Freya Gowrley in this volume (Chapter 7); as Styles notes, the tokens' scant surfaces are "heavily skewed towards patterned and colourful fabrics, because their purpose was to identify a child" (*Threads of Feeling: The London Foundling Hospital's Textile Tokens, 1740-1770* [London: Foundling Museum, 2010], 19). Barbara Burman and Ariane Fennetaux have also examined descriptions of the lost contents of women's pockets in the Old Bailey Proceedings in *The Pocket: A Hidden History of Women's Lives, 1660-1900* (New Haven, CT and London: Yale University Press, 2019), 112–141. See also Kate Smith's forthcoming work on lost things and dispossession, for example: "'Dropt,' 'Lost,' 'Misplaced': Losing Small Things on London's Streets" (paper presented at the Small Things in the Eighteenth Century conference, University of York, June 7, 2019).

[8] Gibson, *Ecological Approach*, 239.

[9] On the links between sight, empiricist science, and magnification, see Barbara Maria Stafford, *Body Criticism: Imaging the Unseen in Enlightenment Art and Medicine* (Cambridge, MA: MIT Press, 1990), 341–375.

[10] On the use of "remarkable" in these contexts, see Margaret Cohen, *The Novel and the Sea* (Princeton, NJ: Princeton University Press, 2010), 23.

In her efforts to recoup items stolen from her home, she swore on October 14, 1741, that "All these things are mine."[11] Itemization such as Smith's recurs across trials for theft, as women and men recount their missing bodkins, coins, lace swatches, rings, seals, snuffboxes, spoons, watches, and innumerable other small items, pinched from their persons and pockets. Testimony from trials such as Smith's present a catalogue of small goods that people touched, handled, and encountered in their daily lives. On June 18, 1730, Elizabeth Eustace lost a "Pair of Silver Buttons, a Pair of Buckles, a Penknife, a Thimble, and two half Crowns, some Shillings, and an Irish Half-penny."[12] On January 16, 1734, Evan Edwards said he was robbed of "a Silver Watch with two Seals, a pair of Silver Shoe-buckles, a pair of Silver Knee-buckles, a pair of Crystal Buttons, a Gold Ring, and a Mother of Pearl Snuff-Box."[13] And on April 4, 1762, as he left a lecture, Anthony Andrews encountered four men who relieved him of "one silver watch, value 40 s. one silver watch chain, value 2 s. and one glass seal, value 6 d."[14] Such testimonies make visible the variety and range of the collections of small things that were valuable enough, either for emotional or monetary reasons, to be accounted for in the courts.

Rather than catalogue the almost endless combinations of stolen small things described by witnesses at the Old Bailey, I want to turn now to a subset of items that were singled out by witnesses for the way their scant surfaces afforded visual recognition. These small things possessed marks, patterns, and designs of particular note to their owner's eyes. Through testimony that centered on a thing's "remarkable" qualities, owners sought to convince the court that they could distinguish their lost property through minute visible markings. Some of these items were commercially produced but were later rendered distinctive through precise signs of wear and tear or mending; others were homemade or marked with family initials. In 1789, Joseph May described a parade of small-scale marks on items stolen from his home while he slept:

[T]he ring is marked with H. C. on the back, that is mine; one of the pepper castors has got a bruise; the sugar-tongs has the initials of my name, J. M. and the spoons also … this pepper-box I am sure is mine; the time-piece I am sure is mine, one of the screws, in taking it off, is broke off, I am sure of it; this shilling is mine, I swear to the paper it is in, because it is marked with two faint yellow spots; this is the bag I kept my money in;

---

[11] *OBP*, October 1741, Mary Reynolds, James Reynolds, James Reynolds, Jane Laws (t17411014-45).
[12] *OBP*, June 1730, Richard Ridgely (t17300704-23).
[13] *OBP*, January 1734, Grace Long (t17340116-42).
[14] *OBP*, April 1762, John Smith (t17620421-3).

I am positive of the bag, it is my wife's make, we used to keep farthings in it; I can swear positively to this bag, because it is rent down on each side.[15]

May's catalogue of telltale markings, peculiars known only to him, runs the gamut of visible affordances: initials engraved on valued items; efforts to secure coins by wrapping them in faded spotted paper; a missing screw that recalls the precise moment it yielded to force; a bag made useless by two holes, but retained because of his wife's handiwork. May conveys his minute attention to the details of his possessions, making the case that they operate as signs of belonging and that marks confer ownership.

May's references to engraved initials on jewelry and cutlery evoke the frequent efforts of other witnesses to recall the ways they added marks in order to individuate possessions. Shopkeepers, such as the linen draper Joseph Bulmer, identified in court the small marks stamped upon goods that would set apart one shop's goods from another's: "here are some handkerchiefs that have got my shop-mark upon them; and a piece of nankeen which has my shop-mark in my own hand; and the fag-end of this gown has my own mark upon it; and the neck-cloth."[16] Other victims of theft pointed to small initials that appeared on their goods, as seen at the trial of Mary Brown, a servant convicted of stealing household linens, handkerchiefs, and neckcloths from her employer, Samuel Whale, a Jewish schoolteacher: "These are all my property, there are the initials of my name in Hebrew letters upon all but two of them."[17] Some witnesses described their other tiny markings, most frequently of coins. Following the theft of coins by a lodger, Ann Hallewall recounted in detail two guineas she had marked. One was a repaired guinea to which she had "made a mark something resembling a T," and the other was memorable for different reasons, but equally worthy of her marking: "A new bright guinea that I thought was a counterfeit from something that I read in the newspaper, I scratched that on the back of the king's head with two or three scratches, and a little scratch on the nose, I think it is a cross; one of these guineas was dated 77 and the other 88."[18] Hallewall demonstrates her sharp memory for the dates and

---

[15] *OBP*, April 1789, John Ward, Edward Church, John Blinkworth (t17890422-71). Dozens and dozens of trials record the presence of initials as means by which to affirm ownership over small things.

[16] *OBP*, December 1797, Robert Penn, Rachel Penn (t17971206-21).

[17] *OBP*, October 1767, Mary Brown (t17671021-17). See also the example of a spoon marked with the initials of the victim's parents: *OBP*, May 1774, Williams Parsons (t17740518-28); for a watch marked with initials see *OBP*, July 1778, Susannah Dunn, Mary Green, Samuel Waitcroft, Jane Gardiner (t17780715-49).

[18] *OBP*, July 1795, John Mullet (t17950701-56). John Mullet was a lodger at a public house and Ann Hallewall's full testimony, with its description of locking and concealing her money box, implies that she aided her husband in the running of the business.

details of coins, as she relays, with precision, the visible affordances of marks and scratches.

Indeed, coins recur as items that could be identified by specific marks, designs, and innumerable visible quirks. Deidre Shauna Lynch has identified how "the material qualities of coins—their graspability, their resemblance to jewelry—provide a basis for their perceived affinity to persons," but here I seek to draw attention to how visible marks developed arguments less for affinity than for repossession.[19] Victims of theft frequently use the term "remarkable" to describe coins whose appearance made them identifiable only to them.[20] Such descriptions relied on claims that some lost coins were not only "striking, unusual, singular" but were also particularly "perceptible, admitting of being observed or noted."[21] Ann Dicker, for instance, remembered a shilling taken from her uncle, a gardener to whom she served as bookkeeper: "it is marked with a name in length on one side, and three letters on the other; the name is Swift, I do not particularly remember the other three letters; one I know is K; it was so remarkable a shilling, that I could not help taking notice of it at the time I took it."[22] The designs of coins were also singled out for being special, as Edward Burke testified about his lost coin: "I told him I had one remarkable shilling, there was something like the figure of a lion, or a dog, I do not know which, and on the other side of it a figure of five or an S, I could not make out which."[23] Such descriptions imply that not all coins were made equally, with some affording more distinctive features than others.

Coins were not the only small things that bore visible affordances accrued through wear and tear, and distinctive marks: other small items also showed signs of use that made their scant surfaces intensely noticeable to former owners. Robert Smith, a surgeon, insisted on his ability to recognize gold buttons taken from his house: "I am surprised to think what the people will do with the gold buttons, whoever they are, for they are so very remarkable, that let me see them wherever I will, I shall know them, and there is a scratch on one of the stones."[24] In 1787, on his way from London

---

[19] Deidre Shauna Lynch, "Money and Character in Defoe's Fiction" in John Richetti (ed.), *The Cambridge Companion to Daniel Defoe* (Cambridge: Cambridge University Press, 2009), 84–101 (90). See also Lynch's discussion of the wear and tear on coins generated by their protracted circulation, and the practice of clipping coins for the illicit trade in bullion (90–91).

[20] Burman and Fennetaux touch on how the trials show the attention paid to "the physical changes to coins caused by wear and defacement" in *The Pocket*, 130.

[21] *OED Online*, s.v. "remarkable, adj., n., and adv.," definitions A1 and 2, accessed March 31, 2021.

[22] *OBP*, October 1776, John Harding (t17761016-24).

[23] *OBP*, May 1799, Ann Williams (t17990508-35).

[24] *OBP*, April 1760, William Price (t17600416-8).

to Hampshire, William Lewer was beset by a highwayman who took his seal and watch:

I can swear positively to them both ... my watch is so very remarkable, that perhaps there is not one in the whole Court like it; among the engravings in the brass work, on the edge of the cock of the watch, is my name engraved ... I only swear to [the seal] as to the colour of the stone, the mode of its setting, and the impression; I have not the least doubt about it, if I had, I would give the seal up.

Where Lewer expresses visual certainty about his "remarkable" watch, he sounds somewhat less confident about the appearance of his seal: he claims it as his own but brushes past its distinctive qualities. Darcy Wentworth, the highwayman (who was acquitted), countered that he possessed a similar Wedgwood seal of his own: "the impressions are so much alike, that it is impossible for any person to distinguish them; a very good judge might, but I could not."[25] Wentworth was not exceptional in his efforts to claim that a plaintiff could not recognize their lost goods or had confused them with others of the same type.[26]

In trials for the receipt of stolen goods (which synch most closely with the resale practices of the Peachums in Gay's play), testimony returns repeatedly to goods that defy their circulation in the secondhand marketplace through their appearance, their movement made difficult through small marks that personalize and individualize. Such trials draw attention to small things – whether a key, medal, mug, nut (for a bolt), thimble (at the top of a cane), seal, or a snuffbox and egg trinket, among other examples – that remained unlike others of their kind: "the Things being pretty remarkable; the Rings being made some of them in Guinea; and some of them in Brazil."[27] Victims relate distinctive features on cherished items, such as the silk sewing case ("huswife") that went missing from Thomas Porter's home. At the trial, Porter's wife noted: "It was, it is very remarkable, it has some writing in it, Greek, or Latin, or something that I do not understand; I had it given me, and I value it."[28] Still other victims drew attention to

---

[25] *OBP*, December 1787, Darcy Wentworth, Mary Wilkinson (t17871212-7).
[26] See, for instance, *OBP*, October 1749, John Johnson (t17491011-38).
[27] *OBP*, April 1730, George Downing, William Downing (t17300408-63). For the remarkable key, see September 1785, Amos Rowsel (t17850914-15); the medal, see May 1770, James Lee, Thomas Cook (t17700530-24); the mug, see December 1784, William Benton, George Green (t17841208-29); the nut, see February 1789, James Underhill, John Comberlege, William Holmes, Francis Fleming (t17890225-66); the thimble cane, see October 1734, John Butler (t17341016-5); the seal, see April 1795, William Barnes (t17950416-73); the snuffbox and egg trinket (both described at length), see April 1787, John Phillips (t17870418-54).
[28] *OBP*, January 1784, Richard Bryan (t17840114-72).

small marks that connected their lost property to their own making, as in the case of Mary Hodges, a servant convicted in 1797 of stealing women's garments, coins, and banknotes from her employers, the Butlers. At the trial, Mary Butler called attention to the evidence of her own needlework: "here is an apron and petticoat of my own mending. I have no doubt that they are all mine."[29] Likewise Ann Hilton affirmed, "this bit of lace I know; I sewed it together to make a lappet to a cap; I have had it many years; I could swear to it any where; and I know it by having sewed it together." Her husband also swore to the details of his missing garments, likely his wife's handiwork: "This is my coat; I know it by the buttons, and a kind of seam that I think is under the left-arm. They are remarkable buttons, in the shape of a heart, inlaid with white."[30] Ariane Fennetaux has compared the visible affordances of such mending to a signature: needlework could be "so deeply idiosyncratic and personal that it could in some cases act as a signature even when no name or initial was used." Fennetaux goes on to note about women's claims of ownership at the Old Bailey that "the peculiarity of a stitch, became meaningful carriers not only of identification but also of identity."[31] Whether witnesses recount marks, scratches, or stitches made by their hands or those of others, their willingness to recall and report the remarkable qualities of their possessions spotlights their commitment to perceiving, noticing, and remembering the tiny traces that made their small things unlike any others.

Concealing Small Things on Stage

Where the Old Bailey trials offer insights into the restitution of small things through sight, Gay's play *The Beggar's Opera* engages the same problem from the opposite angle. In Gay's drama, characters such as Jemmy Twitcher (pickpocket), Crook-fingered Jack (pickpocket), Nimming Ned (stealing), and Jenny Diver (pickpocket) are named for the nimble fingers that displace small things from unknowing owners and into the Peachums' house, a site of material metamorphosis where small things are made unrecognizable. For Gay's thieves and their operator, Peachum, personal marks prove troublesome to their management of stolen goods in an illicit marketplace in which small things are displaced from their owners into,

---

[29] *OBP*, October 1797, Mary Hodges (t17971025-5).
[30] *OBP*, January 1789, Ann Hannaway, John Happy, Richard Cole (t17890114-61).
[31] Ariane Fennetaux, "Work'd pockets," 28, 29.

first, the hands of pickpockets, then into Peachum's hands, and finally to consumers of secondhand goods. Such routes of downward circulation depend on making small things uniform, muting their remarkable characteristics, and turning them into objects that resemble others of the same type.

My discussion comes at the problem of thievery from a different angle to that of literary critic Jonathan Lamb, whose interest in stolen things has centered attention on the similarities between Peachum and the notorious Jonathan Wild, well known for placing advertisements for stolen goods in newspapers, thereby creating "an extraordinarily intimate and conspiratorial connection between thieves and their victims."[32] For Lamb, Wild's practice of selling stolen possessions back to owners, a model that Gay applies to Peachum, works to negotiate a new price for lost things: "what was being priced was the aesthetics of ownership, not the intrinsic, exchange, or fiduciary value of the thing itself."[33] Here, my focus lies less in the spurious advertisements that inflated the cost of stolen goods under the mantle of reunification and more so in the erasure of such tell-tale signs of ownership – an opposite practice upon which Peachum's business model equally depends. The illicit circulation of small things in Gay's drama occurs within a plot that sets economic self-interest and double dealing against love. As Dianne Dugaw establishes, "dramatic plots of love and war take place in the mercantile terms of a newly capitalizing order."[34] Peachum's model of commerce relies on erasing the individualism and particularities of small things and then repurposing cherished possessions into indistinguishable types. In this the play distinguishes itself from the commitment to the remarkable that recurs across legal rhetoric.[35] Peachum thus yanks once-beloved and familiar objects into a secondhand marketplace fueled by detachment and erasure.

Peachum takes clear relish in small things that can be lumped into categories, as we see when he itemizes a long list of pilfered goods delivered by Crook-fingered Jack: "one, two, three, four, five Gold Watches, and seven Silver ones. A mighty clean-handed Fellow! Sixteen Snuff-boxes, five of them of true Gold. Six Dozen of Handkerchiefs, four silver-hilted Swords,

---

[32] Jonathan Lamb, *The Things Things Say* (Princeton University Press, 2016), 37.
[33] Jonathan Lamb, "The Crying of Lost Things," *ELH*, 71.4 (2004), 949–967 (952).
[34] Dianne Dugaw, *"Deep Play": John Gay and the Invention of Modernity* (Newark: University of Delaware Press, 2001), 36.
[35] I seek to avoid reading *Beggar's Opera* as a direct mirror of the actualities of Newgate, following William Empson's lead in identifying the "artificial" qualities of the drama and its range of ironies in *Some Versions of the Pastoral* (1935; London: Penguin, 1995), 173.

half a Dozen of Shirts, three Tye-Periwigs, and a Piece of Broad-Cloth."[36] In this list, Peachum catalogues and classifies stolen items by type, their resale enabled by the absence of identifying marks and designs. The absence of distinguishing marks makes these items less recognizable and thus less likely to be reunited with those who have lost them; their value is determined by the cost of their materials (gold, silver, and "true Gold"). Not long after this moment, Peachum instructs his wife to "rip out the coronets and marks of these dozen of cambric handkerchiefs, for I can dispose of them this afternoon to a chap in the City" (I.iv.106–110). Peachum seeks to remove the individually sewn marks and coronets that would identify their household of origin (the marking and numbering of linens such as handkerchiefs by women was a central component of household management, essential to the tracking of laundered items).[37] The unpicking of marking threads dissociates the handkerchiefs from their aristocratic owners, suggesting the tenuousness of such marks, which can be as easily made as unmade.

Across Gay's drama, Peachum's business benefits from the itemizing and accounting of small, stolen things that must be rendered unfamiliar in order to circulate anew in the marketplace. As Macheath notes, with reluctance, about Peachum, "Business cannot go on without him" (II.ii.29). But some items retain their notable features. The bawd Diana Trapes, for instance, faults Peachum for burdening her with identifiable goods: "that Watch was remarkable, and not of very safe Sale" (III.iii.98–99). Trapes prefers to deal with Peachum for less "remarkable" items, such as velvet scarves and other fine accessories, that will draw fashion-conscious clients to her sex workers: "the gentlemen always pay according to their dress" (III.iii.103–104). Trapes understands that Peachum has unloaded difficult goods into her hands, a tactic affirmed elsewhere when Peachum shares his technique for the disposal of small things "not of very safe Sale." When Lockit challenges Peachum's accounts, which appear to exclude the stolen jewelry he expected to see recorded – "But I don't see any article of the jewels" (III.v.14) – Peachum explains, "Those are so well known, that they must be sent abroad. You'll find them entered under article of exportation"

---

[36] John Gay, *The Beggar's Opera*, in *The Broadview Anthology of Restoration & Early Eighteenth-Century Drama*, gen. ed. J. Douglas Canfield, play ed. Dianne Dugaw (1728; Peterborough, ON: Broadview, 2001), 1332–73, act I, scene iii, lines 6–11. Hereafter cited parenthetically in the text by act, scene, and line number. See John Bender on the outcry generated by Gay's often gleeful depiction of thieves in *Imagining the Penitentiary: Fiction and the Architecture of Mind in Eighteenth-Century England* (Chicago: University of Chicago Press, 1989), 101–103.

[37] In 1776, Solomon Fell described attempts to cross out his name from his stolen clothes and shoes: "there had been an attempt to obliterate the name with ink, but it was not done so as to prevent its being read" (*OBP*, September 1776, William Wood [t17760911-1]).

(III.v.15–17).[38] By contrast, other small things in the same account are so numerous that they have lost their specificity, and Peachum will enter them in his ledger by type: "As for the snuffboxes, watches, swords, etcetera, I thought it best to enter them under their several heads" (III.v.17–19). Peachum's detailed accounts offer insights into how the absence or presence of small marks impedes or facilitates their passage from hand to hand. Jewels are "so well known": their surfaces afford too much recognition – a problem Peachum solves by removing them from London altogether. Some small things are so resistant to resale that they cannot be unmade or unmarked, and only a foreign marketplace can confer anonymity.

The drama raises questions about the mechanics of discernment for both the goods and individuals whose circulation drives the plot forward. The Peachums in particular are committed to a commercial structure in which perception performs an outsized role in the secondhand marketplace for stolen goods. This structure, however, sits in tension with the play's other marketplace, that of marriage. In the introduction, the figure of the player makes a case against visible and material distinctions, arguing that "The Muses, contrary to all other ladies, pay no distinction to dress and never partially mistake the pertness of embroidery for wit" (lines 8–11). But such claims about the greater weight of immaterial virtues over the material signs that distinguish one woman from another are undercut by Peachum's treatment of small things. Mrs. Peachum spots her daughter's interest in Macheath, but Peachum does not; he remains concerned primarily that Polly preserve her separate economic status: "If the Wench does not know her own Profit, sure she knows her own Pleasure better than to make herself a Property!" (I.iv.94–96). With her husband out of view, Mrs. Peachum expresses her contrary perception of a marriage marketplace that thrives on competition: "All Men are Thieves in Love, and like a Woman the better for being another's Property" (I.v.6–7), and then continues in song: "A Wife's like a Guinea in Gold, / Stampt with the Name of her Spouse" (I.v.13–14). For Mrs. Peacham, wives constitute a form of coinage, in which their worth and identity are marked by a new surname, evoking some of the personal marks described in the courts. In this, their identities resemble the small things whose individualized marks make them repellent to the secondhand marketplace.

At the same time, Mrs. Peachum's views around marriage are undercut by the surfeit of wives that circulate in the play. This excess sharpens into

---

[38] Such concerns over jewelry chime with court cases where, for example, witnesses extol the rarity of rings: "It is a yellow rose ring, and a remarkable fine yellow rose it is, I do not think I ever saw one to fellow it" (*OBP*, October 1784, Robert Artz, Thomas Gore [t17841020-9]).

hyperbole in the play's final scene, where in addition to Polly Peachum and Lucy Lockit, four more wives appear onstage, evoking the goods that Peachum groups together in his inventories. As Macheath heads to the gallows, Peachum notes, "This is not a time for a man to be hampered with his wives" (III.xi.5–6). When Macheath finally claims Polly as his wife, he presents a partner to each of the other women and also advises, "If you are fond of marrying again, the best advice I can give you is to ship yourselves off for the West Indies, where you'll have a fair chance of getting a husband apiece, or by good luck, two or three, as you like best" (III.xv.2–6). This vision offers up a model of interchangeability that echoes the circulation of unmarked small things, on which Peachum's trade relies. Macheath proposes a system in which individuals might marry at will and with frequency, most especially in colonized spaces. Such surfeit collapses husbands and wives with Peachum's marketplace of small things, in which small things circulate freely, but only when unencumbered by remarkable, recognizable marks. Here, wives and husbands remain ultimately interchangeable; Mrs. Peachum's claim for the stamping of names and values looks like a nostalgic nod to a past in which coronets could not be unpicked nor remarkable jewelry shipped to France.

Together, *The Beggar's Opera* and the Old Bailey trials record a struggle over small things that centers on the ability to recognize and identify even the smallest of personal marks. If Jonathan Lamb has stressed the voices of lost things that call out to their owners, I have focused here on the particular tensions between the familiar and the small scale. Those who sought to circulate small things as secondhand goods valued the ubiquity that made one commonplace thing appear like any other. In Gay's drama, smallness facilitates the circulation of things from one hand to another and sameness proves a boon to circulation in the secondhand marketplace. But to those who had lost small things, personalized marks held out the promise that they could be returned to their rightful owners, and no thing was too small or too commonplace to be reclaimed by someone. The trials and the stage ultimately reinforce both the economic and emotional importance of studying the surfaces of small things and remembering their tiny, visible marks. Together they return to how the scantest of details could generate a visible affordance with the potential to interrupt unwelcome circulation. Small things, and their even smaller marks, stains, scratches, tears, and mending, made possessions personal and recognizable, rewarding those owners who looked carefully and closely with the possibility of return.

PART II
———

Small Things in Time and Space

5 On the Smallness of Numismatic Objects

CRYSTAL B. LAKE

Early in his *Leviathan* (1651), Thomas Hobbes articulated the basic tenets of materialism when he offered his readers a definition of the imagination as "nothing but *decaying sense*."[1] That phrase, "*decaying sense*," glosses Hobbes's way of describing how we come first to perceive – and then to know as well as to recall – the properties of external objects. Famously, materialists such as Hobbes maintained that all objects exist as particulate and conglomerate bodies in perpetual states of motion and that physical relays of pressure and counterpressure between objects' particles, our bodily senses, and our minds instantiated our apprehension of things and, subsequently, our ideas about them.

Hobbes's conviction that objects communicate information to our senses and thereby ideas to our understanding via movement and collision leads him to attest that our knowledge of external objects is always historical: an encounter with something from the past that we mistakenly experience as an event occurring in the immediacy of the present. By "*decaying sense*," therefore, Hobbes designates as one and the same two cognitive functions that other philosophers deemed to be distinct mental activities; "*Imagination and Memory*, are but one thing," Hobbes writes (1.2.3). "Imagination" names our ability to visualize external objects in our midst; memory names our ability to recall information about objects that we have previously perceived but which no longer remain directly in our perceptual fields; both mental activities of imagining and remembering constitute experiences of "decay" as a consequence of the temporal delay that inevitably occurs while the small, physical components of external objects travel the distances that exist between us and objects.

Although the materialism that underwrites Hobbes's rendering of the imagination and the memory as "*decaying sense*" would seed controversies throughout the long eighteenth century, his account of how distance and delay characterize our encounters with external objects draws our

---

[1] Thomas Hobbes, "Leviathan", in *Three-Text Edition of Thomas Hobbes's Political Theory*, ed. Deborah Baumgold (Cambridge: Cambridge University Press, 2017), part 1, chap. 2, paragraph 2. Hereafter references are given parenthetically in the text.

attention to the ways that materialists enhanced the popularity of numismatics – the collection and study of old coins and medals – throughout the eighteenth century. As small, durable objects encountered as pieces of the past and parts of longer series, old coins and medals figured at relative scale how the particulate components of external objects might move through space as well as time to effect ideas and related chains of associations. More specifically, numismatic objects made manifest the historical aspects of materialist philosophies such as Hobbes's by figuring directly the transfer of information about the past to the senses and the minds of those who collected or studied them. Materialist principles, however, also threatened to undermine the claims that numismatists made on behalf of their prized objects. Numismatics enthusiasts often cast the metallic materiality of old coins and medals as a primary means by which they succeeded at preserving historical facts, reinforcing memory, and thereby strengthening individuals' attachments to moral precepts and imagined communities. Yet privileging the base matter of old coins and medals also made numismatic objects and the tenets of their appreciation susceptible to the charge that old coins and medals conveyed forms of decay that threatened to compromise their popular functions as metaphors of mind, aides-memoires, didactic devices, and historical artifacts.

Not despite but because of their metallic materiality, then, numismatic objects often foregrounded the sense of decay that permeates Hobbes's account of perception; in popular representations of numismatics, the degradation of old coins and medals – as evidenced by rust, especially – testified to the moral decay that attended the decline and fall of historical empires. Consequently, numismatics' apologists often turned to the smallness of their prized objects, celebrating their little size as the means by which old coins and medals delivered valuable information to the memories as well as the imaginations of those who studied and collected them. Reveling in the smallness of numismatic objects maintained many of the benefits that materialism yielded for numismatics while also offering opportunities to highlight the range of associative relationships that old coins and medals could reveal as well as generate between individuals, objects, and communities both historical and imagined. Whereas the metallic materiality of numismatic objects threatened to make manifest the morally decayed and decaying memories of the past that had receded from the present's perceptual fields, the smallness of old coins and medals promised to extend and enhance their influence over the Enlightenment's historical imagination.

As small objects, old coins and medals were especially appreciated for the power they had to accumulate; in writings about numismatics from the period, the smallness of numismatic objects accords with the quantities of old coins and medals that were produced in the past and continued to exist in the present – as well as the range of uses to which they had, and could still be, put. Following the popularization of antiquarianism in the seventeenth century, numismatics became the most widely practiced antiquarian pastime in eighteenth-century England.[2] Many numismatic objects had remained intact throughout the ages; in contrast to other antiquities, therefore, large quantities of coins and medals could still be discovered and purchased affordably. Coins and medals had served prominently as metaphors of mind and memory dating back to the ancients; they were commonly used as everyday mnemonic devices and served as convenient vehicles for explaining how ideas and moral virtues worked in the context of Enlightenment philosophies. Meanwhile, antiquaries – the most ardent of the period's numismatists – insisted that coins and medals were both the most reliable artifacts for determining the facts of history and also the most capable of inculcating sentimental attachments to the past as well as the imagined communities of the present.

All of these aspects of numismatic collection and study have led scholars to recognize that the prominence of place enjoyed by old coins and medals in eighteenth-century English culture depended upon their status as objects made of metal. As Barbara Benedict puts it, numismatic objects' "materiality" constituted their "key virtue" – and as objects that "resist decomposition," old coins and medals were unique among the historical artifacts whose study and collection were popularized by antiquaries.[3] Thanks to the durability of their metal, old coins and medals remained readily available to be found and bought by individuals looking either to establish or expand their numismatic collections throughout the period. The period's antiquaries likewise conflated numismatic objects' metallic durability with their reliability, implying that the sturdy matter of old coins and medals provided a surer and more direct connection to historical conditions than archival texts, for example, which remained vulnerable to loss as well as to forgery. Similarly, the metal of coins and medals proved beneficial for negotiating the relationships between permanence and "ductility"

---

[2] Rosemary Sweet confirms that numismatic objects were the "commonest relics of antiquity" in *Antiquaries: The Discovery of the Past in Eighteenth-Century Britain* (London: Hambledon Continuum, 2006), 13. See also: D. R. Woolf, *The Social Circulation of the Past: English Historical Culture, 1500–1730* (Oxford: Oxford University Press, 2005), 234–349; Francis Haskell, *History and Its Images: Art and the Interpretation of the Past* (New Haven, CT: Yale University Press, 1993), 1–25.

[3] Barbara Benedict, "The Moral in the Material: Numismatics and Identity in Evelyn, Addison, and Pope" in Cedric D. Reverend (ed.), *Queen Anne and the Arts* (Lewisburg, PA: Bucknell University Press, 2015), 65–83 (66).

that characterized Enlightenment theories of mind, as Brad Pasanek also observes; figured simultaneously as both durable and malleable, the metal of numismatic objects enhanced their status as didactic devices capable of conveying to plastic minds both hard facts and enduring virtues.[4]

Yet writings about numismatics in the long eighteenth century frequently take up the signs of decay that attended numismatic objects as a consequence of their metallic materiality. In his *Leviathan*, Hobbes turned to three metaphors in quick succession to explain both how our perception of external objects works and also why he defined the imagination as a "*decaying sense.*" In the first metaphor, external objects emanate information to our senses, like the waves of the ocean washing onto a shore; likewise, our minds continue to apprehend information about external objects even when we can't immediately perceive them – in the same way that the waves of an ocean ripple even after the wind has stopped blowing (1.2.2). In the second metaphor, the sequential appearance of "predominant" objects obscures our ability to perceive other objects that nevertheless persist on their various courses of collision in our perceptual fields – in the same way that the sun occludes our ability to see the stars that continue to shine during the daytime (1.2.3). In the third metaphor, the figure of the aging body helps Hobbes to clarify how, in a manner akin to the dulling and slowing of our senses over time, even our immediate and recent apprehensions of external objects can quickly fade (1.2.3). For Hobbes, all of these metaphors emphasize his point that our minds process information about external objects always at a distance and with a delay.

Joseph Addison's defense of numismatics, *Dialogues upon the Usefulness of Ancient Medals* (1721), offers a representative example of the suspicion with which many regarded the decayed materiality of numismatic objects in the period. Numismatists, complains one character in Addison's *Dialogues*, "value themselves upon being critics in Rust," and consequently, "[t]hey are possessed with a kind of learned avarice, and are for getting together hoards of such money [sic]."[5] Later, Addison's numismatic apologist confirms the complainant's claim; many "Medallists" have been known, he admits, "for hoarding [sic] up such pieces of Money as had been half consumed by time or rust."[6] In his prefatory poem for Addison's *Dialogues*,

---

[4] See Brad Pasanek, *Metaphors of Mind: An Eighteenth-Century Dictionary* (Baltimore, MD: Johns Hopkins University Press, 2015), 50–68; Sean Silver, *The Mind Is a Collection: Case Studies in Eighteenth-Century Thought* (Philadelphia: University of Pennsylvania Press, 2015), 131–134.
[5] Joseph Addison, *Dialogues Upon the Usefulness of Ancient Medals* (London, 1726), 10.
[6] Ibid., 25.

Alexander Pope seizes on these references to rust and makes explicit the links that Addison's characters implicitly draw between an appreciation for numismatic objects' decayed materiality and moral corruptions born out of greed. Pope's poem briefly describes several numismatists whose lust for "rust," which they "adore," evinces vice.[7] One numismatist "employs" nefarious "schemes" to procure a coin minted in the reign of the second-century Roman emperor Pescennius Niger; another "grasps" a coin of the mythical Attican King Cecrops in deluded "ecstatic dreams"; and yet another lies "restless" in his marriage bed, "neglecting his bride" while he longs for "an Otho" instead (39–44). Enchanted by the rust on their time-tarnished objects, Pope's numismatists confirm what the characters in Addison's *Dialogues* imply – that an appreciation for the decayed materiality of old coins and medals, here figured explicitly as an obsession with their metallic surfaces, corresponded to a decay in moral sensibilities.

John Evelyn's early defense of numismatics shows that the period's numismatists valued old coins and medals not just for their metallic materiality but also for their small size.[8] Near the beginning of his influential *Numismata* (1697), Evelyn famously insisted that many details about the past would have been lost if they hadn't been preserved on old coins and medals: "these small pieces of Metal, which seem to have broken and worn out the very Teeth of Time, that devours and tears in pieces all things else."[9] Although Evelyn's imagery contends that old coins' and medals' metallic strength breaks the teeth of time, their small size also protects them from being broken. The smallness of numismatic objects enhanced their ability not only either to endure or escape the crush of history's vicissitudes but also, in so doing, to proliferate and accumulate. For Evelyn, the smallness of old coins and medals stands initially in contrast to the immensity and implied permanency of monuments such as pyramids, but monuments' enormity and endurance conceptually shrink in contrast to the quantities of numismatic objects that have amassed and circulated throughout the ages. Though one of his briefer productions, Evelyn's *Numismata* is

---

[7] Alexander Pope, "To Mr. Addison, Occasioned by his Dialogues on Medals" in *The Poems of Alexander Pope*, ed. John Butt (New Haven, CT: Yale University Press), 215–216, line 36. Hereafter, line numbers are cited parenthetically in the text.

[8] Evelyn was personally acquainted with Hobbes, and his diary describes both a visit he made to "the famous philosopher of Malmesbury" and the two men's "long acquaintance." See *The Diary of John Evelyn*, ed. E. S. de Beer, 6 vols. (Oxford: Clarendon Press, 1955), vol. 3, 163; Gillian Darley, *John Evelyn: Living for Ingenuity* (New Haven, CT: Yale University Press, 2006), 108–109.

[9] John Evelyn, *Numismata: A Discourse of Metals* (London, 1697), 2. Hereafter, page numbers are cited parenthetically in the text.

similarly remarkable for its scale, suggesting that the smallness of old coins and medals tendered varieties of plenitude.

Evelyn first invokes the small size of numismatic objects in order to define them as objects and then to encourage their study and collection. Evelyn offers novice numismatists a basic definition they can use to distinguish between coins and medals – coins, in short, are usually smaller than medals, although both are small compared with other antiquities (8); Evelyn next implies that because "smaller *Monies*" were used for "Commerce," they communicate more democratic histories into the present than many larger medals, which were used to commemorate the deeds of exemplary individuals. Evelyn encourages the collection of old coins as well as medals by noting that the smallest numismatic objects are often valued more highly than the "largest" specimens, especially when the smaller items are also rare (18). Evelyn's withdrawal here from the numerous to the singular by way of attesting to the rarity of some old coins and medals is, however, remarkably quick; he immediately returns to encouraging his readers' numismatic pursuits by appealing, once again, to the types of quantity that characterized numismatic study and collection. Evelyn helps his readers to visualize rare numismatic objects by comparing them with the modern-day coins that were familiar because plentifully in circulation. He reminds his readers that although the rarest of the smallest gold Greek coins are "most esteem'd" by collectors, "not a few" copper Greek coins continued to be available on the numismatic market because of "the vastly spreading Conquests" that the ancient Greeks achieved and the "wonderful and successful Expeditions of the Great *Alexander*" (19).[10] Taken together, those "vastly spreading Conquests" and the expeditions of the "Great" Alexander meant that "innumerable" old "*Medals* and Coins" were "scattered" far and wide in the past (19). And as they proliferated throughout the ancient world, numismatic objects likewise circulated images of historical figures as well as of the far-flung "Cities and Places" that the Greeks conquered.

The innumerability of old coins and medals and the kinds of scale produced by such quantities of small numismatic objects stands as a refrain throughout Evelyn's *Numismata*. The global diffusion of coins and medals occurred throughout the historical eras dominated by Rome as well as ancient Greece. Ancient Romans, Evelyn explains, produced astonishing

---

[10] See also Susan Stewart's observation that, in the form of the miniature, "[s]cale is established by means of a set of correspondences to the familiar." *On Longing: Narratives of the Miniature, the Gigantic, the Souvenir, the Collection* (Baltimore, MD: Johns Hopkins University Press, 1984), 46. Likewise, Gaston Bachelard remarks, "correlatively, familiar objects become the miniatures of the world." *The Poetics of Space* (1958; Boston, MA: Beacon Press, 1994), 170.

amounts of coins and medals because they appreciated, as the Greeks had before them, numismatic objects as records of historical figures as well as events and moods. Consequently, "instead of Ensigns and painted Banners," ancient Romans purportedly "carried" numismatic objects with them "in Pomps and Processions of State" (69). The ancients also, Evelyn claims, "adorned the Vestibules and Porches of their Temples, Halls and Palaces" with coins and medals, which likewise inspired the display of even more antiquities – "Armour, Weapons, Trophies, Statues, Urns, Tables and Inscriptions" – all attesting to the "Veneration" that the ancients had for their ancestors, their virtues, and their heroic exploits (64).

In contrast with the other antiquities that amassed around them, numismatic objects were the most celebrated "*Memoirs*" of the past to be found in ancient Rome not only because they were understood to be stamped on metal, the "the most lasting Materials," but also because their small size meant that they were portable and produced in quantities that ensured many of them would survive over time (64). As both small and "lasting" objects, old coins and medals were plentifully available in the past and remained so in the present, according to Evelyn. Evelyn leads his readers to imagine, for example, that "much" of the ancient "Money and *Medals*" that were already so "innumerable" throughout historical ages "is yet remaining, much more 'tis probably than what is yet come to light" (69). There are the numismatic objects "found here and there casually in single pieces" – but just as "often," numismatists find their objects "in heaps, full *Urns* and Jars" in modern Rome as well as Britain (69). These old coins and medals were, Evelyn recognizes, one means by which the Romans "inlarg'd [*sic*] their Conquests over Men," and they subsequently "shew the immense Treasure of that once flourishing State" as well as "the vast Extent of its numerous *Colonies*" (69).

Evelyn's enthusiasm for numismatic quantity, however, risks leading him into the dubious moral territory occupied by Addison's and Pope's hoarding medalists. Evelyn seems aware that his zeal for numismatic plenitude might gloss as greed and unwittingly appear, therefore, as an endorsement of the vices commonly associated with the fall of the Roman empire throughout the long eighteenth century. Immediately after he raises the specter of Rome's "inlarg'd" conquests, "numerous" colonies, and the "vast" extent of its empire, as evidenced by the multitude of old coins and medals that could still be found in present-day Britain, Evelyn demurs. All those numismatic objects, he muses, offer "recompense of the Changes and Devastations" wrought by Rome's imperial rule and confirm that the Romans brought "Laws and Learning, useful Arts, and Exemplary Virtues" to the "Barbarous World," despite the violence their armies inflicted (69). Although Evelyn here finds "recompense" in the timeless "Virtues" enshrined in historical figures commemorated by the numismatic objects that were produced partly as a consequence of Rome's regrettable excesses, he mitigates the avarice that numismatic quantity might belie or stimulate by tethering such vices, as Pope would also later do, to the metallic materiality of old coins and medals – thereby preserving their virtues in their small size. In other words, the substance of numismatic objects emerges as the site where moral virtues are most likely to be undermined, while the size of old coins and medals proves to be the means whereby vices can be moderated and moral virtues can be preserved, recovered, or inculcated.

For Pope, the smallness of numismatic objects mitigates the qualities of moral decay they evince and threaten to convey. His prefatory poem for Addison's *Dialogues* begins with expansive imagery of Rome's decline in terms that invoke monumental modes of duration, distance, and size. After conjuring in the first stanza Rome's "Imperial wonders" – the "Huge Theatres" and "Huge moles [massive structures], whose shadow stretch'd from shore to shore" – which were built by "Slaves" and in which "the groaning Martyr" also "toil'd," the second stanza describes the figure of Ambition now in the present (lines 5–6). Ambition "sigh[s]," "contracts her vast design," and "shrinks" Rome's history "into a Coin" where "a narrow orb each crouded conquest keeps" (lines 19–25). "Beneath [Ambition's] Palm" (a pun that raises both the image of a miniaturized tree that might appear on a numismatic object as well as the hand of Ambition) "sad Judea weeps," while a "proud Arch" (another pun that again raises both the image of miniaturized architecture that might appear on a numismatic object as well as the shape of the round numismatic object itself) "confine[s]" the Roman empire to "scantier limits" (lines 26–27). The stanza concludes by emphasizing the "small Euphrates" and the "little Eagles" that can also be seen on the object (lines 29–30).

The small size, circumscribed shape, and minute representations that characterize the numismatic object correspond in Pope's rendering to a welcomed "short view" of Rome's history (line 33). The "pale Antiquaries" whose lust for rust Pope condemns notably spend too long lingering over the metallic materiality of their old coins and medals, "por[ing]" over the objects and admiring, in particular, their "blue" and "green" "varnish" (lines 35–37). The duration of attention that numismatists pay to their objects correlates to the attention they give to the objects' physical indicators of age. The effect is ironic; attending too long to the material surfaces of old coins and medals makes them relatively outsized – large in the imagination in contrast to their physical diminution – and interrupts the distance and delay that would make the Roman empire seem perceptually small and instructively short-lived in the larger timescale established by the present. Returning to the metaphors that Hobbes used to explain his materialist theories of perception, the metallic matter of numismatic objects threatened to carry with it the foibles of the ancients, like flotsam washing onto the shores of the present from the past; similarly, valuations of old coins and medals as pieces of mere metal undermined their status as artifacts by eclipsing their function as itemizable records of individual historical figures and events; as pieces of metal, finally, numismatic objects were liable to degradations and transformations that compromised their legibility, thereby producing the kind of interpretive slowness, confusion, and ambiguity that Hobbes attributes to the aging body and its senses.

For Evelyn, the smallness of numismatic objects productively channels their qualities of decay into quantities of more usefully distanced and delayed associations. Appreciated for their smallness, old coins and medals could still be celebrated for their ability to convey factual particulars, bit by bit, from the past to the present, while also ensuring that varieties of historical information remained available as universal, applicable, and transferrable data for the present and the future. In order to mitigate the kinds of decay that old coins and medals threatened to introduce into present-day Britain, therefore, Evelyn returns throughout his *Numismata* to clarify the relationship that exists between the size and quantity of numismatic objects, ultimately disassembling numismatic objects' smallness from their substance and reframing their relationship to scale accordingly. For example, he follows his claim that modern-day numismatists continue to discover "heaps" of old coins and medals with a "digression" on how the surfeit remainders of the ancients' mass productions of numismatic objects faired before numismatists such as Evelyn appreciated their uses as small historical artifacts and transferrable moral devices. "A *Venetian* Merchant," Evelyn reports, was said in the sixteenth century to have "melted down [an] abundance of rare *Coins* to make a Chain of Gold for his Wife to wear"; likewise, a "*Spanish* Apothecary" purportedly "cast a Mortar for the use of his shop [from] an invaluable Collection of *Medals*"; "at *Rome* a Goldsmith was wont to cast little Shrines and Statues of gold and silver *Medals*"; and in "the *Ottoman* Court," when a "Pagan *Tinker*" was asked if he had any old coins or medals to sell, he replied that he did not because he had "melted" them all down "to make *Pots* and *Kettles*" (70).

The plentitude of old coins and medals makes the merchant's, apothecary's, goldsmith's, and tinkerer's actions possible, but they are lamentable actions not only because they reduce numismatic objects to their metal but also because they negate old coins' and medals' boundedness as small and distinct objects. The merchant, the apothecary, the goldsmith, and the tinkerer combine many numismatic objects into a few notably longer (the merchant's gold chain), larger (the goldsmith's statues and the tinkerer's pots), or more ineffably distributive (the apothecary's mortar) commodities. Though newly made and shaped, the necklace, mortar, shrines, and pots manifest a material degradation of numismatic objects as well as the moral decay of those who would value old coins and medals primarily for their metal. The merchant who flatters his wife with a gold chain made of old coins and medals, we can infer, nurtures lust; the apothecary trades in the falsehoods of a mountebank; the goldsmith stokes idolatry; the tinkerer is a pagan.

Although an antiquary himself, Evelyn similarly condemned those antiquaries who – like the merchant, the apothecary, the goldsmith, and the tinkerer – valued old coins and medals for their materiality at the expense of appreciating them for their smallness. Echoing the implicit condemnation that he levels at the merchant who made a necklace for his wife out of an "abundance" of melted coins, Evelyn insists that for "all" that he has said "in favour" of numismatic objects, he hopes his readers will recognize that he is "far from approving or encouraging that abandon'd and passionate love which some have shew'd, in a restless and expensive pursuit of these Curiosities" (69). Evelyn here singles out those "Luxurious Antiquaries" who, "to the prejudice of their Fortunes or any nobler Parts of Life," have "rang[ed] over all the world, and compass[ed] Land and Sea to feed an unbounded Appetite" (69). These antiquaries "turn" the "laudable and useful Diversion" of numismatic collection and study "into Fault and Vice" (70). In contrast to the merchant, the apothecary, the goldsmith, and the tinkerer, Evelyn's luxurious antiquaries appreciate old coins and medals as distinct objects, but they still fail to heed the affective responses demanded by their smallness. "[R]anging over all the world" in order to "feed an unbounded Appetite," the actions of luxurious antiquaries are notably outsized in relation to the objects they prize. "*Est modus in rebus*," Evelyn quips; there is a proper measure in things (70).

In his castigation of luxurious antiquaries (and the merchant, the apothecary, the goldsmith, and the tinkerer), Evelyn admonishes those who disrupt the experience of distance and delay that materialist philosophers such as Hobbes ascribed to the mechanical processes of perceiving external objects. The merchant, the apothecary, the goldsmith, and the tinkerer all interrupt old coins and medals in the course of their spatiotemporal trajectories, halting their ability to transmit specific historical facts and universal virtues by shaping them into new material objects for consumption in the present. Evelyn's luxurious antiquaries impose artificially extended delays on numismatic objects' transmission of facts and virtues by either taking too long and going too far to find them, by neglecting to spend sufficient time examining one item in their "restless" and "unbounded" pursuit for yet another and then another, or by lavishing too much "passionate" attention on one prized object at the expense of considering other or different objects. In their perception of numismatic objects as unbounded matter, the merchant, the apothecary, the goldsmith, the tinkerer, and luxurious antiquaries all fail to appreciate the particularities of historical knowledge and experience encoded in materialist philosophies such as Hobbes's and invoked by numismatists such as Evelyn. In other words, the inevitable distance and delay in perception that leads Hobbes to describe both the imagination and the memory as "decayed" manifests as material and moral degradation when numismatic objects are prized solely for their substance.

Evelyn prioritizes, therefore, the ways in which numismatic objects' smallness yields quantities not of substance but of associations that could be textually assembled and remediated. Throughout Evelyn's *Numismata*, the smallness of numismatic objects ensures that they continue to function as the physical conduits of historical information while remaining available for the present's ideological as well as aesthetic needs, and the distance and delay that attend the consideration of small objects become welcome opportunities for introducing meaningful associations that, in turn, recover as well as establish new networks of relations – or, when necessary, delimit problematic historical inheritances and moral transgressions. Evelyn, in other words, reveres old coins and medals not just because their small size appears to be pleasingly juxtaposed to their many functions but rather precisely because their small size appears to afford what Evelyn describes early on in the *Numismata* as the "knowledge of a thousand useful things of twice a thousand years past" (3). He notes, for example, that the portraits of figures on the ancients' coins and medals were designed not only to "delight the Eye" of their beholders but also to "[call] to their minds the glorious actions [the depicted figures] had perform'd," which, in turn "inflam'd" the objects' beholders "with an Emulation of [the depicted figures'] Virtues" (66). The transitory pleasure of visual "delight" gives way here to the recall of biographical details, the exercise of moral contemplations, a swelling of sentimental feeling, and forms of replication; lest the time spent in seeing the numismatic object, appreciating it aesthetically, recollecting the history of the figure it depicts, and feeling "inflam'd" to emulate that individual's character seems correspondingly quick relative to the object's small size, Evelyn continues to explain that the delighted, reminded, and inspired beholders of ancient numismatic objects did not "rest" until "they themselves had also done something worthy" (66).[11]

Evelyn's assessment of old coins' and medals' reverses similarly revels in the kinds of expansive proliferation that numismatic objects afforded. Evelyn, in fact, prefers the reverses of numismatic objects to their obverses; whereas the obverses of old coins and medals might be said to remain somewhat delimited by their referential relationship to the individuals whose faces they depict, their reverses – which often feature "*Inscriptions*, with *Figure* and *Emblem* representing Action" – are "preferred," "desirable," and "enquir'd" about by "the Learned," according to Evelyn, because they are "infinitely fruitful and full of Erudition" (48). "[H]ad we a perfect and uninterrupted Series" of just numismatic objects' reverses, Evelyn declares, "we should need almost no other History" (48). Reverses, Evelyn continues, present not only "the Successions of the noblest and most illustrious Families, their Names, Titles, Impreses [*sic*], Honors, Dignities, Crowns, Garlands, Marks and Rewards of Magistracy," but also representations of

> the Habits and Robes of *Consuls, Kings* and *Emperors, Flamens, Vestals,* and other Royal and Sacerdotal Garments … *Tripos, Lituus, Patera, Sistrum, Simpulum,* Knife, Ax, the Lustral Sprinklers, and other *Vasa,* and Utensils of Sacrifice, *Libations* and *Augury* … Chariots, Arms, *Ancilia,* Shields, Ensigns, Engines, Harness, and Weapons of War. … antient Gallies, and other Vessels, with their manner of Naval Combat … the Actions and Exploits of the greatest Captains; their Military Expeditions, Legions, Cohorts, Colonies, Discipline, Stations, Castrametations, Victories, Trophies, Triumphs, Largesses, Benefactions, Remissions, Confederations, Truces, Cessations, Indulgences, Relaxations of Tribute, *Encaenias,* Dedications, and Vows … the *Lectisternia,* Marriages, Births, Funeral Pomps, *Pyrae, Apotheoses,* and Consecrations … the most magnificent and stately Buildings that ever stood upon the Face of the Earth: *Basilics* and Royal Palaces, Temples, Altars, *Asyla,* Sacrifices, *&c.* … stupendious [*sic*] Amphitheatres, Theatres, Forums, *Thermae, Xysti,* Portics, *Naumachiae,* Hippodroms, Mausolea, and Sepulchres … Aquaeducts, Fountains, Bridges, *Cryptae, Viae, Castra, Metae, Termini, Cippi,* Bases … Triumphal Arches, *Obelisks, Pyramids, Colossus's,* and other Royal and Magnificent Fabrics of venerable Antiquity. (49–50)

The list goes on; after delineating the incredible range of historical minutiae that can be excavated from just the reverses of numismatic objects, Evelyn

---

[11] For a similar argument about small bodkins' power to "puncture and reassemble," see Chloe Wigston Smith, "Bodkin Aesthetics: Small Things in the Eighteenth Century," *Eighteenth-Century Fiction*, 31.2 (2019), 271–294.

turns to consider the symbolic meanings of various details that are also to be seen on the reverses of old coins and medals – and, fourteen pages later, he concludes: "And thus all that was heroical and great, peculiar and eminent, and properly regarding Antient History, its Circumstances and Accessories, is, we see, fetch out of *Medals* and their *Reverses*" (64). As passages like these suggest, a sense of Evelyn's enthusiasm for the ways small numismatic objects could convey so very many things can be seen in the style that Evelyn's own treatise assumes. Sean Silver notes, for example, that the longest interpretation Evelyn provides for a single numismatic object corresponds to the smallest object illustrated in his treatise, the Kineton medal.[12] More significantly, Evelyn's *Numismata* consistently translates the quantities afforded by numismatic objects' smallness stylistically as accumulating lists that establish both a range of historical particulars and more enduring networks of relations. Long lists are one of *Numismata*'s most prominent features – a formal aspect that illustrates the conceptual content of Evelyn's praise for numismatic objects by transforming their smallness into quantities of associations that can be compiled into various arrangements.

Evelyn's interest in the quantities of associations that accumulate around old coins and medals finds its fullest expression, however, in the penultimate chapter of his treatise. Following a discussion of the clipping and debasement that corrupted England's coinage during the seventeenth century, he continues to further disassemble the metallic matter of old coins and medals from their functions by recommending that his readers undertake the work of creating a comprehensive "Collection of the *Heads* and *Effigies* of Famous Illustrious Persons" in the format of a catalogue of prints (257). To this end, Evelyn offers his readers a list of the individuals whose visages might be documented in print – but in the style of medals – for posterity. For Evelyn, these are the people from the past as well as the present who are "worthy the Honor of *Medal*" (257). He begins his list as columns and rows enumerating more than five hundred individuals by name, but he eventually returns to running his lists in line. And Evelyn's lists are prolific, constituting thirty total pages of the treatise and encompassing everyone from "*Emperors, Kings, Princes*" (257) to "illustrious Strumpets" (266), someone named "*Farley*, who slept fourteen Days and Nights" (267), and "Imposters, Heresiarchs, and Heterodxi, &c." (276).

---

[12] Evelyn's interpretation is, in fact, mistakenly premised on a very small change imposed on a transcription of the medal's inscription. See Sean Silver, "John Evelyn and Numismata: Material History and Autobiography," *Word & Image*, 31.3 (2015), 331–342.

Even Evelyn recognizes the seeming absurdity of his listing style at this point in *Numismata*. After concluding his list of individuals whose faces might be engraved in a numismatic style for posterity, he writes: "And now I confess it may be wonder'd, why I should call over so extravagant a list of *Names*, and what my meaning is" (288)? Evelyn defends his commitments to plenitude by appealing to a quantity of as-yet-unrealized possibilities; by such a list, he writes, "I endeavour to point out how some of all Capacities, signal for any Thing or Action extraordinary, and that possibly may enter into any part of History, may at some time, or upon some occasion or other, fetch Matter and Subject proper for Use" (289). Evelyn's proliferating particulars, in other words, are assembled in order to prevent the historical decay of the present for an imagined future, when – after a delay and at a distance – their moral significance might be better understood. Moreover, as his willingness to include the faces of "Imposters, Heresiarchs, and Heterodxi, &c." shows, Evelyn does not shy away from representing individuals known for their vices in his imagined catalogue of numismatic prints; these are the people "worth the honor of … some memory" (257). When rendered as lines and shapes on paper rather than in metal, the visages of the corrupt might further mitigate the kinds of moral decay that attended more materialistic appreciations for numismatic objects, not least because the period's numismatic print style could readily correct the kinds of physical damage that compromised the appearance and legibility of old coins and medals.

Evelyn's way of expressing the value of numismatic collection and study confirms some of Melinda Alliker Rabb's findings in her study *Miniature and the English Imagination*. Rabb argues that, for Evelyn, old coins and medals "both mediate the realities of the past and displace them."[13] Yet in Evelyn's hands, numismatic objects are not quite the "miniatures" on which Rabb focuses her attention. The smallness of old coins and medals means that they work differently than miniatures. Although old coins and medals present little versions of people and things, Evelyn maintains that their power inheres not necessarily in the ways that they shrink, or scale down, that which they represent so that their beholders and their holders might better cognitively comprehend "difficult" and large-scale events, such as "financial revolution, war, globalization, and natural disasters."[14] Evelyn's small numismatic objects make sense of sociocultural phenomena

---

[13] Melinda Alliker Rabb, *Miniature and the English Imagination: Literature, Cognition, and Small-Scale Culture, 1650–1765* (Cambridge: Cambridge University Press, 2019), 150.
[14] Ibid., 4.

by preserving a seemingly inexhaustible range of historical particulars for ongoing and future assemblages. Moreover, Rabb finds that miniatures remained "steadfastly inanimate" throughout the long eighteenth century; they did not, she insists, "become animated and/or anthropomorphized" in the way that distinguishes the kinds of objects that emerge as the narrators of the period's it-narratives, for example.[15] Numismatic objects, however, were ubiquitous as just such narrators. In *Artifacts*, I argued that the materiality of old coins and medals afforded competing, diametrically opposed interpretations of their historical significance that kept them circulating throughout the long eighteenth century as narrative devices; as Evelyn suggests, however, their smallness yielded quantities of particulars and associations that likewise established them as vehicles for variety, explaining in part how individuals might imagine numismatic objects as the progenitors of the kinds of episodic adventures that characterized the period's it-narratives.[16]

At the same time, however, Evelyn's interest in numismatic objects' smallness also correlated to a sense of their value relative to memorable – and, notably, short – literary forms.[17] By way of concluding his treatise, Evelyn's proposal for a universal catalogue of faces modeled on the style of numismatic objects leads him into *Numismata*'s final chapter: a lengthy "digression" on physiognomy that reflects Evelyn's attempt to parse a wide range of historical and then-contemporary writings, often indebted to materialist principles, which considered the possibility that the facial features belied ineffable qualities of moral character. In his turn to the problem of the relationships between faces and characters, Evelyn also considers the relationships between the blood, the mind, the body, and the environment – and the scale of *Numismata* accordingly toggles between the microscopic and the universal. Although Evelyn reports that those of his readers who "remember Mr. Hobbs [sic], as I perfectly do" will recognize that the portraits made of Hobbes were "perfectly like him" and confirm that "his very Looks" matched his "supercilious, Saturnine, [and] *Opiniatrety*" character, Evelyn ultimately remains unconvinced by the "*Science*" of physiognomy (340–341). Unable to settle the matter of physiognomic science's validity, Evelyn takes recourse in the "*Proverbs*, trite and vulgar Sayings" that seem to confirm many of physiognomy's tenets (300).

---

[15] Ibid., 30.
[16] Crystal B. Lake, *Artifacts: How We Think and Write about Found Objects* (Baltimore, MD: Johns Hopkins University Press, 2019), 79–108.
[17] Stewart similarly observes that the miniature often gives way to "aphoristic thinking." *On Longing*, 43.

If the generalized nature of such a literary form seems initially to stand in contrast to the quantities of particulars that Evelyn finds to be commensurate with old coins' and medals' smallness, his way of clarifying the nature of proverbs returns again to emphasize plenitude as a means of achieving endurance. Proverbs, Evelyn explains, are "by no means to be slighted" (300). Proverbs can, in fact, be trusted because they are "gathered from the long and constant Observations, confirmed by much Experience, and founded upon the most infallible Reasons and Philosophical Resolutions" (300). For Evelyn, then, the smallness of numismatic objects made it possible for them to proliferate, materially and imaginatively, in the expanse of the distances and delays that Hobbes maintained existed in our experiences of perceiving external objects – while they also persisted as little vehicles for the memorable transference of history's most enduring lessons.

6 | Crinoidal Limestone and Staffordshire Teapots

Material and Temporal Scales in Eighteenth-Century Britain

KATE SMITH

Teapots have long been recognized as "indispensable props in the genteel performances that constituted politeness" in eighteenth-century Britain.[1] They were crucial objects in practices of tea drinking and remained central to the workings of the tea table, a key site of female sociability and gentility.[2] The tea table simultaneously acted as "the very headquarters of female opinion, a byword for feminine confederacy, gossip and slander," and as "a forum for business dealings in the widest possible sense."[3] Rather than simply sites for the performance of politeness, tea tables were distinctly active spaces in which knowledge was exchanged and transactions completed.

By 1760, tea was recognized as a universal habit among all social groups in England, and as early as the 1820s commentators identified the British as "a tea-drinking nation."[4] While eighteenth-century Britons worked hard to construct tea-drinking as a distinctly polite, domestic, and British activity, the commodities central to such rituals – the tea and sugar crucial to the beverage, the mahogany of the tea table, and the ceramic material that made up the multiple vessels required – alluded to the expansive geographies, violence, and exploitation central to eighteenth-century global trade.[5] Recent research on ceramic goods has shown how these commodities emerged from evermore complex global networks of influence and

---

[1] John Styles, "Georgian Britain 1714–1837: Introduction" in Michael Snodin and John Styles (eds.), *Design and the Decorative Arts: Britain 1500–1900* (London: V&A, 2001), 184.
[2] Amanda Vickery, *Behind Closed Doors: At Home in Georgian England* (New Haven, CT and London: Yale University Press, 2009), 272.
[3] Ibid., 274; Amanda Vickery, *The Gentleman's Daughter: Women's Lives in Georgian England* (New Haven, CT and London: Yale University Press, 1998), 208.
[4] Vickery, *Behind Closed Doors*, 247.
[5] For more on the cultural work at stake in making tea drinking a polite activity, see Markman Ellis, Richard Coulton, and Matthew Mauger, *Empire of Tea: The Asian Leaf that Conquered the World* (London: Reaktion Books, 2015), 31–52. For more on the geographies and violence at stake in sugar and mahogany production, see James Walvin, *Slavery in Small Things: Slavery and Modern Cultural Habits* (Chichester, W. Sussex: Wiley, 2017), 11–36; Jennifer L. Anderson, *Mahogany: The Costs of Luxury in Early America* (Cambridge: Cambridge University Press, 2012), 89–124.

exchange.⁶ While teapots were important props, then, they also prompted eighteenth-century Britons to reflect on the movement of knowledge, skills, styles, and materials across seemingly disparate cultures.⁷

Over the last twenty years, eighteenth-century tea tables, and the practices of tea drinking they accommodated, have increasingly come to be understood as complex sites in which the people *and* objects present encouraged questions, discussion, and reflection. Building on such work, this chapter seeks to further interrogate the tea table as a complex site by focusing on how teapots themselves provoked a range of questions. This chapter examines a particular series of teapots produced in Staffordshire, and possibly Yorkshire, in the late 1750s and 1760s (see, for example, Figure 6.1), to show how objects could raise questions about issues important to, and controversial within, eighteenth-century British culture. Featuring depictions of fossils and rock formations, these particular pots invited conversations about time and the natural world in a period when understandings of the scale and extent of these things were in flux.

Diminutive in size (see the measurements in the captions to Figures 6.1 and 6.2), the teapots under examination all feature a particular design that sought to mimic the patterns, shapes, and colors found in crinoidal limestone. This chapter argues that reading such objects in their eighteenth-century contexts shows the multiple juxtapositions at play and suggests how small objects, such as teapots, were capable of asking big questions about scale. By decorating items with a pattern that mimicked fossilized forms, eighteenth-century potters raised questions of temporal scale: they alluded to contemporary discussions about fossils and the questions they raised about the earth's history and deep time. Similarly, by including a pattern

---

⁶ Robert Batchelor, "On the Movement of Porcelains: Rethinking the Birth of Consumer Society as Interactions of Exchange Networks, 1600–1750" in Frank Trentmann and John Brewer (eds.), *Consuming Cultures, Global Perspectives: Historical Trajectories, Transnational Exchanges* (Oxford and New York: Berg, 2006), 95–122; Maxine Berg, "Cargoes: The Trade in Luxuries from Asia to Europe" in David Cannadine (ed.), *Empire, the Sea and Global History: Britain's Maritime World c. 1763–c. 1840* (New York and Basingstoke: Palgrave, 2007), 60–82; Robert Finlay, *The Pilgrim Art: Cultures of Porcelain in World History* (Berkeley and London: University of California Press, 2010); Meha Priyadarshini, *Chinese Porcelain in Colonial Mexico: The Material Worlds of Early Modern Trade* (London: Palgrave, 2018); Anne Gerritsen, *The City of Blue and White: Chinese Porcelain and the Early Modern World* (Cambridge: Cambridge University Press, 2020).
⁷ David Porter, *The Chinese Taste in Eighteenth-Century England* (Cambridge: Cambridge University Press, 2010); Anne Gerritsen and Stephen McDowall, "Global China: Material Culture and Connections in World History," *Journal of World History*, 23.1 (2012), 3–8; Stacey Pierson, "The Movement of Chinese Ceramics: Appropriation in Global History," *Journal of World History*, 23.1 (2012), 9–39; Kate Smith, *Material Goods, Moving Hands: Perceiving Production in England, 1700–1830* (Manchester: Manchester University Press, 2014), 25–48.

Figure 6.1 Side view of white stoneware teapot and cover with enamel and salt glaze, Staffordshire, c. 1760. H.: 10.8 cm; Diam. (body): 10.5 cm; Diam. (handle-spout): 17.5 cm. Photo credit: Gavin Ashworth. © The Chipstone Foundation, Milwaukee, 1997.19.a–b.

that spoke to rock formations, manufacturers and decorators also ensured that the teapots provoked questions of solidity and material longevity. Rather than being perceived as breakable and momentary, through their decoration the teapots gestured towards permanence. Finally, their shapes and forms raised questions of mortality and human scale. The form of the teapot, particularly its crabstock handle, was both familiar and strange, producing an uncanny experience that underlined the object as a non-human "other." In their use, teapots reaffirmed the centrality of the human and human scale. The aesthetic and material formations of particular objects asked challenging questions about the material and temporal scales that broad swathes of eighteenth-century Britons sought to grapple with in the later decades of the century. As such, these small things provoked important questions through their display and use on the tea table.

Deep Time

At first glance, the decorative schemes featured on these teapots appear unknowable (see particularly Figure 6.1). Rather than the opulence or order often associated with eighteenth-century British aesthetics, the pattern contains an abstract chaos usually associated with early twentieth-century European art and design. A closer look might reveal seemingly identifiable elements: eyes, jaws, vertebrae, and flowers. For eighteenth-century Britons increasingly well versed in the order and symmetry of neoclassical designs, the scattering of seeming body parts may have appeared threatening and unsettling. Similarly, the sharp contrasts in color (black and white in Figure 6.1; red, black, and cream in Figure 6.2) further exaggerate the motifs at stake, allowing the decoration to seem aggressive in its occupation of visual space. Nevertheless, rather than a pattern featuring different elements, the decorative scheme of the teapots carefully depicted a known and particular rock formation: crinoidal limestone. Such limestone features encrinus or fossilized elements of crinoids, marine animals that, in their adult form, are attached to the seabed via a stalk and are popularly known as sea lilies. There are also unstalked varieties of crinoids, called feather stars or comatulids. The patterns included on the teapots under discussion here carefully represent crinoidal limestone; their surfaces speak of deep temporal spans and the era's new interest in fossils.

During the period in which these teapots are commonly thought to be made, the late 1750s and 1760s, knowledge accessed through imperial projects and imperial networks provided natural historians with a more detailed understanding of the "creature" fossilized within these rock formations. A broader interest in fossils was also growing in Britain and rapidly increased in the early nineteenth century.[8] At the same time, with the growth of geology as a particular discipline, understandings of temporal spans and the earth's history were changing substantially.[9] Fossils became linked to wider questions of temporal scale and came to symbolize an immense view of time. Featured on a diminutive teapot, the object's size further highlighted the importance of such temporal spans: in contrast to the small thing (the teapot), the temporal span of fossils pointed to vastness and enormity.

---

[8] For more on the interest in fossils, see Deborah Cadbury, *The Dinosaur Hunters: A True Story of Scientific Rivalry and the Discovery of the Prehistoric World* (London: Fourth Estate, 2000).

[9] For more on the development of geology, see Roy Porter, *The Making of Geology: Earth Science in Britain, 1660–1815* (Cambridge: Cambridge University Press, 1977); Rhoda Rappaport, *When Geologists Were Historians, 1665–1750* (Ithaca, NY and London: Cornell University Press, 1997); Hugh Torrens, *The Practice of British Geology, 1750–1850* (Aldershot: Ashgate, 2002); Kenneth L. Taylor, *The Earth Sciences in the Enlightenment: Studies on the Early Development of Geology* (Aldershot: Ashgate, 2008).

In 1761, the natural historian John Ellis published "An Account of an Encrinus" in the *Philosophical Transactions of the Royal Society*.[10] Ellis had previously worked on attempts to grow tea plants in Europe, but here he engaged with other imperial networks to produce knowledge on sea lilies.[11] Ellis wrote the article after receiving a specimen of the animal from "Mr. Mason of Barbadoes [sic], remarkable for his curious experiments in magnetism."[12] The specimen had come from Ellis's friend Dr. Alexander Bruce, also a resident of Barbados.[13] Although it first "fell into the hands of my worthy friend Dr. John Fothergil [sic]" (as Ellis was "in the country"), it was swiftly delivered to Ellis to enable him to describe and show it to the Royal Society.[14] Ellis's receipt of Mason's specimen was timely. In his article, Ellis described how in 1761 Mr. Guettard had published "a most minute description and dissection of an animal of this kind," which was from the French colonial island of Martinique and which he had been given from the "curious cabinet of Madam Bois Jourdain of Paris."[15] Cabinets of curiosity provided important spaces in which specimens could be brought together and thought through in the seventeenth and eighteenth centuries.[16] According to Ellis, other collectors, such as Mr. Francomb, also held specimens, but these were in fossilized form.[17] Ellis's description of the "animal" itself offered something new and exciting to the readers of the *Philosophical Transactions*. It noted how the encrinus was an "animal" with a "stem and head," measuring "about fourteen inches." The stem was made up of vertebrae, which were "capable of bending at the will of the animal."[18] In his description, Ellis regularly switches between

---

[10] John Ellis, "An Account of an Encrinus," *Philosophical Transactions of the Royal Society*, 52 (1761), 357–362. For more on Ellis's life and career, see Roy A. Rauschenberg, "John Ellis, FRS: Eighteenth-Century Naturalist and Royal Agent to West Florida," *Notes and Records of the Royal Society of London*, 32.2 (1978), 149–164.

[11] Ellis, Coulton, and Mauger, *Empire of Tea*, 108–112.

[12] Ellis, "Account of an Encrinus," 357.

[13] For more on the importance of go-betweens and the "how" of specimens moving around the world, see Simon Schaffer, Lissa Roberts, Kapil Raj, and James Delbourgo, introduction to *The Brokered World: Go-Betweens and Global Intelligence, 1770–1820*, ed. Schaffer, Roberts, Raj, and Delbourgo, Uppsala Studies in History of Science 35 (Sagamore Beach, MA: Science History Publications, 2009), xxv.

[14] Ellis, "Account of an Encrinus," 357.

[15] Ellis, "Account of an Encrinus," 358.

[16] Arthur MacGregor, *Curiosity and Enlightenment: Collectors and Collections from the Sixteenth to the Nineteenth Century* (New Haven, CT and London: Yale University Press, 2007); Stacey Sloboda, "Displaying Materials: Porcelain and Natural History in the Duchess of Portland's Museum," *Eighteenth-Century Studies*, 43.4 (2010), 455–472.

[17] Ellis, "Account of an Encrinus," 361.

[18] Ibid., 358.

plant, human, and animal descriptors – while at one moment he describes the "arms," in another he describes its "branches." Likewise, he notes how this animal had "small jointed claws, like fingers."[19] Despite the minute detail of Ellis's description, the "animal" seemed to lie precariously between categories.

Ellis thought his description would be of great interest to fellow "writers on natural history" who have been "much at a loss to discover to what kind of animals those petrified bodies have properly belonged."[20] Clearly, he and his fellow natural historians were not only interested in the living animal itself but also in its fossilized form. Ellis was right in his belief that others would find his description of interest. His article was reprinted in full in other publications, such as the *Universal Magazine* in May 1763.[21] Publication in a well-established and more mainstream periodical such as the *Universal Magazine* (which continued to be published between 1747 and 1814) allowed a wider variety of readers to engage with the subject. The manufacture of the teapots suggests that these articles made an impact beyond those with an established interest in natural history.

In the 1760s, the potteries of North Staffordshire began making teapots whose decoration closely imitated the fossilized form of the "Encrinus," namely crinoidal limestone (see Figure 6.1). Such limestone contains different elements of the encrinus, such as its head, stem, and branches, which have become broken up and fossilized over time. While the teapots' decoration seems to include a range of teeth, eyes, and vertebrae, these elements are in fact parts of an encrinus and appear in crinoidal limestone in fossilized forms. Two extant examples of teapots featuring crinoidal limestone as their decorative design are held in the collections of Chipstone Foundation in Milwaukee.[22] The Metropolitan Museum of Art in New York, the Nelson Atkins Museum of Art in Kansas City, Winterthur Museum in Delaware, and the Potteries Museum & Art Gallery in Stoke-on-Trent, Staffordshire,

---

[19] Ibid., 361.
[20] Ibid., 357.
[21] John Ellis, "An Account, with a Representation, finely engraved of an Encrinus, or Starfish, with a jointed Stem, taken on the Coast of Barbadoes, which explains to what Kind of Animal those Fossils belong, called Starstones, Asterioe, and Astropodia, which have been found in many Parts of this Kingdom," *Universal Magazine of Knowledge and Pleasure*, 32.223 (1763), 266–268.
[22] Teapot and cover (Figures 6.1 and 6.3), Staffordshire, c. 1760, white stoneware with enamel and salt glaze, 1997.19.a–b, Chipstone Foundation, Milwaukee; Teapot and cover (Figure 6.2), Yorkshire or Staffordshire, c. 1785, creamware, 1995.1.a–b, Chipstone Foundation, Milwaukee.

Figure 6.2 Teapot and cover, c. 1785. Creamware: 13 × 20 (with handle and spout) × 10 cm (diam). Photo credit: Gavin Ashworth. © The Chipstone Foundation, Milwaukee, 1995.1.a–b.

also each have one in their collections.[23] One of the teapots at the Chipstone Foundation and those at the Metropolitan Museum of Art and the Nelson Atkins Museum of Art each feature black and white decoration (the latter two being similar to the design of the Chipstone example in Figure 6.1). The other teapot at the Chipstone Foundation has a red, white, and black color scheme, while that at Winterthur Museum (see Figure 6.2) features a red, white, and black color scheme. The one held in the collection at the Potteries Museum & Art Gallery is glazed in a liver-brown base with a white and black design overtop. Each teapot in these collections is dated to the late 1750s and 1760s. Alongside the publication of John Ellis's article in the *Transactions* and its dissemination through other periodicals, other events in the 1760s illuminate why potters in Staffordshire (and possibly Yorkshire) would have been motivated to create teapots featuring fossilized forms.

[23] Teapot, Staffordshire, 1760–1765, salt-glazed stoneware with enamel decoration, 37.22.6a,b, Metropolitan Museum of Art, New York; Teapot, Staffordshire, c. 1755–1760, salt-glazed stoneware, 41-23/717 A,B, The Nelson-Atkins Museum of Art, Kansas City; Teapot, Staffordshire, c. 1760–1765, salt-glazed stoneware, 1977.0113 A,B, Winterthur Museum, Delaware; Teapot, Staffordshire, c. 1760, salt-glazed stoneware, no accession number, Potteries Museum & Art Gallery, Stoke-on-Trent. A further example of this type of teapot is listed in Robin Emmerson, *British Teapots and Tea Drinking* (London: HMSO, 1992), 93 and pl. 8, but no details on its location are provided.

In February 1768, Josiah Wedgwood wrote to his soon-to-be business partner Thomas Bentley. Wedgwood wanted to inform Bentley of the "wonderfull [sic] & surprising curiositys [sic]" the laborers had found whilst digging the Trent and Mersey Canal, the bill for which had been authorized by Parliament in 1766.[24] Wedgwood was financially and operationally invested in the creation of the canal, as it would provide an important means by which raw materials could be transported to his new site at Etruria in Stoke-on-Trent (which opened in 1769), and by which finished products could be transported out. His letter reported to Bentley how the canal bed was seemingly littered with the bones of monstrous animals. They had found "a prodigious rib, with the back bone of a monstrous sized Fish," which some connoisseurs thought had belonged "to the identical Whale that was so long ago swallowed by Jonah!" They also found another bone "of a very considerable thickness" and "several able anatomists" could not decide whether it was the "first, or last of the vertebre [sic] of some monstrous animal," which might have been "an inhabitant of the Sea, or Land." The monstrous nature of the animals that they imagined these bones might belong to was directly related to their scale. Too large to bear consideration, these animals were incomprehensible.

Wedgwood's laborers also found other fossilized forms within the canal bed. Wedgwood notes that there was a "Great variety of impressions from vegetables such as Fern, Vetches, Crowfoot, Hawthorn, yew, Withy & many other kinds, with roots & trunks of Trees, some of them two feet diameter, & all of them converted into a kind of soft stone which moulders, or shivers to atoms in the open Air." With perhaps some knowing humor, Wedgwood admits to Bentley that in trying to understand the fossils and rock formations he had found he had "got beyond my depth." He states that "These wonderfull [sic] works of Nature are too vast for my narrow ... comprehension." Wedgwood ends the letter by asserting that he needed to "attend to what better suits my Capacity, The forming of a Jug or Teapot." With such finds being revealed so near to his manufactory, it is perhaps unsurprising that potters in 1760s Staffordshire did just that: they produced a series of teapots that featured fossilized forms.

As W. J. T. Mitchell argues, fossils are "the natural sign par excellence."[25] They are both mortal and immortal, acting as both evidence of past life and relics from death. They also represent an epic temporal landscape, what

---

[24] Josiah Wedgwood to Thomas Bentley, February 1768, Etruria Factory Collection, E. 18188-25, Wedgwood Museum, Stoke-on-Trent.

[25] W. J. T. Mitchell, "Romanticism and the Life of Things: Fossils, Totems and Images," *Critical Inquiry*, 28.1 (2001), 167–184 (177).

William Wordsworth referred to as "time's abyss," something "unimaginably greater than human history," and evidence of the distinctly short and mortal nature of human life.[26] Fossils became increasingly important over the later eighteenth century, principally thanks to the work of Georges-Louis Leclerc, Comte de Buffon (1707–1788), and Georges Cuvier (1769–1832). Buffon's 1778 work *Les Époques de la Nature* made explicit a speculation already widespread among naturalists, that human history was but a brief final chapter in a much longer story. *Les Époques de la Nature* explored the Earth's origins and estimated its age as 77,000 years, opening up a much broader sense of time.[27] Similarly, Cuvier developed a theory of fossils that saw them as traces of life-forms extinguished by climatic events.[28] For Michel Foucault, the study of fossils by Cuvier and Buffon among others led to a new "historicity of things," something operating across a much longer temporal span and independent of human affairs and human history.[29] In featuring fossilized forms, therefore, these small teapots pointed towards new questions of historicity and vast temporal spans.

Solidity and Permanence

Alongside decoration, the materiality of ceramic wares – their scale and perceived fragility – was important in defining their cultural place and the meanings they might hold. Small in size and breakable, these teapots when used encouraged a set of gestures that might be interpreted as graceful and refined. As such they contributed to the construction of tea-drinking as a polite activity.[30] Together with these haptic engagements, contemporaries

---

[26] William Wordsworth, "Forth from a Jutting Ridge, around Whose Base" in *The Complete Poetical Works* (London, 1888), line 21, as cited in Mitchell, "Romanticism and the Life of Things," 175.

[27] Christophe Bonneuil and Jean-Baptiste Fressoz, *The Shock of the Anthropocene* (London and New York: Verso Books, 2016), 28.

[28] Martin J. S. Rudwick, *Georges Cuvier, Fossil Bones, and Geological Catastrophes: New Translations & Interpretations of the Primary Texts* (Chicago: University of Chicago Press, 1997).

[29] Mitchell, "Romanticism and the Life of Things," 176; E. C. Spary, "The 'Nature' of Enlightenment" in William Clark, Jan Golinski, and Simon Schaffer (eds.), *The Sciences and Enlightened Europe* (Chicago and London: University of Chicago Press, 1999), 272–304 (274).

[30] For more on how the material world shapes human gestures, see Tim Dant, "The Work of Repair: Gesture, Emotion and Sensual Knowledge," *Sociological Research Online*, 15, nos. 3 and 7 (2010), n.p.; Richard Sennett, *The Craftsman* (London: Yale University Press, 2008); Tim Ingold, *Making: Anthropology, Archaeology, Art and Architecture* (Abingdon: Routledge, 2013). For more on how eighteenth-century objects taught people how to move, see Jennifer Van Horn, *The Power of Objects in Eighteenth-Century British America* (Chapel Hill: University of North Carolina Press, 2017), 301.

learned to understand ceramic wares as fragile through interacting with cultural renderings of these objects. In the eighteenth century, ceramics were regularly used by satirists, commentators, and painters as a means by which to consider the role of women in society. Throughout the period, a variety of authors wrote of porcelain, and ceramics more broadly, to denote women and their perceived weaknesses.[31] Ceramic, and especially porcelain, gave "form through its very materiality to fears and pleasures which, in the absence of a suitable substitute, might otherwise have remained hauntingly inchoate."[32] The material qualities of ceramic wares were particularly important to these cultural renderings. In the early decades of the eighteenth century, for example, writers such as Alexander Pope (1688–1744) and Joseph Addison (1672–1719) used "china" as a means through which to discuss female sexuality, desire, and subjectivity. In these texts, authors conflated women's bodies with the material qualities of porcelain. Despite the material's hardness and ability to withstand hot liquids, porcelain was consistently identified as delicate, translucent, fragile, and breakable – as such, it was equated with characteristics that increasingly came to define a specific view of femininity marked by class and race.[33] While such cultural constructions distinctly shaped the lives of women, they also effected cultural understandings of ceramics, marking them as delicate and fragile entities. In contrast to such cultural understandings of its material, the decorative scheme included on the teapots under consideration here referenced solidity and permanence. The juxtaposition of material and decoration allowed these pots to form questions about the diverse nature and scale of materialities. The teapots feature a pattern that highlights not only fossils but also the limestone in which the fossils are embedded. As such, the configuration references a carbonate sedimentary rock formed over hundreds of thousands of years and often composed of skeletal fragments of marine organisms. Like the fossilized organisms, the rock itself speaks to epic temporal spans, solidity, and permanence.

In contrast to the majority of teapots and ceramic wares produced in this period, the decorative scheme on the teapot in the Chipstone Foundation collection is continued on the base of the pot (see Figure 6.3). The teapot appears like a rock fragment, extracted whole from the earth. Here,

---

[31] Elizabeth Kowaleski-Wallace, *Consuming Subjects: British Women and Consuming Cultures in the Eighteenth Century* (New York: Columbia University Press, 1997), 53. Also see Porter, *Chinese Taste*, 141.
[32] Porter, *Chinese Taste*, 139.
[33] Patricia A. Matthew, "A Taste of Slavery: Sugar Bowls, Abolition, and the Politics of Gender," *Eighteenth-Century Fiction* (forthcoming, 2022).

Crinoidal Limestone and Staffordshire Teapots 105

Figure 6.3 View of base of white stoneware teapot with enamel and salt glaze, Staffordshire, c. 1760. H.: 10.8 cm; Diam. (body): 10.5 cm; Diam. (handle-spout): 17.5 cm. Photo credit: Gavin Ashworth. © The Chipstone Foundation, Milwaukee, 1997.19.a–b.

the choices made with regards to *where* the decoration is included further underlines how this particular pot spoke to questions of solidity and permanence. Featuring the decorative scheme on the base of the pot and thus creating the idea of the pot as a piece of rock was powerful in the eighteenth century, because the burial theories expounded by European travelers to China in the sixteenth and seventeenth centuries continued to exist as a means of trying to understand the nature of porcelain.

From the end of the fifteenth century onwards, European travelers journeyed to China in greater numbers, providing accounts (often speculative) of the origins and making of Chinese porcelain. Portuguese navigator Vasco da Gama (c. 1460–1524) returned from his voyage to Asia in 1499 and presented the king of Portugal with sacks of black pepper, cinnamon, and cloves and a dozen pieces of Chinese porcelain. By 1520, elite consumers throughout Europe considered Chinese porcelain a highly desirable commodity; however, there was little understanding as to how it was made. European attempts to understand how Chinese porcelain was made often asserted that it was stone or was produced through burial. In the early sixteenth century, the Portuguese writer Duarte Barbosa (d. 1545) recorded that ceramic was made from "fish ground fine, from eggshells and the whites of eggs and other materials." Similarly, a compatriot of Barbosa told an Ottoman naval commander of how porcelain was a stone "closely resembling rock crystal and passed down like an heirloom from father to son." The philologist and physician Justus Caesar Scaliger (1484–1558) reasoned that porcelain was produced by pounding eggshells into dust, mixing it with water, and forming it into vases before hiding it underground. According to Barbosa's account, Scaliger reckoned that "A hundred years later they are dug up, being considered finished, and are put up for sale." Similar ideas involving burial and time were voiced in the seventeenth century by the likes of Sir Francis Bacon (1561–1626), who noted that the Chinese kept porcelain "in the ground for forty or fifty years, and to be transmitted to their heirs as a sort of artificial mine." Even in the early eighteenth century, commentators remarked on how such theories were still believed.[34] Made from white stoneware, the Chipstone teapot (Figures 6.1 and 6.3) was fabricated from a material that sought to imitate porcelain, a material that had long been understood to be produced through burying materials or working stone. At the same time, it featured a design that referenced stone formations, and, by including decoration on the base, created the idea of it being wrenched from the earth fully formed. By contrasting broader cultural constructions of ceramic wares as fragile objects, this small teapot could articulate ideas of solidity and permanence through its decoration, a design evoking a long, material temporal scale.

That contemporaries understood the solidity and permanence of crinoidal limestone is further evidenced by its ornamental uses in the seventeenth and eighteenth centuries. Crinoidal limestone was an expensive and desirable material, and was used in country house interiors. Substantially rebuilt in the 1680s and 1690s, Chatsworth House (not far from Stoke-on-Trent) is fitted with various crinoidal limestone fireplaces, floors, and windowsills. Refined and polished, the limestone continues to act as an important element of the house's interior today. Including such a material in elements that are perceived as largely permanent demonstrates how crinoidal limestone was valued not only for its aesthetic qualities but also for its solidity and heft. As "power houses," country houses and stately homes acted as units of power that were dependent on land, space, and symbolic stature.[35]

[34] For these historical accounts and perspectives, see Finlay, *Pilgrim Art*, 65–66.
[35] Mark Girouard, *Life in the English Country House: A Social and Architectural History* (New Haven, CT and London: Yale University Press, 1978), 2.

Country houses also acted as power houses through their longevity. They were built to last and were perceived as intergenerational investments that would (hopefully) remain within families for centuries. With their solidity and heft, materials such as crinoidal limestone spoke to such ambitions: the fireplaces, floors, and windowsills would remain. Similarly, the teapot decoration (particularly in its juxtaposition with the perceived fragile nature of the object) gestured towards solidity and permanence. Rather than being a fleeting thing, it could evoke intergenerational longevities, a scale beyond the singularity of an individual human life.

Humanity and Immortality

The form and affordances of eighteenth-century teapots required manual dexterity and experience from their users. These small crinoidal teapots were particularly difficult to use, with finials and handles that challenged hands and fingers.[36] Teapots demanded handling in order to play their role in tea-drinking practices: they did not have lipped lids until the later eighteenth century. To ensure that the lid did not fall off while pouring, the user would have to reach out and touch the finial atop the lid. Small in size, these finials allowed for one finger at most. The other hand would have been required to grasp the handle of the pot and raise it up. Again, the dimensions of the object meant that only two or three fingers could be utilized. The Chipstone teapot features a crabstock handle and spout (see Figure 6.1). The tactile quality of these features was a popular decorative innovation of the later eighteenth century. The position of this tactile motif on the handle would particularly resonate on an object whose main functional purpose was to pour tea. Yet grasping the handle would have been at once familiar and disturbing, owing to the knuckled quality of the crabstock form. The smooth surface and bulging form of the handle made it seem almost animal or human like. While seeming animate, however, the teapot would not respond; it would not move in that moment of grasping and use. Unmoving in itself, the teapot was an actant with the capacity to determine the actions of the user.[37] The teapot animated gestures but was

---

[36] For the importance of form in material-culture analysis, see Jules David Prown, "The Truth of Material Culture: History or Fiction?" in Jules David Prown and Kenneth Haltman (eds.), *American Artifacts: Essays in Material Culture* (East Lansing: Michigan State University Press, 2000), 18–19.

[37] Bruno Latour, *Reassembling the Social: An Introduction to Actor-Network-Theory* (Oxford: Oxford University Press, 2007), 71–72.

itself seemingly inanimate. In providing such a contrast and underlining its own lack of animacy, the teapot highlighted the animacy of the user, stressing their mortality in contrast to the otherness of the thing at hand. While, as Wordsworth understood, the fossils featured on the teapot were reminders of the short length of human lives, so too the form of the object encouraged reflections on human mortality. The teapot showed how different scales were constantly at work in the world. Finally, by including a handle designed for the human hand, the teapots brought the question of scale full circle. In moments of use, they reminded their users that the human-made material world was designed to a human scale. In questions of scale, the human body was the central reference point.

While their decorative elements called forth the solidity and permanence of rock formations, and thus a temporal span far beyond the human, in their form the teapots sought to affirm human mortality and the scale of the human. Through their decoration and form, the teapots marked themselves as distinctly different and, as such, had the capacity to underline human mortality and the centrality of human scale and perspective. As this chapter has shown, small things were particularly adept at asking questions. Small relative to their human possessors, their very size began conversations about conceptions of scale. As this chapter has also shown, such conversations were further extended by the material and aesthetic forms of the object at hand. With the teapots under discussion here, a decorative scheme that referenced fossils and stone formations prompted questions of permanence, longevity, and a new sense of deep time. Bringing such questions to bear on an object perceived as delicate and fragile underlined the issues of enormity at stake. At work in the homes of eighteenth-century Britons, such objects engaged with debates concerned with geology and natural history. Examining a wide set of aesthetic registers and inspirations reveals the diverse roles these diminutive, densely patterned teapots played in the cultural and social life of eighteenth-century Britain. In pointing towards geographical, material, and temporal enormity, these small things were deeply engaged in the world around them.

7 | "Joineriana"

The Small Fragments and Parts of Eighteenth-Century Assemblages

FREYA GOWRLEY

This chapter takes its title from a letter written by Anna Letitia Barbauld (1743–1845) to her brother John Aikin (1747–1822) in 1775, in which she playfully suggests that they might someday "sew all our fragments, and make a *Joineriana* of them," going on to list a range of incomplete literary productions, including "half a ballad," "the first scene of a play," and some "loose similes," that might form part of a collected volume of miscellaneous pieces.[1] Barbauld clearly references Samuel Paterson's multivolume work *Joineriana: Or, the Book of Scraps* (1772), a compilation of *bon mots* on specific topics, gathered, as Paterson claimed, for the profit of the reader.[2] In his discussion of Barbauld's letter, Daniel E. White argues that her use of the term "sew" evokes the structure of a patchwork quilt, stitched together from many fabric fragments to create a complete whole, to explain the form of her imagined text.[3] This chapter, however, places renewed attention on the act of joining that Barbauld's "sewing" also denotes. Indeed, Barbauld's phrasing brings to mind not only the metaphorical connections between the miscellaneous literary pieces that she cites but also the complex physical relations that characterized a range of eighteenth-century literary, visual, and material objects that attached small fragments together into a new larger form, creating a dialogue of part and whole.

This fragmentary culture encompassed a range of objects made from small things, with scraps, clippings, patches, and pieces all presented together within larger material assemblages. Quilts, specimen tables, mosaics, shellwork, and decorative furnishings were generated from many parts that were joined through various material and intellectual acts to make a new complete form. Likewise, in literary and bibliographic culture, commonplace

---

[1] *The Works of Anna Laetitia Barbauld. With a Memoir by Lucy Aikin*, 2 vols. (London, 1825), vol. 2, 9. See William McCarthy, *Anna Laetitia Barbauld: Voice of the Enlightenment* (Baltimore, MD: Johns Hopkins University Press, 2008), 190.
[2] Samuel Paterson, *Joineriana: Or, the Book of Scrap*, 2 vols. (London, 1772).
[3] Daniel E. White, "The 'Joineriana': Anna Barbauld, the Aikin Family Circle, and the Dissenting Public Sphere," *Eighteenth-Century Studies*, 32.4 (1999), 510–533 (510).

books, herbaria, albums, miscellanies, and anthologies made use of a variety of constituent elements, linked through their joining together and proximate display in the codices in which they were contained. Previous studies of the eighteenth-century fragment have tended to focus on several interrelated areas of enquiry, investigating topics such as literary fragments, ruins, and artifacts.[4] This chapter, by contrast, will consider the fragment through its relationship with the new wholes into which it was placed in the long eighteenth century, focusing particularly on how the process of joining allowed small fragments, together, to materialize emotional connection. It examines several of these highly complex objects, united through their scrappy and fragmented materiality, and the fact that they were all owned by women, or made by women craft practitioners, whose assemblages have so often been removed from the broader history of collage.[5] Specifically, it will discuss the production of herbaria as a reflection of the knowledge and memories of their makers; collaged stained-glass windows as displays of personal significance at Plas Newydd, the home of the "Ladies of Llangollen," Lady Eleanor Butler (1739–1829) and Sarah Ponsonby (1755–1831), in Llangollen, North Wales; interior decoration and furnishings as a site of embodied memory constructed through assembled souvenir objects at A la Ronde, in Exmouth, Devon, home to cousins Jane and Mary Parminter (1750–1811 and 1767–1849); and the production of eighteenth-century patchwork as a technique that affirmed the emotional significance of fragments across class lines. In so doing, the chapter will reinforce how the tiny objects that constituted these assemblages, whether

---

[4] First, scholarship has examined the "fragmentary mode" in contemporary literary production, particularly within texts such as James Macpherson's 1760 *Fragments of ancient poetry*, in which the piecemeal nature of the "collected" poetic prose reinforced ideas of authenticity, as well as Romantic poetry such as Samuel Taylor Coleridge's *Kubla Kahn* (1797). See Sandro Jung, *The Fragmentary Poetic: Eighteenth-Century Uses of an Experimental Mode* (Bethlehem, PA: Lehigh University Press, 2009). Secondly, research on the fragment has also focused on interest in the ruin and artifact, often inflected with antiquarian and picturesque motivations, relating fragments to ideas of history, chronology, and the picturesque. For example, see Crystal B. Lake, *Artifacts: How We Think and Write about Found Objects* (Baltimore, MD: Johns Hopkins University Press, 2020).

[5] For example, Dawn Ades writes that "when Pablo Picasso and Georges Braque started gluing bits to their pictures in 1912, this had nothing to do with long-standing popular past-times like pasting cut out images onto fire screens, and everything to do with art," in an account that deliberately and actively separates eighteenth- and nineteenth-century craft practices from Modernist collage. Dawn Ades, "Collage: A Brief History" in Dawn Ades, Peter Blake, and Natalie Rudd (eds.), *Peter Blake: About Collage* (London: Tate Gallery, 2000), 37–43 (37). On women's craft practices during this period, see Amanda Vickery, *Behind Closed Doors: At Home in Georgian England* (New Haven, CT and London: Yale University Press, 2009), 232. For the foundational discussion of women's creative work and its lack of critical attention within art historical scholarship, see Rozsika Parker and Griselda Pollock, *Old Mistresses: Women, Art & Ideology* (New York and London: Bloomsbury Academic, 2013).

individual shells, bits of ribbon, scraps of paper, fragments of glass, or cuttings from plants, were given meaning through their relationship with and subsumption within a larger whole.

In studying how minute pieces of paper, glass, leaves, and shells contributed to eighteenth-century culture, I seek to demonstrate the centrality of the small fragment to understanding larger collections, assemblages, and composite manuscripts. By considering these objects as forms of "collage" or "assemblage" – disparate art forms unified by the act of joining – the chapter most closely follows important work by Ariane Fennetaux, who has argued for the significance of women's craft practices during this period by conceptualizing them as a kind of "bricolage."[6] This approach is appropriate for the analysis of the fragment, a term whose Latin root, *frangere*, means to break into pieces. This etymological reference reinforces the dynamics of both part and whole, size and scale, that characterize all fragments, whether separate or joined.[7] Even Barbauld's fragmentary texts, which were themselves separate and incomplete at the time she wrote the letter, were conceptualized by her as potentially belonging to a new whole, her "joineriana." As Deborah Harter highlights, the fragment is always "a part in a larger system," whether that whole relates to the fragment's former state or its new or even potential material relationships. This included those relationships established between objects belonging to a similar class (such as collected dried seaweed or pieces of stained glass displayed together), or those made through the bringing together of different kinds of fragments.[8] As such, this chapter not only studies the fragment in and on its own terms but also its status as a small object that gains particular significance when assembled into a larger whole; that is, when placed in dialogic juxtaposition with and against other objects. This was facilitated through the process of joining, and the various practices of acquisition, curation, and selection, of combination, placement, and creation, that it encompassed. Anke te Heesen argues that such objects can be understood through a framework of "visual variety," the defining characteristic of which was "independent

---

[6] The chapter follows recent work that has sought to expand conceptions of collage beyond a literal definition based on the idea of *papier collé*. See, for example, Patrick Elliott, *Cut and Paste: 400 Years of Collage* (Edinburgh: National Galleries of Scotland, 2019); Ariane Fennetaux, "Female Crafts: Women and Bricolage in Late Georgian Britain" in Maureen Daly Goggin and Beth Fowkes Tobin (eds.), *Women & Things, 1750–1950: Gendered Material Strategies* (Farnham: Ashgate, 2009), 91–108.

[7] Camelia Elias, *The Fragment: Towards a History and Poetics of a Performative Genre* (Bern: Peter Lang, 2004), 1.

[8] Deborah Harter, *Bodies in Pieces: Fantastic Narrative and the Poetics of the Fragment* (Redwood City, CA: Stanford University Press, 1994), 29.

parts coexist[ing] next to one another."[9] Notably, te Heesen understands this through the lens of scale, noting that "the existence of small elements" was essential to the creation of assemblage, in which "individual bits of knowledge or their visually valuable parts were assembled and pasted up with no attempt to hide their form."[10] This material dialogue of small parts within a larger whole is key to how the objects discussed in this chapter embedded meaning and sentiment within their form. Their makers relied on the several simultaneous registers of viewing experience that those who encountered these objects would have had to engage with in order to understand them fully, initially seeing the object as a whole, then looking at its disparate parts in order to intellectually pursue the various connotations and narratives that each fragment could tell, before coming back to the whole again, finally recognizing its status as a biographical object.

If we return to Barbauld's reference to joining, we spot how her assumption of a relatively jovial approach to her scrappy texts implies their relative insignificance, a position echoed by a secondary literature often uninterested in fragmentary objects. Yet the composite objects of this chapter all point to the deeply personal and emotional component of pieced and joined objects, showing that together small scraps and fragments made up resolutely tender and emotional wholes. An examination of these diverse assemblages thereby invites us to reconsider the deeply meaningful nature of these small fragments, revealing a culture obsessed not only with small things but also with compiling, collecting, and reconstituting them into assemblages, potent with personal meaning, history, and emotional significance. In this account, apparently trivial things disclose deeply felt sentiment. Despite their small scale, individual fragments collectively reflected and expressed much larger emotional significance, as accomplished through the meaningful act of joining.

Consuming Fragments and Producing Intimate Histories

Women's production of their "joinerianas" allows us to consider patterns of consumption and production on an intimate scale, in which individual acts of acquisition and transformation constituted examples of knowledge construction, identity formation, and emotional expression.

---

[9] Anke te Heesen, *The Newspaper Clipping: A Modern Paper Object* (Manchester: Manchester University Press, 2014), 227.
[10] Ibid., 232.

Eighteenth-century women found many ways to work with fragments, reflecting a wide range of creative practices and various modes of consumption and production. The making of elaborate shellwork pieces, for instance, was the result of both the collection of found objects and the purchase of shells from vendors such as Rudolph Ackermann, whose Repository of the Arts, established on the Strand in London in 1796, sold materials for the fabrication of a wide variety of craft practices.[11] Likewise, the individual production of commonplace books demonstrates how the transcription of excerpted texts, copied and transplaced into a new whole, functioned as a means of processing and preserving information, ideas, and texts.

The herbarium, or *hortus siccus*, constituted one of the most popular forms of fragment-making and display in the period. Their makers collected and preserved plant specimens together in elaborate volumes, designed for both botanical research and as a place to preserve memory and sentiment. In so doing, their creators often included as much of the plant's parts as possible, from stems and leaves to flowers and seeds, as well as contextual information about the plant's discovery, location, and appearance, as herbarium specimens were often intended to be model examples of the collected plant. The production of such volumes involved practices of observation, collection, annotation, preservation, and gathering, and therefore participated in the era's systematization and classification of the natural world; what Foucault has called the desire for an "order of things."[12] As Fennetaux argues, bricolage made in this manner was "a meaningful process whereby women not only expressed themselves as individuals, but above all organized, appropriated and made sense of the world around them."[13]

Snipped from the plants that these cuttings were collected to represent, the botanical specimen is an exemplary eighteenth-century fragment. Cut, clipped, detached, it is a fragment of the bigger whole of which it was once part. The makers of herbaria pasted such plant clippings onto sheets of paper and subsequently bound them into albums, creating compendia of tiny pieces cut from plants and flowers, underlined with evocative information about the dates, places, and conditions in which they were collected. The diarist Dorothy Richardson (b. 1748), for instance, recorded treating

---

[11] Ann Bermingham, *Learning to Draw: Studies in the Cultural History of a Polite and Useful Art* (New Haven, CT and London: Yale University Press, 2000), 127.

[12] Michel Foucault, *The Order of Things: An Archaeology of the Human Sciences* (London: Routledge, 2005).

[13] Fennetaux, "Female Crafts," 92.

the individual seaweed samples she collected on her travels in water before pressing them ready for preservation within an album.[14] Such volumes allowed collections of specimens to be sorted and organized, facilitating both their practical display and ease of subsequent consultation. As such, small clippings from surviving plants represent an attempt to document, preserve, and understand the natural world on the one hand, but also to consume, own, and process this floral materiality on the other.

Women frequently imbued their botanical specimens and small cuttings with emotion, as exemplified by those exchanged by Eleanor Butler and Sarah Ponsonby, who frequently gifted cuttings, seeds, and parts of plants to their friends to convey their affection. For instance, Butler and Ponsonby maintained a long-standing floral correspondence with their friends Thomas Netherton Parker and his wife, Sarah, of Sweeney Hall in Oswestry, a relationship characterized by their shared interest in botanical specimens and horticultural techniques.[15] For example, a gift of cuttings given to the Parkers was accompanied by a letter from Ponsonby that expressed their "Wishes that their progeny may flourish through many Generations," showing how fragmented sections of plants and flowers taken from larger wholes were understood as carriers of sentiment by contemporaries.[16] As part and whole in two senses (as whole plant and part removed, and as individual specimen bound into a codex), we might theorize that the selection, separation, and collection of fragments of chosen plants, along with processes of pasting and arranging that made herbaria, were acts that were key to making these small things acquire emotional significance.

The interiors of Plas Newydd, the home that Butler and Ponsonby shared for almost fifty years, similarly reinforce how individual identity was expressed and consolidated through the creation, viewing, and ownership of small fragments placed in new wholes. A key example of this is Butler and Ponsonby's commission of a series of stained-glass windows for the house's library (Figure 7.1). Made sometime after their arrival at the property in 1788, the windows form an intricate bricolage of small pieces of brightly colored and fragmented glass, whose designs encompass representations of

---

[14] Dorothy Richardson, "Yorkshire (West Riding), Derbyshire, Nottinghamshire and Lancashire," Dorothy Richardson Papers, GB 133 Eng MS 1122, 1761–75, John Rylands Library, 266.
[15] Ponsonby to Parker, DD/LL 7, 1809–16, Denbighshire Record Office, Ruthin. Jill Casid has also discussed the women's presentation of flowers to their friends, although she focuses specifically upon Ponsonby's presentation of a rose to Anne Lister, and the metaphorical possibility of queer intimacy indicated by this gift. See *Sowing Empire: Landscape and Colonization* (Minneapolis: University of Minnesota Press, 2004), 174–175.
[16] Ponsonby to Parker, October 1811, DD/LL 7, 1809–1816.

Figure 7.1 View of the library window, Plas Newydd, Llangollen. Photograph, the author.

biblical figures, heraldry, foliate designs, abstract patterns, and block color, set into lead cames. Comprising individual fragments of glass with distinct origins, displayed together in their new casings, the windows illustrate how small things could be implicated within a dynamic, larger, and meaningful whole, whose proximate display transformed their meaning.

Based on contextual information from Butler and Ponsonby's diaries and records, we can assume that the windows comprise both found and purchased fragments, including small pieces of glass reputedly collected from the nearby ruined Valle Crucis Abbey, the site of much contemporary picturesque admiration, as well as colored glass bought from the Birmingham glassmaker Francis Eginton and glass gifted to the women by local landowners.[17] For example, Butler and Ponsonby recorded in their diaries the donation of "a casement window of Painted Glass, the arms of Trevor, Owen, the Godolphin Family with their different Quarterings: a present from Mr. Owen of Porkington."[18] The designs that appear in the completed windows are indeed suggestive of the black lion of the Owen family crest and the golden lion of the Trevor family. While the installation of heraldic stained glass in one's house was established antiquarian practice by this time, the

---

[17] *Plas Newydd: A Brief History* (Denbigh: Denbighshire County Council, 2003), 14; Elizabeth Mavor (ed.), *A Year with the Ladies of Llangollen* (Harmondsworth: Penguin Books, 1986), 31; G. H. Bell (ed.), *The Hamwood Papers of the Ladies of Llangollen and Caroline Hamilton* (London: Macmillan, 1930), 63.

[18] Mavor, *A Year with the Ladies of Llangollen*, 64.

fragmentation and (re)arrangement of these designs at Plas Newydd shows how such visual histories were complicated through the process of juxtaposition and joining.[19] Indeed, their current arrangement – namely, their display together in a series of diamond shaped sections, alongside the pieces of figurative and plain colored glass – disrupts the expected formal genealogical display of such stained glass. Instead, the heraldic glass included within the windows resonates provocatively with the more random fragments surrounding it, whether patches of green, red, and blue plain glass, or the abstracted head of a cherub. In their current joineriana, these parts therefore evoke much more than antiquarian contemplation; they evoke the personal histories of their owners. Like the herbaria above, the windows negotiate the relationship between small part and larger whole on two levels; first, between the stained glass and its original window display, and second through its subsumption within a later scheme of fragmented stained glass collected from a range of sources. Through the joining together of small disparate fragments in Butler and Ponsonby's commission, the windows unify the women's Welsh locale through the installment of glass from local landmarks alongside pieces gifted to the women from local landowners, which in turn reference their affective relationships.

Although likely not installed by the women themselves (indeed, their accounts record payments to glazers for work done on the property), the stained glass's complex arrangement reinforces Butler and Ponsonby's agency and active role in decorating their house with objects redolent with personal meaning.[20] The library's stained-glass windows speak to the thriving gift culture that Butler and Ponsonby, and their friends, participated in, and demonstrate the connectedness between themselves and their locale. From the preservation of their friends' coats of arms within the windows of Plas Newydd, to the glass pieces sourced from Valle Crucis, which recalled shared experiences in the Welsh countryside, the women joined together small pieces to produce wholes that showcased personal connections and experiences. As such, these objects illuminate how individual fragments were sourced, acquired, and collected before being transformed into new objects imbued with complex narratives, personal meaning, and emotion.[21]

---

[19] See for example Michael Peover, "Horace Walpole's use of Stained Glass at Strawberry Hill," *British Art Journal*, 5.1 (2004), 22–29.

[20] Mavor, *A Year with the Ladies of Llangollen*, 38.

[21] See for example, Goggin and Tobin (eds.), *Women & Things*; John Styles and Amanda Vickery (eds.), *Gender, Taste, and Material Culture in Britain and North America, 1700–1830* (New Haven, CT and London: Yale University Press, 2007); Jane Hamlett, Hannah Greig, and Leonie Hannan (eds.), *Gender and Material Culture in Britain Since 1600* (London: Palgrave, 2015).

Whether made from cloth, natural materials, or man-made objects, small (or diminutive) fragments were a vital constitutive element in a number of women's craft practices, many of which were typified by the physical process of bringing small objects into new configurations. This characterized the production of crafts such as shellwork, quilting, and various forms of interior decoration, all of which were predicated upon the translation, or movement, of pieces, patches, and other small things into dialogue with each other. An important example of this female-centric form of making is A la Ronde in Devon, the sixteen-sided home of first cousins Jane and Mary Parminter, which was likely inspired by their extensive continental tour of c. 1784–1791. As various commentators have noted, a number of surfaces and spaces within the house are ornamented with diverse forms of collage, which mix shells, feathers, and other natural materials with paper and paint.[22] The Parminters decorated their drawing room, for example, with a featherwork border that runs around the perimeter of the room and sits above its fireplace, itself a composite structure comprising shellwork and engravings clipped and stuck onto the wall. The house is perhaps most remarkable for its crowning shell gallery, decorated in a manner reminiscent of a number of contemporary grottos, with an array of shells, bones, pieces of spar and mica, and other small found objects stuck into plaster. The gallery was accessed via a steep and narrow staircase, also decorated with densely packed shellwork, and this ascent would have brought the viewer into close contact with the small specimens and geological fragments embedded into its walls. This proximity to these large-scale works would have accordingly recalled and reinforced the close engagement and careful handling of tiny objects necessary to creating such expansive yet highly detailed surfaces.

The Parminters' creation of shellwork reflects common craft practice in the period, in which makers joined shells into patterns destined to decorate a range of objects. Collected from beaches and acquired with friends, the small size of the shells ensured their transportability and facilitated their easy integration into broader decorative schemes. At A la Ronde, shells

---

[22] Colin Cunningham, "'An Italian house is my lady': Some Aspects of the Definition of Women's Role in the Architecture of Robert Adam" in Michael Rossington and Gilly Perry (eds.), *Masculinity and Femininity in Eighteenth-Century Art and Culture* (Manchester and New York: Manchester University Press, 1994), 63–77 (71); Vickery, *Behind Closed Doors*, 248. A number of scholars have explored the particular popularity of shellwork as a pastime during this period. See, Katherine Sharp, "Women's Creativity and Display in the Eighteenth-Century British Domestic Interior" in Susie McKellar and Penny Sparke (eds.), *Interior Design and Identity* (Manchester: Manchester University Press, 2004), 10–26 (15).

Figure 7.2 Jane and Mary Parminter, Specimen table, Exmouth, Devon, 1790s. Glass, mineral, shell, paint, paper, and wood. 1312249, National Trust Collections, A la Ronde, Devon. © National Trust Images/James Dobson.

were incorporated into these designs alongside other small-scale souvenir objects, such as micromosaics, cameos, and found objects such as fragments of mineral. Displayed together with such evocative objects, shells might conjure shared and treasured memories, maritime landscapes, and connections between families, lovers, and kin. That A la Ronde's shellwork production is in reference to the imagined contexts of travel and the evocation of its memory is suggested by the survival of two shellwork souvenir pictures in their collections, likely purchased during their tour. The two constructions depict fantastical architectural forms using shell, paper, and painted wood, and are labelled "Isola Bella" on the reverse, a reference to the Italian island on Lake Maggiore. Famous for its large-scale grottos encrusted with shells, these shellwork souvenirs suggest a potential source of inspiration for the Parminters' decoration of A la Ronde. This connection was reinforced by their display of the images in the house's drawing room, where they sat decorating the house's fireplace, itself comprising an intricate shellwork display.

A specimen table likely made by the Parminter cousins testifies to the connection between collage, their travels, the processes of visual and material commemoration, and the expression of emotion (Figure 7.2). The construction of the table demonstrates how pervasive this form of decoration was throughout their home, where it functioned as a microcosm of the collaged space of the house's shell gallery. The small octagonal worktable comprised a hollow rosewood base decorated with floral paper decoupage; its top was formed from a collaged surface of small-scale souvenir objects covered with a pane of glass. The table's design recalls the marble tabletops acquired by Grand Tourists during this period. Often made by Italian craftsmen and subsequently purchased by British tourists, specimen tables took their name from the various specimens of rock and mineral from which they were produced, whose rarity and historical significance made them particularly sought after by mineral enthusiasts and antiquarians alike. At the same time, the table's form also highlights the narrative potential of an object made from fragments, and how these smaller pieces might tell the histories of their owners and makers. By joining together natural materials, such as shells and minerals, alongside typical Grand Tour souvenirs such as plaster cameos and micromosaics, the makers of the Parminters' table created a newly evocative whole, which, like the women's other shellwork souvenirs, clearly referenced the experience of travel as well as their location on the Devonshire coast.

At the very center of the table sits a ceramic plaque that reads "Life Shall Triumph Over Death." The plaque depicts a vestal virgin pouring libations onto a burning pyre; its image and text reflect the visual and material cultures of eighteenth-century mourning, suggesting that the cousins included the plaque to mark the death of Elizabeth Parminter (d. c. 1796), Jane's sister and their travelling companion, who likely died shortly after their tour.[23] As I have argued elsewhere, through the combining of mourning devices and travel souvenirs, the collaged table's maker created a biographical object.[24] Uniting distinct personal histories into a single object through meaningful juxtaposition, the maker's physical arrangement of the table's many small fragments created metaphorical connections that collapsed boundaries between home and tour, past and present, and the generic and the personal in order to share the various narratives of its owners and makers. Although it is not clear who made the table, thanks to the lack of documentary evidence that characterizes the house as a whole, it is

---

[23] For biographical information on Jane and Mary Parminter, including the Parminter family tree, see Trevor Adams, *The A la Ronde Story: Its People* (Exmouth, Devon: National Trust, 2011). On contemporary mourning culture, see Christiane Holm, "Sentimental Cuts: Eighteenth-Century Mourning Jewelry with Hair," *Eighteenth-Century Studies*, 38.1 (2004), 139–143.

[24] Freya Gowrley, "Craft(ing) Narratives: Specimens, Souvenirs, and 'Morsels' in A la Ronde's Specimen Table," *Eighteenth-Century Fiction*, 31.1 (2018), 77–97.

nonetheless significant that the table uses the same kind of joined decoration done throughout the house by the Parminters themselves, suggesting that its making was conceptualized as part of a larger evocative whole of house and furnishings, in which assemblages communicated the identities and family histories of those who lived there. In any case, the table exemplifies how the processes of joining enabled individual souvenir objects to contribute to a larger autobiography, transforming small fragments into complex material stories that women told of themselves.

Fabric Lives

While the objects so far discussed were made, produced, and purchased by women at the upper echelons of British society, this final section gestures towards how non-elite women likewise gathered small fragments together in larger joinerianas.[25] The practice of joining crossed class lines, specifically through the technique of patchwork. Unlike the stained glass and specimen tables, patchwork was both beautiful and useful in its form, making it much more likely to be made by women of the laboring classes. Such constructions affirm women's consumer skills and deep knowledge as well as their understanding of forms of material production, skills, and learning that Serena Dyer and Chloe Wigston Smith have described as "material literacy."[26] Both elite and non-elite women displayed their comprehensive understanding of textiles through the savvy use of fabric remnants and scraps to construct patchwork for a number of functions, including dress, quilts, and pockets.[27] According to Maxine Berg's study of consumer inventories of women of the "industrial classes," clothing and other linens had simultaneously practical and symbolic functions, and so were "expressive goods, conveying identity, personality and fashion."[28] Quilt-tops exemplified these dually functional and decorative concerns. In patchwork or pieced quilts, decorative top layers were formed from small

---

[25] The practice of making assembled objects such as shellwork was also undertaken by women from the middling classes. See Vickery, *Behind Closed Doors*, for discussions of such "accomplishments."

[26] Serena Dyer and Chloe Wigston Smith, "Introduction," *Material Literacy in Eighteenth-Century Britain: A Nation of Makers*, Serena Dyer and Chloe Wigston Smith (eds.) (London and New York: Bloomsbury Academic, 2020), 1–15.

[27] See, for example, Ariane Fennetaux and Barbara Burman, *The Pocket: A Hidden History of Women's Lives, 1660–1900* (New Haven, CT and London: Yale University Press, 2019), 207.

[28] Maxine Berg, "Women's Consumption and the Industrial Classes of Eighteenth-Century England," *Journal of Social History*, 30.2 (1996), 415–434 (421).

patches of fabric pieced together in geometric patterns. An example from the Victoria and Albert Museum made in Cornwall in the 1740s features a top layer entirely made of fabric ribbons in a remarkable range of colors and patterns, likely sourced as unused yardage from clothes makers and haberdashers.[29]

Attention to eighteenth-century patchwork also reveals how, through the process of joining, smaller objects with distinct resonances and meanings could be incorporated into wider wholes, where they became comfortable, decorative, and, crucially, sentimental objects to be (re)used in a domestic context. The records of the Old Bailey document numerous instances of patchwork being stolen, examples that stress their importance to the families to which they belonged.[30] These accounts show how knowledge of a specific patchwork design could be used as proof that a stolen quilt was under a person's ownership, as in the case of James Hammerton, whose quilt was stolen by Samuel Wallis in 1783. When asked by the court, "What do you know them by?," Hammerton replied, "My wife made this out of a bit of patchwork."[31] This kind of intimate knowledge of laboring-class women's work is also affirmed by the case of Mary Smith, ultimately found not guilty of stealing some patchwork in 1712. Although Anne Cross, the woman Smith was supposed to have stolen the patchwork from, claimed it as her own work, several of Smith's friends gave evidence that they "knew the Patch work produc'd, and help'd her to make it; and others who gave her some of the Pieces," highlighting the role of such textile practices within Smith's social relationships.[32]

An important collection of poorer women's textile fragments is held by the London Foundling Hospital, whose collection features tokens made from tiny scraps of ribbons, embroidery, and textiles used for clothing (alongside other kinds of non-textile tokens).[33] Like many of the other objects analyzed within this chapter, the dynamics of part and whole and their attendant registers of small and large work on several levels in these

---

[29] Bedcover, 1740–1800, T.117-1973, Victoria & Albert Museum, London.
[30] See for example, Samuel Chester, who was found not guilty of stealing a "looking-glass, value 12 d. the goods of Edward Cannon; a pair of linen sheets, a pair of blankets, a quilt made of cloth patchwork, and a copper saucepan, the goods of Peter Sinclair," in 1741. *Old Bailey Proceedings Online* (www.oldbaileyonline.org, version 8.0, March 2018, hereafter *OBP*), October 1741, trial of Samuel Chester (t17411014-6).
[31] *OBP*, February 1783, Samuel Wallis (t17830226-1).
[32] *OBP*, September 1712, Mary Smith (t17120910-27).
[33] The museum's collection of over 5,000 small pieces of textile was the subject of John Styles's 2010 exhibition, *Threads of Feeling*. See John Styles, *Threads of Feeling: The London Foundling Hospital's Textile Tokens, 1740–1770* (London: Foundling Hospital, 2010).

objects. With small parts of textile cut and fragmented from larger pieces of cloth before being donated alongside babies whose mothers could no longer care for them, the separation of these tiny fabric scraps facilitated their use as forms of potential or eventual identification. As John Styles writes, each fragment is thereby suggestive of "the life of a single infant child and that of its absent parent," while evoking a potential future in which mothers could return for their children, using another piece of the same fabric in order to prove their relationship with the child in question.[34]

Through their disentanglement from their fabric whole – specifically, the dresses of their mothers – and their subsequent integration into the pages of the ledgers that recorded the children left at the hospital, the tokens performed weighty emotional labor relative to their size. At the same time, the fragments also recall an immaterial joining and separation that is also vital to understanding these objects, namely the enduring bond that connected child to mother. As referents to the entities from which they were cut, like the plant specimens discussed earlier, the textile tokens symbolize the physical separation of family members through the material distance between these objects. At the same time, the potential future reunion of two parts of a fragment made whole again, could conceptually and literally signify the joining together of mother and child once more. Such fragmentary and highly quotidian textiles allow us to recenter lived experiences for which there are no textual records in order to mark and reveal the lives of poorer men and women, their economic ingenuity and entrepreneurship, and the splintering of their familial bonds.

Where printed fabric was not available to make these tokens, plain swatches were also embroidered upon, adding another layer of haptic attachment and meaning through the addition of tiny details that created embellished surfaces. One telling example is a small fragment of a patchwork needle case embroidered with a red heart (Figure 7.3). Cut in half, it was eventually used to reunite mother and child, a rare outcome for foundling children.[35] The act of joining was crucial to both the construction and various uses of this needle case: made from fabric pieces seamed together through the act of sewing (reminiscent of Barbauld's phrasing), it would once have held the very tools used to stitch these pieces. These ties between form and function persist as an evocative culmination of the needle case's meaning and physicality, even before its eventual fragmentation and transformation into a smaller token. As a fragment made of many

[34] Ibid., 9.
[35] Ibid., 70.

"Joineriana": Small Fragments and Parts of Assemblages 123

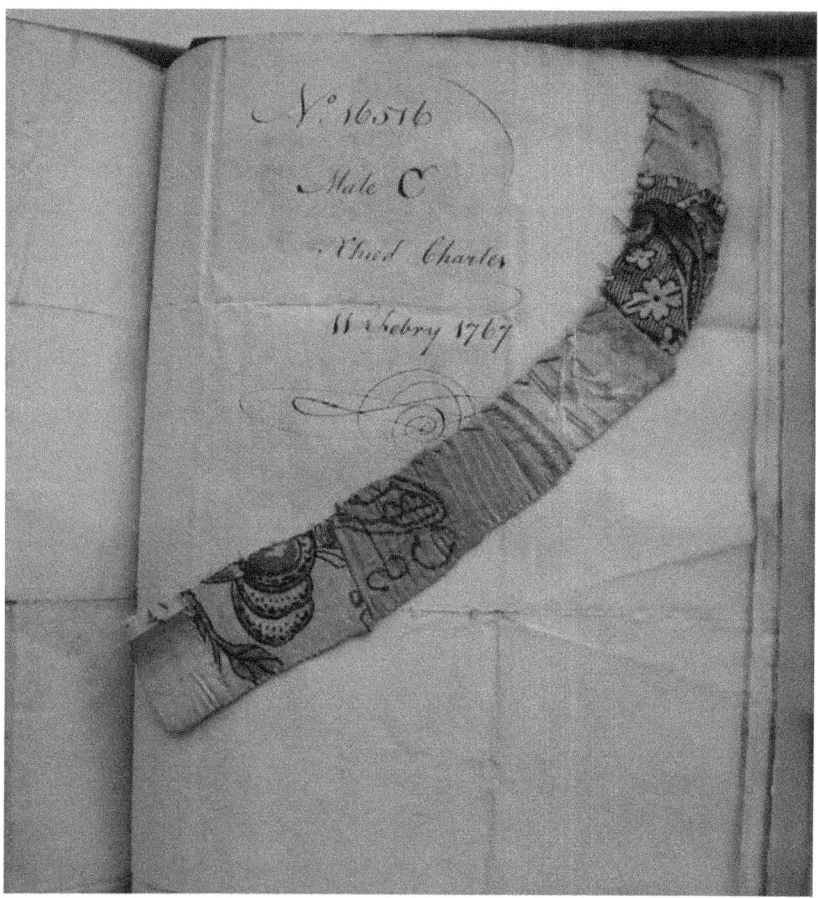

Figure 7.3 Patchwork needle case, made from printed and woven fabrics, embroidered with a heart and the initials SC, and cut in half, made in c. 1767. Foundling 16516. © Coram.

smaller fragments, and decorated with a stitched emblem of love, this example makes clear how such objects represented more than the sum of their (sometimes many) constituent parts, highlighting how individually they might physically embody broken families and lost relationships, and collectively the opposite. As the needle case shows, smaller parts, pieces, and fragments maintained and materialized these powerful emotional resonances.

This chapter has shown how fragments and the assemblages through which they were joined together were of deep importance to those that made, owned, and viewed them, not least evidenced by the sheer proliferation of these kinds of objects that survive from this period. Across classes, such objects preserved and recorded knowledge, demonstrated the complex and varied material literacies of their makers, and expressed emotions and intimacies. Although the fragment was often diminutive when measured on its own, fragmentary forms, which followed Barbauld's invitation to "sew all our fragments" together, grew in significance, connecting with their makers' identities and articulating affective bonds. Joined across a variety of forms of cultural production, assembled fragments transformed the minute into the meaningful object, a repository of memory, emotion, and experience. Despite the very nature of fragments as incomplete, ephemeral, evanescent, and small, they constituted more than the sum of their joined parts, as demonstrated by their contributions to the expansive cultural, artistic, and personal canvases of the eighteenth century's joineriana.

8 | "Pray What a Pox Are Those Damned Strings of Wampum?"

British Understandings of Wampum in the Eighteenth Century

ROBBIE RICHARDSON

Wampum is best known today for the belts used as records of early treaties between First Nations and European peoples, and for the Two-Row Wampum treaty between Europeans and the Haudenosaunee, which legal scholars and Indigenous people recognize now as an important model for reconciliation in settler countries.[1] However, wampum comes in a variety of forms.[2] Composed of marine shells formed into small tubular beads, which were then exchanged on strings or woven into patterns as belts, wampum was used in Native cultures in complex ways, functioning as an object of exchange, at times diplomatic, ceremonial, or financial; as inscription or as a mnemonic device to record a treaty or event; and as ornamentation on clothes, weapons, and other objects.[3] Today wampum is often viewed as an important form of literacy and cultural memory for Indigenous people.[4] In the eighteenth century, its complexity was at least somewhat understood in the colonies, where Europeans had to grapple with its various uses to maintain alliances and economic relationships; in Britain, however, collectors and writers struggled with its meaning.[5] The earliest pieces of wampum came to Britain in the mid-seventeenth century, as ethnographic specimens and curios in museums and private collections. They arrived with an influx of North American Indigenous material culture, a part of

---

[1] For a history of Two-Row wampum and its legal implications, see Robert A. Williams, Jr., *Linking Arms Together: American Indian Treaty Visions of Law and Peace, 1600–1800* (London: Routledge, 1999), 40–61.
[2] For a discussion of wampum in Haudenosaunee tradition, see Penelope Myrtle Kelsey, *Reading the Wampum: Essays on Hodinöhsö:ni' Visual Code and Epistemological Recovery* (Syracuse, NY: Syracuse University Press, 2014).
[3] For a more detailed overview of its differing uses, see James W. Bradley, "Re-Visiting Wampum and Other Seventeenth-Century Shell Games," *Archaeology of Eastern North America*, 39 (2011), 25–51.
[4] See Angela M. Haas, "Wampum as Hypertext: An American Indian Intellectual Tradition of Multimedia Theory and Practice," *Studies in American Indian Literatures*, 19.4 (2007), 77–100.
[5] For European impressions of wampum in the colonies, see Paul Otto, "'This is that which … they call Wampum': Europeans Coming to Terms with Native Shell Beads," *Early American Studies: An Interdisciplinary Journal*, 15.1 (2017), 1–36.

the expanding collecting practices in Britain that were catching up to the established collections on the continent.⁶ Sylvia Spitta argues that Indigenous objects from the Americas challenged and unsettled European epistemologies.⁷ Wampum, with its uncertain meaning as knowledge, fashion, and currency, destabilizes categories of understanding. Spitta notes also that the "misplaced objects" from the Americas "signal the destruction of indigenous cultures."⁸ This is often true, as in the case of the Aztec objects that were plundered by Hernán Cortés and marveled at by Albrecht Dürer at Brussels in 1520.⁹

But this is not a narrative about the destruction of Indigenous cultures, but of their endurance, their survival, and, to use Anishinaabe critic Gerald Vizenor's term, their "survivance": these objects could provide "renunciations of dominance, tragedy and victimry."¹⁰ They could actively shape meaning. This chapter will consider the evolving interpretations of wampum in Britain from the mid-seventeenth to the late-eighteenth centuries, and suggest that its unclear and often unacknowledged signification as knowledge and commodity speaks to Britain's own struggles over the meaning and origin of language and writing just as this understanding was becoming secularized.¹¹ Though wampum beads were typically just a few millimeters in length and diameter, woven together they could form expansive historical records. Europeans often perceived the Indigenous desire for small beads and other trinkets as proof of their gullibility or uncivilized nature, thus diminishing such items.¹² Yet they also found themselves using wampum and attempting to make it fit into their Western epistemologies.

---

[6] On the belated appearance of British collecting, see Arthur MacGregor, "The Cabinet of Curiosities in Seventeenth-Century Britain" in Oliver Impey and Arthur MacGregor (eds.), *The Origins of Museums: The Cabinet of Curiosities in Sixteenth- and Seventeenth-Century Europe* (London: House of Stratus, 2001), 201–215.

[7] Sylvia Spitta, *Misplaced Objects: Migrating Collections and Recollections in Europe and the Americas* (Austin: University of Texas Press, 2009), 5.

[8] Ibid., 29.

[9] See Peter Hess, "Marvelous Encounters: Albrecht Dürer and Early Sixteenth-Century German Perceptions of Aztec Culture," *Daphnis*, 33.1/2 (2004), 161–186.

[10] Gerald Vizenor, *Manifest Manners: Narratives on Postindian Survivance* (1994; London: University of Nebraska Press, 1999), vii.

[11] See Margreta de Grazia, "The Secularization of Language in the Seventeenth Century," *Journal of the History of Ideas*, 41.2 (1980), 319–330.

[12] Ned Ward sarcastically remarked in 1699 that "[t]he Ground upon which *Boston* ... stands, was purchas'd from the Natives, by the first *English* Proprietors, for a Bushel of *Wampum peag* and a Bottle of *Rum*, being of an inconsiderable Value." *A trip to New England* (London, 1699), 8.

First British Encounters with Wampum

The earliest recorded pieces of wampum to come to Britain appear in museum catalogues; both the catalogues of the Tradescant collection, printed in 1656, and Nehemiah Grew's account of the Royal Society from 1681 contain various wampum materials.[13] The Tradescant text describes the collection of the father and son John Tradescants, whose collection was first held at the Ark at South Lambeth in London; it later became the Ashmolean Museum at Oxford, named after antiquarian and alchemist Elias Ashmole, who funded and helped to write its catalogue.[14] This museum catalogue, the first to be published in English and to use the word "museum" in its contemporary context, describes "Black Indian girdles made of Wampam peek, the best sort."[15] The provenance of these items is unclear, but the younger Tradescant likely gathered them during one of his three voyages to Virginia.[16] The girdles are grouped under "Garments, Vestures, Habits, Ornaments," indicating they were understood as an adornment. Yet earlier accounts, as in John Underhill's *News from America* (1638), explain that "*Wampam Peke* ... is their money," and John Eliot similarly calls it "Indian money" in a letter from 1648.[17] Indeed nearly all mentions of it prior to the Tradescant catalogue describe it as a form of currency. This early inconsistency illustrates the gap in understanding between colonists and the collectors in Britain.

Wampum was, in fact, legal tender in the colonies from the 1630s to the 1660s, and had been steadily commodified by European trade since the late-sixteenth century. Outside the Tradescant catalogue, this colonial understanding became increasingly prevalent in Europe. In his *Second Treatise* (1689), for instance, John Locke notes that money has a "[p]hantastical imaginary value" as opposed to a natural basis, and as an example he notes that "the Wampompeke of the *Americans*" is of little meaning

---

[13] *Museum Tradescantuanum* (London, 1656); Nehemiah Grew, *Musaeum Regalis Societatis* (London, 1681).

[14] See Marjorie Swann, *Curiosities and Texts: The Culture of Collecting in Early Modern England* (Philadelphia: University of Pennsylvania Press, 2001), 45–46.

[15] Sarah Irving, *Natural Science and the Origins of the British Empire* (London: Pickering & Chatto, 2008), 106. *Museum Tradescantuanum*, 51.

[16] Tradescant visited in 1637, 1642, and 1654, primarily gathering plant species. See Catherine Armstrong, *Writing North America in the Seventeenth Century: English Representations in Print and Manuscript* (Burlington, VT: Ashgate, 2007), 103.

[17] John Underhill, *News From America* (London, 1638), 11; Caspar Sibelius, *Of the conversion of five thousand and nine hundred East-Indians* (London, 1650), 28.

to "an *European* Prince," while "the Silver Money of *Europe*" is equally valueless to "an *American*."[18] In Nehemiah Grew's catalogue of the Royal Society's Repository, wampum is listed along with other currencies in the section "Chiefly of Mechanicks [...] Relating to Trade." He describes "Several sorts of *Indian* MONEY, called WAMPAMPEAGE," explaining: "'Tis made of a sort of Shell, formed into small *Cylinders*, ... and so being bored, as *Beads*, and put upon *Strings*, pass among the *Indians*, in their usual Commerce, as *Silver* and *Gold* amongst us." He compares wampum's value relative to British currency, noting the "meanest" is worth "Five shillings the Fathome" or "Six a penny," and so on. As in Tradescant's catalogue, Grew asserts that the best wampum "is woven into Girdles" and is "used in great Payments, esteemed their Noblest Presents, and laid up as their Treasure," yet also acknowledges that this sort is "sometimes worn as their richest Ornaments."[19] Ken Arnold notes that the "straightforward translation of wampum as Indian currency was, of course, difficult to sustain on closer examination," and suggests that "this somewhat nuanced gesture towards a dual purpose for the shell indicates—through categorical indecision if nothing else—a glimmer of awareness that assuming a one-to-one relationship between commercial systems was not unproblematic."[20]

The word "wampum," of Algonquian origin, is consistently used across British texts in various iterations, which both locates its exoticism and value as a rare object and gestures to its untranslatable nature.[21] And Grew hints at a third possibility for this material when he describes the "girdles," with one sort consisting of "fourteen pieces in a Row, woven, for the most part, into black and white Squares," and the other being "Woven into black *Rhombs* or *Diamond-Squares*, and *Crosses* within them."[22] The description of these patterns grants them a potential legibility and meaning beyond their more instrumental interpretation.[23] The rhombus or lozenge shape was well known in heraldry and in other antiquarian pursuits for its symbolism, and

---

[18] John Locke, *Two Treatises of Government*, ed. Peter Laslett (1689; Cambridge: Cambridge University Press, 1988), 391.
[19] Grew, *Musaeum Regalis Societatis*, 370.
[20] Ken Arnold, *Cabinets for the Curious: Looking Back at Early English Museums* (New York: Routledge, 2006), 121–122.
[21] "Wampum" became the accepted word by the late seventeenth century in most European languages. The Dutch had previously called it *sewan* or *zeewant*, while the French used *porcelaine*. See Bradley, "Re-Visiting Wampum," 25.
[22] Grew, *Musaeum Regalis Societatis*, 370.
[23] In his preface, Grew asserts that "instead of medling with Mystick, Mythologick, or Hieroglyphick matters," his descriptions will more simply "remarque some of the Uses and Reasons of Things" (ibid., iii).

seventeenth-century writers such as the polymath Thomas Browne saw in geometric shapes such as these transcendent meanings that connected the human and the natural world across cultures.²⁴ These belts from the Royal Society no longer survive; already in 1710, when German traveler Zacharias Conrad von Uffenbach visited the collection with an "exalted idea" of the Society formed thanks to "the fine description of the Museum by Grew," he found that "[h]ardly a thing is to be recognized, so wretched do they all look."²⁵ By the time the Repository was donated to the British Museum in 1781, most of it had been ruined by "time and dirt."²⁶ However, the girdles in the Tradescant collection survive, and they are similar to those described by Grew, with both likely originating from Virginia in the same period. They contain three diamond or rhombus shapes in white, against the purple or so-called "black" wampum. The broader interest in hieroglyphics and symbolic language at the time can illustrate how these objects might challenge or be placed within the period's epistemologies. Certainly, Browne would have noted the lozenge shape as gesturing to a transcendent meaning.²⁷ And Ashmole himself, the driving force behind the Tradescant catalogue, had written on the heraldic significance of the lozenge shape in his 1672 work *The Institution, laws & ceremonies of the most noble Order of the Garter*.²⁸

Thus, at the same time that the first pieces of wampum arrived in Britain and the first English grammars of Indigenous languages were produced, such as Roger Williams's *A Key into the Language of America* (1643), European writers were fascinated by the possibilities of symbolic language. Hieroglyphs, in particular, featured prominently; while Renaissance thinkers believed the hieroglyph concealed mystical and hidden knowledge known by the ancients and since forgotten, the universal language schemers of the mid-seventeenth century saw in hieroglyphs a non-alphabetic way of representing thought.²⁹ They were a "mute language" (Vico) or "dumb signs"

---

[24] See Thomas C. Singer, "Sir Thomas Browne's 'Emphaticall decussation, or fundamentall figure': Geometrical Hieroglyphs and The Garden of Cyrus," *English Literary Renaissance*, 17.1 (1987), 85–102.

[25] Richard Altick, *The Shows of London* (London: Harvard University Press, 1978), 14.

[26] Jennifer Thomas, "Compiling 'God's great book [of] universal nature': The Royal Society's Collecting Strategies," *Journal of the History of Collections*, 23.1 (2011), 1–13 (2).

[27] Thomas Browne's work *The Garden of Cyrus, or The Quincuncial Lozenge* (London: 1658) explores its appearance among plants and among cultures.

[28] He notes that the lozenge is typically used in heraldry to indicate "unmarried Ladies and Gentlewomen" (Elias Ashmole, *The Institution, laws & ceremonies of the most noble Order of the Garter* [London, 1672], 126).

[29] Thomas C. Singer, "Hieroglyph, Real Characters, and the Idea of Natural Language in English Seventeenth-Century Thought," *Journal of the History of Ideas*, 50.1 (1989), 49–70 (56).

(Cave Beck) that circumvented speech; potentially, they unified signifier and signified without reference to the spoken word, and both Chinese and Aztec symbols also became included in this conversation.[30] In the first European description of a Mesoamerican text, from 1520, a Spanish writer compares it to Egyptian scripts, and by the early 1550s these symbols were called "hieroglyphs," thus connecting the New World to the ancient world.[31]

While the writing systems of Mesoamerica have their own separate history from North American systems, for many critics the fate of these early Mexican scripts provide a paradigmatic account of conquest across the Americas; for Walter Mignolo, the colonization of Indigenous language systems, and the privileging of the European book above them, was a fundamental part of the destruction of Indigenous cultures.[32] Indeed, in the first grammar of a European vernacular language, printed the same year as Columbus's landing in 1492, Antonio de Nebrija declares that "language has always been the companion of empire."[33] Mignolo argues that colonial literacy was "a massive operation in which the materiality and the ideology of Amerindian semiotic interactions were intermingled with or replaced by the materiality and ideology of Western reading and writing cultures."[34] Thus the spread of the European book, the production of grammars of Indigenous languages, and the dismissal of Native epistemologies and inscription represents the colonization of Indigenous memory itself. And doubtless it was a question of scale, for no matter how many small wampum beads composed a string or belt, they could not equal the voluminous text of a book. Drew Lopenzina adds that European accounts of Indigenous societies consistently engaged in what he calls "unwitnessing"; writing became the key distinction between civilized and uncivilized, and "to maintain this dichotomy, European explorers have to unwitness Native models of signification such as hieroglyphs, birch bark writing, rock drawings, and wampum."[35]

---

[30] See Byron Ellsworth Hamann, "How Maya Hieroglyphs Got Their Name: Egypt, Mexico, and China in Western Grammatology since the Fifteenth Century," *Proceedings of the American Philosophical Society*, 152.1 (2008), 1–68.

[31] Ibid., 24.

[32] Walter Mignolo, "On the Colonization of Amerindian Languages and Memories: Renaissance Theories of Writing and the Discontinuity of the Classical Tradition," *Comparative Studies in Society and History*, 34.2 (1992), 301–330.

[33] Don Paul Abbott, *Rhetoric in the New World* (Columbia: University of South Carolina Press, 1996), 6.

[34] Walter Mignolo, *The Darker Side of the Renaissance: Literacy, Territoriality, & Colonization* (Ann Arbor: University of Michigan Press, 1995), 76.

[35] Drew Lopenzina, *Red Ink: Native Americans Picking Up the Pen in the Colonial Period* (Albany: SUNY Press, 2012), 24–25.

In John Wilkins's book on cryptography, *Mercury: or the secret and swift Messenger* (1641), he reflects on wampum and quipu, the Peruvian system of knot-writing, as providing useful ways to convey secret knowledge: "For who would mistrust any private News or Treachery to lye hid in a Thread, wherein there was nothing to be discerned, but sundry confused Knots, or other the like Marks?"[36] He provides an illustration of one code system for making this knotted language, which resembles wampum patterns. Wilkins also proposes a universal language for trade in this work, which would express things rather than words; as Cordula Neis suggests, wampum was a mystery to European scholars, but helped provide inspiration for the invention of both cryptographies and universal characters.[37] It could contain hidden meaning, like the hieroglyph, but its materiality, and its commercial use, gestured to transcendence. While wampum and quipu would later be perceived as the earliest civilizational stage of writing, lacking the complexity of alphabet script, at this moment these signs of inscription embody the utopian merging of word, concept, and object.[38]

By the early eighteenth century, however, universal language schemes were widely discredited. This was due in part to Locke's *Essay Concerning Human Understanding* (1689), which, in Rivett's words, "rendered the universal language program scientifically untenable by making the case for words as mere human constructs."[39] Language as an arbitrary, cultural invention hardly inspired a search for divine universality. In *Gulliver's Travels*, Swift mocks universal language schemes in his depiction of Lagado's Academy of Projectors: the professors propose "a scheme for entirely abolishing all words whatsoever [and] since Words are only Names for *Things*, it would be more convenient for all Men to carry about them, such *Things* as were necessary to express the particular Business they are to discourse on."[40] This leads, naturally, to comic effect, and Gulliver observes adherents to this new scheme "almost sinking under the weight of their packs." For Swift, the comic unwieldiness of this scheme flags the problem of scaling up printed letters into cumbersome things. It is hard not to see the supposed unification of word and concept in the hieroglyph, and even more so the unification of

---

[36] Quoted in Cordula Neis, "European Conceptions of 'Exotic' Writing Systems in the Seventeenth and Eighteenth Centuries," *Language & History* 61.1–2 (2018), 39–51, 44. Wilkins does not mention quipu or wampum by name but Neis argues that they explicitly inspire his thought.
[37] Ibid.
[38] Ibid., 41.
[39] Sarah Rivett, *The Science of the Soul in Colonial New England* (Chapel Hill: University of North Carolina Press, 2011), 171.
[40] Jonathan Swift, *Gulliver's Travels*, ed. Claude Rawson and Ian Higgins (1726; Oxford: Oxford University Press, 2005), 172–173.

word and object in wampum, as being evoked by Swift. The dream of pure meaning in a world of multiplying significations seemed more impossible than ever before, and even tiny beads could become enormous.

Wampum and Cross-Cultural Relations

While wampum was collected and perceived as an object of Indigenous origin, the form in which it appeared in Britain was in fact a product of intercultural systems of meaning in the contact zone. The small tubular beads known as "true wampum" by anthropologists only emerged in North America following European contact, and this was the form in which it initially traveled to Britain and the form in which it is most recognizable today.[41] While wampum use and trade among First Nations dates back more than a thousand years, the introduction of new European manufacturing tools led to its spread and to its commodification and accumulation by nations who previously did not have access to it. In 1628, William Bradford commented on its widespread adoption, noting that wampum had been a "current commodity" for roughly twenty years in New England, and worried that "it may prove a drug in time."[42] Prior to the early seventeenth century, wampum was primarily discoidal in shape, but metal drilling implements allowed for the easier manufacture of tubular shapes; these small uniform cylinders of "true wampum" spread rapidly.[43] It was often manufactured by Europeans. The mass-produced beads could more easily be made into belts, and their greater number meant that belts themselves could become larger, often composed of thousands of beads and measuring over 60 cm in length and 10 cm in width. These belts increasingly depicted figures in their woven patterns, such as people holding hands, buildings, and animals. Wampum became legal tender owing to a currency shortage in the colonies, leading to its widespread commodification among white settlers.[44]

For the Haudenosaunee, wampum is fundamentally part of the foundation of the Great Law of Peace of the fifteenth century. The Great Law formed

---

[41] Paul Otto, "Wampum: The Transfer and Creation of Rituals on the Early American Frontier" in Axel Michaels (ed.), *Ritual Dynamics and the Science of Ritual*, 5 vols., *Transfer and Spaces*, ed. Gita Dharampal-Frick, Robert Langer, and Niles Holger Peterson (Wiesbaden: Harrassowitz Books, 2010), vol. 5, 171–188 (175).

[42] Bradley, "Re-Visiting Wampum," 34.

[43] William Engelbrecht, *Iroquoia: The Development of a Native World* (Syracuse, NY: Syracuse University Press, 2005), 157.

[44] David Graeber, *Toward an Anthropological Theory of Value* (New York: Palgrave Macmillan, 2001), 118. Graeber notes, however, that there is no evidence that Native groups bought and sold wampum to each other, instead maintaining their traditional understandings of it.

the Iroquois Confederacy between five separate peoples: the Mohawk, Onondaga, Oneida, Cayuga, and Seneca, with the Tuscarora making six in 1722.[45] The peace was brokered by the Great Peacemaker and Mohawk leader Hiawatha. According to one version of the story, Hiawatha was grieving the loss of his family and sat down by a lake. Suddenly a flock of ducks flew away, magically taking all the water with them. Wampum beads were revealed in the bottom of the lake. Forming them into strings, he declared:

> This would I do if I found anyone burdened with grief even as I am. I would take these shell strings in my hand and console them. The strings would become words and lift away the darkness with which they are covered. Holding these in my hand, my words would be true.[46]

Wampum was from then on used in condolence ceremonies for grief and healing and in diplomacy, uniting word and object. The smallness of the beads could perhaps function metaphorically to diminish and externalize mourning, while when woven together they gave weight and manifestation to spoken words. It was most often made from the common hard-shell clam, the quahog, but could also be made from other shells. Mario Schmidt notes that the production of beads made from such creatures was likely charged with value owing to its transformative power: "As gastropods, they existed between water and land, fish and mammal, and each shell had a unique form … the production of wampum beads entailed the destruction of uniqueness in favour of generality."[47] Wampum was ceremonially "read" at treaties by orators, and this performance had to be periodically repeated to keep the agreements current and to ensure the details and spirit were committed to memory (Figure 8.1). Yet Linnaeus named the hard-shell quahog clam *Mercenaria mercenaria*, a reference to wages, since he understood it to be used solely as currency.

The earliest pictorial representation of wampum in England appeared in 1710; that year, four representatives of the Haudenosaunee were given an audience with Queen Anne at St. James's Palace.[48] The so-called "Four

---

[45] For a history of the Iroquois Confederacy, see William N. Fenton, *The Great Law and the Longhouse: A Political History of the Iroquois Confederacy* (Norman: University of Oklahoma Press, 1998). For a Haudenosaunee perspective, see Rick Monture, *We Share Our Matters: Two Centuries of Writing and Resistance at Six Nations* (Winnipeg: University of Manitoba Press, 2015).
[46] Kelsey, *Reading the Wampum*, xiv.
[47] Mario Schmidt, "Wampum as Maussian objet social totalitaire" in H. P. Hahn and H. Weiss (eds.), *Mobility, Meaning and Transformation of Things* (Oxford: Oxbow Books, 2013), 133–146 (137).
[48] See Eric Hinderaker, "The 'Four Indian Kings' and the Imaginative Construction of the First British Empire," *William and Mary Quarterly*, 53.3 (1996), 487–526; Kate Fullagar, *The Savage Visit* (Los Angeles: University of California Press, 2012), 37–64.

Figure 8.1 The Indians Giving a Talk to Colonel Bouquet in a conference at a Council Fire Near his Camp on the Banks of Muskingum in America, Benjamin West, c. 1765. Yale Center for British Art, Paul Mellon Collection, B1975.4.798.

Indian Kings" appeared widely in popular literature, but there is little direct evidence today of how the Iroquois themselves actually felt during their trip.[49] The closest document to providing this perspective is the speech that

[49] I discuss this literature in Robbie Richardson, *The Savage and Modern Self: North American Indians in Eighteenth-Century British Literature and Culture* (Toronto: University of Toronto Press, 2018), 25–33.

they gave through their interpreter in the presence of Queen Anne, which was widely circulated as a broadside and in newspapers across Britain. It was even written into verse and reproduced twenty years later, such was its perceived cultural importance. This speech, delivered through an English translator while the men stood silently beside him, likely reflects the interests of the European men who organized their visit. Yet the vocabulary and metaphors of "forest diplomacy" permeate the text, with the Iroquois assurances of having "hung up the kettle, and took up the Hatchet" to fight alongside their English brothers. These phrases would become ubiquitous to the point of parody in later accounts of Indian warfare and diplomacy, but were not widespread in British texts until midcentury. In the end the kings declare that "as a Token of the Sincerity of the Six Nations, we do here in the Names of All, present Our Great Queen with these Belts of Wampum."[50] Or, as the verse version of 1730 proclaims, "In sincerity of the Nations whence we come / Great Queen we do present the Belts of Wampum."[51] Relatively little has been made of this exchange, yet it is the first wampum given directly from North American Indigenous people to any European monarch and an important Haudenosaunee intervention into eighteenth-century print and visual culture. And while the meaning of this gesture appears to be fairly straightforward, it reveals an "unwitnessing" in British understandings of wampum and presents unresolvable notions around both this cultural artifact and the question of Indigenous literacy.

It is likely that one of the belts mentioned in the speech appears in Jan Verelst's portrait of Theyanoguin, also known as Hendrick (Figure 8.2). It makes sense if read alongside the speech to Queen Anne, in which they ask for more missionaries to help instruct them in their "Knowledge of the Saviour of the World" and to combat the "Insinuations of [French] Priests."[52] This pictographic belt of crosses appears to commemorate this agreement, and Mohawk historians confirm that there was a desire among the Haudenosaunee for more Christian missionaries, but have suggested that this was to ward off witchcraft, not to preach and convert.[53]

It's hard to know how the court of Queen Anne would have understood these protocols. The wampum in British museum collections and antiquaries' cabinets were usually single pieces, strings, or smaller girdles, so this larger belt constituted a new scale and form to British viewers. In the

---

[50] *The Four Indian Kings Speech to Her Majesty* (London, 1710), n.p.
[51] *The Four Indian Kings Speech* (London, 1730), n.p.
[52] *The Four Indian Kings Speech to Her Majesty* (London, 1710), n.p.
[53] Stephanie Pratt, "The Four Indian Kings" in J. Hackworth-Jones (ed.), *Between Worlds: Voyagers to Britain 1700–1850* (London: National Portrait Gallery, 2007), 22–35 (35n10).

Figure 8.2 Tee Yee Neen Ho Ga Row, Emperour of the Six Nations, mezzotint by John Simon c. 1755, after Johannes Verelst, 1710. Yale Center for British Art, Paul Mellon Collection, B2001.2.1509.

painting the belt appears to translate relatively clearly as a textual record of their agreement in the form of Indigenous inscription. Small individual beads are woven into a pattern of crosses to communicate a significant moment in diplomacy and political relations. The codes of portraiture seem to dictate its importance as a diplomatic text, displayed by the only Indian king without any fierce weapons or tattoos. Yet in at least one printed edition of the speech of the Indian kings, a footnote explains that this wampum is "the money of their country, or beads form'd out of the shells of a certain fish."[54] The text later explains this fish has a "singular Virtue for stenching of Blood; for which End they make Bracelets of them, not only for their own Use, but to vend to others."[55]

How could the British reconcile this obviously diplomatic inscribed object with its explanation as money? In treaty negotiations in the colonies during this same period, wampum was frequently exchanged with British officials, but this knowledge was slow to translate at home. However, the English appropriated the tradition of the Iroquois when seven Cherokee visited London in 1730, in a kind of wampum belt intertextuality. The Lord commissioners for Trade and Plantations declared to the Cherokee in their London offices:

> You are to understand all what we have now said to be the Words of the great King whom you have seen, and as a Token that his Heart is open and true to his Children and Friends the Cherrokees, […] he gives his Hand in this Belt, which he desires may be kept and shown to all your People, and to their Children, and Childrens Children, to confirm what is now spoken; and to bind this Agreement of Peace and Friendship between the English and Cherrokees, as long as the Mountains and Rivers shall last, or the Sun shine; whereupon we give this Belt of Wampum.[56]

Mirroring the speech of the Indian kings twenty years earlier, the lessons of forest diplomacy finally came to the metropolis. It is unclear where this English wampum belt was made or what it looked like. In response, one of the Cherokee chiefs "lay[ed] down his Feathers upon the Table, [and] added, 'This is our Way of Talking, which is the same Thing to us, as your Letters in the Book are to you; and to you, beloved Men, we deliver these Feathers, in Confirmation of all that we have said.'"[57] The Cherokee, it turns out, did not yet use wampum in their protocols, valuing eagle feathers instead.[58]

Newspaper accounts of Indians as well as books such as Cadwallader Colden's *The History of the Five Nations* (1727) changed British understandings beginning in the late 1720s. In John Shebbeare's 1755 novel *Lydia*,

---

[54] *The Four Kings of Canada* (London, 1710), 5.
[55] Ibid., 8. This is describing *esurgni*, which predominantly appears in early French accounts but is most likely wampum. Paul Otto, "'This is that which … they call Wampum'," 4–5.
[56] *Daily Journal*, London, October 7, 1730.
[57] Ibid.
[58] Nancy Shoemaker, *A Strange Likeness: Becoming Red and White in Eighteenth-Century North America* (Oxford: Oxford University Press, 2004), 74–76. Cherokee increasingly began to use wampum in the 1750s.

or filial Piety, there is an awareness of wampum's role in diplomacy; at one point the Iroquois character Cannassatego declares, "I had prepared the Strings of Wampum to ratify the Treaties of Alliance to be concluded with the Great King," and elsewhere says to the British, "the tree of friendship, which we will plant together, shall put forth fresh shoots, and shield us with its leaves; and the hospitable wampum bind us for ever in one cause."[59] The Indians in the novel are also frequently depicted with wampum as an adornment; in the introductory description of Cannassatego, the text notes, "Around his manly Neck shone the beauteous beads of wampum, composed of shining shells of variously reflecting hues."[60] In Henry Mackenzie's novel *The Man of the World* (1773), the European character Billy is given a belt of wampum around his neck to symbolize his adoption into Cherokee society.[61] This is also the case in William Richardson's *The Indians: A tale* (1774), which explains that girdles of the beads "served as tokens of friendship to their kindred, allies, and the captives whom they adopted into their tribe."[62] While its ornamental value continued to confuse its significance, and diminish its legibility as a political document in British eyes, wampum is clearly more than currency.

This shift in the understanding of wampum also came about from the rise in stadial theory, and more particularly in a greater interest towards the origins and development of writing. Yet even in these accounts, wampum could confound interpretation. Perhaps the most well-known history of writing from the period is William Warburton's *The Divine Legation of Moses* (1737), a conjectural history that presents writing as a process of emergence across human cultures. He discusses Mayan pictographs, Egyptian hieroglyphs, and Chinese ideograms, now separated in a scale of progress, and finally the European alphabet as the pinnacle of writing.[63] Warburton does not discuss wampum, but mentions the Peruvian quipu. Quipu appears more frequently than wampum in the period as representative of Indigenous writing, though it is also more often attacked as inadequate.[64] In a 1781 letter to the Countess of Ossory, Horace Walpole positively speculates on

---

[59] John Shebbeare, *Lydia, or Filial Piety*, 4 vols. (London, 1755), vol. 1, 13.
[60] Ibid., vol. 1, 5.
[61] Henry Mackenzie, *The Man of the World*, 2 vols. (London, 1773), vol. 2, 181.
[62] William Richardson, *Poems, Chiefly Rural* (Glasgow, 1774), 122.
[63] See Hamann, "Maya Hieroglyphs," 37–39.
[64] For a discussion of quipu in French Enlightenment discourse, see Lorraine Piroux, "The Encyclopedist and the Peruvian Princess: The Poetics of Illegibility in French Enlightenment Book Culture," *PMLA*, 121.1 (2006), 107–123. In *The History of America*, 2 vols. (London, 1777), William Robertson dismisses quipu as containing "no accession of light or knowledge" (vol. 2, 305).

quipu; the Countess had loaned him some strings to study, and he admits in returning them that he has not been able to decipher their meaning. Nonetheless, he writes, "I am so pleased with the idea of knotting verses, which is vastly preferable to anagrams and acrostics, that if I were to begin life again, I would use a shuttle, instead of a pen, and write verses by the yard."[65] Walpole imagines Indigenous writing to amplify the size of humble verse, not reduce it. In James Beattie's *The theory of language* (1788), he notes that quipu "supplied the place of writing":

> The knowledge of the Quipos is said to have been a great mystery, handed down by tradition from fathers to their children, but never divulged by the parent, till he thought his life near an end.—Belts of *wampum* (as it is called) are probably contrivances of a like nature, made of a great number of little beads of different colours artfully, and not inelegantly, interwoven. These belts are used by the Indians of North America in their treaties; and are said to express, I know not how, the particulars of the transaction.[66]

While many antiquaries and philosophers denied the possibility of Indigenous writing in North America, others admitted that perhaps European systems of understanding were unable to describe them. In John Dove's *An essay on Inspiration* (1756), he writes:

> The strings of wampam [sic] the American Indians deliver, exchange, or give, to ratify their treaties with their friends, the exact care they take to keep them whole and unbroken, as a proof that they have inviolably kept their terms; if they are not hieroglyphical or emblematical [referring to Warburton's account], I want a name … to express myself more properly (they are strings of shells, which they never break till they break their treaty).[67]

An essay in *The Connoisseur* features a country gentleman obsessed with current affairs who proclaims: "I am a great admirer of the Indian oratory; and I dare say old Hendrick the Sachem would have made a good figure in the House of Commons. There is something very elegant in the *Covenant-Belt*; but pray what a pox are those damned *Strings of Wampum*? I cannot find any account of them in Chambers's Dictionary."[68] The gentleman admires wampum in patterned-belt form, which is legible, but cannot understand it stringed in smaller form. Yet even the belt is simply "very elegant," almost an adornment, and not a political document. It so happens

---

[65] *The Letters of Horace Walpole*, ed. Peter Cunningham, 9 vols. (London: Richard Bentley & Son, 1891), vol. 7, 490.
[66] James Beattie, *The Theory of Language* (London, 1788), 113.
[67] James Dove, *An Essay on Inspiration* (London, 1756), 56–57.
[68] George Colman and Bonnell Thornton, *The Connoisseur*, no. 76 (July 10, 1755), 41.

that Chambers does have a definition of wampum, but it is taken directly from Grew's definition as currency almost one hundred years earlier.

There are increasing calls from Indigenous people and from scholars to address wampum as a form of literacy.[69] Germaine Warkentin argues that "writing" should be looked at as a spectrum and not a hierarchy. She notes that historians of writing still divide systems into semasiographic (pictography) and phonographic (language-based); this does not fall far from Warburton's treatise, and wampum, as John Dove pointed out in 1756, does not fit into such a paradigm.[70] In assuming that "written signs must be interpretable without intervention," the performative aspects of Indigenous texts are lost. Warkentin notes that "many Native sign systems are distinguished from alphabetic ones by their character as process rather than as representation," which suggests that reading itself needs to be redefined.[71] Arjun Appadurai similarly reminds us that Western common sense frequently opposes "words" and "things," but, as seventeenth-century British writers began to realize, Indigenous cultures do not have such divides.[72] Wampum is even still perplexing to such sensory regimes, with scholars divided between claiming it as currency, as mnemonic device, or as inscription. Lorraine Piroux suggests that Indigenous scripts such as wampum and quipu were singularly misunderstood in Enlightenment discourse and that their illegibility unmasked the literariness of all texts.[73] Yet if we look at the commodification of wampum, its transformation through mass reproduction from sacred object to currency and then to written record, from small beads into strings and larger belts, Britain's own struggles with the commodification of culture in the period – and indeed the rise of popular literature itself – can be illuminated through its epistemological shortcomings.

---

[69] See Barbara A. Mann, "The Fire at Onondaga: Wampum as Proto-Writing," *Akwesasne Notes: A Journal of Native and Natural Peoples*, 26th Anniversary Issue, 1.1 (1995), 40–48. See also Haas, "Wampum as Hypertext"; Kelsey, *Reading the Wampum*.

[70] Germaine Warkentin, "In Search of 'The Word of the Other': Aboriginal Sign Systems and the History of the Book in Canada," *Book History*, 2 (1999), 1–27.

[71] Ibid., 7.

[72] Arjun Appadurai, "Introduction: Commodities and the Politics of Value" in *The Social Life of Things*, ed. Arjun Appadurai (Cambridge: Cambridge University Press, 1986), 3–63 (4).

[73] Piroux, "The Encyclopedist," 115.

PART III

Small Things at Hand

9   "We Bought a Guillotine Neatly Done in Bone"

Illicit Industries on Board British Prison Hulks, 1775–1815

ANNA MCKAY

In 1797, Elizabeth Wynne Fremantle visited a prisoner of war depot at Portchester Castle in Hampshire with her husband. She noted in her diary that 3,000 French prisoners were on site and that many were "very industrious and make all kinds of little works. We bought a guillotine neatly done in bone."[1] Fremantle's observation captures the complex dynamics of the manufacture and exchange of prisoner-made items. Illicit industries of "little works" commonly occurred across places of confinement during the long eighteenth century; these crafts fostered sociability between prisoners, and between prisoners and tourists, and also worked against the restrictions imposed upon prisoners by the authorities. This chapter focuses on the years 1775–1815, a period in which British prisons struggled to house an enormous influx of prisoners. While war captives of the officer class were released on parole, lower ranks of soldiers and seamen were held in depots such as Portchester Castle, or on board decommissioned and partly dismantled warships known as hulks.[2] During the same period, convicts sentenced by the criminal justice system were imprisoned on board neighboring ships, awaiting transportation.[3] The markets and manufacture that took place on board prison hulks have received little scholarly attention. This chapter, however, takes seriously the small things made by prisoners on board the hulks to show how they represented sociability, human resilience, and adaptability.

---

[1] Elizabeth Wynne Fremantle, diary entry dated October 21, 1797, in *The Wynne Diaries*, ed. Anne Fremantle, 3 vols. (London: Oxford University Press, 1935–1940), vol. 3, 288. Examples of such bone-work guillotines can be found in Clive Lloyd, *Arts and Crafts of Napoleonic and American Prisoners of War, 1756–1816* (Woodbridge: Antique Collectors' Club, 2007), 164–171.

[2] There is very little academic literature on prison hulks. See W. Branch Johnson, *The English Prison Hulks*, rev. ed. (London: Phillimore, 1970); and Charles Campbell, *The Intolerable Hulks: British Shipboard Confinement, 1776–1857* (Tucson, AZ: Fenestra Books, 2001).

[3] For more on penal transportation, see Hamish Maxwell-Stewart, "Convict Transportation from Britain and Ireland 1615–1870," *History Compass*, 8.11 (2010), 1221–1242; Clare Anderson (ed.), *A Global History of Convicts and Penal Colonies* (London: Bloomsbury, 2018); and A. G. L. Shaw, *Convicts and the Colonies: A Study of Penal Transportation from Great Britain and Ireland to Australia and Other Parts of the British Empire* (London: Faber and Faber, 1966).

Studies of prisoner-of-war archaeology have viewed handicrafts as responses to the boredom of captivity, understanding them as outlets for creative expression or as practical means for prisoners to sell or exchange for goods.[4] Objects were created from whatever materials prisoners could scavenge or barter for, from bone and straw to copper sheathing. While previous work on Napoleonic and American prisoner-of-war crafts has provided insight into the types of materials that were used and the locations of depots, the problem of provenance makes it difficult to identify the makers of most pieces made by prisoners of war.[5] In contrast to convict-made objects, there are no shortages of prisoner-of-war handicrafts to consider; yet for both types of object, identifying individual makers is close to impossible. With few textual records attached to specific items, it remains a challenge to identify the location – hulk, depot, prison, or on parole – in which these small things were made and sold. Excavations at penal colony sites in Australia, such as the Hyde Park Barracks and Paramatta Female Factory in New South Wales or the prisoner barracks at Port Arthur, Tasmania, have offered insights into the institutional life of convicts there.[6] These sites may have been partially demolished or rebuilt over time, but their locations are fixed. Prison hulks, conversely, were mobile by their nature and often towed across locations. When decommissioned, they could be sold on, broken up for parts, or scuttled. In Bermuda, the recovery of convict-made objects from the *Dromedary* has provided a rare opportunity to examine artifacts undisturbed by modern dredging.

In snatched moments of time, both prisoners of war and convicts made, bought, and sold small things. These items were illicit, and were miniature in nature as they had to be concealed, smuggled, and hidden from authorities. This chapter examines the values – monetary, national, and emotional – that prisoner-made objects held for their makers and consumers. I examine

---

[4] Gilly Carr and Harold Mytum (eds.), *Cultural Heritage and Prisoners of War: Creativity behind Barbed Wire* (London: Routledge, 2012); Gilly Carr and Harold Mytum (eds.), *Prisoners of War: Archaeology, Memory, and Heritage of 19th- and 20th-Century Mass Internment* (London: Springer, 2012); Fransjohan Pretorius, "Boer Prisoner of War Art," *History Today*, 56.3 (2006), www.historytoday.com/archive/boer-prisoner-war-art, accessed February 10, 2020.

[5] Lloyd, *Arts and Crafts*; Jane Toller, *Prisoners-of-War Work, 1756–1815* (Cambridge: Golden Head, 1965).

[6] For example, see Fiona Starr, "An Archaeology of Improvisation: Convict Artefacts from Hyde Park Barracks, Sydney, 1819–1848," *Australasian Historical Archaeology*, 33 (2015), 37–54; Caitlin D'Gluyas, Martin Gibbs, Chloe Hamilton, and David Roe, "Everyday Artefacts: Subsistence and Quality of Life at the Prisoner Barracks, Port Arthur, Tasmania," *Archaeology in Oceania*, 50 (2015), 130–137; Robyn Stocks, "New Evidence for Local Manufacture of Artefacts at Parramatta, 1790–1830," *Australasian Historical Archaeology*, 26 (2008), 29–43.

first the objects made by French prisoners of war before moving to those made by convicts. As I will show, their small crafts served a range of social, devotional, and personal functions. In my final section, I turn to prisoners who crafted coins and forged banknotes, illuminating the risks and rewards associated with this type of surreptitious making, which required varied tools, resources, skills, and networks of communication. As we shall see, the small things of illicit shipboard industry reveal prison hulks to be spaces not only of confinement but also of sociability, creativity, and industry.

Small Things Made by Prisoners of War

Prisoner-of-war handiwork was a product of significant changes made within the bureaucratic systems of war. After the Seven Years' War, combatants – including soldiers, sailors, and merchantmen or privateers – were generally exchanged through cartel exchange systems, on the basis of grade for grade, or man for man.[7] Women, children, and civilians were also sent home. During the American, French Revolutionary, and Napoleonic Wars, prisoners hailed from territories including France, the American colonies, Denmark, Prussia, and Spain.[8] These decades saw changes in attitude and governance that significantly weakened the exchange system, resulting in far higher numbers of prisoners of war being forcibly detained in Britain.[9] From 1792, over 200,000 prisoners of war were estimated to have passed through Britain, while the highest prisoner population in any one year was 72,000 in 1814.[10] The Admiralty managed prisoner of war depots across Britain and its colonies. In England, captured servicemen were stationed in prisons and depots, while the higher classes, such as officers, were paroled. As numbers increased, forty-three prison ships – stationed at Chatham, Plymouth, and Portsmouth – were put to use by the Admiralty and held as many as 35,000 prisoners over time.[11] The large number of detainees

---

[7] Gavin Daly, "Napoleon's Lost Legions: French Prisoners of War in Britain, 1803–1814," *History*, 89.295 (2004), 361–380 (365).

[8] See Renaud Morieux, *The Society of Prisoners: Anglo-French Wars and Incarceration in the Eighteenth Century* (Oxford: Oxford University Press, 2019); Daly, "Napoleon's Lost Legions"; Paul Chamberlain, *Hell upon Water: Prisoners of War in Britain, 1793–1815* (Stroud: History Press, 2008).

[9] Daly, "Napoleon's Lost Legions," 366.

[10] Francis Abell, *Prisoners of War in Britain 1756–1815: A Record of Their Lives, Their Romance and Their Sufferings* (London: Humphrey Milford, 1914), 10.

[11] James Davey, *In Nelson's Wake: The Navy and the Napoleonic Wars* (New Haven, CT: Yale University Press, 2015), 172.

created a ripe environment for the production of handicrafts, as prisoners sought ways to occupy their time.

Captives held on board prison ships adhered to naval routines and were destined to spend months, even years, stooping under beams, breathing close air, and breaking moldy bread with messmates. While some prisoners were given the opportunity to earn money by carrying out minor tasks – either on board or on shore – men and boys were generally left to their own devices. Boredom could be stifling. As ships were not divided by cells and instead remained as they had been when captured at sea, prisoners could roam the decks freely, day and night. These undivided decks enabled prisoners to come together, leading to the formation of unofficial social hierarchies on board. French prisoners of war were known to divide themselves into roughly three classes that reflected their station before capture: *les officiers* (officers), who were released on parole unless they were demoted to the hulks; *les messieurs ou bourgeois* (gentlemen), who gave lessons in drawing, mathematics, fencing, and languages; and *les raffalés* (gamblers), who were the lowest class of prisoner.[12]

Between these categories sat another key group: that of skilled craftsmen or artisans, including working-class naval and military servicemen. These prisoners were seen to be the most practical and industrious, with many making a comfortable living buying and selling items and making objects from wood, bone, and straw. Their work invites comparisons with sailor-made art, such as scrimshaw carvings, canvas, and ropework.[13] Hand-making skills were often learnt from others while at sea, and we can assume that prisoners of war – many of whom were seamen – possessed making skills prior to their capture or acquired knowledge and techniques during captivity. Craftsmen on the hulks were noted by prisoner Jacques-Louis Chieux at Chatham in Kent: "the cobblers and tailors set up their boutiques. The soldiers and sailors with no trade amused themselves making small ships from bone, dice, dominoes."[14] Chieux describes the kinds of small handcrafted objects now held by the National Maritime Museum, Greenwich (see Figure 9.1). Alongside a significant number of bone-work ship models in the Museum's collections, these items are representative of the handiwork of prisoners of war from this period. Figure 9.1 shows a bone-work domino box with cribbage board, a

[12] Abell, *Prisoners of War in Britain*, 59.
[13] Maya Wassell Smith, "'The fancy work what sailors make': Material and Emotional Creative Practice in Masculine Seafaring Communities," *Nineteenth-Century Gender Studies*, 14.2 (2018), para. 3.
[14] Jacques-Louis Chieux, quoted in Terry Crowdy, *French Warship Crews 1789–1805: From the French Revolution to Trafalgar* (Oxford: Osprey, 2005), 58.

Figure 9.1 Domino box, watch stand, and straw work casket, AAA0002, AAA0004, AAA0005. © National Maritime Museum, Greenwich, London. Sutcliffe-Smith Collection.

watch stand made of the same material, and a straw-work box or casket.[15] Other extant crafts range from decorative straw-work snuff boxes and watch stands to elaborate bone-work guillotines and spinning jennies. In some rare cases, the names of individual craftsmen are known, such as Corporal Jean De Laporte, whose straw-work pictures were made during confinement at Norman Cross (near Peterborough), or the marine artist Louis Garneray, whose paintings of prison hulks moored in Portsmouth Harbour illustrate his own confinement on board the *Prothee* between 1806 and 1814.[16] Not all craftsmen worked alone, however, and many of the items produced by prisoners were the result of collective making.

---

[15] Further collections of prisoner-made objects can be found at the Peterborough Museum and Art Gallery in Cambridgeshire, close to the original site of the Norman Cross Barracks, which were in use between 1797 and 1814. The museum holds around eight hundred prisoner-of-war handicrafts.

[16] Toller, *Prisoners-of-War Work*, 2; and Louis Garneray, *The Floating Prison: The Remarkable Account of Nine Years' Captivity on the British Prison Hulks during the Napoleonic Wars, 1806–1814*, trans. Richard Rose (London: Conway Maritime Press, 2003).

Prisoner-made small things tell us much about access to materials, prisoner diets, encounters with the public, and eighteenth-century consumer culture. Straw marquetry was popular in the eighteenth century and a major industry in some regions of France and Holland.[17] The fashionable appetite for miniature pieces of furniture provided opportunities for captives who had the skills – and materials – to capitalize on these trends. Unless there was an issue with supply, prisoners of war were given a thin mattress, a straw-filled pillow, and one blanket.[18] Although tools and paints were required to produce higher quality items, prisoners undoubtedly used straw from their mattresses and created dyes by boiling down their clothing and rations. Straw-work produced by prisoners ranged from cabinets and tea caddies to pictures and snuff boxes. The decorative box in Figure 9.1 is one of many that feature insets of intricate patterns, made by changing the direction of the straw to achieve differences in light and shade. Interiors of these boxes varied from simple to elaborate, with drawers of different sizes, compartments, mirrors, and carved bone handles. Plaiting straw to make hats, bonnets, and baskets became such a productive – and lucrative – industry in some depots that it began to threaten the revenues of local hatmakers, leading to orders from the Transport Board governing body to stop the practice in 1799 and 1807.[19] Bones used for handicrafts, such as the domino box and watch stand in Figure 9.1, were available in large quantities as they were sourced from prisoners' rations. When not troubled by a lack of supply, the daily rations for each prisoner on board the prison ship *Sultan* in Portsmouth Harbour were one and a half pounds of bread, half a pound of fresh beef, one-quarter of a pint of pease – split yellow peas – and one-third of an ounce of salt.[20] Salvaged bones could be boiled down into glue, or polished, shaped, and carved into a variety of small objects, with ship models proving the most popular.

The sight of prisoners of war on land and at sea quickly became a tourist attraction, and many captives took advantage of the trading possibilities presented by contact with the public. In port towns, the sea presented no obstacle to this; visitors paid boatmen to row them up to the ships that housed prisoners. One such tourist was the recently widowed Lady Jerningham, who, in 1810, visited Portsmouth with her son Edward. She wrote to her daughter that together they spent two hours in a boat, "Roving round

---

[17] Toller, *Prisoners-of-War Work*, 4.
[18] Admiralty to Captain Isaac Cotgrave, June 14, 1803, folio 14, ADM 98/212, The National Archives, London (hereafter TNA).
[19] Lloyd, *Arts and Crafts*, 63.
[20] Transport Office to Mr. William Boulton, Portsmouth, June 11, 1803, fo. 11, ADM 98/212, TNA.

tremendous Men of War [and] Ships full of French Prisoners."[21] Crafts made on board could be sold directly to tourists by being lowered down on string to those in the boats below, or indirectly through exchanges for a commission by members of the ship's company who could ferry goods to shore. In depots such as Edinburgh Castle and Norman Cross, weekly – sometimes daily – prisoner markets provided structured opportunities for prisoners to trade and buy tools and materials. Prisoner handicrafts formed part of a network of small items passed between rowboat and hulk. In reaction to "disturbance and insurrection" at the depot in Portchester Castle in 1797, authorities stopped the prisoner market there, which had been "allowed to be held, for the purpose of putting it in the power of the prisoners, by disposing of various articles which they manufactured, to supply themselves with vegetables and other little comforts."[22] It was in this depot that Elizabeth Wynne Fremantle bought her miniature "guillotine neatly done in bone." Stopping trade was a means to exercise power over prisoners, but Fremantle's purchase – which occurred in the same year as restrictions were placed upon the market – suggests that prisoners still found ways to sell their wares.

Small things crafted by French prisoners of war were particularly popular with the British public. Despite the anti-French sentiment that commonly appeared in news media reports, British fascination with French fashions and styles frequently overrode hostility.[23] French prisoners of war monetized this status as "other" to the British by tapping into the fame and celebrity cults of Napoleon, the Revolution, and the infamous guillotine. Thousands of bone-work guillotines, such as that purchased by Elizabeth Fremantle, and domino boxes depicting Napoleon were crafted, the latter in the same style as that depicted in Figure 9.1. However, the domino box in Figure 9.1 is noteworthy as its pull-out slide is illustrated with an image of a sailor mourning beside a monument with a bust flanked by Union Jack flags, inscribed with the words "Lord Nelson." This example shows that French prisoners could transcend their own national loyalties to make items that specifically appealed to – even celebrated – British patriotism. After the Battle of Trafalgar in 1805, Nelson memorabilia increased in popularity. The domino box indicates that prisoners of war took advantage

---

[21] Lady Frances Jerningham to her daughter Charlotte, September 23, 1810, JER546, Cadbury Research Library, Birmingham (CRL).
[22] House of Commons Parliamentary Papers (HCPP), *Report on Treatment of Prisoners of War*, House of Commons Sessional Papers (1798), vol. 118, article nos. 5, 6.
[23] For example, see the public fascination surrounding the trial of French prisoner Charles Mausereaux on board the *Sampson*: "Horrid Murder," *Royal Cornwall Gazette*, July 24, 1813 (via GALE Historical Newspapers).

of this trend, altering designs from Napoleon to Nelson.²⁴ Handiwork by French prisoners of war tapped into the sense of national loss prompted by Nelson's death, suggesting that sites of confinement were far from sealed off from the latest in fashionable commodities. Instead, they were places where news flowed between captive, captor, and the public. As such, prisoners altered their handicrafts to reflect shifts in consumer culture, from the celebration of victories to the mourning of losses.

Small Things Made by Convicts

When prisoners of war were sent home in 1815, neighboring convict hulks remained in Portsmouth, Plymouth, and along the Thames Estuary. In 1776, the Criminal Law Act authorized the punishment of offenders awaiting transportation with hard labor.²⁵ The previous method of transporting convicts to the American colonies was halted by the American Revolutionary War.²⁶ Convicts were instead housed on hulks and put to work dredging channels in dockyards, hauling ballast and timber, and constructing administrative buildings and barracks. With an entire daily routine structured around work, they labored eight hours in the winter months and nine hours in summer.²⁷ Strict routines were designed to impose order and aid the reform of bad habits. For convicts, imprisonment on the hulks was a harsh life, designed to have few idle moments. Despite the restrictions placed upon them, men and boys on board found time to make and sell small things.

Before being transported, many convicts sought to exchange material love tokens with their families. However expedient a solution prison hulks might at first appear, they could only absorb 60 percent of those under sentence of transportation.²⁸ As such, the embarkation of the so-called First Fleet of eleven convict ships to New South Wales in 1787 eased

---

[24] See in particular the commemorative sampler of fourteen-year-old Mary Gill, from Dudley, as discussed by Marianne Czisnik, "Nelson, Navy, and National Identity" in Quintin Colville and James Davey (eds.), *Nelson, Navy & Nation: The Royal Navy & the British People 1688–1815* (London: Conway, 2013), 188–207.

[25] The Criminal Law Act, 1776, 16 Geo. 3, c. 43.

[26] See A. Roger Ekirch, *Bound for America: The Transportation of British Convicts to the Colonies, 1718–1775* (Oxford: Clarendon, 1987); and Gwenda Morgan and Peter Rushton, *Eighteenth-Century Criminal Transportation: The Formation of the Criminal Atlantic* (Basingstoke: Palgrave Macmillan, 2004).

[27] HCPP, *Reports Relating to Convict Establishments*, February 10 and 3, 1816, Sessional Papers, vol. 18, 1–20, report no. 3 (Instructions to John Henry Capper), p. 10.

[28] Simon Devereaux, "The Making of the Penitentiary Act, 1775–1779," *The Historical Journal*, 42.2 (1999), 405–433 (406).

overcrowding. When a convict was transported, they faced sentences of seven years, fourteen years, or life. Many did not return. Engraving coins with messages of affection to give to loved ones became a means of leaving a personal memento behind.[29] These were deeply personal small objects, shaped by the conditions of incarceration. They played a vital role in preserving the identity of the giver, and acted as an important site of memory – and emotion – for the recipient.[30] Made by smoothing down copper pennies and halfpennies, then pricking the surface with small dots, using a sharp tool or stipple, these tokens record the personal and emotional responses of convicts. They often included names of prisoners and loved ones, the length of the sentence, and popular phrases and rhymes. Making a token was illegal, as it involved tampering with legal tender and the defacing of a monarch.[31] Even so, the physical conditions of the coins themselves often meant that altering pennies into love tokens required very little work.[32] Tokens were easy to conceal, pass on, and hold in the palm of the hand. Their messages of hope, fear, and love spoke of the individual – as opposed to the consumer-driven objects crafted by prisoners of war.

While existing objects such as coins were altered to become personal keepsakes, the dockyards in which convicts undertook hard labor provided them with the means to acquire raw materials to make new items. Many royal naval dockyards were in need of modernization at the end of the eighteenth century, and convicts became a key, cheap workforce.[33] In the midst of the daily comings and goings, it was possible to escape detection and pillage storerooms for copper, lead, wood, even tools. It may have been a practical necessity for free dockyard workers to converse with convicts while at work, but this risked the formation of friendships and alliances that supported illicit industries. Dockyard workers delivered convicts' letters and love tokens to their friends and families and sold on their handicrafts. Convicts sometimes also encountered members of the public who

---

[29] Michele Field and Timothy Millett (eds.), *Convict Love Tokens: The Leaden Hearts the Convicts Left Behind* (Kent Town, Australia: Wakefield Press, 1998). The National Museum of Australia holds the world's largest collection of convict love tokens: "Collection Highlights: Convict Love Tokens," National Museum of Australia, www.nma.gov.au/explore/collection/highlights/convict-love-tokens, accessed February 1, 2020.

[30] Sally Holloway, *The Game of Love in Georgian England: Courtship, Emotions, and Material Culture* (Oxford: Oxford University Press, 2018), 69.

[31] Tom Gretton, "Last Dying Speech and Confession" in Field and Millet, *Convict Love Tokens*, 39–46 (43).

[32] Bridget Millmore, "Love Tokens: Engraved Coins, Emotions and the Poor, 1700–1856," unpublished PhD thesis, University of Brighton (2015), 33–34.

[33] See Roger Morriss, *The Royal Dockyards during the Revolutionary and Napoleonic Wars* (Leicester: Leicester University Press, 1983).

visited the yards in a tourist capacity. Indeed, Lady Jerningham, who had made note of the prisoner-of-war ships in Portsmouth, commented that on the same trip she had also seen "Convicts in Prison Vessels with the Windows grated with Iron."[34] As hubs of activity, dockyards therefore provided convicts with multiple opportunities to sell or pass on their handicrafts.

Food rations offered another means for convicts to access resources, and salvaged bones from rations did not go to waste. For example in 1812, one chaplain reported that on board the convict hulks at Langstone Harbour, near Portsmouth, he had found that "indecent toys were manufactured from bone for sale."[35] No further detail was given, but a surviving example of prisoner-of-war-made erotica – a small wooden figure of a Dartmoor countrywoman wearing a hinged long skirt, which, when lifted, revealed her naked body – might have proven similar.[36] In 1798, London authorities issued orders that "obscene figures and indecent toys and all such indecent representations tending to disseminate Lewdness and Immorality exposed for sale or prepared for that purpose are to be instantly destroyed."[37] A decree such as this could well have forced the production of pornographic objects further underground, upping the risks for prisoners caught making or selling them, while also increasing the market price once smuggled outside. Other illicit convict-made items also raised alarm. For example, in 1815, the captain of the *Portland* noted that he had discovered the manufacture "of what are called skeleton-keys, made for the purpose of opening locks."[38] Made from salvaged metal or bone, skeleton keys could serve as the route to escape; their small scale made them easy to conceal in pockets and sleeves, and to pass between hands. In the cases where convicts worked together, entire groups could be punished by having their rations reduced or by being excluded from recommendations for pardon.

The largest collection of convict-made objects, recovered from the *Dromedary* hulk, belongs to the National Museum of Bermuda. Convicts were first sent to Bermuda – an island situated in the North Atlantic Ocean, some 800 miles from New York – in 1824, after the passing of an act of parliament that authorized the combination of transportation and hard labor "in any colony designated by the King."[39] Until 1863, when the

---

[34] Jerningham, September 23, 1810, JER546, CRL.
[35] HCPP, *Confinement of Offenders in the Hulks*, June 22, 1815, Commons Sitting, series 1, vol. 31, cols. 944–968, col. 951.
[36] For an image of this object, see Lloyd, *Arts and Crafts*, 173.
[37] Quoted by Toller, *Prisoners-of-War Work*, 21.
[38] HCPP, *Confinement of Offenders in the Hulks*, col. 951.
[39] Male Convicts Act, 1823, 4 Geo. 4, c. 47.

convict establishment there was disbanded, Bermuda's dockyards were transformed into a strongly fortified and well-equipped supply, maintenance, and repair base. At the closure of the convict station, the *Dromedary*, which had been docked in Bermuda since 1826, was scuttled. The objects in Figure 9.2 were among those recovered by marine archaeologists examining the site of the mooring. The site's varied items included cannons, miniature bibles, rosaries, chess and draught pieces, dice, and dominoes, indicating that convict-made objects could serve a variety of functions. The *Dromedary*'s objects present a unique insight into the social and devotional lives of convicts on the hulks. While gaming pieces suggest gambling and social activities, the carving of crucifixes, rosaries, and books marked with crosses (resembling bibles) found in Bermuda point to the influx of Roman Catholic Irish prisoners who were sent there during the famine years of the 1840s. Their presence led to tensions between Catholic and Protestant prisoners, and culminated in the appointment of a Roman Catholic chaplain to deliver separate devotional services.[40] Chaplains were employed by the hulk establishment to conduct services for inmates and staff, in addition to prayers every morning and bible classes or general schooling most evenings. Devotional objects made by convicts may have been sold to members of the public, but they also evoke images of individuals clinging to the solace offered by religion, murmuring prayers before bed and remembering loved ones.

We can assume that items recovered from the *Dromedary* were similar to those made from bone, slate, and scraps of metal in England. However, one raw material stands out as specific to Bermuda: calcite-cave flowstone. On the island, convicts were put to work finishing the Commissioner's House and also built surrounding dwelling houses for dockyard workers, magazines for ordnance stores, and any other buildings associated with the efficient running of the yard.[41] Convicts were also tasked with quarrying the raw materials used for construction. They cut and moved blocks of hard limestone and were often blinded from the reflected glare. Convicts quarried in caves underneath the Commissioner's House and Casemates Barracks, which became sources of multicolored calcite flowstone, as seen in Figure 9.2.[42] Cave flowstones are composed of sheet-like deposits

---

[40] C. F. E. Hollis Hallett, *Forty Years of Convict Labour: Bermuda 1823–1863* (Bermuda: Juniperhill Press, 1999), 92. Note also the chapter "Floating Hells: Bermuda, Gibraltar and the Hulks, 1850–1875" in Hilary Carey, *Empire of Hell: Religion and the Campaign to End Convict Transportation in the British Empire, 1788–1875* (Cambridge: Cambridge University Press, 2019), 257–281.

[41] General report on the state of the colony, "Public Works," no. 10, fo. 44, CO 37/87/10, TNA.

[42] Chris Addams, "Counterfeiting on the Bermuda Convict Hulk Dromedary," *Journal of the Numismatic Association of Australia*, 18.1 (2007), 3–17 (12).

Figure 9.2 Convict-made objects recovered from the *Dromedary* hulk in Bermuda, 1824–1863. Photograph courtesy of the National Museum of Bermuda.

of calcite or other carbonate materials, and are formed when water flows down the walls or along the floors of a cave. Convicts smuggled fragments of flowstone back to the hulks, spending hours chipping, carving, and polishing them to build up a pearlescent sheen. They were made into various objects, including the dice, draughts pieces, dominoes, and chessmen in Figure 9.2. In the dockyards, these objects could be traded with free and enslaved workers for fresh fruit and vegetables, or prohibited goods such as tobacco and rum (clay pipes recovered from the *Dromedary* show that prisoners were able to smoke tobacco).[43] In England and Bermuda, convicts displayed a willingness to use whatever resources they could obtain to make social, emotional, and devotional small things. Excepting love tokens, the objects they crafted were adaptable and not defined by material. Wood could therefore be substituted for bone, cave flowstone, or anything else that came to hand.

[43] For further images of objects recovered from the *Dromedary* hulk, including clay pipes (p. 9), see Chris Addams and Michael Davis, "Bermuda Hulks," www.bermudahulks.com/brochure.pdf, accessed November 5, 2019.

Shared Experiences: Gambling and Forgery

While prisoner-of-war artisans made bone-work ships and guillotines to sell to the public and convict craftsmen worked on indecent toys and items for prayer, others turned to more lucrative and entertaining activities. Many of the small things that prisoners made were linked with gambling; the activity provided entertainment for individuals and social groups alike. Both convicts and prisoners of war made dice, dominoes, and chess and draughts pieces, such as those seen in Figures 9.1 and 9.2. Their small size enabled prisoners to quickly sweep away games and conceal their existence. Gambling was facilitated by ease of movement. When convict hulks entered into use in 1776, they were not separated into cells; instead, like prisoner-of-war hulks, convicts could move freely at night. Games staved off boredom when hatches were locked down and prisoners were out of the sight of overseers and guards. Crucially, much like the making and selling of handicrafts, winnings could lead to increased welfare. Money could buy better sleeping quarters, extra food, and writing materials, pay for letters to be sent home, or settle debts. As gambling was forbidden, the act of making dice, dominoes, and gaming chips was inherently illicit.

Coining and forgery were further workarounds for deprivation and life on a hulk, connected to material objects by virtue of their being made or crafted. Between 1775 and 1815, prisoners of war received small monetary allowances from the Admiralty, but little was paid out during captivity. Conversely, convicts were paid for their labor, but only a third of their wages, amounting to one penny, was given to them per day, at the discretion of the master shipwright or officer overseeing their work.[44] The rest was saved and given out at the end of their sentences. Currency clearly had a place on board the hulks as coining and forgery became commonplace among both groups of prisoners. In 1815, a parliamentary committee stated that convicts had stolen materials from the dockyards worth between thirty and forty pounds.[45] Pieces of metal and wood that could be taken and easily concealed were sold to those who could use them, in many cases to make money. Indeed, the captain of the *Portland* convict hulk at Langston Harbour stated that beating out half crowns into sixpences had gone on for many years on board his vessel, and that "he himself had taken thirty-nine of these sixpences from one of the convicts, at one time: they now coin

---

[44] Samuel Bentham, Inspector General of Naval Works, Portsmouth, to Evan Nepean, May 11, 1802, ADM 1/3526/3, TNA.

[45] HCPP, *Confinement of Offenders in the Hulks*, col. 954.

copper at Sheerness, and it is some aggravation of the offence that the metal of which the false money is made is stolen from the King's stores."[46] In Bermuda, convicts allegedly used Spanish dollars and English half crowns and shillings to forge molds for Mexican, Peruvian, and English coinage, reflecting a circulation of multinational currency.[47] Crude coinage was in evidence at most prisoner-of-war depots too: at Dartmoor in Devon, shillings were made from Spanish dollars supplied to prisoners from outside the market. Out of every four dollars, eight full-weight shillings were made.[48] In other cases, lead prized from the barrack roofs was used.[49]

Coining required tools and access to resources. Cut off from land – and, by extension, raw materials – skilled prisoners of war on hulks found that forging banknotes from scraps of paper was more practical. Counterfeit notes became a major problem during the Restriction Period, when the Bank of England was unable to pay out gold in exchange for banknotes.[50] The practice was punishable by death, as clipping, coining, and counterfeiting were seen to threaten the stability of the kingdom.[51] In 1809, two prisoners of war on the *El Firme* at Plymouth were convicted of forging banknotes using smooth halfpennies and sail-makers' needles to emulate the perforated stamp of Bank of England, Naval and Commercial Bank, and Okehampton Bank notes.[52] They were among the first war captives executed for forgery. In 1812, two more prisoners of war, Beury and Dubois, taken from a Portsmouth hulk, attempted suicide after being condemned to hang for forging Bank of England notes. While counterfeiting served as a means to gain limited freedoms on board, the resulting suicides were more a fundamental rejection of authority. Beury left a suicide note, stating that he preferred to take his own life and disgrace himself, his family, and his country, rather than suffer "so ignominious a death" as hanging.[53]

Despite their minute scale, the small things made by prisoners of war and convicts held immense value for their makers, fulfilling a wide range of social, devotional, and personal functions. The straw- and bone-work items crafted

---

[46] Ibid., col. 951.
[47] Addams, "Counterfeiting," 13.
[48] Toller, *Prisoners-of-War Work*, 20.
[49] Abell, *Prisoners of War in Britain*, 256.
[50] The Bank Restriction Act was passed in 1797 and the period lasted until convertibility was restored in 1821. See Bank Restriction Act, 1797, 37 Geo. 3, c. 45.
[51] Peter Linebaugh, *The London Hanged: Crime and Civil Society in the Eighteenth Century* (London: Verso, 2003), 55.
[52] Abell, *Prisoners of War in Britain*, 97.
[53] "Forgery of Bank of England Notes, by French Prisoners of War," *Hull Packet*, April 7, 1812 (via GALE Historical Newspapers).

by prisoners of war provide insight into the nature of prisoner diets, sleeping arrangements, and collaborative working. They also prompt further questions about their access to materials and relationships with the outside world, from guards and overseers to supply contractors and tourists. What is striking about the objects made by prisoners of war is their adherence to cultural tropes and fashions, such as the guillotine purchased by Elizabeth Fremantle and domino boxes depicting Napoleon. Prisoners capitalized on the public's fascination with their status and foreignness, targeting their market and producing popular items. Conversely, the narrative of convict-made objects tells us a different story. When materials such as copper and iron were stolen while laboring in the dockyards, convicts not only risked their hopes of pardon and early release but also damaged relations with overseers. As with prisoners of war, bones salvaged from meat rations could be used to make toys – in certain cases "indecent" ones – to sell to the public, while the illicit manufacture of skeleton keys increased chances of escape. Convict-made objects arguably give us a greater sense of the individual; tokens made from smoothed and stippled coins were made for loved ones prior to transportation, while flowstone rings, rosaries, and miniature bibles found in Bermuda mark the scant material traces of their devotional lives.

Isolated by water, prison hulks essentially functioned as islands, cut off from land and society. Making and selling small things brought prisoners into contact with the outside world. For convicts, objects were fed through a network of supply facilitated by dockyard workers, both at home and in overseas stations such as Bermuda. For prisoners of war, the public appetite to see "the enemy" brought a steady stream of tourist boats directly to them. The act of making – and selling – illicit items provided both sets of prisoners with the means to gain some freedoms on board. However, when apprehended by authorities coining and forging banknotes, punishment was severe, and the law made little distinction between groups. Ultimately, crafts fostered sociability between prisoners and the various civilians that they encountered. The presence of prisoner-made material culture on board prison hulks shows us that individuals worked together, bartered, traded, and stole to ameliorate their daily life. Crucially, their small objects speak of human resilience, adaptability, and ingenuity in the face of hardship.

10 | "What Number?"

Reform, Authority, and Identity in Late Eighteenth-Century Military Buttons

MATTHEW KEAGLE

Fort Ticonderoga, on the shores of Lake Champlain in the state of New York in the United States, barely 75 miles from the Canadian border, is located at a point of multiple conflicts over several centuries, first between Indigenous nations, then between those nations and European imperial powers, and at various times between European colonizers. Between the Seven Years' War (1754–1763) and the American War of Independence (1775–1783), tens of thousands of soldiers served at Ticonderoga. The presence of these soldiers can be found in the archaeological collections of the Fort Ticonderoga Museum. The clothing worn by French, British, German, Colonial, and Indigenous soldiers and civilians is reflected by over 2,500 individual metal, wood, and bone buttons recovered from the site. Hundreds of these buttons once adorned military uniforms. More than just an acknowledgment of the migration of European-style uniforms to North America, the collections at Fort Ticonderoga reveal an historical shift in the development of military buttons. The earliest military buttons from the Seven Years' War are plain brass or pewter. More detailed buttons cast with regimental numbers or insignia constitute an important development, which occurred in the wake of that conflict. This shift in button design materializes broader changes to military dress and European institutions.

Despite their ubiquity on the dress uniforms of armies and police forces to the present, marked military buttons are a distinct creation of the second half of the eighteenth century. Their widespread presence at military sites, however, has not turned them into subjects of extensive scholarly study.[1] Buttons have received some attention as a diagnostic tool by

---

[1] Military buttons have rarely been taken seriously as a subject of academic study. Some recent scholars of material culture, such as Mary Beaudry, have even consciously avoided exploring them, while others address them in passing only as they pertain to a specific cultural style. See Mary C. Beaudry, *Findings: The Material Culture of Needlework and Sewing* (New Haven, CT: Yale University Press, 2006), 8; Peter McNeil, *Pretty Gentlemen: Macaroni Men and the Eighteenth-Century Fashion World* (New Haven, CT: Yale University Press, 2018), 90–92. There is a rich literature on military buttons by and for collectors: see Warren K. Tice, *Uniform Buttons*

archaeologists, which will be addressed at the end of this chapter. As I will show, the origin of military buttons carrying numbers and insignia following the Seven Years' War makes them compelling markers of a period that I will refer to as the "age of reform." This period, from roughly 1763 to at least 1789, overlaps with the more familiar periodization of the Age of Revolution, often dated from the outbreak of the American War of Independence in 1775.[2] That definition, however, obscures a surge of innovation that preceded and overlapped with the political revolutions of the end of the century and into the next. This included significant attempts to rationalize and systematize institutions, particularly the military, to preserve and extend order and authority. Throughout this period, uniforms were dynamic objects, capable of representing changes in the military as well as civil society, not simply static, conservative artifacts of the past. In the early modern era, uniforms represented the tensions between new and old, signifying, on the one hand, the growing centralization and consolidation of nation states and, on the other, the continuance of archaic power structures from the recent feudal past. By the eighteenth century, uniforms communicated more than just military function or identification.[3] Uniforms encoded meaning, and alterations often reflected changes to underlying systems that highlighted evolving institutions and contested ideas, making them particularly powerful during historical moments of great change. During the age of reform, changes to military dress spoke to the revision and even rejection of established norms.[4] Military buttons reflect, in microcosm, the contingent and negotiated authorities that

---

of the United States: Button Makers of the United States, 1776–1865 (Gettysburg, PA: Thomas Pubs, 1997); Marian L. Hurley, *A Collector's Guide to French Military Buttons of the American Revolution, 1775 to 1783* (Suffern, NY: M. L. Hurley, 1998); Don Troiani and James Kochan, *Insignia of Independence: Military Buttons, Accoutrement Plates, & Gorgets of the American Revolution* (Gettysburg, PA: Thomas Publications, 2012). The limited analytic studies that exist are often reductive and fail to consider other sources, contexts, and disciplines, see Penny Le Couteur and Jay Burreson, *Napoleon's Buttons: How 17 Molecules Changed History* (New York: J. P. Tarcher/Putnam, 2003).

[2] Wim Klooster, *Revolutions in the Atlantic World, New Edition: A Comparative History* (New York: NYU Press, 2018), 1. On the dating and scope of the Age of Revolution, see also David Armitage and Sanjay Subrahmanyam, *The Age of Revolutions in Global Context, c. 1760–1840* (Basingstoke: Palgrave Macmillan, 2010), xii–xxxii.

[3] Brendon Simms, *Three Victories and a Defeat: The Rise and Fall of the First British Empire, 1714–1783* (New York: Basic Books, 2009), 318–319, 324.

[4] For example, doctrinal and technological debates in France over reforms of the artillery were couched terms of "reds" and "blues," using the metonym of changing uniform colors. See Ken Alder, *Engineering the Revolution: Arms and Enlightenment in France, 1763– 1815* (Princeton, NJ: Princeton University Press, 1997), 39; *Ordonnance du Roi Concernant le Corps-Royal de L' Artillerie. Du 3 Octobre 1774* (Paris, 1774), 53.

characterize the early modern era and the ability of military dress to reflect broader societal and cultural issues.[5]

This chapter will explore the origin of marked military buttons in the age of reform. As we shall see, buttons constituted the smallest piece of military dress, yet their minuscule surfaces articulated significant changes in military administration and authority. As we shall see in the first section, France initiated the use of marked military buttons in the wake of the Seven Years' War, a moment of military and cultural reckoning for the nation. From the experience of France in the heated context of the 1760s and 1770s, to Britain and its colonies, this chapter will examine how the introduction of marked military buttons raised questions of representation and identification on both sides of the Atlantic. The chapter ends with a pivot to what military buttons found in archaeological sites such as Ticonderoga can tell scholars and archaeologists about the systems and ideas they represent.

Minuscule Reforms

The introduction of patterned military buttons is one of the first material manifestations of the age of reform in the military. Military uniforms relied on distinct relationships of materials to differentiate soldiers from civilians and to distinguish different military units from each other. This generally took the form of distinctively colored cloth for the body of their coats, set off by contrasting cuffs, collars, and/or lapels, called "facings." These allowed spectators to identify soldiers and to further denote regiments or branches of service. Until the 1760s, the buttons worn on these uniforms were relatively plain. The development of numbered military buttons marks a precise point in the evolution from civilian to military styles. Rather than using buttons that could also be found on civilian clothing, numbered buttons inscribed the efforts of military reformers to centralize and rationalize military institutions into the very materiality of uniforms.

---

[5] For detailed examples of broader French military reforms, see Alder, *Engineering the Revolution*; Jonathan Abel, *Guibert: Father of Napoleon's Grande Armée* (Norman: University of Oklahoma Press, 2016). For an example from the Atlantic world, see Ben Vinson, *Bearing Arms for His Majesty: The Free-Colored Militia in Colonial Mexico* (Stanford, CA: Stanford University Press, 2004). On the persistence of privilege and proprietorship, see Alan J. Guy, *Oeconomy and Discipline: Officership and Administration in the British Army 1714-63* (Manchester University Press, 1985), 2–3, 13–14, 162; Sanborn C. Brown (ed.), *The Collected Works of Count Rumford*, 5 vols. (Cambridge, MA: Belknap Press of Harvard University, 1968–70), vol. 5, 398–401; Rafe Blaufarb, *The French Army 1750-1820: Careers, Talent, Merit* (Manchester: Manchester University Press 2017), 25.

Prior to the Seven Years' War, the French Army maintained a complicated system in which button metal (cast brass or pewter) combined with facing color, as well as the unique shape of the pocket flap and the arrangement of buttons on it, identified individual regiments. This was a holdover from the late seventeenth century when modern military uniforms were adopted, and the system persisted through the middle of the eighteenth century. While the buttons on the breast of the coat were functional, allowing the soldier to open and close his coat, the majority of the buttons were vestigial and decorative, corresponding only to blind buttonholes. Despite allowing for discreet identification, no unifying program underlay this system, and regimental distinctions were not even described in the official *ordonnances* that governed the dress of the army. The limited detail provided room for the officer corps to exert their own influences and tastes at regimental or company level. By the mid-eighteenth century, the French and the British, as well as others, had nominally numbered the regiments of their armies to assign seniority. In practice, regiments were typically still referred to by the names of their colonels, or any royal or regional sobriquet, harkening back to their feudal origins. Published charts, correspondence, and orderly books of the French or British armies during the War of the Austrian Succession or the Seven Years' War reveal limited use of numbers to refer to regiments in the field.[6]

The French soldier marched to the Seven Years' War dressed in a uniform relatively little changed since the beginning of the century, which even French officers disparaged as impractical and unhealthy. As French political and military ambitions declined and collapsed by the end of the war, military reforms increased dramatically, especially after the appointment of the Duc de Choiseul as minster of war in 1761. The reforms begun after this period have been characterized as a "watershed moment in military thought during the Enlightenment," and among them was the first serious reexamination of French military dress since the turn of the century.[7]

---

[6] Alan Forrest, *Soldiers of the French Revolution* (Durham, NC: Duke University Press, 1990), 28–29; Nora Waugh, *The Cut of Men's Clothes 1630–1900* (New York: Routledge, 1964), 52, 85; *Septième abrégé de la carte générale du militaire de France* (Paris, 1741); Ryan R. Gale, *"A Soldier-Like Way": The Material Culture of the British Infantry 1751–1768* (Elk River, MN: Track of the Wolf, 2007). On the use of titles rather than numeric designations, see "Moneypenny Orderly Book," *Bulletin of the Fort Ticonderoga Museum*, 13.2 (1971), 151–184 (184); "Troupes du Roi, Infanterie française et étrangère, année 1757," tome I, 10858 BIB, A1J 12, Musée de l'Armée, Paris; Sieurs de Montandre-Lonchamps, *Etat militaire de France, pour l'année 1758* (Paris, 1759).

[7] On the appearance of the French army in the early eighteenth century, see Aaron Wile, *Watteau's Soldiers: Scenes of Military Life in Eighteenth-Century France* (New York: Frick Collection, 2016); David D. Bien, "The Army in the French Enlightenment: Reform, Reaction and Revolution," *Past & Present*, 85.1 (1979), 68–98 (69).

Clothing regulations became more specific, diminishing the proprietary role of the officers. To read the 1747 *ordonnance* on clothing against that issued twenty years later in 1767 is to see how the king, through the minister of war, was exerting influence in an increasingly minute way. While it may seem a minor point that something as small as a button less than an inch wide became an object of royal concern, it remains important evidence of how deeply the state was willing to assert its control.[8]

In his posthumous *Reveries*, the French marshal Maurice, Comte de Saxe, one of the most influential military authors of the day, asserted that "Matters of the utmost importance depend sometimes on trifles, which escape our notice."[9] Saxe urged that "the custom of calling troops … after the names of provinces or commanding officers, ought to be abolished." He recommended a brass marker worn on the shoulder with the soldiers' legion and regiment number (anticipating the shoulder sleeve insignia of the nineteenth and twentieth centuries). Saxe even suggested that the men be tattooed with the number of the regiment, including the remarkably optimistic idea that the noblemen of the officer corps should set the example. He reasoned that "the exploits of a corps which has any fixed title, are not so soon forgotten, as those of one which bears the name of its colonel only; because that is subject to be changed, and the remembrance of their former actions will then be apt to cease, together with that of their name."[10] Officers and men would be accordingly encouraged to reflect on their own contributions to an institution that would outlive them, granting them a greater stake in the honor and history of their regiment. Saxe's opinion was a rather profound acknowledgment of the personal motivation of the private soldier, itself a growing interest among military theorists in the age of reform. His recommendation that members of the officer corps lead the way with regimental tattoos illustrates how reforms of this era were often couched or implemented along traditional lines of authority and hierarchy. Although the French army adopted numbered buttons, they never implemented Saxe's full proposal.[11]

---

[8] James C. Riley, *The Seven Years War and the Old Regime in France: The Economic and Financial Toll* (Princeton, NJ: Princeton University Press, 2014), 82; Christy Pichichero, "Le Soldat Sensible: Military Psychology and Social Egalitarianism in the Enlightenment French Army," *French Historical Studies*, 31.4 (2008), 553–580 (574).

[9] Maurice de Saxe, *Reveries, or, Memoirs Concerning the Art of War* (Edinburgh, 1759), 57. Louis Ph. Sloos, *Gewapend met Kenis: 500 Jahr Militaire Boekcultuur in Nederland* (Nijmegen: Utgeverij Vantilt, 2012), 181–200.

[10] Saxe, *Reveries*, xi, 39, 56–57, 325.

[11] Pichichero, "Soldat Sensible," 566–567.

In an *ordonnance* issued on December 10, 1762, the buttons of French soldiers' uniforms were ordered to be marked with the number of their regiments. For some time, uniforms continued to combine functional buttons and buttonholes with decorative buttons on cuffs and pocket flaps. The increasing presence of numbered buttons – made in a uniform "scroll and dot" pattern, as collectors refer to them – privileged the numeric designation of a soldier's regiment as opposed to the name of its commander or nominal regional title. The numbers cast into the metal of these buttons reflects the centralization of the French military in the late eighteenth century as well as the monarchy's increasing organizational control over the military. Although regional designations were retained, numbering clearly indicated that these regiments belonged to a centralized organization with a rational structure.[12]

These early moves towards reform culminated in regulations issued in 1779 and 1786 that made numbered military buttons part of a complex and highly developed system of identification. The infantry was organized into classes of six regiments. Each class was further broken down into divisions of three regiments, and each division was identified by either yellow or white metal buttons and one of two pocket flap styles, worn vertically or horizontally. In addition, every class bore a distinctive facing color, which could be applied as solid-colored lapels, cuffs, or both. This formalization of regimental identification was in keeping with broader Enlightenment impulses to categorize and quantify. This systematic structure made every regiment completely distinct from every other, shifting authority towards the crown and away from proprietary colonels who had hitherto exercised extensive authority over their own corps.[13]

French reforms achieved the greatest level of control over military dress, but the system was undercut by the dynamism of reform as well as by the official persistence of noble privileges these very systems were designed to police. The pace of reform, the passion expressed by partisans, and the relatively rapid succession of ministers of war led to a dizzying number of regulations issued from the end of the Seven Years' War to the fall of the Bastille. Comprehensive uniform regulations were promulgated for clothing beginning in 1762 and subsequently in 1767, 1775,

---

[12] *Ordonnance du Roy Concernant l'Infanterie Françoise. Du 10 Décembre 1762* (Paris, 1762); Troiani and Kochan, *Insignia of Independence*, 260–85. Numbered buttons were worn on coats and waistcoats; breeches used cloth-covered buttons.

[13] *Règlement Arrêté par le Roi, Pour l'Habillement & l'Équipment de ses Troupes. Du 21 Février 1779* (Paris, 1779); *Règlement Arrêté par le Roi, Pour l'Habillement & l'Équipment de ses Troupes. Du 1er Octobre 1786* (Paris, 1786).

1776, 1779, and 1786. In each of these there was typically a renumbering of the army's regiments, which ultimately undercut the clarity of the numbering program itself. Additionally, units such as the Swiss regiments and some guards retained privileges such as plain buttons throughout the period. Explicit exceptions were made for the *regiments des princes*, who were often allowed to incorporate elements of their own coats of arms into the buttons of their regiment.[14]

Buttons in Britain

The British adopted numbered buttons through an Order in Council in September 1767, formalizing their use in a royal clothing warrant issued in 1768. Some regiments moved quickly to introduce the new buttons, such as the 28th Regiment of Foot, which commissioned "buttons with the number of the regiment" just two months after the order.[15] The production and use of numbered buttons, however, reflects the relatively diffuse authority of the British military. This is highlighted by the lack of a uniform pattern for British military buttons, even from those recovered from a single site of British occupation and operations in North America (Figure 10.1). All made of a pewter alloy, the largest, that of the 16th Regiment of Foot at the top left, measures 1 in wide, while the smallest, from the 24th Regiment of Foot at the center bottom, is 11/16 of an inch. British military regulations provided for buttons to be largely functional, to hold up cuffs and button-down lapels, and noted that buttons should be numbered but gave no instructions or designs for how that was to be done. Regimental uniforms were approved and "sealed" annually by a clothing board; colonels hired agents, who negotiated with contractors and subcontractors in England and Ireland to manufacture uniform components. As the examples in Figure 10.1 illustrate, this produced a wide variety of patterns, some with Arabic numerals, some with Roman numerals, and with a range of designs including rope-like borders, insignia like wreaths and crowns, geometric shapes, abbreviations, heraldic emblems, and even copies of the French "scroll and dot," such as those of the 9th and 62nd Regiments. As far away as Rhode Island in New England, Britons were informed about buttons of

---

[14] Hurley, *French Military Buttons*, 27–28; Troiani and Kochan, *Insignia of Independence*, 260–261.
[15] H. G. Parkyn, "Buttons of the British Regular Army," *Journal of the Society for Army Historical Research*, 13.51 (1934), 159–169; Percy Sumner, "Notes of Regimental Uniforms, from the Irish Treasury Papers, 1713–1782," *Journal of the Society for Army Historical Research*, 14.56 (1935), 206–220 (214).

Figure 10.1 British military buttons recovered at Fort Ticonderoga in the United States, 1768–1781. Fort Ticonderoga Museum Collection. Photo: Gavin Ashworth.

a "new make, marked with the number of the regiments." Like the French, there were also exceptions to the new buttons, with some regiments retaining privileges, such as the senior regiment of the English household infantry, the 1st Foot Guards, who continued to wear plain buttons throughout the period, as did the Royal Regiment of Artillery through the mid-1780s.[16]

The change to numbered buttons in Britain and its colonies was not welcomed by all. A piece in *The Dublin Mercury* as late as 1770, which circulated to North America, reported:

some officers of the army are highly displeased with the late orders from the war office for numbering the buttons on their regimental cloaths: "D—n me, says a young ensign, at St. James' coffee-house, the other day, what a degradation here! Why, it was but this day I was passing the Temple and a ticket-porter came up to me and insolently accosted me with, Brother, what number?"

Although humorous, the anecdote acknowledges the increasingly impersonal use of regimental numbers. Alongside orders that "No Colonel is to put his arms, crest, device, or livery, on any part of the appointments of the

---

[16] Hew Strachan, *British Military Uniforms 1768–1796: The Dress of the British Army from Official Sources* (London: Arms and Armour Press, 1975), 11, 14, 172, 174; Troiani and Kochan, *Insignia of Independence*, 1–6, 21, 31; William Y. Carman, "Early Buttons of the Foot Guards," *Journal of the Society for Army Historical Research*, 68.276 (1990), 226–231; *Newport Mercury*, June 6–13, 1768.

Regiments under his command," numbered buttons further diminished expressions of proprietorship and reinforced centralized royal control.[17]

New Buttons for a New Nation

As we have seen so far, the reforms and the debates surrounding military buttons traveled to North America both on the clothing of soldiers and through print culture. Changes to military dress occurring in Europe were followed by American settlers and informed their own approach to uniforms during the Revolutionary War. As the Continental Congress tried to legitimize its military forces and create national unity from the disparate peoples of British North America, military buttons became a key location and test of their ability to institute and centralize authority.[18] Prior to 1776, individual colonies had started to follow recent European practices by authorizing numerically designated buttons. In 1775, only three months after the commencement of hostilities, the colony of Massachusetts ordered numeric buttons for the regiments of its "Grand Army" laying siege to the British in Boston. Despite the lack of any real industrial infrastructure, over 70,000 cast pewter-alloy buttons were produced in at least twenty-two patterns, and other colonies instituted similar measures on a smaller scale. In the end, the logistical reality of matching coats manufactured across the colony with buttons designed for specific regiments in the field proved too complex, and officials resolved that the buttons "be set on those Coats that they now have or may hereafter receive without Buttons as soon as may be, and this without any respect to the Numbers of the Regiments as was first propos'd," threatening to undermine the whole project.[19]

By 1776, the commander of the Continental Army, George Washington, troubled by the division and faction that regional distinctions prompted within the army, lobbied to create a national force. He proposed numerically numbering the whole Continental Army and drawing its officers from across the states of the young nation. While he failed in the latter, he was

---

[17] *Dublin Mercury*, August 23–25, 1770; *Massachusetts Spy*, November 15–19, 1770. On proscriptions against livery and proprietary insignia, see the text of the warrant, reprinted in Strachan, *British Military Uniforms*, 171–178.

[18] To John Adams from Henry Knox, May 16, 1776, *Founders Online*, National Archives, https://founders.archives.gov/documents/Adams/06-04-02-0081, accessed April 11, 2019 [Original source: *The Adams Papers, Papers of John Adams*, vol. 4, *February–August 1776*, ed. Robert J. Taylor (Cambridge, MA: Harvard University Press, 1979), 189–191.]

[19] Henry M. Cooke, IV, "The Massachusetts Bounty Coat of 1775," *Brigade Dispatch*, 28 (1998), 2–10 (2–4); Troiani and Kochan, *Insignia of Independence*, 220–222.

successful in numerically designating the regiments under his command without regard to state identification. This led to a Continental Army of twenty-seven numbered regiments like any other European force. However, the archaism of referring to regiments by the name of their colonels continued in the Continental Army. Furthermore, regional divisions and the relative lack of authority of the Continental Congress undercut even this limited success. The numbered army only counted the regiments under Washington's direct control, mostly from New England, leaving economically prosperous or distant states to go their own way. These states produced their own regimental buttons, which represented their own state identities and even parallel attempts at numerical ordering of their state forces. The experience of the Continental Army reveals the reach and the limitations of enlightened military reforms in the face of political and cultural division and economic realities.[20]

Buttons in the Ground

From North America to the Caribbean, from Africa to Australasia, military buttons, similar to those found at Fort Ticonderoga, are markers of the spread of European colonization across the globe.[21] Owing to the durability of the pewter and copper alloys they were made from, military buttons are among the most datable and identifiable features in archaeological excavations. Their presence, and their clarity, can lull archaeologists and historians into a false sense of security.[22] For instance, some buttons recovered at Fort Ticonderoga belong to British regiments with no known presence there. The

---

[20] Robert K. Wright, Jr., *The Continental Army* (Washington, DC: Center of Military History, 1986), 45–47, 50; Troiani and Kochan, *Insignia of Independence*, 191–254.

[21] Horacio De Rosa, Nicolás Ciarlo, and Hernan Svoboda, "Estudio sobre botones de peltre hallados en la corbeta HMS Swift (1770)" in *Arqueometría Latinoamericana: Segundo Congreso Argentino y Primero. Latinoamericano* (Buenos Aires: Comisión Nacional de Energía Atómica, 2009), 227–32; Chuck Meide, "'Cast away off the bar': The Archaeological Investigation of British Period Shipwrecks in St. Augustine," *Florida Historical Quarterly*, 93.3 (2015), 354–386 (378); Laurie A. Wilkie and Paul Farnsworth, "Trade and the Construction of Bahamian Identity: A Multiscalar Exploration," *International Journal of Historical Archaeology*, 3.4 (1999), 283–320 (296); Martin Hall, Antonia Malan, Sharon Amann, Lyn Honeyman, Taft Kiser, and Gabrielle Ritchie, "The Archaeology of Paradise," *Goodwin Series*, 7 (1993), 40–58 (58). For a later example of military buttons marking European colonization in Australasia, see Nigel Prickett, "The History and Archaeology of Queen's Redoubt, South Auckland," *Records of the Auckland Museum*, 40 (2003), 5–37 (33–35).

[22] Ivor Noël Hume, *A Passion for the Past: The Odyssey of a Transatlantic Archaeologist* (Charlottesville: University of Virginia Press, 2010), 268.

distribution of marked military buttons archaeologically, in fact, often represents the tensions they embody more than the precision of identification that reformers sought to impose and that archaeologists rely on to understand sites. Like the military regulations that governed their use, small numbered buttons represent ideal structures of authority, developed through negotiations of power between the crown, proprietary colonels, captains, and occasionally even the rank and file. As such, archaeological recoveries express not only the evolving and negotiated relationship of individuals and authority in the early modern state but also the exigencies of wartime, in which logistical systems to support imperial war were still developing.[23]

Eighteenth-century states, especially maritime empires such as France and Great Britain, became increasingly successful at projecting their power at great distances. By the time numbered military buttons became commonplace in the late 1760s, both nations were sending tens of thousands of soldiers across the globe, supported by a vast infrastructure of shipping, finance, and supply. Despite this, the communications lag, compounded by local and regional exigencies, often mitigated against the seamlessness of these operations. Troops on distant stations sometimes waited months, even years, for supplies from Europe, adopting in the meantime any number of local expedients, which operated against the power of uniforms to represent centralized authority to soldiers, their enemies, and surrounding subjects. This was especially true for states in the process of formation such as the United States, where the logistical realities outstripped the ability of officials to enact the authority buttons reflected even into the early nineteenth century.[24]

---

[23] It should also be noted that the adoption of numbered buttons was not uniform across the Atlantic world; the dynamism of the French experience, the diffuse authority represented by the British, or even the mixed results of the American experiment stand in contrast to other nation states, such as Prussia or Spain, that persisted with the identification of regiments with colonels and regions and thus maintained the use of plain buttons combined with distinctive regimental lace and facings until much later in the century. See Daniel Hohrath, *Freiderich der Grosse und de Uniformierung der Preussischen Armee von 1740 bis 1786*, 2 vols. (Vienna: Verlag Militaria, 2011); Troiani and Kochan, *Insignia of Independence*, 286; John T. Powell, "Spanish Colonial Artifacts of the Gulf Coast Region, Part I: Cast Metal Military Buttons, ca. 1700–1795," *Military Collector & Historian*, 46.1 (1994), 2–11.

[24] On the local challenges of maintaining military dress for British imperial garrisons, see Michael N. McConnell, *Army & Empire: British Soldiers on the American Frontier, 1758–1775* (Lincoln: University of Nebraska Press, 2004), 64–65. One Spanish militia regiment was not resupplied with new uniforms for twenty years; see Christon I. Archer, "Bourbon Finances and Military Policy in New Spain, 1759–1812," *The Americas*, 37.3 (1981), 315–350 (334). For similar challenges in the young US army, see Alan D Gaff, *Bayonets in the Wilderness: Anthony Wayne's Legion in the Old Northwest* (Norman: University of Oklahoma Press, 2008), 91, 227; Robert J. Moore and Michael Haynes, *Lewis & Clark, Tailor Made, Trail Worn: Army Life, Clothing & Weapons of the Corps of Discovery* (Helena, MT: Farcountry Press, 2003), 161–163.

Even for the largest and most developed empires, the nature of long-distance military campaigns and the practices of early modern militaries calls the classifying function of military buttons into question. Both the British and the French relied on a practice described in English as drafting, which consisted of stripping units of all available manpower to augment regiments remaining in theater or being shipped overseas, leaving the officers and noncommissioned officers to recruit their regiments anew. Given the cumbersome apparatus of military clothing procurement, which sometimes required over a year from orders being placed to clothing being delivered (longer for manufacturers to receive payment), men shifted from one regiment to another would often remain in their old uniforms for a year or more afterward. Similarly, transfers of units often outstripped the ability of their clothing to keep up, with shipments arriving where the regiments had been months or years after they had departed. Stocks of such clothing were often raided by units that remained in theater to equip recruits or to alleviate deficiencies in their own clothing supply owing to shipwrecks or capture by the enemy. It could take years to balance accounts for the use of such clothing.[25]

While drafting occurred in peacetime, circumstances like these increased during wartime, especially during the most notable conflict of this period, the American War of Independence, which involved substantially more operations across the Atlantic than in Europe. Both the French and British drafted men from regiments in Europe into those serving in North America. At various times, American troops relied heavily on captured British clothing. A broad range of French buttons are found in North America as a result of the changes in regimental numbering systems between 1767 and 1779 as well as the influx of army soldiers serving on ships who were landed to serve on shore. Together these circumstances mean buttons regularly turn up at archaeological sites from regiments with no history of service there.[26]

Certain small objects, such as coins and pottery sherds, are deeply important to dating and interpreting archaeological sites, and the clear

---

[25] Don N. Hagist, "What the Drunken Soldier Wore: Non-Uniform Clothing in British Regiments," *The Brigade Dispatch*, 24.3 (1994), 16–18; Hurley, *French Military Buttons*, 29–31. On the timing of clothing issues in the British off-reckoning system, see "The Custom and Practice of the Army Concerning Off Reckonings," April 25, 1772, WO 30/105/2, The National Archives, London (TNA). For regiments outstripping the ability of their clothing to keep up, see Charles Jenkinson to Henry Clinton, November 1, 1783, PRO 30/55/4/187, TNA. For an example of a unit being offered the clothing of another, see Adam Gordon to Guy Carleton, November 17, 1782, PRO 30/55/30/77, TNA.

[26] Troiani and Kochan, *Insignia of Independence*, 148–150, 191–192, 260–261.

numbering of military buttons would seem to mark them as one of these artifacts. From an archaeological and historical point of view, however, the physical intentionality the numbers on these small objects represent often stands in contrast to the actual circumstances and practices in which they were used. Marked military buttons are commonly used to identify specific units and confirm their presence. The military regulations of the era are among the most referenced sources by archaeologists and historians since they were actively and widely circulated. Yet military regulations, and the physical buttons themselves, represent how military officials attempted to assert authority over the physical world, and archaeologists' interpretations of such numbered buttons have sometimes revealed a lack of understanding of how historical forces such as drafting of soldiers, long-distance imperial service, and overlapping regulations acted against the uniformity and centralization that buttons represent. The archaeological record of small buttons complicates our understanding of complex and dynamic institutions such as eighteenth-century militaries. The precise composition of military forces at a particular place and time, down to the level of individuals, can seem like military minutiae, or worse, trivia, but these factors have a profound value for understanding the outcome of historic events. The transfers of manpower that archaeological buttons materialize shaped the personal and professional bonds between soldiers and the capabilities of units, affecting the outcome of battles and campaigns.[27]

To conclude, numbered military buttons remind us that the objects around us, however small, and the concepts they represent are, in fact, historical artifacts that embody the convergence of many cultural factors. For the time period under scrutiny in this chapter, numbered military buttons

[27] For a case of using archaeological buttons to shift the historical record, see John M. Bingeman and Arthur T. Mack, "The Dating of Military Buttons: Second Interim Report Based on Artefacts Recovered from the 18th-Century Wreck Invincible, between 1979 and 1990," *International Journal of Nautical Archaeology*, 26.1 (1997), 39–50. This analysis has been hotly contested between archaeologists, historians, and "uniformologists." See A. T. Mack, D. R. Houghton, and William Y. Carman, "'Invincible' Buttons," *Journal of the Society for Army Historical Research*, 69.279 (1991), 192–196; René Chartrand, "Buttons of the 50th and 51st Foot, 1754–1757," *Journal of the Society for Army Historical Research*, 70.281 (1992), 60–62; Brian D. N. Stevens, "'Invincible' Buttons," *Journal of the Society for Army Historical Research*, 70.283 (1992), 205–207. The drafts, recruits, and detachments that button deposits such as those at Ticonderoga often represent are increasingly being understood as contributing meaningfully to combat effectiveness, compounding additional factors, and ultimately impacting the outcome of military campaigns; see David L. Preston, *Braddock's Defeat: The Battle of the Monongahela and the Road to Revolution* (Oxford: Oxford University Press, 2018), 56–58; Eric Schnitzer, "The Tactics of the Battles of Saratoga" in William A. Griswold and Donald W. Linebaugh (eds.), *The Saratoga Campaign: An Embattled Landscape* (Hanover, NH: University Press of New England, 2016), 39–79 (57, 67).

articulate a perspective on centralization and authority that was still developing. Their small, cast, metallic surfaces physically embody evolving structures of power. On its surface, military dress might be seen as among the most authoritarian forms of material culture, but social, cultural, and economic factors as well as the realities of increasingly long-range imperial service prevented uniforms from fully enacting their authoritarian intentions. Far from self-evident historical markers, military buttons reflect the dynamic nature of the age of reform, and the power of even small pieces of material culture to reflect and encode societal change.

11 | Two Men's Leather Letter Cases

Mercantile Pride and Hierarchies of Display

PAULINE RUSHTON

Thousands of examples of small personal possessions from the eighteenth century survive in UK museum collections.[1] For a variety of reasons, the vast majority of them may never be displayed or even fully researched. For some objects, this neglect stems from a lack of opportunity for exhibition or scant details of provenance, but many others have been overlooked owing to the materials from which they were made. There is a long-established, but largely unacknowledged, hierarchy of materials in the museum discipline of the decorative arts. This ranking of objects has often been closely connected to the rarity and sometimes the monetary value of small things, as well as the aesthetic appeal of the piece in question. In many museum collections, items made by the goldsmith, silversmith, enameller, and jeweler, for example, have taken precedence in curatorial regard over those made by the potter or weaver. This chapter studies one example of small, personal objects from the eighteenth century: men's letter cases, an early form of wallet, which on average measured around 20 cm by 12 cm and were made to fit in the capacious pockets of greatcoats.[2] Such cases were mostly, but not exclusively, made of leather, which, however finely worked, settled them near the bottom of the hierarchy of materials in the world of decorative arts curation.

My focus here is on two particular examples of the letter case, both of them dated and belonging to two named individuals involved in trade.[3] Despite their limited embellishments, small size, and leather

---

[1] I would like to acknowledge the financial assistance I received from the Art Fund, in the form of a Jonathan Ruffer Curatorial Grant, to attend the conference "Small Things in the Eighteenth Century," University of York, June 5–6, 2019, at which I presented a preliminary version of this chapter.

[2] The pockets of men's waistcoats and breeches were not large enough to hold them during most of this period.

[3] These two objects have been in the decorative art collections of the National Museums Liverpool for many years, but until recently neither had ever been researched or exhibited. In 2018–2020, they were displayed for the first time at the Walker Art Gallery, Liverpool, as part of the temporary exhibition "Dressed to Impress: Fashion in the Eighteenth Century": Black leather letter case, embossed with *Jno. Bridge, Liverpoole, Mercht, 1750*, the gift of Mrs. Laithwaite, 1976, 1976.557; Red leather letter case, embossed with *Harold Hillam, Newry, 1767*, the gift of James H. Robinson, via Leicester Museum, 1958, 58.4.

material, these letter cases prove to be just as effective in providing us with insights into some of the key social and economic developments of the eighteenth century as any refined porcelain teapot or cup. The cases, through the biographies of their owners, provide tangible links to several aspects of eighteenth-century commerce: the transatlantic slave trade; the growth of the mercantile elite and their commercial networks within the consumer revolution; and the development of manufacturing and retail networks in English towns. The cases' material details and composition find further significance when compared with other extant examples and also when placed within the contexts of contemporary print culture, including their appearance in trade cards, novels, criminal trials, and accounts of slave trade voyages.[4] Such letter cases were acquired and carried by their owners not just as a means of transporting bills of exchange, letters, and sometimes notebooks but also as a way of establishing and signaling to contemporaries mercantile class identity and rising social status.[5]

Until now, the obscurity of letter cases held in museum collections has perhaps inhibited research into their consumption and social significance. Some research has already been directed towards merchants' houses and their furnishings, and to their owners' taste in paintings and fashionable dress as markers of social status.[6] Much less attention has been paid to their small personal possessions. In this chapter, beginning with the biographies of these cases' owners, I demonstrate

---

[4] My interpretations are informed by a group of eighteen very similar letter cases that I have traced so far in seventy other British collections, both public and private, and which I refer to here as the sample group. In the sample group, I compare the distinctive features of manufacture found in the letter cases, consider the likely circumstances of their production and retail, and seek to establish if they were typically owned primarily by the merchant and the high-level tradesman, as opposed to those in other social groups such as yeoman farmers, husbandmen, laborers, or servants.

[5] Bills of exchange were the forerunners of the modern check, financial instruments by which payments were made and credit extended between individuals via a third party. See B. L. Anderson, "The Lancashire Bill System and Its Liverpool Practitioners: The Case of a Slave Merchant" in W. H. Chaloner and Barry M. Ratcliffe (eds.), *Trade and Transport: Essays in Economic History in Honour of T. S. Willan* (Manchester: Manchester University Press, 1977), 59–97. Liverpool slave merchants in particular made use of such bills from the 1750s onwards in long-term credit arrangements. See Kenneth Morgan, "Liverpool's Dominance in the British Slave Trade, 1740–1807" in David Richardson, Suzanne Schwarz and Anthony Tibbles (eds.), *Liverpool and Transatlantic Slavery* (Liverpool: Liverpool University Press, 2007), 14–42, (32–33).

[6] Mireille Galinou (ed.), *City Merchants and the Arts* (London: Oblong Creative for the Corporation of London, 2004).

how such small, plain objects link up with the web of commercial and colonial networks that bound eighteenth-century Liverpool to enslaved labor in the Atlantic world. The size and ordinariness of the leather cases contrast sharply with the violence and exploitation with which their owners were involved within that world. I then turn to an exploration of the making and selling of letter cases as part of the growth of a flourishing consumer culture. Finally, I show how these small, unassuming objects articulated the social and commercial complexities associated with the emerging mercantile class, acting as markers of status and prestige.[7]

Liverpool's Letter Cases and the Slave Trade

The earlier of the two letter cases (Figure 11.1, top) examined here is made from black leather, with an interior of tan and green leather, and its internal compartments lined with red and white marbled paper. Its original scrolling silver clasp, although broken, is still attached. The case is embossed beneath the front flap in gold leaf with the abbreviated words "Jno. Bridge, Liverpoole, Mercht, 1750"; this name, profession, and date allow us to gather a history of its owner and his place within the slaving trade of eighteenth-century Liverpool. John Bridge was born on February 5, 1714, the son of Edward Bridge, a cooper, and his wife, Mary.[8] When, in July 1737, aged twenty-three, John Bridge married Mary Aspinwell, he was described as a mariner in their marriage record (there is no record of the couple's address during their early married life).[9] Bridge likely learned the mariner's craft from his teenage years, but since the muster rolls of Liverpool ships' crews survive only from 1775 onwards, it is not known which vessels he served on as a young man.[10] He was heavily involved in the Liverpool slave trade, both as

---

[7] See Simon Gikandi, *Slavery and the Culture of Taste* (Princeton, NJ and Oxford: Princeton University Press, 2011), 81. He argues that "the more they became entangled in the business of transforming black bodies into objects of trade, the more the slavers sought to secure their own identity as cultured subjects."

[8] Baptismal record, February 17, 1713/14, baptismal register 1704–1737, p. 20, entry 22, St. Peter's Church, Liverpool.

[9] Marriage record, July 6, 1737, marriage register 1737–1754, p. 1, entry 20, St. Peter's Church, Liverpool.

[10] Stephen D. Behrendt, "The Captains in the British Slave Trade from 1785 to 1807," *Transactions of the Historic Society of Lancashire and Cheshire*, 140 (1990), 79–140 (81).

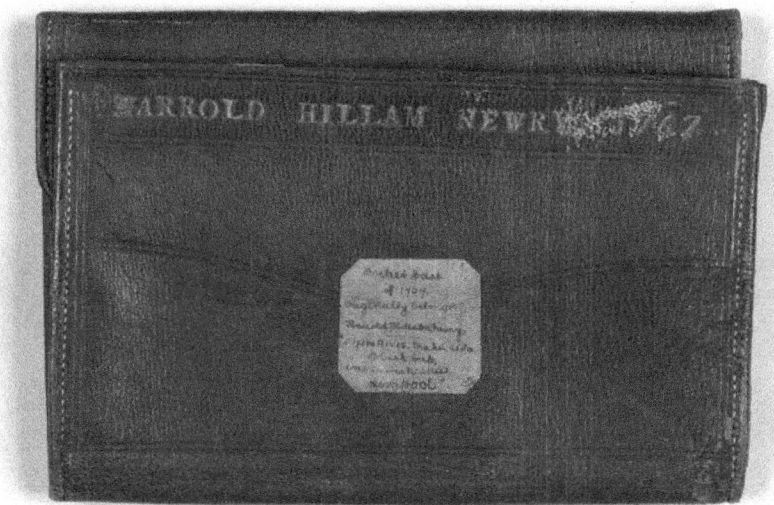

Figure 11.1 Letter cases of John Bridge, 1750 (top), and Harold Hillam, 1767 (bottom). Photograph courtesy of National Museums Liverpool.

an investor in many voyages and, on two occasions, as a ship's master. Between 1745 and 1769, Bridge is listed as a partner in fifty separate slaving voyages, involving sixteen different ships and forty-nine different co-investors, many of them members of Liverpool's ruling elite, including three mayors of the town.¹¹ In 1745, he captained his first voyage of a slave vessel, the *Nancy*.¹² In 1749, Bridge acted for the second, and last, time as a slave-ship captain when he took co-command of another ship named *Nancy*.¹³ In taking command only twice, Bridge was typical of his fellow captains involved in slavery, in that, on average, the majority of them made no more than four voyages as master, before concentrating on investment rather than the captaining of the forced transportation of enslaved people.¹⁴

Bridge acquired his small leather case after he had firmly established himself in the slave trade. In 1750, aged thirty-six, he bought the letter case to hold his documents and bills of exchange and had his name stamped upon it, proudly proclaiming himself a "merchant." Bridge may have used the case to carry a copy of a daily pocket journal in which to record his business appointments, cash flow, and receipts, while keeping an eye on the fortunes of his fellow merchants and competitors whose ships were also detailed therein.¹⁵ The label "merchant" was used mainly to describe a member of the mercantile elite, someone who dealt in overseas trade and could extend credit to others. But during this period a multitude of traders at different levels might also describe themselves as "merchants," as shown in surviving street and trade directories from towns and cities across

---

[11] *Slave Voyages Database* (www.slavevoyages.org/voyage, accessed January 3, 2019), voyage identification numbers (in chronological order) 90028, 90029, 90097, 90248, 90236, 90196, 90198, 90249, 90199, 90360, 90250, 90197, 90237, 90409, 90200, 90238, 90251, 90432, 90517, 90252, 90518, 90433, 90253, 90594, 90595, 90254, 90677, 90519, 90434, 90757, 90520, 90435, 90255, 90785, 90521, 90256, 90758, 90522, 90804, 90257, 90523, 91005, 90998, 90805, 91006, 90999, 90524, 90806, 91000, 90807. The last of these voyages that Bridge can have personally invested in was 90805, that of *The Prince of Wales*, which embarked on March 31, 1763. According to his will, Bridge died sometime before April 1763, but he left to his only son James "*all my shares in the shipping and their effects.*" This would explain why Bridge's name appears as an investor until 1769, some six years after his death. James Bridge evidently invested in his father's name, as well as on his own account, on four occasions, voyages 91101, 91102, 91258, 91277. See the will of John Bridge, April 15, 1763, WCW/Supra/C446A/56, Lancashire Archives.

[12] *Slave Voyages Database*, voyage identification number 90028.

[13] *Slave Voyages Database*, voyage identification number 90248. Bridge is listed as captain together with Francis Bare.

[14] Behrendt, "Captains in the British Slave Trade," 87.

[15] Bridge would, undoubtedly, have been aware of *The Liverpool Memorandum Book, or Gentleman's, Merchant's and Tradesman's daily pocket journal for the year 1753* (Liverpool, 1753). The section headed "a list of vessels trading from Liverpool to the coast of Africa … December 1752" includes details of one of his ships: *Vigilant*, Wm. Freeman [master], Wind and Gold Coast (missing) J. Bridge & Co [owners]. See the *Slave Voyages Database*, voyage identification number 90360. The *Vigilant* is recorded as either shipwrecked or destroyed after the disembarkation of its enslaved people.

Britain.[16] It is clear that contemporaries held those who traded overseas in particular esteem, with one commentator referring to the merchant as "the Life, Spring and Motion of the Trading World ... wherever he comes, wherever he lives, Wealth and Plenty follow him: the Poor is set to work, Manufactures flourish, Poverty is banished and Public Credit increases."[17] The timing of his purchase and the addition of his professional status, then, suggest Bridge's eagerness to proclaim his mercantile status on his small letter case.

Bridge's active participation in Liverpool's slave trade was not the only way in which he amassed his fortune. John and Sheryllynne Haggerty, in their work on the visualization of Liverpool's eighteenth-century merchant networks, have identified John Bridge as one of the lesser-known actors in the tangled web of the transatlantic slave trade.[18] However, he also took part in privateering.[19] During the Seven Years' War, Bridge invested in at least one privateering voyage, along with one of his long-standing co-investors in the slave trade.[20] By both these means, he became sufficiently well established for David Pope to consider him one of the 201 leading Liverpool slave merchants of the period 1750–1799, if not one of the most high profile.[21] When he died in 1763, Bridge left his wife, Mary, £3,000 in his will and his son, James, all his shares in his shipping interests, together with those in a rope works, a sugarhouse, and a pottery. At the time of his death, he was among the wealthiest of Liverpool's merchants.[22]

---

[16] Sheryllynne Haggerty, "The Structure of the Trading Community in Liverpool," *Transactions of the Historic Society of Lancashire and Cheshire*, 151 (2002), 97–125 (108–109). See also David Hancock, *Citizens of the World: London Merchants and the Integration of the British Atlantic Community, 1735–1785* (Cambridge: Cambridge University Press, 1995), 9–10; Penelope J. Corfield, "Giving Directions to the Town: The Early Town Directories," *Urban History Yearbook*, 11 (1984), 22–35.

[17] R. Campbell, *The London Tradesman* (1747; David & Charles reprints, 2014), 284.

[18] John Haggerty and Sheryllynne Haggerty, "Networking with a Network: The Liverpool African Committee 1750–1810," *Enterprise and Society*, 18.3 (2017), 566–590.

[19] Sheryllyne Haggerty, "Risk, Risk Networks and Privateering in Liverpool during the Seven Years War, 1756–1763," *International Journal of Maritime History*, 30.1 (2017), 30–51 (44–45). See also Gomer Williams, *History of the Liverpool Privateers and Letters of Marque, with an account of the Liverpool Slave Trade* (London, 1897), 155.

[20] Haggerty, "Risk, Risk Networks and Privateering," 44. The co-investor in privateering with whom Bridge associated most frequently on his slaving voyages was William Gregson, while his associates in privateering were Henry Hardwar, Edward Fryer, Thomas Pinnwold, and James Sanders.

[21] David Pope, "The Wealth and Social Aspirations of Liverpool's Slave Merchants of the Second Half of the Eighteenth Century" in Richardson, Schwarz, and Tibbles, *Liverpool and Transatlantic Slavery*, 164–226.

[22] In today's terms, £3,000 equates to more than £431,000; see www.measuringworth.com/calculators//ppoweruk/, accessed October 12, 2020. The will of John Bridge, April 15, 1763, WCW/Supra/C446A/56, Lancashire Archives. William Gregson, with whom Bridge co-invested in forty-one voyages, was one of the wealthier merchants, leaving £12,500 in his personal estate when he died in 1801. See Pope, "Wealth and Social Aspirations," 211.

The second letter case (Figure 11.1, bottom) under discussion here looks similar in appearance to that owned by Bridge but is made from red Morocco leather. It, too, is lined with tan-colored leather and the compartments are lined with red and white marbled paper. While its original metal clasp is now missing, it is also embossed beneath the front flap in gold, with the words "Harrold Hillam Newry" and the year "1767." This example bears the maker's paper label, "Joseph Rives, Maker, At the Black Cap, in Fenwick-Street, Liverpool." Harold Hillam was born in Newry (now in Northern Ireland) in 1744 and died there, aged seventy-eight, in 1822.[23] The town's earliest street directories reveal that he lived in Boat Street, near the Newry River, and list him under the heading "Merchants and Traders."[24] However, Hillam's name does not appear in other slave-voyage records, either as a ship's master or as an investor. Unlike John Bridge, he had no direct connection with the transatlantic slave trade. By 1760, at the age of sixteen, Hillam was working as a collector's clerk in the Custom House at Newry.[25] He held this post for almost the next fifty-eight years. It is not known why he traveled to Liverpool in 1767, aged twenty-three, where he visited Joseph Rives's shop in Fenwick Street and bought this letter case. If his trip was business related it may have been linked to the trade between Liverpool and Newry with which he would have been familiar as a customs officer.[26]

By the end of Bridge's life, he had established himself as a prominent Liverpool merchant, but Hillam's position was decidedly more modest. When Hillam retired in 1818, aged seventy-four, his salary stood at £100 per year and he still held his original post of collector's clerk, although he was also working as the clerk of the cheque, organizing workmen in the Newry Custom House and keeping accounts of their earnings.[27] Despite

[23] Harold's gravestone in the churchyard of St. Patrick's Church of Ireland in Newry reads, "Here are interred the remains of Mary Hillam who departed this life on the 6th Apl. 1820 aged 73yrs. And of her husband Harold Hillam who departed this life on the 29th September 1822 aged 78 yrs. This stone was erected to their memory by Thomas Hillam of Liverpool." R. S. J. Clarke (ed.), Old Families of Newry and District, from Gravestone Inscriptions, Wills and Biographical Notes (Belfast: Ulster Historical Foundation, 1998), 51.

[24] Thomas Bradshaw, *The General Directory of Newry, Armagh and Others* (Newry, 1820), 11.

[25] Parliamentary Papers, Finance Accounts of Ireland for the Year Ended Fifth January 1811, Appendix A.3, p. 4.

[26] In the 1760s, when Hillam visited Liverpool, the export trade from his hometown was dominated by linen. See David Dickson, Jan Parmentier, and Jane H. Ohlmeyer, *Irish and Scottish Mercantile Networks in Europe and Overseas in the Seventeenth and Eighteenth Centuries* (Ghent: Academia Press, 2007), 308.

[27] Parliamentary Papers, *Public Offices, 23 January–11 July 1821*, vol. 14, part II, Ireland, 64. His annual pension, after such long service, was £340 per annum, or a very respectable £24,380 in today's money. Hillam's will was proved on October 15, 1822, and was originally held in the Public Record Office of Ireland, now the National Archives of Ireland, but unfortunately was destroyed in 1922, together with many other records, during the Civil War. No copy survives.

the differences in their financial circumstances and social standing, and the different points in their careers at which they acquired their letter cases, both Bridge and Hillam were attracted to the ownership and use of these small objects as a means of signaling to contemporaries their membership of an admired group in society, the mercantile body. Their aspirations were fully realized in the next generation, when Bridge's son, James, and Hillam's younger brother, Thomas, both took advantage of their social mobility, by moving into a more select area and calling themselves merchants and gentlemen.[28]

Making and Selling Small Letter Cases

During the eighteenth century, letter cases were made and retailed as part of the ever-expanding demand for consumer goods of all descriptions. John Bridge's letter case bears no maker's label so its place of production cannot be confirmed, but the materials for its manufacture are likely to have been readily available in Liverpool. The town's first street directory of 1766 lists two tanners and a leather seller, who may have supplied the main material, but letter-case makers also required marbled paper for the linings. Imported by stationers and booksellers from France and Germany, often via Holland, it was known as "Dutch paper." Some of these papers were made in Britain too. The retailer of one of the letter cases in my sample group, Thomas Davenport of Birmingham, makes it clear on his label that not only did he make letter cases himself, "stitched with gold or silver wire, neatly gilt," but that he also "makes marble paper as near as the Dutch."[29]

The same maker also stated that he "sets on silver and steel locks." The metal clasps on the letter cases in my sample group show that a limited

---

[28] James Bridge is listed in the 1766 and 1767 Liverpool street directories in Paradise Street in the town center. By 1773, he had moved to the gentrified northern suburb of Everton, where many other upwardly mobile merchants had settled. For the gentrification of Everton, see Pope, "Wealth and Social Aspirations," 170. Thomas Hillam (1752–1834) married a Liverpool linen draper, Mary Lathom (1753–1829), in 1789. First listed in the town's 1790 street directory as a bookkeeper, by 1815 he was described as a merchant (*The New Monthly Magazine*, 3 [1815], 480). By 1824, he too had moved to Everton, where Baines's street directory for that year described him as a gentleman, living at 12 Great Homer Street.

[29] Letter case, dated 1767, made by Henry Hall, Wednesbury, for Samuel Caldecot, Birmingham, and retailed by Thomas Davenport, T.211-1996, Collection of the Victoria & Albert Museum, London. Davenport is listed in the Birmingham street directory for 1770 as a letter-case maker at 107 Park Street, Birmingham. See *Sketchley's and Adams's Tradesman's True Guide or an Universal Directory for the towns of Birmingham, Wolverhampton, Walsall, Dudley* (Birmingham, 1770), s.v. "Davenport, Thomas."

number of designs were used, in steel, brass, and silver, meaning that customers could select the design and material that best suited their financial circumstances. Extant cases reveal that customers were most frequently drawn to elliptical and scrolling clasp shapes in comparison with rectangular, oval, and diamond-shaped ones.[30] The close similarity of clasp design across the sample group, especially the elliptical and scrolling examples made from stamped brass or steel, indicates a centralized location for their mass production. This is most likely to have been in the independent workshops of Birmingham and its surrounding villages, such as Wednesbury and Bilston, where small-scale metal components of all kinds were produced in a process characterized by extensive division of labor.[31] The button, buckle, and allied trades included the production of all sorts of other fastenings and mounts. Letter-case makers could select such components from printed catalogues and price lists offered by the manufacturers' agents and ordered by post.[32] The metal clasps and the embossed gold lettering, spelling out the owner's name and the date, were then applied to each order. In the majority of surviving examples, the names are embossed beneath the front flap and could only be clearly seen when the letter case was opened and in use. As with the clasps, close similarities in the embossed decoration on all the letter cases in the sample group indicate the same common source for the embossing tools, undoubtedly the metal workshops of the Midlands.

Exactly how many letter-case makers were working in Liverpool in 1750, when John Bridge bought his example, is unknown. Later eighteenth- and early nineteenth-century sources list only a limited number of craftsmen describing themselves specifically as case makers. Many of them traded under much wider descriptions as booksellers, print sellers, and stationers, meaning that making and selling letter cases constituted one small part of their trade. In 1785, eight tradesmen described themselves by these various terms in Liverpool, twenty-one by the period 1792–1798, and thirty-two by 1811.[33] Some combined their trades with other activities, advertising themselves as printers, auctioneers, grocers, music sellers, bookbinders, carvers

---

[30] In the sample group of eighteen letter cases, six of them have elliptical clasps and five have scrolling designs.

[31] Eric Hopkins, *Birmingham: The First Manufacturing Town in the World, 1760–1840* (London: Weidenfeld & Nicolson, 1989).

[32] W. B. Stephens (ed.), *Victoria History of the County of Warwick*, 8 vols., *The City of Birmingham* (London: Victoria County History, 1964), vol. 7, 81–139.

[33] Exeter Working Papers in British Book Trade History, 20. The British book trades 1784–1811: a tabulation of national directories, Localities: L. https://bookhistory.blogspot.com/2009/03/britain-1784-1811-l.html, accessed April 4, 2019.

and gilders, and makers of mathematical instruments. Engaging in more than one trade at a time was a common feature of the eighteenth-century retail world.[34] In 1750, for instance, one London-based cutler, John Brailsford of St. Martin's Court, Leicester Fields, advertised cases for sale on his trade card, among the many everyday metal implements that his customers could buy.[35]

Social Status in Small Cases

Despite their rather plain external appearance, Bridge's and Hillam's letter cases communicated ownership, via their embossed names, and constituted one avenue for members of the mercantile class to signal peer-group identity. In purchasing and paying to have their names added to their new cases, Bridge and Hillam participated in broader cultural practices, in which there is some evidence to suggest that contemporaries did indeed recognize the letter case as a material marker of the mercantile body. For instance, literary sources include references to letter cases owned by wealthy men at the gentry level, noting their use as receptacles for letters and other papers. The male protagonists in Samuel Richardson's novels *Pamela* (1740) and *Clarissa* (1748–1749), and in Oliver Goldsmith's *The Vicar of Wakefield* (1766), all make use of letter cases.[36] But some earlier literary evidence for their use by merchants in particular may be found in Daniel Defoe's novel *The Life of Colonel Jack* (1722). In this work, the title character recounts his instruction in the art of pickpocketing when he was a fifteen-year-old beggar boy on the streets of London; his companion and instructor, Major Jack, steals a "little Leather Letter Case" from the Custom House in Thames Street, containing a bill of exchange for £300 and another from a goldsmith for £12 10s. Aware that he may raise suspicion

---

[34] For details of the many other commodities sold by booksellers, besides letter cases, see John Feather, *The Provincial Book Trade in Eighteenth-Century England* (Cambridge: Cambridge University Press, 1985), 83–87. For multiple trades, see Penelope J. Corfield, "Business Leaders and Town Gentry in Early Industrial Britain: Specialist Occupations and Shared Urbanism," *Urban History*, 39.1 (2012), 20–49.

[35] Printed trade card, c. 1750, Prints and Drawings Collection, Heal, 52.22, British Museum, London.

[36] Samuel Richardson, *Pamela; or Virtue Rewarded*, ed. Thomas Keymer and Alice Wakeley (1740; Oxford: Oxford University Press, 2001), 256; Richardson, *Clarissa, or the History of a Young Lady*, ed. Angus Ross (1748–1749; London: Penguin, 2004), 786; Oliver Goldsmith, *The Vicar of Wakefield*, ed. Arthur Friedman and Robert L. Mack (1766; Oxford: Oxford University Press, 2008), 65.

and be apprehended should he try to cash the larger bill, Major Jack takes the smaller bill to the goldsmith's shop in Lombard Street. There, he "pull'd out the Letter Case, as if he had been a Merchant's Boy, acquainted with Business, and had other Bills about him ... They paid him the Money in Gold."[37] His self-presentation relies on the practice of shopkeepers and other contemporaries recognizing merchants, and indeed their servants, by the carrying and use of a letter case.

Trial testimony from the Old Bailey confirms the association between merchants and leather cases, as seen in the brief information about the owners of the ten letter cases recorded as stolen between 1716 and 1783. Although their names, and sometimes their addresses, are included in the trial proceedings, in most incidents it has not been possible to confirm their social status, with one notable exception. William Galley, like Harold Hillam, was a customs officer, a tidewaiter at the Customs House in Southampton, whose job it was to board vessels on their arrival in port in order to enforce customs regulations. In 1747, Galley was set upon and brutally murdered by a gang of tea smugglers, to prevent him from informing on one of their number.[38] They beat him to death and buried his body in a shallow grave. When it was discovered some months later, having been dug up by animals, Galley's letter case was found in what remained of his coat pocket, which was subsequently identified by his son at the trial of his father's murderers. The placement of the letter case in this gruesome and notorious incident, although apparently lacking its owner's name, offers further evidence that it was likely commonplace for customs officers, similar to merchants, to own a letter case – an everyday accessory for their profession.

The extant examples I have examined to date, while not exhaustive in their numbers, do provide further evidence that cases were small personal possessions closely associated with the merchant class. Sixteen of the eighteen are dated examples, spanning a forty-year period between 1738 and 1778, while two of them are undated. Ten of the sixteen dated letter cases have a proven mercantile provenance or can be attributed to a high-end tradesman. Two letter cases from the sample group of eighteen have no traceable provenance because they are neither dated nor bear their owner's name; two have an unconfirmed provenance; another one

---

[37] Daniel Defoe, *Colonel Jack*, ed. Gabriel Cervantes and Geoffrey Sill (1722; Peterborough, ON: Broadview Press, 2016), 77–88.

[38] *Old Bailey Proceedings Online* (www.oldbaileyonline.org, version 8.0, March 2018), January 1748, trial of Benjamin Tapner et al. (t17480116-1).

is dated but has no owner's name; and three have provenances that place them outside the mercantile class, although indicating membership of a social elite.[39] Despite being worn, through repeated handling and use, the majority of these letter cases remain in good condition. They were bought at all stages of an owner's career, at ages ranging from the twenties to the fifties, but most were acquired during their owner's early twenties, when a career might have been taking off, or during their forties, when it had become well established. In the case of the former, such a purchase might have been purely aspirational, while in the latter it was perhaps indicative of the owner's sense of achievement and belonging in his field. Harold Hillam and John Bridge are broadly reflective of this apparent trend in terms of the ages at which they purchased their letter cases.[40]

However, one letter case (Figure 11.2) from the sample group is of particular significance because, like that carried by John Bridge, it bears a date and its owner's name and occupation as a merchant.[41] Made of black leather, lined inside with both black and red Morocco leather, it is embossed in gold on both outer and inner surfaces with "Hesketh Yarburgh, Merchant in Bristol, 1738." In contrast to most of the other letter cases in the sample group, it has no clasp and simply folds in two to close. Unlike John Bridge of Liverpool whose father was a cooper, his near contemporary Hesketh Yarburgh (1714–1754) was a member of a long-established gentry family, originally from Lincolnshire. His mother, Anne Hesketh (1676–1718) of Heslington Hall, York, married his father, Sir James Yarburgh of Snaith, Yorkshire, in 1692.[42] Hesketh was their seventh son and was raised principally at his mother's former home, Heslington Hall.

As was acceptable for and indeed often expected of the younger sons of gentry families during the eighteenth century, Hesketh embarked upon a mercantile career. By January 1736, aged about twenty-one, he had moved

---

[39] Two of those with non-mercantile provenances are black leather letter cases, made for Richard Moss, Registrar of Norwich Cathedral, 1751, and Charles Lay, attorney and Sword Bearer of Norwich, 1765. Both are in the collection of Norwich Castle Museum, accession numbers 1922.135.934 and 1894.27.1. The third is most likely to have belonged to the landowner and gentleman Henry Yarburgh (1707–1748) and is now in the Borthwick Institute for Archives, University of York.

[40] In the sample group, when they purchased their letter cases four men were aged between 20 and 26; one was aged 39; four were aged between 40 and 49; and one was aged 51.

[41] In the collection of the Borthwick Institute for Archives, University of York, reference number YM/MB/7. I am grateful to Holly Day of the University of York for drawing my attention to this object.

[42] J. W. Clay (ed.), *Dugdale's Visitation of Yorkshire, with additions*, 3 vols. (Exeter: W. Pollard, 1899–1917), vol. 3, 66.

184　PAULINE RUSHTON

Figure 11.2 Letter case of Hesketh Yarburgh, Bristol, 1738. Photograph courtesy of the Borthwick Institute for Archives, University of York.

to Bristol.[43] It is likely that Hesketh chose Bristol owing to its dominance during the 1730s and 1740s in the transatlantic slave trade.[44] In December 1737, Hesketh was admitted to the Society of Merchant Venturers of Bristol, and it is perhaps telling that his letter case, made in the following year, possibly to mark his acceptance into that body, describes him as being a merchant in Bristol, rather than simply recording the location alone as if he were a native of the city.[45] Like John Bridge in Liverpool, Hesketh was clearly proud of his standing as a merchant, despite his gentry ancestry, and proclaimed it on this personal possession.

[43] Letter dated January 28, 1736, ref. YM/CP/2, the Borthwick Institute for Archives, University of York. I am grateful to Alexandra Medcalf for her assistance in relation to the thirty-five letters in this collection, none of which provide any conclusive evidence of the nature of Hesketh's mercantile business, unfortunately.
[44] David Richardson (ed.), *Bristol, Africa and the Eighteenth-Century Slave Trade in America, vol. 2, The Years of Ascendancy, 1730–1745* (Bristol Record Society, 1987).
[45] Hesketh was admitted by apprenticeship on December 1, 1737. See W. E. Minchinton (ed.), *Politics and the Port of Bristol in the Eighteenth Century: The Petitions of the Society of Merchant Venturers, 1698–1803*, Bristol Record Society's Publications 23 (Bristol: Bristol Record Society, 1963), 213.

The surviving documentary evidence does not establish the exact nature of Hesketh's business as a merchant. Like Harold Hillam, Hesketh does not appear in the slave-voyages records, either as a direct investor in the trade or as a ship's captain. Judging by his close associates, it is likely that he was engaged in one or more of the ancillary occupations that the slave trade engendered, such as sugar baking, distilling, or supplying trade goods. From 1742 onwards, he was living at premises in Guinea Street, St. Mary Redcliffe, an area of Bristol in which many slave-ship captains were also based. He shared the house with a number of tradesmen, and, significantly, the only other two men who, like Hesketh, were described in the lease of the premises as merchants: John Macie and Joseph Percivall.[46] Macie worked as a sugar baker.[47] Percivall controlled the Coster copper-smelting company at Upper Redbrook, Bristol, producing the metal used in the manufacture of "Guinea kettles," made expressly for export as part of the slave-trade economy.[48] Hesketh may have been engaged in similar activities to both men. He was certainly acquainted with a number of well-known slave-ship captains from the port, including Edmund Saunders and Joseph Wilson.[49] Given such connections, it would seem highly improbable that Hesketh himself was not involved in the trade in some capacity, even if conclusive evidence for his involvement is now lacking. In 1748, Hesketh inherited the Heslington and Snaith estates when his older brother, Henry Yarburgh (1707–1748), died childless.[50] It is unclear if he continued with his mercantile career in Bristol or returned home to Yorkshire to administer his land. Hesketh was not to enjoy his inheritance for long. In May 1754, he too died, unmarried and childless, leaving his letter case as the only tangible evidence of his life as a merchant in Bristol.[51]

---

[46] Deeds relating to house in Guinea Street, ref. 4052/5/3/4, Bristol Archives.

[47] Will of John Macie, sugar baker of the city of Bristol, signed June 20, 1746, proved, London, May 25, 1750, PRO PROB 11/799, The National Archives, London.

[48] Barrie Charles Blake-Coleman, *Copper Wire and Electrical Conductors; The Shaping of a Technology* (Chur and Philadelphia, PA: Harwood Academic, 1992), 100–101.

[49] On November 15, 1740, Joseph Wilson wrote to Hesketh concerning the safe arrival in Barbados of the slave ship *Berkley*, mentioning its owner, Captain Saunders. Borthwick Institute, ref. YM/CP/2. *Slave Voyages Database*, voyage identification number 16981. Wilson was the owner of the slave ship *Leopard*, which in 1741–1742 transported 271 enslaved people from an unspecified African port to St. Kitts. *Slave Voyages Database*, voyage identification number 17050.

[50] One of the letter cases in the sample group may have belonged to Henry Yarburgh. Made from brown leather with a scrolling brass clasp, engraved *Heslington 1746/7*, it is now in the Borthwick Institute for Archives, University of York, ref. YM/MB/7.

[51] Hesketh died intestate, which may indicate a sudden and unexpected demise. A grant of administration of his goods was made to his youngest brother, Charles Yarburgh (1716–1789), who inherited the family estates. Borthwick Institute for Archives, University of York, ref. YM/prob/7. No subsequent list of them survives to indicate the nature of his business.

The leather letter cases of the eighteenth century were relatively unassuming objects within the period's vast market for domestic-made and imported goods. Durable and portable, they took rather uniform shapes and dimensions, but offered some scope for difference, from the color of their external leather and internal marbled papers, to the shape and materials of their clasps and the level of their decorative embossing. Often tucked away in pockets, they were carried close to the body and moved between their owners' residences and places of business. The letter cases highlighted here reflect the social aspirations of men who were eager to indicate their belonging to a rising mercantile class through the ownership of this small personal possession. When the contents of their leather cases included the bills and papers associated with the transatlantic slave trade, these small objects held whole worlds within them.

12 | The Aesthetic of Smallness

Chelsea Porcelain Seal Trinkets and Britain's Global Gaze, 1750–1775

PATRICIA F. FERGUSON

Seal trinkets are the smallest of British porcelain "toys" and the least-studied class of wares produced at the two most prestigious porcelain manufactories operating in London in the mid-eighteenth century, the Chelsea and the St. James's manufactories. These rival factories both specialized in pocket-sized toys – paraphernalia associated with the person, variously defined as a thing of little or no value, a trifle, a piece of nonsense, something contrived for amusement and not for use, as well as a thing of small estimation. Their toy production included figural scent or smelling bottles; small boxes for sweets, snuff, or patches; étui cases for needles or bodkins, tweezers, toothpicks, or ear-scoops; cane-handles; and seal-trinkets or fob seals.[1]

The smallest of these toy trifles, and indeed of all eighteenth-century porcelain objects, are fob seals (trinkets for watch chains), the focus of this chapter. In charm and inventiveness, these novelties, in numerous variations, rivaled the wares of the great European factories. British manufacturers had a global monopoly on these diminutive, sculptural wares because of the slip-cast technique employed in their creation. Finely detailed miniaturization was not possible with the press-molding process used by continental competitors such as the royal Saxon porcelain factory at Meissen and, in France, the porcelain factories at Saint-Cloud, outside Paris, and at the château de Villeroy, near Mennecy. These factories also produced novel *galanterien*, *bijou*, *bagatelles*, and *breloque* – the eighteenth-century German and French terms describing small objects or toys – but not seals.

Toys easily conform to the generic aesthetic of smallness, which has been defined by Samina Najmi "as an artistic emphasis on small-scale objects and material realities, which include not only the ordinary, unadorned, and the everyday, but also the personal and the particular."[2] Many were given as gifts on St. Nicholas Day or New Year's Day, presents exchanged

---

[1] Chloe Wigston Smith, "Bodkin Aesthetics: Small Things in the Eighteenth Century," *Eighteenth-Century Fiction*, 31.2 (2019), 271–294 (280–281).

[2] Samina Najmi, "Naomi Shihab Nye's Aesthetic of Smallness and the Military Sublime," *MELUS*, 35.2 (2010), 151–171 (156).

between individuals who were bound by ties of attraction and intimacy, typically gendered.³ The creators of these toys understood and exploited the rhetoric around token gifts, evoking in their designs the feminine sphere and the qualities of cuteness, vulnerability, ambiguity, and wonder in objects that could fit in the palm of the receiver's hand. A small group of these miniature sculptures, however, address themes and subjects that privilege the elite market for these wares, exposing the passions, pursuits, and prejudices of their owners and collectors.

Seal trinkets, unlike any other ceramic objects, were routinely carried on the person and were strongly connected with touch and tactility: fingers mindlessly caressed and rubbed the features on these miniature sculptures, thrust deep into a pocket or dangled from metal chains. Through repeated familiarity, the glazed and enameled surfaces evoked intimate memories of the presenter – a forgotten lover or a presumed partner – and are evidence of the new obsession with sentimentality. Their true charm, as suggested by Mimi Hellman in the case of scent bottles, was when they were held; their forms encouraged graceful hand gestures, and, when they were shared, created a sense of intimacy.⁴ Few other ceramic objects were either as intimate or as personal. This chapter considers their history and production as well as the legibility of the details hidden in their designs. Many of the almost two hundred models depict familiar eighteenth-century tropes – chickens, shepherdesses, cupids holding hearts – to reference, in miniature, the everyday material culture of elite Britain. Another group of these pocket-sized toys incorporates a global sphere of imagery, by showing exoticized and enslaved persons on their surfaces. These toys, and their engagement with colonialism and race, have received less attention; as we shall see, their imagery illuminates the uncomfortable currents of toys that afforded their owners aesthetic and tactile delight and pleasure, while exploiting imagery of global commerce, empire, and slavery, all on their small forms.

Making Small Seal Trinkets

A fob seal (Fr. *cachet*) has an engraved or carved intaglio matrix, designed to make an impression in hot sealing wax to secure the contents of important documents and private correspondence, ensuring they will

---

³ For the "economies of exchange," see Jacques Derrida, *Given Time: 1. Counterfeit Money*, trans. Peggy Kamuf (Chicago: University of Chicago Press, 1992).

⁴ Mimi Hellman, "Scents and Sensibilities" in Rachel Gotlieb and Karine Tsoumis (eds.), *30 Objects 30 Insights: Gardiner Museum* (London: Black Dog, 2014), 104–111 (107).

not be tampered with while also identifying the sender. Made of metal or hardstone, the matrix contained a graphic element in the form of a coat-of-arms, crest, or cipher used to attest the authority of its bearer. The matrices mounted on porcelain seal trinkets are typically carnelian, a reddish semiprecious gemstone, imported from Sweden or India through the East India Company. They were pre-engraved with generic motifs and mottoes by independent seal engravers and lapidarists, such as James Wicksteed (act. 1754–1778), a seal engraver based in Bath, the heart of the toyshop trade catering to the visiting nobility and gentry.[5] Rather than family armorials or even personal monograms, the motifs on matrices mounted on porcelain seal trinkets for commercial purposes were accessible to as wide an audience as possible. The matrices were attached to the porcelain with mounts in gold, silver, gilt base metal, or pinchbeck – an alloy of copper and zinc resembling gold invented by Christopher Pinchbeck (1670–1732) as an affordable substitute for such – each aimed at a different price point.

Metal fob seals, along with other articles of household use such as watch keys, thimbles, *bonbonnières* (filled with small breath-freshening sweets), nutmeg graters, cork screws, and étui, were typically suspended from an ornamental metal appendage hung from the waist by a flat hook known in eighteenth-century Britain as an "équipage" and, after the 1820s, as a "châtelaine."[6] The French term *équipage* was defined in James Buchanan's *Linguæ Britannicæ Vera Pronunciato: or a New English Dictionary* (1757) as "Ornaments for a lady," but they were equally ornaments for men.[7] These trinkets were visual symbols of social status, but the tinkering sound of the metal elements also announced the wearer's body movement, adding a pleasing auditory experience that resulted from the fashion to load them with ornaments. In addition, like the ceremony of taking snuff, the toying with these porcelain *breloques* offered the owner an opportunity to display an etiquette of elegance with the motion of the hands and arms when revealing them to confidantes.[8]

---

[5] Trevor Fawcett, *Bath Entertain'd: Amusements, Recreations & Gambling at the 18th-Century Spa* (Bath: Ruton, 1998), 84.

[6] Ariane Fennetaux, "Toying with Novelty: Toys, Consumption, and Novelty in Eighteenth-Century Europe" in Bruno Blondé, Natacha Coquery, Jon Stobart, and Ilja Van Damme (eds.), *Fashioning Old and New: Changing Consumer Patterns in Western Europe (1650–1900)* (Turnhout: Brepols, 2009), 17–28; Genevieve E. Cummins and Nerylla D. Taunton, *Chatelaines: Utility to Glorious Extravagance* (Woodbridge: Antique Collectors' Club, 1994), 16.

[7] James Buchanan, *Linguæ Britannicæ Vera Pronunciato: or a New English Dictionary* (London, 1757), s.v. "équipage."

[8] Fennetaux, "Toying with Novelty," 24.

These tiny porcelain seals had a global market; they were purchased by French, Dutch, and other foreign merchants and consumers, as evidenced by an elite international assemblage on an équipage at the Rijksmuseum, Amsterdam.[9] This rare intact survivor includes two English seals, possibly together since their original purchase, along with a Parisian pocket watch, c. 1755, suspended from a gold équipage made in Hanau, Germany, in 1762–1764 (Figure 12.1).[10] The two English seals include a black-spotted hound, or dalmatian, with a painted motto, "JE SUIS FIDELLE," and a figure of Cupid, also with a dalmatian, and the amorous inscription, "AMOUR FIDELLE."[11] Made at the St. James's factory, both are mounted in gold with carnelian intaglio seals; the first has a crowned-heart crest and the other the inscription "P A X" above a bird with an olive branch. The pocket watch belonged to a governor of the Dutch East India Company, Jan Albert Sichterman (1692–1764), and was left to his daughter Johanna Maria, who had a jeweler add the German équipage and personalize it with imported, English, porcelain seal trinkets as an expression of her taste and interests.

Such fob seals typically measure less than 1 in or 2.5 cm in height. Porcelain examples were produced at the Chelsea porcelain factory from at least around 1754 until 1770 (when the works were acquired by the owners of the Derby factory) and perhaps slightly earlier at the St. James's factory. The first reference to examples made at Chelsea, founded in about 1745 by the inventive silversmith and Liège-born entrepreneur Nicholas Sprimont (1716–1771), appears in an auction advertisement. On November 23, 1754, the *Public Advertiser* listed a sale on December 16 that included, "Trinkets for Watches, (mounted in Gold and unmounted) in various beautiful Shapes, of an elegant Design, and curiously painted in Enamel." It noted that "nothing of the kind was in their former sale," suggesting that these trinkets were a new enterprise.[12] They are never mentioned in subsequent auctions held by the factory, leading to speculation that they were wholesaled, unmounted, to retail jewelers.[13] They are

---

[9] Seals in the Schreiber Collection, at the Victoria and Albert Museum, London, were purchased before 1885 in Amsterdam, Vienna, Berlin, Seville, and The Hague. For examples in the Musée du Louvre, see Catherine Cardinal, *Catalogue des montres du Musée du Louvre, Tome 1* (Paris: Réunion des Musées Nationaux, 1984), cat. nos. 159, 177, 208, and 325.

[10] Suzanne van Leeuwen, "'En Quatre Couleur': An Eighteenth-Century Gold Watch Chatelaine in the Rijksmuseum," *The Rijksmuseum Bulletin*, 64.4 (2016), 328–46.

[11] Gilbert Ernest Bryant, *The Chelsea Porcelain Toys* (London: Medici Society, 1925), plates 38-14 and 36-10.

[12] Frank Severne Mackenna, *Chelsea Porcelain: The Red Anchor Wares* (Leigh-on-Sea: F. Lewis, 1951), 5.

[13] See *A catalogue of Part of the Large and Valuable Stock in Trade of Mr. James Cox of Shoe-Lane, Jeweller* (London, 1772), for an auction held by James Christie, July 1–2, 1772, which listed almost four hundred unmounted porcelain seals.

Figure 12.1 Two seal-trinkets of a dalmation and a cupid with dalmation, soft-paste porcelain, St. James's factory, c. 1751–1759, suspended from an équipage made by Daniel Marchand and Company, Hanau, Germany, c. 1762–1764, with a pocket watch by Jean Baptiste Baillon, c. 1755. Length 4.5 cm. BK-NM-11238. © Rijksmuseum, Amsterdam.

described as "trinkets" rather than "seals," indicating that they were considered ornamental rather than functional, as many were never mounted with a matrix.

Sprimont's chief rival was a former business partner, the Huguenot Charles Gouyn (d. 1785) who had a jewelry warehouse at the Turk's Head on Bennet Street in St. James's. Their partnership had dissolved in around 1748–1749 and Gouyn continued to produce porcelain toys until at least

1760.[14] Gouyn and Sprimont may have developed porcelain seals when they were still in partnership. Shortly after their split, Sprimont announced in the *Daily Advertiser* on January 9, 1750, "a great Variety of Pieces for Ornament in a Taste entirely new," hinting at objects, such as seals, scent bottles, or cane handles, that needed mounting in precious metal.[15] These may have been inspired by figural scent bottles or a series of miniature figures of court ladies, gallants, peasants, and farmyard animals produced by the Meissen factory from the late 1740s.[16]

Little is known about production at the St. James's factory, but both manufactories employed a soft-paste or low-fired porcelain, an artificial material resembling "true" Asian porcelain or European hard-paste or high-fired porcelain, ideal for slip casting. Before 1760, the Chelsea soft paste contained frit, a glassy substance made from siliceous sand, soda, alum, sea salt, and niter, but after that date, frit was replaced with calcined bone ash from cattle, which added strength to the small toys. The slip-cast technique was designed for mass production and involved taking plaster of Paris molds from unique master models in lead. The plaster molds were filled with liquid clay and the excess water was absorbed into the plaster as the clay solidified, quickly becoming leather-hard. The object was then removed from the mold. Each seal was drilled vertically to create a tubular hole. The molded clay object was then glazed, fired, painted in enamels, and fired again. Jewelers purchased them unmounted and inserted metal pins through the holes to attach suspension rings or secure mounts on the base, set with a gemstone seal matrix. Considering the diminutive size of these toys, this was extremely intricate and detailed work.

Painters decorated specific models, say "Gentle Man with a Muff," with identical patterns and details in groups of twelve, twenty-four, or thirty-six.[17] At least one decorator is identified in the overtime records, c. 1770–1773: "31 seals, Indian, Painted by Jinks," probably the gilder known only as "Jenks" who was paid five shillings and twopence.[18] The enamel details, although not of fine workmanship, critically make the features more legible and the subjects identifiable. The end result, if appearing

---

[14] Between 1961 and 1993, it was identified as the "Girl-in-a-Swing" factory, after a figure in the Victoria and Albert Museum, C.587-1922.

[15] Elizabeth Adams, *Chelsea Porcelain* (London: Barrie and Jenkins, 1987), 58–59.

[16] For a Meissen figural scent-bottle, see the Gardiner Museum, Toronto, G83.1.1043, and for miniatures, see Fenton House, Hampstead, London, The National Trust, NT1448179 and 1448165.

[17] Llewellyn Jewitt, *Ceramic Art of Great Britain* (London: Virtue, 1878), 180.

[18] Bryant, *Chelsea Porcelain Toys*, 111.

naïve and crude in its execution, remains charming, witty, and to our eyes – and perhaps to those of Georgian society – irresistible.

A factory motto painter added the designated romantic inscription in French in iron-red enamel. Generic French inscriptions, as Sally Holloway suggests, were part of the language of love and often based on John Cleland's *Dictionary of Love* (London, 1753), a translation of J. F. Dreux du Radier's *Dictionnaire d'amour* (Paris, 1741).[19] In the early 1770s, payments were recorded to specialist motto painters: "30 Seals painted in Mottows by Boarman and Wollams, 0.3.1.1½," a reference to the painters Zachariah Boreman (1738–1810) and the brother (n.d.) of the celebrated Chelsea sculptor Joseph Willems (1715–1766); and elsewhere to "Boyer," probably Robert Boyer (n.d.), who trained as a painter under Sprimont.[20] Bibliographic sources for their obscure, gallant catchphrases, such as "Pour Divertir Les Filles," have not been identified; the frequent misspellings suggest motto painters were either illiterate, had transliterated spoken instructions, or were simply unfamiliar with the French language. At around 0.3 cm in height, these minute texts, neatly inscribed on the bases, enhanced the beholder's pleasure, but contributed to ocular diseases among the painters straining to complete their work by candlelight.

Seal trinkets were still in production from 1770 to 1784, during the "Chelsea-Derby" period when Chelsea was taken over by William Duesbury (1725–1786), owner of the Derby porcelain factory. The weekly overtime records for painters working at the Chelsea decorating studio between 1770 and 1773 indicate thousands of seals were painted: "3 dozen Cupid crying by a Urn," "1 Dozen and 6 fine Gentle Man with a Muff," and "6 Arlequens."[21] When the London studio closed in 1784, casks full of seals, probably unpainted, were transferred to Derby, where they were subsequently decorated in a strong palette with apple-green bases and gold line bands, or remained white.[22] Few are inscribed with mottoes or mounted with seal matrices or suspension rings. Technically, this latter group were not seals per se, but were rather trinkets sold as keepsakes or mementoes. Many hands, including perhaps those of children, were involved in the various stages of making of these minuscule mass-produced wares, clearly feeding a voracious appetite for these tiny, intricately decorated pieces of novel design.

---

[19] Sally Holloway, *The Game of Love in Georgian England: Courtship, Emotions, and Material Culture* (Oxford: Oxford University Press. 2019), 100–102.
[20] Adams, *Chelsea Porcelain*, 161; and Arthur Lane, *English Porcelain Figures of the Eighteenth Century* (London: Faber and Faber, 1961), 135.
[21] Jewitt, *Ceramic Art of Great Britain*, 180.
[22] Bryant, *Chelsea Porcelain Toys*, 108–109, plates 42 and 44.

Small Designs

The standard and most comprehensive work on the subject of seal trinkets is Gilbert Ernest Bryant's *Chelsea Porcelain Toys* (1925). Bryant (1878–1965) applied his methodical and observational training as an entomologist to the publication, in which he recorded over two hundred models, loosely arranged by subject, albeit with some duplication. Through access to numerous private and public collections, he carefully and meticulously illustrated these minute specimens, assisted by Olive Florence Tassart (d. 1953), a scientific illustrator, and H. Haase (n.d.); each example was accompanied by a cursory description. The list is not exhaustive, as many unrecorded models have subsequently appeared. The two-dimensional watercolors, reproduced as color plates (Figure 12.2), capture the fine details of the three-dimensional designs, lost in the tonal reproductions of black-and-white photography found elsewhere in the book. Bryant stated that he chose this method as "so much detail is lost by direct photography."[23]

Seals were, of course, never intended to be illustrated; they are not particularly photogenic and photography exposes their crudeness and blemishes. They are instead cartoon-like figures, caricatures of theatrical, musical, and literary characters – now unrecognized – lightly satirizing contemporary society. Compromised not only by the diminutive scale representing human-sized objects and people, details were further distorted when covered with thick glaze. Forms were designed to be compact and arms and limbs were close to the body to limit breakages, which resulted in generally stocky and thick-set figures. In the process of mass-produced miniaturization, details were lost and meanings obliterated, losses made visible in unfinished seal trinkets and those that lack painted markings or were left "in the white." While porcelain is typically perceived as fragile and delicate, and small things commonly read as vulnerable, the design of these figural seal trinkets made them far more durable, creating an awkward ambiguity.

Bryant's survey permits the study of the inventive designs of these two factories, most of which were original models and not based on larger Meissen figural models, while the rest were compressed translations of scent-bottle designs.[24] Collectively, they help to form a picture of the types

---

[23] Ibid., 1.
[24] The Victoria and Albert Museum has two pen and ink drawings depicting models of children and putti in various guises, c. 1765, which resemble seal-trinkets, see E.1667–1931 and E.1666–1931.

Figure 12.2 Gilbert Ernest Bryant (1878–1965), watercolor, depicting twenty-four seal trinkets, reproduced in *The Chelsea Porcelain Toys* (London: Medici Society, 1925), Plate 38, 31 × 25 cm. Photograph, the author.

of consumers for these porcelain miniatures, referencing the obsessions of elite British society: pets, hunting, music, theater, and romantic aspirations. They also use humor to introduce issues around politics and power; inequality; and class, gender, and marriage – as well as to entertain readers and audiences. Animal subjects are prominent, largely domestic and familiar, including cats, dogs, squirrels, and sheep; birds are represented by parrots, bullfinches, swans, and hens with chicks. The eighteenth century saw the invention of pet-keeping and the affection of upper-class women for "parrots, monkeys and lap dogs"; loved for their assumed traits of intelligence, affection, and loyalty, many of them were fed and treated better than most servants.[25] These symbols of fidelity enjoyed the "hall mark of modernity," a bourgeois phenomenon linked to urbanization, commercialization, and alienation, as Laura Brown has argued.[26] There are also models of objects associated with the everyday: clock cases, baby walkers, wicker bird cages, and sandglasses.

Figural models include sportsmen with hunting dogs, soldiers with pipes and drums, ladies dancing, gardeners, and players in Lilliputian theatrical production. Harlequin, Punch, Pierrot, and Columbine, entertainers from the Italian Comedy, were also popular. Many are "petites amours," identified as Cupid or Venus depending on their gender (though the majority are male) – scantily garbed putti holding hearts, billing doves, nets, letters, bows, and arrows, emphasizing even more than the mottoes that these are love tokens dripping with sexual innuendo. Other Cupid figures underscore the popularity of masquerades under the theme of "love in disguises," for example "Cupid as Doctor" or "Cupid as Backus," inspired by larger figures introduced at Meissen in the late 1740s.[27] These semi-erotic, coquettish figures satirized the vanity of members of the French court and, by association, the English aristocracy.[28]

In their reductions, many of the childlike figures have large heads, a number of which exhibit the physical characteristics of dwarfism.[29] For example, a male figure is theatrically garbed, with a feathered cap, large ruffled collar, breeches, and long ermine-lined cloak; his exceptionally long hair is worn in an unfashionable loose queue (Figure 12.3, middle). Bryant describes the model as a "Grotesque," a derogatory term that appeared in a late eighteenth-century list of models used by the Derby factory. The term was partially based on the phrase "Grotesque Punch," which was used to describe porcelain figures known as "Mansion House Dwarves," after the

---

[25] Laura Brown, *Fables of Modernity: Literature and Culture in the English Eighteenth Century* (Ithaca, NY and London: Cornell University Press, 2001), 233–234.
[26] Ibid., 223.
[27] Carl Berling, *Das Meissner Porzellan und seine Geschichte* (Leipzig: F. A. Brockhaus, 1900), 195.
[28] Maureen Cassidy-Geiger, "Turkish Delights: Meissen Figures for the Marchand Mercier Gilles Bazin in 1756," *The French Porcelain Society Journal*, 5 (2015), 47–52 (48–49).
[29] British Museum, 1887,0307,II.229; and Victoria and Albert Museum, 414:324–1885.

engraved series *Varie figure Gobbi* (1622), based on drawings by Jacques Callot.[30] While the precise identities of this figure and a corresponding dancing woman are now lost, eighteenth-century shoppers may have recognized these and other popular entertainers from plays and street theaters, such as a puppet show held at the corner of Shoe Lane and Fleet Street consisting of "one hundred figures in miniature" and based on Samuel Richardson's *Pamela* (1740).[31] Given the rise of the cult of celebrity in the second half of the eighteenth century, it is surprising that so few of these figural seals depict identifiable personalities, living or dead. Only one reproduces in miniature a monumental, life-size sculpture or historical figure. This is a seal trinket of William Shakespeare, modeled after the well-known memorial statue in Poets' Corner in Westminster Abbey, executed in 1740 by Peter Scheemakers (1691–1781) after designs by William Kent (1685–1748).[32] Whether or not their subjects are recognizable to us, these seal trinkets demonstrate their ability to capture likeness and personal features on their small forms.

Global Trade and Empire in Seal Trinkets

This final section examines figural seal trinkets that represent Britain's global gaze towards Asia, the Middle East, and the Americas. Similar to other goods of the period, this collection of trinkets demonstrates the widespread consumer interest in depictions of foreign places and peoples, yet their scale yields discomforting insights into how minute objects sought to contain, control, and diminish these regions, cultures, and persons. One group of fashionable chinoiserie seals, whose figures wear Asian-style costumes, fans, or conical hats and play European musical instruments, was inspired by larger Meissen and Chelsea models as well as by print sources. These were originally based on a series of engravings, *Recueil de diverses figures chinoise* (1738–1745), after paintings by

---

[30] Bryant, *Chelsea Porcelain Toys*, 138; Franklin A. Barrett and Arthur L. Thorpe, *Derby Porcelain* (London: Faber and Faber, 1971), 185; and for a Chelsea Mansion House Dwarf, c. 1750–1752, see Victoria and Albert Museum, 414:167–1885. The figures may represent Robert (d. 1764) and Judith Skinner (d. 1763), a dwarf couple who exploited their physical condition for personal gain and amassed a fortune of £20,000; see Edward J. Wood, *Giants and Dwarfs* (London: Richard Bentley, 1868), 350.

[31] Melinda Alliker Rabb, *Miniature and the English Imagination* (Cambridge: Cambridge University Press, 2019), 13.

[32] The trinket was produced at the St. James's factory, c. 1749–1760, and an example is Victoria and Albert Museum, 414:313–1885. See also Bryant, *Chelsea Porcelain Toys*, plate 36–11.

François Boucher (1703–1770).³³ Two chinoiserie seals were described in the 1770–1773 Chelsea painters' overtime records: "2 dozen of Indian Boys with handscreen" (Figure 12.3, left) and "1 dozen and six Chinease Men a smoking."³⁴ These loosely descriptive terms "Chinease" and "Indian" – which were, of course, shorthand for objects associated with Asia and the East India Companies – reflect how the small seals presented English figures dressed as mock-Chinese characters, all in the guise of adorability.

In the past, the phenomenon of chinoiserie has been dismissed by scholars of the decorative arts, but more recently, scholars have drawn attention to how the idea of China was central to the making of modernity.³⁵ Chi-ming Yang, for instance, has argued that chinoiserie was "a theoretical deconstruction of the idea of authenticity." In the case of the play *The Orphan of China* (1759), Yang identifies how China was perceived as a source of unruly luxury that created rampant materialism in Europe, but was also represented as a place of Confucian virtue capable of moral exemplarity.³⁶ Eugenia Zuroski Jenkins has demonstrated that Chinese material culture helped shaped emergent conceptions of taste and modern subjectivity in Britain, and notes that by 1760, chinoiserie presented an opportunity for designers of mass production to "abandon order in pursuit of pleasure divorced from reason."³⁷ This license for fantasy under the banner of the hybridity of chinoiserie was also critiqued at the time for its effeminization, sensuality, and frivolity.³⁸ All of these notions are encapsulated in the diminutive nonthreatening scale of these chinoiserie figures, especially when presented as an eroticized gift. These trinkets illustrate the fully fledged commercialization of chinoiserie, which integrated the exotic into British culture on the small surfaces of handheld toys.

The second and last group of figural models considered in this chapter are depictions of Black people, rare in porcelain, whose small, bright surfaces offer a jarring counterpoint to the complicated, and often harrowing, histories of people of African descent in eighteenth-century

---

[33] Nicolas Surlapierre, Yohan Rimaud, Alastair Laing, and Lisa Mucciarelli (eds.), *Une des Provinces du Rococo: La Chine Rêvée de François Boucher* (Paris: In Fine éditions d'art, 2019).

[34] Bryant, *Chelsea Porcelain Toys*, 111 and plates 37–6 and 42–3.

[35] Peter J. Kitson, *Forging Romantic China: Sino-British Cultural Exchange 1760–1840* (Cambridge: Cambridge University Press, 2013), 1.

[36] Chi-ming Yang, *Performing China: Virtue, Commerce and Orientalism in Eighteenth-Century England, 1660–1760* (Baltimore, MD: Johns Hopkins University Press, 2014), 108–109.

[37] Eugenia Zuroski Jenkins, *A Taste for China: English Subjectivity and the Prehistory of Orientalism* (Oxford: Oxford University Press, 2013), 183.

[38] David Beevers, *Chinese Whispers: Chinoiserie in Britain, 1650–1930* (Brighton: Royal Pavilion & Museums, Brighton & Hove, 2008), 24.

Figure 12.3 Three seal trinkets, "Indian boy with handscreen," "Grotesque Punch," "Cupid disguised as an Eunuch," soft-paste porcelain, Charles Gouyn, proprietor, St. James's factory, London, c. 1751–1760. Height 3.75 cm and smaller [1887,0307,II.209 at 3.75 cm; 1887,0307,II.229 at 3 cm; 1887,0307,II.198 at 3.10 cm]. © Trustees of the British Museum, London.

Britain. Typically, such imagery in the decorative arts has been identified as "blackamoors," a racist term that addresses neither ethnic distinctions nor geographical origins among people of the African diaspora.[39] These seal types are often grouped with other figures that depict "Cupid in disguises," but their designs obscure whether their figures perform as personifications of sub-Saharan Africans, "Moors" (the Muslim peoples of North Africa), or enslaved Africans in the Americas. When clothed in extravagant European costume, these figural seals romanticize the slave trade, and when in Turkish costume, they evoke stereotypes of the sensual seraglio – the sequestered living quarters used by wives and concubines in an Ottoman household.[40] As objects of curiosity, desire, and fascination that reference the exotic, erotic, and servile, these seals exemplify Simon Gikandi's reading of how the violence and ugliness of enslavement shaped theories of taste, notions of beauty, and practices of high culture, providing a powerful counterpoint built around Black difference, exclusivity, and absence.[41]

One figural seal shows a seminaked male with skin enameled to represent a Black body; the figure kneels with hands clasped at his breast in the act of pleading (the piece is attributed to Chelsea or Chelsea-Derby, c. 1760–1775).[42] The base is inscribed in iron-red, "*JE BRULE D'AMOUR*" (I am burning with love).[43] The seal appears to anticipate Wedgwood's famous abolitionist medallion of an enslaved Black figure, "Am I Not A Man And A Brother," introduced in 1787.[44] The figure does not wear the visual signals of enslavement, such as a gold earring, collar with padlock,

---

[39] Adrienne L. Childs, "Sugar Boxes and Blackamoors: Ornamental Blackness in Early Meissen Porcelain" in Alden Cavanaugh and Michael E. Yonan (eds.), *The Cultural Aesthetics of Eighteenth-Century Porcelain* (Farnham, Surrey, and Burlington, VT: Ashgate, 2010), 159–178.

[40] The small porcelain figures discussed in this chapter do not resemble the elegantly garbed Black page or servant found in portraiture and visual culture of eighteenth-century Britain; see Agnes I. Lugo-Ortiz and Angela Rosenthal, *Slave Portraiture in the Atlantic World* (New York: Cambridge University Press, 2013), 2.

[41] Simon Gikandi, *Slavery and the Culture of Taste* (Princeton, NJ: Princeton University Press, 2011), 21–27.

[42] Christie's, London, *British and Continental Ceramics*, June 27, 2005, auction catalogue, lot 100.

[43] Bryant, *Chelsea Porcelain Toys*, plate 42–5.

[44] Mary Guyatt, "The Wedgwood Slave Medallion," *Journal of Design History*, 13.2 (2000), 93–105. For a similar kneeling figure that appears as America in a porcelain group commemorating William Pitt, c. 1766, see David Bindman and Henry Louis Gates (eds.), *The Image of the Black in Western Art*, vol. 3, *From the "Age of Discovery" to the Age of Abolition*, part 3, *The Eighteenth Century* (Cambridge, MA: Belknap Press of Harvard University Press in collaboration with the W. E. B. Du Bois Institute for African and African American Research and the Menil Collection, 2011), 34–35, fig. 27; and see British Museum, 1887,0307,II.48.

or shackles. Instead, he wears a crown and a skirt of multicolored feathers, traditionally emblematic of the Americas rather than of Africa, but frequently misinterpreted in art.[45] His supplicating pose remains at odds with his regal accessories, which perpetuate the trope of servitude – but to whom? Europe? In this instance, the figure's small scale, where texture and detail are lost to roughness and manufacturing, compromises our understanding. On the one hand, the design clearly shows a racist depiction of a regal figure in supplication, whose body has been whitened by the techniques of toy production. On the other hand, the figure's servitude lacks an audience, unless we count the owner as the recipient of the gesture. The inscription further folds the figure's kneeled position into the rhetoric of love, turning the African figure into a love token to be exchanged.[46]

Other examples of "black-skinned," standing figural seals were produced at the St. James's factory, c. 1751–1759. One turbaned male figure, for instance, is dressed in loose-fitting striped trousers with a matching jacket and a green sash at his waist, from which a long sword (*kilij*) is suspended; his shoulders are draped in a long, ermine-edged red cape (Figure 12.3, right).[47] He wears a prominent single gold earring, a mark of servitude, which ultimately glamorized slavery.[48] The seal's base is inscribed in iron-red enamel, "*VAINCRE OU MOURIR*" (conquer or die).[49] The figure resembles the eunuch guarding the seraglio in an engraving in Aubry de la Motraye's *Travels through Europe, Asia, and into Part of Africa* (1723/1724)

---

[45] Childs, "Sugar Boxes and Blackamoors," 163.

[46] Another context for this seal includes the many products that showed the religious redemption of a heathen, a subject that appealed to Protestant and Catholic consumers; see Bindman and Gates, *Image of the Black in Western Art*, vol. 3, part 3, 48. A different seal, made during the Chelsea-Derby period (c. 1770–1775), potentially offers Christian allusions (see Waddesdon Manor, Buckinghamshire, inv. 8580). This genuflecting figural seal model wears a feathered crown and regal robe with short sleeves over a classical chiton (knee-length shift) tied with a belt, exposing a glimpse of his calf-length boots; his skin is enameled in black. The figure either represents an actor playing a stage role, such as William Shakespeare's Othello, which until the 1820s was performed by white actors in blackface, or is an allusion to Balthazar, the Black Magus in the biblical Nativity story, as signaled by the object he clutches (perhaps a gift of gold, Frankincense, or myrrh). On Othello and blackface, see Olivia Bloechl, "Race, Empire, and Early Music" in Olivia Bloechl, Jeffrey Kallberg, and Melanie Lowe (eds.), *Rethinking Difference in Music Scholarship* (Cambridge: Cambridge University Press, 2015), 77–107 (91). No other seal-trinkets represent biblical subjects (although there are two models of nuns shown in Bryant, *Chelsea Porcelain Toys*, plates 36-4 and 39-5).

[47] British Museum, 1887,0307,II.198.

[48] Bindman and Gates, *Image of the Black in Western Art*, vol. 3, part 3, 202.

[49] For the same model depicted as a white-skinned European see, Victoria and Albert Museum, 414:327/E-1885.

by William Hogarth after Jean-Baptiste Vanmour.[50] During the pre-Ottoman and Ottoman empires, harem guards were traditionally enslaved, non-Muslim East Africans who had converted to Islam and learned Turkish.[51] Given its inscription, which toys with Petrarchan rhetoric around romance, this figural seal may have served as an overtly erotic love token; its status as a love token makes the turbaned figure secondary to the exchange of gifts between lovers.

The St. James's factory also produced a female figure, whose head is covered in a white head wrap. She clasps a striped shawl over her shoulders, which matches her wrapped skirt, and holds a mirror in her hand.[52] Her costume associates her with Caribbean or Creole culture, where such fashions were appropriated by women of all colors and classes: enslaved people, free people of color, and white planters.[53] On arrival in the Americas, as Steeve O. Buckridge has identified, enslaved and free African women maintained their fashion and style of dressing as a symbol of resistance to slavery and to accommodation to white culture in pre- and post-emancipation society, in order to prevent European attempts at cultural annihilation.[54] Striped costume fabric has its origins in the Middle East in the twelfth century, but in the eighteenth century it became a "visual geographic or racial marker" aligned with the Caribbean and slave status.[55] Such costumes would have been familiar to the many wealthy British plantation owners and merchants, who, financed by slavery, spent voraciously on luxurious commodities.[56]

These diminutive exoticized and enslaved persons were designed to be dangled from chains as conversation pieces and held up for scrutiny by their owners as evidence of their taste. By nature of their hard usage, shoved into pockets or dangled from metal fobs or ribbons with other

---

[50] Aubry de la Motraye, *Travels through Europe, Asia, and into Part of Africa*, 2 vols. (London, 1723/4), vol. 1, plate 18 (which can be viewed online at Metropolitan Museum of Art, New York, inv. no. 17.3.2838).

[51] Jane Hathaway, *The Chief Eunuch of the Ottoman Harem: From African Slave to Power-Broker* (Cambridge: Cambridge University Press, 2018), 12–39.

[52] Bonham's, London, *Gentleman's Library Sale*, January 29, 2013, auction catalogue, lot 20. The base is inscribed in red enamel: "JE LE PORT AVEC GRACE" (I wear it with grace).

[53] Amelia Rauser, *The Age of Undress: Art, Fashion, and the Classical Ideal in the 1790s* (New Haven, CT: Yale University Press, 2020), 140 and figs. 43, 122–123.

[54] Steeve O. Buckridge, *The Language of Dress: Resistance and Accommodation in Jamaica, 1760–1890* (Kingston, Jamaica: University of the West Indies Press, 2004).

[55] Michel Pastoureau, *The Devil's Cloth: A History of Stripes and Striped Fabric*, trans. Jody Gladding (New York: Columbia University Press, 1991), 110n51.

[56] See the engravings after sketches by Agostino Brunias, in Bindman and Gates, *Image of the Black in Western Art*, vol. 3, part 3, 271–275.

objects, surviving seals are often damaged – bits are missing, mounts have been replaced – or they have been adapted for different uses, such as finials on hatpins. The results are generally unphotogenic and rarely published. As a result, they have been overlooked by scholars, other than as polemical personifications of luxury and excess among Britain's elite. However, these tiny, sculptural trinkets reference important, consequential issues, specifically Britain's global ambitions and imperial ventures in their trade with the Caribbean, the Levant, and the Ottoman court as well as with Asia. Many of the mostly female possessors of such trinkets had directly profited through the capital ventures of their fathers, brothers, and spouses, overlooking the sources of their family's affluence. Rather than simply mocking foreign persons, these seal trinkets offered British consumers the opportunity to touch and hold their nation's mastery (or aspirations thereof) over the world. These small toys thus turned Britain's burgeoning empire into handheld trinkets and accessories, whose rough surfaces smoothed over extensive and far-reaching forms of oppression and exploitation. Manufactured just as Britain was gaining commercial pre-eminence on the back of multinational trading firms, the subject matter of this small group of porcelain seal trinkets miniaturized global trade and imperial ambitions, fitting them into the palm of one's white hand. The power of the gazer, the owner of these toys, enjoyed all the benefits of this trade, accepting, and indeed supporting commercially, the cultural hegemony of the British elite, the market for these wares. On their scant surfaces, within their diminutive shapes and their cuteness of design, these porcelain trinkets register how smallness and tactility signaled the British consumer's uneasy desire to touch and hold these inauthentic representations of the erotic, the exotic, and of Blackness, and the market of small toys that grew up to satisfy such consumer demands.

13   "Small Gifts Foster Friendship"

Hortense de Beauharnais, Amateur Art, and the Politics of Exchange in Postrevolutionary France

MARINA KLIGER

In early August 1813, Hortense de Beauharnais (1783–1837), stepdaughter and sister-in-law of Emperor Napoleon Bonaparte, invited the painter Fleury Richard to paint her portrait.[1] Sensing an opportunity, he came armed not only with compositional sketches for the full-length likeness but with a small painting as well, *Madame de la Vallière Carmélite*, in which the former mistress of Louis XIV sits by the window of her cell at the convent of Faubourg Saint-Jacques in Paris. In a letter to a friend, Richard proudly announced that his quiet historical scene was a "complete success" with Queen Hortense, who had not only purchased it but also "undertaken to copy it."[2] This full-scale replica would not, however, be Hortense's last. Some years later, she also painted a miniature version of the composition (Figure 13.1). Preserved under glass, in a metal frame mounted to a leather toothpick case, it captures all the salient details of the original on a surface only one-tenth its size. This essay examines this second, tiny copy within the unique context of its diminutive scale and seemingly trivial purpose.

As a member of the imperial family, Hortense was the subject of imposing state portraits, the mistress of exquisitely crafted garments and jewelry,

---

[1] Hortense de Beauharnais was the second child of Rose Tascher de La Pagerie, better known as Empress Joséphine, and her first husband vicomte Alexandre de Beauharnais, who was guillotined during the Reign of Terror. The widowed Joséphine married Napoleon in 1796. On Hortense's life, see Marie-Hélène Baylac, *Hortense de Beauharnais* (Paris: Perrin, 2016). The letter of invitation to Richard was written on Hortense's behalf by her reader, Louise Cochelet. Fleury Richard, "Mes Souvenirs rassemblés et mis en ordre en 1847, 1848, 1849," ms p. 41, Fonds Richard, Musée de Beaux-Arts de Lyon (typewritten transcript, p. 64, Bibliothèque-Documentation, Musée de Beaux-Arts de Lyon). The portrait is preserved at the Fondation Dosne-Thiers, Paris.

[2] Letter from Fleury Richard to Pierre-Toussaint Dechazelle, Aix-les-Bains, August 8, 1813; in Richard, "Mes Souvenirs," ms p. 98 (typewritten transcript, p. 148). Unless otherwise noted, all translations are my own. In 1802, Hortense was compelled to marry Napoleon's younger brother Louis, who became king of Holland in 1806. She retained the title of queen even after his abdication in 1810. Both Richard's original *Madame de la Vallière Carmélite* and Hortense's copy, which bears the inscription "Painted by the mother of Napoleon III" on its verso, are preserved at the Napoleon Museum Thurgau, Switzerland.

Figure 13.1 Hortense de Beauharnais, after Fleury Richard, *Madame de La Vallière Carmélite*, c. 1813–1824. Miniature mounted on a leather toothpick case. 3 × 2.5 cm (miniature), 9 × 3.8 cm (case). The collections of H.M. the King of Sweden, Stockholm. Inv. no. MR 526. © The Royal Court, Sweden, photo Lisa Raihle Rehbäck.

and a prominent patron of the arts.[3] Yet her own tiny copy after Richard's picture, likely executed after the fall of the First French Empire, did not belong to this public realm of official commissions, luxurious adornments, and state exhibitions. Nor was it, like the full-scale replica she executed under Richard's tutelage, simply a technical exercise of the sort central to the education of both professional and amateur artists.[4] Rather, it operated

---

[3] On Hortense's patronage of and participation in the arts, see Bernard Chevalier (ed.), *La Reine Hortense: Une Femme Artiste* (Paris: Réunion des musées nationaux, 1993); and Marina Kliger, "Une Histoire Particulière: The Troubadour Style and Gendered Historical Consciousness in Early Nineteenth-Century France," unpublished PhD thesis, New York University (2020).

[4] On the role of copying in amateur art practice, see Charlotte Guichard, *Les Amateurs d'art à Paris Au XVIIIe Siècle* (Seyssel: Champ Vallon, 2008), 239–299; and Ann Bermingham,

within an altogether different realm, one that was more intimate and personal but no less consequential to its maker.

Less than an inch and a half tall, the toothpick case fits easily inside the palm of the hand, where its miniature can be examined by only one or two individuals at a time. Though normally kept hidden, it would have emerged in a variety of social situations when its contents were needed, for toothpicks were wielded regularly, if discreetly, when in the company of others.[5] Indeed, the example once preserved inside this delicate receptacle was handled frequently enough to break the clasp intended to secure its smooth satin interior. Such modest utilitarian objects are typically lost to time through use, deterioration, and eventual disposal. However, when linked to historically significant individuals such as Hortense, they are sometimes preserved as secular relics within cults of historical nostalgia or familial remembrance.[6] Accordingly, Hortense's toothpick case is today preserved in the private collection of the Swedish royal family, to whom she was related through her older brother, Eugène de Beauharnais (1781–1824), viceroy of Italy and later Duke of Leuchtenberg. Like the many other mementos in the collection, this one is accompanied by a note written in the hand of Queen Josephine of Sweden (1807–1876), Hortense's niece: "This toothpick case, painted by Queen Hortense, belonged to my late father, the duke Eugène de Leuchtenberg."[7] In revealing the author and the original owner of the object, this simple epigraph indicates the intended social function of Hortense's miniature beyond the utilitarian purpose of its support. It was created as a gift.

Hortense's letters to her brother, and her correspondence with others, reveal that she frequently gave and received similarly intimate objects: small portraits of herself and her children; "pretty little" rings and necklaces; "a little heart of emeralds"; "a pretty mosaic"; "a little *necessaire*"; a purse; books;

Learning to Draw: Studies in the Cultural History of a Polite and Useful Art (New Haven, CT: Yale University Press, 2000), 111–174. On its role in academic art training, see Albert Boime, *The Academy and French Painting in the Nineteenth Century* (New Haven, CT: Yale University Press, 1971), 42–43, 122–132.

[5] The toothpick, fashioned from wood, quill, or precious metal, was a ubiquitous instrument of oral hygiene during the long eighteenth century, when a new emphasis on dental appearance swept elite European society. See Colin Jones, *The Smile Revolution in Eighteenth-Century Paris* (Oxford: Oxford University Press, 2014). On the etiquette surrounding tooth-picking, see Henry Petroski, *The Toothpick: Technology and Culture* (New York: Vintage Books, 2008).

[6] On secular relics, see Teresa Barnett, *Sacred Relics: Pieces of the Past in Nineteenth-Century America* (Chicago: University of Chicago Press, 2013).

[7] The text of the note is published in Alain Pillepich (ed.), *Eugène de Beauharnais, honneur et fidélité* (Paris: Réunion des musées nationaux, 1999), 68, cat. no. 33. Eugène's eldest daughter, Josephine, married Prince Oscar Benadotte of Sweden in 1823. They ascended to the throne in 1844.

sheets of music; drawings; and various other "little ornaments."⁸ These small items are diverse in form and function: some are *objets d'art* commissioned from highly skilled artisans; others are commodities purchased from local shops; many are handmade items produced by the sender herself. All, however, like the toothpick case, were items of small scale or modest value. This chapter will first demonstrate how the exchange of such small, seemingly trivial, gifts was a strategic social practice within elite social networks in early nineteenth-century Europe, one to which amateur artworks were particularly well suited. It then returns to the composite object Hortense made for her brother to argue that Richard's *Madame de la Vallière Carmélite* held a unique personal significance for the siblings, one that was amplified through its miniaturization and its exchange as a sentimental gift.

Trifles into Precious Objects: The Gift in the Age of Sensibility

The French language has three terms for the English word "gift": *don*, *present*, and *cadeau*. The objects exchanged by Hortense and her contemporaries were referred to as *présents* or more colloquially as *cadeaux* – that is, things of little economic value or something that might be consumed through use – rather than as *dons*, which signified something of more considerable value, such as property or favors granted by a sovereign. In all three senses, however, the gift was conceived, much as it is today, as something freely and liberally given. Yet as anthropologist Marcel Mauss established in his classic *Essai sur le don* (1923–1924), the act of giving creates not only the obligation to receive but also, and perhaps more importantly, to give in return. Unlike a commodity exchange within a market economy, which is terminated once payment is complete, the giving of a gift always demands a return, creating an unending cycle of reciprocity and obligation.⁹ In this way, gift exchange functions as a means of establishing and maintaining social relationships.

Hortense's correspondence shows that she was intimately familiar with these aspects of gift giving. For instance, in a letter to her old schoolmate and lifelong friend Aglaé Auguié Ney, later Duchess of Elchingen and

---

⁸ Hortense mentions such items in letters to her brother and her friend Aglaé Augiué from the Empire period into the 1830s. See boxes 6–18 of the Spencer Napoleonica Collection, Newberry Library, Chicago (hereafter abbreviated as SNC). Further references to gifts appear in another cache of letters to Aglaé, transcribed in Thierry Bodin and Christian Galantaris, (eds.), *Autographes, livres*, sale cat., Paris, Drouot Richelieu, December 9, 2011 (Paris: Jean-Marc Delvaux, 2011), 19–50, cat. nos. 96–193.
⁹ Marcel Mauss, *The Gift: The Form and Reason for Exchange in Archaic Societies*, trans. W. D. Halls (New York and London: Routledge, 2002).

Princess of the Moskova (1782–1854), Hortense wrote: "Small gifts foster friendship. That was said long ago, my dear Eglé [sic], but without needing to keep up what we shall always feel, I send you four little crosses."[10] Unlike dictionary definitions of the gift, the old French proverb "les petits cadeaux entretiennent l'amité" lays bare the reciprocal nature and social purpose of gift giving in traditional French society.[11] Yet in her letter to Aglaé, Hortense uses it to not only invoke the significance of her small gifts but also to question the necessity of reinforcing their friendship through material means. Indeed, Hortense frequently trivialized the social purpose of her gift giving. "You must have laughed over my little gifts," she modestly presumed in a letter to her brother.[12] These rhetorical strategies not only disguise the obligation of reciprocity but they also show the influence of the era's culture of sensibility on friendship and gift giving.

Though proper friendly intercourse had always required the expression of affection, friendship in the early modern period was conceived as explicitly beneficial to both parties, with each defined by his or her position in a hierarchical social order. Gift giving reaffirmed rather than challenged this social hierarchy.[13] *Sensibilité*, by contrast, reconfigured friendship into an elective and equalizing bond between individuals, one based on feelings of emotional communion.[14] It also modified the discourse and cultural conventions that surrounded the exchange of gifts. As a story in Arnaud Berquin's influential children's book *L'Ami des Enfants* (1782) demonstrates, the social value of the gift shifted from the material to the emotional. Entitled "Le Cadeau," it describes a little girl's efforts to give her brother a birthday present. "A good gift," her mother advises, "is when we give through friendship something that pleases us and that must also please the person to whom we give it...."[15]

---

[10] Hortense to Aglaé, December 9, 1807, box 7, folder 719, SNC.

[11] This proverb was already in common usage by 1694, when it appeared in the first edition of the *Dictionnaire de L'Académie française*.

[12] Hortense, Mayence, to Eugène, January 11, 1807, box 7, folder 638, SNC.

[13] See, for example, Brigitte Buettner, "Past Presents: New Year's Gifts at the Valois Courts, ca. 1400," *The Art Bulletin*, 83.4 (2001), 598–625.

[14] On the distinction between early modern and sentimental friendship, see Irma Thoen, *Strategic Affection? Gift Exchange in Seventeenth-Century Holland* (Amsterdam: Amsterdam University Press, 2007), 13–17; and Sarah Horowitz, *Friendship and Politics in Post-Revolutionary France* (University Park: Penn State University Press, 2013), 21–40.

[15] Arnaud Berquin, *L'Ami des Enfans*, 12 vols. (London: Elmsley, 1782), vol. 9, 40. The word *cadeau*, which was defined as a feast given principally to women in the first edition of the *Dictionnaire de L'Académie française* (1694), only became synonymous with the word *présent* in the late eighteenth century. It was first linked to the idea of pleasure in the fourth edition of the *Dictionnaire* (1762), though only in reference to a *cadeau* given to oneself. By the fifth edition (1798), the word *cadeau* was described as "un petit présent" and the act of giving it to someone else as "faire ou donner à quelqu'un quelque chose qui lui soit agréable."

After some missteps, the young protagonist ultimately gives her brother a little lamb, which she trains to follow and caress him – in effect, collapsing the very idea of a gift into that of a friend. Her mother approves, concluding: "This delicate attention doubles the price of your gift. It is in this way that the slightest trifle becomes a precious object."[16]

A revealing anecdote described in the memoirs of Hortense's reader and confidant Louise Cochelet demonstrates the impact of sensibility on gift giving even within the hierarchical court culture of the First Empire.[17] In early 1813, Cochelet presented her mistress with a small portrait drawing. That same day two other women arrived with similar gifts. Madame Mollien, Hortense's former lady-in-waiting, gave her a drawing that represented the queen's visit to her bedside during a recent illness. Similarly, Madame de Boucheporne, "who owed her husband's position" to Hortense, gave her a drawing that "depicted the instant when the queen handed over the brevet for this appointment."[18] Although these gifts reinforced, and in the latter case even explicitly represented, hierarchical and political relationships, they were presented and received as emblems of authentic friendships based on feelings of affection. Cochelet thus concluded that "It was by similar care that we sought to show her our sentiments."[19] In describing the three gifts, Cochelet also expressed surprise that "without us saying a word to each other, we would have all made such drawings for the queen." Yet amateur artworks were precisely the kind of economically insignificant objects that became intimate and precious within the gift economy of the age of *sensibilité*.

Her Little Talents: Gender and the Gift in a Changing Age

Despite the widespread embrace of gift giving within the culture of sensibility, a distrust of gifts in public life was emerging in the period's liberal political theory, which viewed them as signs of corruption rather than as obligatory signs of regard.[20] An article published in the *Journal des Dames*

---

[16] Ibid., 42.
[17] Louise Cochelet, *Mémoires sur la reine Hortense et la famille impériale*, 4 vols. (Brussels: Chez Ladvocat, 1837), vol. 1, 23–24.
[18] René Bertrand de Boucheporn (1770–1842) became *préfet du Palais* to Louis Bonaparte in 1806 and *receveur général des finances de la Haute-Marne* in 1810.
[19] Cochelet, *Mémoires*, vol. 1, 25.
[20] See Harry Liebersohn, *The Return of the Gift: European History of a Global Idea* (Cambridge and New York: Cambridge University Press, 2011).

et des Modes in May 1819, for example, spotlighted how gifts might be wielded for personal gain rather than for the pleasure of others:

> It is said, small gifts foster friendship. I will add that … one can, when one has a certain tact, captivate the protection of the great, the favors of the beautiful, and sometimes the votes of a rival … I offer myself as the proof of what I advance: with little wit and talent, I have been able to push myself into the world, and I owe the fortune which I enjoy only to the constant habit that I had to spread gifts right and left whenever my purse allowed me.[21]

Although the article's anonymous male author ostensibly sought to warn the magazine's female readers about the potentially self-serving purposes of gift giving, he in fact simply adopted and hyperbolized tactics with which women like Hortense were already intimately familiar. Indeed, his satirical tale reveals that the new skepticism about promiscuous gift giving colored even the gifts given to and by women, especially where they overlapped with arenas of public life such as literature, the arts, and politics.

Within postrevolutionary society, such misgivings coexisted with a renewed need for sincere friendships. As Sarah Horowitz has shown, the Revolution's ideological factionalism and political violence, followed by the state surveillance and censorship of the Napoleonic era, initiated a climate of suspicion and social atomization in the public life of the early nineteenth century. Within this atmosphere of public uncertainty, private forms of solidarity such as friendship became increasingly important as unique sources for trust and social cohesion.[22] The trend was only exacerbated during the Bourbon Restoration, when Hortense experienced the repercussions of this political climate firsthand.

Following Napoleon's initial defeat in the spring of 1814, Hortense was the only member of the Bonaparte family to remain in France. With the support of Tsar Alexander, whose admiration she had won during the occupation of Paris by the Allied powers of Europe, Hortense obtained a royal ordinance that granted her the title of Duchess of Saint-Leu and a perpetual income of 400,000 francs. Nevertheless, she remained a catalyst for the hopes of Bonapartists and very quickly began to be accused of "intrigues" at her salon. Things only worsened with Napoleon's return in 1815. In the absence of his second wife, Empress Marie-Louise, who had absconded to Austria, Hortense took on the role of official hostess at the Tuileries Palace. Upon Napoleon's final defeat at the Battle of Waterloo,

---

[21] "Les Présents," *Journal des Dames et des Modes*, 23.26 (1819), 203–204.
[22] Horowitz, *Friendship and Politics*, 41–64.

she was accused of plotting in favor of the emperor and ultimately exiled from France. Even outside French borders, however, French authorities viewed Hortense as a threat, tracking her movements and her correspondence across Europe for the rest of her life.

Reliant on successive Bourbon and Orléans monarchs for her income and freedom of movement – as well as for a hoped for, though never achieved, return to France – Hortense sought to protect her interests by maintaining an apolitical persona and vigilantly refuting what she claimed was her false reputation as a political intriguer. In her letters to Aglaé during these years, she frequently swung from descriptions of her quiet life in Germany, Switzerland, and Italy, to denunciations of the government's false suspicions, to rapturous gratitude for her remaining true friends.[23] Those in Paris, like Aglaé, were not only an emotional but also a practical necessity. Hortense relied on them for errands in the city's shops as well as for legal and political interventions. In this context, gift giving was more essential to her than ever. Yet as a politicized actor on the world stage, Hortense also recognized the need to be cautious. Overt representations of social alliance were ill advised, while expensive gifts crafted from precious materials were now out of reach financially. Amateur artworks and art practices, on the other hand, were perfectly poised to bolster friendships within the period's politically polarized atmosphere.

In France, drawing and painting had become part of a well-rounded aristocratic education, alongside more traditional *arts d'agrément* such as dancing and music, in the second half of the eighteenth century.[24] Hortense herself received particularly rigorous artistic training at Henriette Campan's famed school at Saint-Germain-en-Laye in the late 1790s.[25] Though newly prescribed as a "useful resource against the great reverses of fortune," artistic skill remained an important marker of distinction in postrevolutionary society, especially for women.[26] Often practiced within

---

[23] See, for example, Hortense to Aglaé, October 25, 1816, box 14, folder 1322; April 26, 1820, box 15, folder 1411; and January 25, 1827, box 16, folder 1543, SNC.

[24] Guichard, *Les Amateurs d'art à Paris Au XVIIIe Siècle*, especially chapter 6, "Practiques d'amateurs."

[25] Catherine R. Montfort and J. Terrie Quintana, "Madame Campan's 'Institution d'Education': A Revolution in the Education of Women," *Australian Journal of French Studies*, 33.1 (1996), 30–44.

[26] Jeanne-Louise-Henriette Campan, *De l'éducation*, 2 vols. (Paris, 1824), vol. 1, 197. On the complex discourse about women's training in the *arts d'agrément*, see Bermingham, *Learning to Draw*, 127–228; and Rebecca Rogers, *From the Salon to the Schoolroom: Educating Bourgeois Girls in Nineteenth-Century France* (University Park, PA: Penn State University Press, 2010), 38–39, 67–71.

arenas of sociability, art making was also a convenient vehicle for social and political maneuvering. For instance, Louise Cochelet described the "gay evenings" she and Hortense spent at the house of the latter's cousin Stéphanie de Beauharnais, Grand Duchess of Baden, during the politically tenuous summer of 1814. Hortense "made portraits of all the people there," each of whom "came to pose in front of her for five minutes."[27] Significantly, her sitters on this occasion included several members of Stéphanie's illustrious extended family, who would prove essential to her search for a home outside France in the years that followed.[28]

In her correspondence, however, Hortense emphasized the private and inconsequential nature of her practice of the *arts d'agrément* in order to emphasize its benign femininity and her political neutrality. In a letter to her brother dated December 16, 1814, in the midst of rumors about intrigues at her salon in Paris, where she hosted outspoken Bonapartists, Hortense declared:

I lead the life that suits me: I have a small society. Every night we play music ... To take care of her children, to amuse herself with her little talents and not to talk about herself, that is the life of a woman.[29]

Knowing her correspondence was surveilled, she added falsely, "at all times, we never speak of politics at home, and it is a conversation that I will always forbid." Writing to Aglaé once she was settled in Augsburg, Bavaria, Hortense contrasted the "worldly" part of her life to her practice of the *arts d'agrément*: "Once a week I receive a great many people; but the rest of the time, reading, painting, music and that's all."[30] In creating this distinction between a worldly, politicized sociability in the salon and a private, feminine practice of the arts, and emphasizing the latter, Hortense sought to veil her politicized position during the Restoration.

Yet even when made in private, amateur artworks took on social and political significance when exchanged as gifts. Their economic inconsequence, however, concealed their strategic value. In another letter to Aglaé, Hortense asked her friend to facilitate the return of a portfolio of prints

---

[27] Cochelet, *Mémoires*, vol. 2, 55.
[28] Stéphanie's sister-in-law Elizabeth Alexeievna was wife of Tsar Alexander of Russia, who provided Hortense a passport to travel to Geneva in 1815; Stéphanie's husband, Charles, the Grand Duke of Baden, allowed Hortense to live in the town of Constance in the Duchy of Baden in 1816; and her brother-in-law King Maximilian I Joseph of Bavaria (also the father of Hortense's sister-in-law Augusta) allowed her to live in the city of Augsburg in 1817, after she was compelled to leave Constance in late 1816.
[29] Hortense to Eugène, December 16, 1814, box 12, folder 1178, SNC.
[30] Hortense to Aglaé, January 12, 1819, box 14, folder 1379, SNC.

forgotten in Venice. "I consent to your giving *my print* to those who may attach some value to it," she wrote.[31] This value may well not have been strictly aesthetic, but when linked to the appropriately feminine accomplishment of amateur art making, in this case lithography, it was also not overtly political.

We can now more clearly see the social function of the small object (Figure 13.1) with which this chapter began. When Hortense gave her brother Eugène a leather toothpick case mounted with her miniature copy after Richard's *Madame de la Vallière Carmélite*, she knew that her gift would demand a return and thus strengthen the bond between brother and sister. Affective ties, even familial ones, were not assured; they had to be reinforced through material and emotional means. Writing to Aglaé of financial troubles during her exile, Hortense stated: "You will tell me perhaps that I have a rich brother. It is true, but he has children. He owes me nothing and I will never accept anything from anybody, even him."[32] Though Hortense did rely on her own financial means during her exile – selling property in France and Switzerland as well as her mother's immense collection of jewelry – she depended on her brother in other ways. The toothpick case Hortense gifted her brother would have been one of the objects she used to maintain their friendship, and consequently her good standing at the Bavarian court.[33]

Unlike the period's many ostentatious miniature-mounted snuffboxes, made from precious materials and exchanged as diplomatic gifts, Hortense's toothpick case was not intended to demonstrate the economic worth of its giver. On the contrary, constructed from inexpensive textiles and base metals, it was a deliberately modest item of sentimental value. Though its soft leather exterior and smooth satin lining provide a pleasing tactile experience, its simplicity encourages the viewer to focus their attention on the finely detailed image at its center. As Susan Stewart has suggested, the diminution of dimensions tends to shift signifying practice from the mimetic to the symbolic.[34] That is, the small scale of Hortense's miniature copy enhanced rather than diminished its meaning. Isolated in the hand of its intended recipient, it could transcend its origins as a historical painting and become a symbol.

---

[31] Hortense to Aglaé, October 31, 1818, box 14, folder 1374, SNC (my emphasis).
[32] Hortense to Aglaé, October 29 [c. 1816–23], box 18, folder 1748, SNC.
[33] Tellingly, following Eugène's death in 1824, Hortense lost her social footing in Bavaria and moved permanently to Arenenberg castle, a sixteenth-century chateau she had purchased in Switzerland in 1817.
[34] Susan Stewart, *On Longing: Narratives of the Miniature, the Gigantic, the Souvenir, the Collection* (Durham, NC and London: Duke University Press, 1993), 48.

In one sense, the miniature represented something shared between brother and sister, for Richard's first version of *Madame de la Vallière Carmélite*, which he had exhibited at the Salon of 1806, was purchased by none other than Eugène.[35] Thus, the particular subject represented on the toothpick case was one both brother and sister owned and admired. More than this, the genre to which the painting belonged and which Richard had pioneered, the *genre anecdotique* (also known as the troubadour style), was a favorite of the siblings' mother, Empress Joséphine.[36] Joséphine's collection included twenty-four examples of these highly detailed, illusionistic scenes from the French national past, with eight by Richard alone.[37] Upon her death in 1814, these pictures were divided between her two children, who displayed them prominently in each of their homes in exile.[38] Hortense's tiny copy of Richard's picture thus not only represented their shared taste but also that of their much admired mother, reinforcing the potency of the familial tie. Yet the symbolic nature of miniatures and sentimental gifts also heightened the allusive potential of this small painting's unique iconography and authorship.

The Gift of the Self: Portrait of the Artist as a Sentimental Heroine

Most of the many objects Hortense mentions in her letters have a self-referential quality, either bearing her likeness or signifying her person in some other capacity, and as such dovetail with Marcel Mauss's insight that "to make a gift of something is to make a present of some part of oneself."[39] Small portraits comprised a significant percentage of the items Hortense sent to her correspondents both during the Empire and from exile. An account book, kept for her by Louise Cochelet from May 1805 to December 1810, confirms that Hortense made numerous payments to artists for portrait miniatures in particular, as well as for the *petits bijoux* in which

---

[35] Marie-Claude Chaudonneret, *Fleury Richard et Pierre Révoil: La Peinture Troubadour* (Paris: Arthena, 1980), 70, cat. no. 17.

[36] On the troubadour style, see Stephen Bann, Magali Briat-Philippe, and Stéphane Paccoud, *Invention du passé*, 2 vols. (Paris: Hazan Editions; Lyon: Musée des Beaux Arts, 2014).

[37] See Alain Pougetoux, *La collection de peintures de l'impératrice Joséphine* (Paris: Éditions de la Réunion des Musées nationaux, 2003).

[38] On the display of Eugène's collection, see France Nerlich, *La peinture française en Allemagne: 1815–1870* (Paris: Maison des sciences de l'homme, 2010), 21–50. On Hortense's installation of her collection at her residences in Augsburg and Rome, see Kliger, "Une Histoire Particulière."

[39] Mauss, *The Gift*, 19.

they would be mounted.⁴⁰ Such ambulant portrait-objects were particularly common sentimental gifts during the early nineteenth century, serving as surrogates for absent lovers, friends, and family.⁴¹ Yet a likeness was not the only means by which Hortense invested her gifts with a "portion" of herself. A portrait miniature of Hortense mounted on a silver pendant and encircled with diamonds contains a second hidden sign of its giver, plaited strands of her hair concealed on its verso (Figure 13.2). Though the early provenance of this portrait-object is unknown, such a tactile piece of Hortense's body would have reinforced the sense of personal intimacy between her and the intended beholder. Like a synecdoche, such bodily fragments need not have been accompanied by a likeness to represent the larger whole to which they once belonged. In December 1806, for example, Hortense simply sent "a little cross with a little lock of my hair" to her sister-in-law Princess Augusta of Bavaria.⁴² Embedding hair into jewelry had been a popular mode of remembrance since the rise of *sensibilité* in the eighteenth century, and the early years of the nineteenth century saw a new inventiveness in this vein.⁴³ Hortense herself not only placed her hair inside jewelry but used it to create bracelets, necklaces, and chains. Unlike portrait miniatures, hair jewelry did not publicly display the identity of its giver, which was known only to the wearer, making their relationship into a materialized secret from which other viewers were necessarily excluded.⁴⁴

If we understand the gift as a sign of the self – either bearing an iconic relationship to the giver, as does a portrait, or consisting of a synecdoche, as does jewelry made from hair – then amateur artworks are an index of the giver. They are the result of her hand, her observation, her imagination, and her time. From the description of the small toothpick case left by Eugène's daughter, it is clear this object was especially valued for having been made by Hortense herself. Some recipients of such gifts, such as Hortense's last reader and lady-in-waiting Valérie Mazuyer, even inscribed this indexical quality on the item in order to reinforce their implicit bond with the giver. Nearly all the drawings by Hortense that come from Mazuyer's collection prominently bear the inscription *fait et donné par la reine*

---

⁴⁰ "Livre de dépenses de Mlle Cochelet," Ms Masson 65 (A), Bibliothèques Theirs, Paris.
⁴¹ On the nomenclature for such objects, see Marcia Pointon, "'Surrounded with Brilliants': Miniature Portraits in Eighteenth-Century England," *The Art Bulletin*, 83.1 (2001), 48–71 (48).
⁴² Hortense to Eugène, January 11, 1807, box 7, folder 638, SNC.
⁴³ See Deborah Lutz, "The Dead Still among Us: Victorian Secular Relics, Hair Jewelry, and Death Culture," *Victorian Literature and Culture*, 39.1 (2011), 127–142.
⁴⁴ Christiane Holm, "Sentimental Cuts: Eighteenth-Century Mourning Jewelry with Hair," *Eighteenth-Century Studies*, 38.1 (2004), 139–143 (140).

Figure 13.2 Jean Urbain Guerin, *Portrait of Queen Hortense*, c. 1804–1814. Miniature on ivory mounted in a silver pendant framed with diamonds and backed with an arrangement of hair. 3.5 × 2.5 cm. Musée du Louvre, Paris. RF 30721. © RMN-Grand Palais / Art Resource, NY.

Hortense, along with the date and place of its execution and/or presentation.[45] Even a drawing Hortense made years before Mazuyer entered her service – a small view of Lake Geneva in Switzerland – was significant enough to merit an inscription: "Fait par la reine à Prégny le matin de son départ peril en 1815 / donné à Arenenberg avril 1832" (Figure 13.3). In this context, the drawing's subject becomes more than a simple landscape. Sketched on the morning of Hortense's perilous departure from the Château de Pregny-la-Tour, a property at which Hortense stopped briefly after being exiled from France, it becomes a cipher for the beginning of her identity as an émigré. As self-referential signs, small amateur artworks given as gifts thus have the potential to stealthily carry complex meanings about their creators.

When read as an index of the artist's hand, Hortense's miniature copy of Richard's *Madame de la Vallière Carmélite* becomes a free-floating signifier seeking a symbolic meaning within Hortense's own life. Such symbolic links would not have been difficult for Eugène to find, for in 1804, two years before Richard exhibited his first version of the subject, the celebrated author Stéphanie de Genlis had published an immensely successful historical novel entitled *La Duchesse de la Vallière*. In it, Genlis took a royal mistress who had abandoned the glittering court of Versailles in order to become a religiously austere penitent and transformed her into the heroine of a sentimental novel caught between her deeply felt moral principles and her passionate love for Louis XIV. As is typical of a sentimental plot, this fundamental ethical conflict is reiterated again and again in numerous narrative incidents in order to heighten the reader's sympathy for the heroine.[46]

Significantly, Hortense read the novel shortly after its publication and kept a copy in her library until her death.[47] Her life, moreover, corresponded to that of Louise de la Vallière in numerous ways: she found herself trapped in an unhappy sexual relationship (though with her husband

---

[45] The comte Octave d'Esdouhard d'Englène, nephew of Valérie Mazuyer, gave a collection of objects related to Hortense, including her drawings, to the Musée national des châteaux de Malmaison et Bois-Préau between 1927 and 1937.

[46] On the typical double-bind plot of sentimental novels, see Margaret Cohen, *The Sentimental Education of the Novel* (Princeton, NJ: Princeton University Press, 1999).

[47] Madame Campan discussed the book, which she assumed Hortense had already read, in an undated letter from early 1804. Jeanne-Louise-Henriette Campan, *Correspondance inédite de Mme Campan avec la Reine Hortense*, Jean Alexandre C. Buchon (ed.), 2 vols (Paris: A. Levavasseur, 1835), vol. 1, 235–236 (lettre CVI). "La Duchesse de Lavallière par Mme Genlis 2 vols" is listed in the inventory of Arenenberg castle's library after Hortense's death. "Livres," no. 77029, Staatsarchiv Thurgau, Switzerland (photocopy in the collection of the Napoleon Museum Thurgau).

Figure 13.3 Hortense de Beauharnais, *View of Lake Geneva at Prégny*, 1815. Watercolor and graphite on paper. 50 × 68 cm. Musée national des châteaux de Malmaison et Bois-Préau, Rueil-Malmaison. M.M.47.7060. © RMN-Grand Palais / Art Resource, NY.

rather than a lover); she had an extramarital affair that produced an illegitimate child (though with a military officer named Charles de Flahaut rather than a king); and she retreated from public life into relative isolation (though through enforced political exile rather than religious penance).[48] I cite these biographical parallels neither to assert that Hortense *must* have identified with Louise de la Vallière nor to perpetuate the misogynist eighteenth-century trope that women mindlessly imitated the things they read in novels. Rather, I suggest that the events of Hortense's life provided ample material for a sentimental tale of her own, which, in fact, she wrote between 1816 and 1820 in the form of her memoirs.[49] Published in the twentieth century by her grandson, Hortense's manuscript was read during her

---

[48] Hortense's marriage to Louis Bonaparte was unhappy and ended in permanent separation by 1810. She gave birth to her son by Flahaut, Charles de Morny (1811–1865), the following year.

[49] Hortense de Beauharnais, *Mémoires de La Reine Hortense*, ed. Jean Hanoteau, 3 vols. (Paris: Plon, 1927).

lifetime by a small circle of friends, including her brother Eugène, whom she invokes in the first pages of her text.[50]

In her story, Hortense chronicled the cruel behavior of her husband, the romantic attentions of numerous admirers, the many injustices inflicted by fate, and the intense yet (in her memoirs at least) unconsummated love she felt for Flahaut, all the while demonstrating her own moral virtue and scrupulously avoiding any political opinions on the tumultuous events that surrounded her sentimental biographical tale. As Henri Rossi has shown in his important study of early nineteenth-century women's memoirs, Hortense was not alone in thus sentimentalizing the story of her life.[51] Sentimental plot points appear in some of the most important memoirs of the period, including those by the Duchesse d'Abrantès and the Comtesse de Boigne. It is the conclusion to Hortense's memoir, however, that links it most closely to Genlis's novel and to Richard's composition.

Typically, the sentimental novel has an unhappy ending, in which the story's underlying emotional conflict is resolved with the woeful isolation and ultimate death of the heroine. In her preface, Genlis explicitly announces her divergence from this convention. "I may, perhaps be reproached," she writes, "for not having presented Madame de la Vallière as dying and in a state of despair when she finally abandoned Louis XIV."[52] As Suellen Diaconoff has pointed out, Genlis's conclusion depicts the heroine's choice to enter a convent not as a species of suicide committed on account of disappointed love but as a positive triumph of will over passion, as an embrace of independent tranquility, and as an opportunity for self-improvement.[53] Near the end of the novel, Louise de la Vallière herself articulates a unique defense of her choice to enter religious seclusion, where she proclaims:

Ah! when I enter this holy asylum, in which I want to spend the rest of my days, I shall atone for both the faults and the idleness of my past life. I shall no longer misapply the faculty of my mind and my heart; I shall no longer profane my sensibility; I shall no longer have any activity except for the good![54]

---

[50] "Mon frère me connaît assez; quelle est celle de mes pensées dont une confiance mutuelle et une vive affection ne l'aient rendu dépositaire?" Beauharnais, *Mémoires*, vol. 1, 2.

[51] Henri Rossi, *Mémoires Aristocratiques Féminins: 1789-1848* (Paris: H. Champion, 1998), 101–188.

[52] Stéphanie Félicité de Genlis, *La Duchesse de la Vallière*, 2 vols. (Paris: Maradan, 1804), vol. 1, xxv.

[53] Suellen Diaconoff, "The Romance as Transformative Reading: Félicité de Genlis" in *Through the Reading Glass: Women, Books, and Sex in the French Enlightenment* (New York: State University of New York Press, 2005), 77–100.

[54] Genlis, *Duchess of La Vallière*, vol. 2, 220.

Isolated yet content, the seventeenth-century woman painted in Genlis's novel is a model of feminine virtue. She is thus the perfect persona for a politicized woman of the nineteenth century to project to her own readers. Hortense concludes her memoirs in the same spirit:

> Isolated as I am, exiled from my homeland ... I often say to myself: "I no longer need to fear passions. I have conquered them. I no longer fear misfortune. I have been able to bear it. And if I have found a way in which to live quietly and to improve myself, what else can I hope for?"[55]

Echoing the repetition of Vallière's decisive negative phrasing ("I shall no longer ...") in her own voice ("I no longer need ..."), Hortense recalls Genlis's ascetic yet autonomous conclusion to a woman's unhappy existence at the heights of court society.

Hortense's representation of her life story in sentimental terms, on the quietly triumphant model of Genlis's novel, thus amplifies the symbolic significance of her miniature copy of Richard's *Madame de la Vallière*. Though the painted scene – in which Louise de la Vallière "glances at a lily, emblem of her love, and lets her prayerbook fall from her hands"[56] – is not found in the novel itself, the painting produces a corresponding sentimental narrative through its careful orchestration of symbolic contrasts. The heroine's internal conflict between passion and piety arises from the juxtaposition of lily and prayerbook, inside and outside, light and shadow. Depicted at the conclusion of her sentimental tale, Richard's contemplative la Vallière thus becomes a metonym for Hortense in her exile – an identity that she fashioned both in word and image through the parallel strategies of literary and visual imitation.

Within the intertwined contexts of gift exchange, sentimental friendship, amateur art practice, and miniature portraiture, Hortense's tiny copy of Richard's *Madame de la Vallière Carmélite* functioned not only as a reminder of the taste and familial ties shared by brother and sister but also as a poignant yet veiled sign of the giver, as a sort of non-mimetic self-portrait recognizable to a select few. When wielded in the company of Eugène's influential in-laws and other acquaintance, this allegorical portrait-object might have elicited closer examination and the disclosure of its maker, thus disseminating an appropriately virtuous and politically shrewd image of Hortense within an elite social network,

---

[55] Beauharnais, *Mémoires*, vol. 3, 159–160.
[56] *Explication des ouvrages de peinture, sculpture, architecture et gravure, des Artistes vivans, Exposés au Musée Napoléon* (Paris, 1806), cat. no. 431.

much like the reading of her memoirs to select visitors at her salon. Both modes of self-fashioning reframed Hortense's identity on a culturally familiar model that was, nevertheless, executed on her own terms. A lightening rod for partisan politics in uncertain times, Hortense employed seemingly trivial amateur artworks as gifts precisely because they were viewed as sentimental, economically inconsequential, and apolitical. They obscured the socially and politically strategic value of her gift giving while concentrating complex narratives of self into small, discreet, portable, and inexpensive items.

PART IV

Small Things on the Move

14 | Hooke's Ant

TITA CHICO

This is the story of Robert Hooke's ant.

Robert Hooke – microscopist and member of the Royal Society, serving as Curator of Experiments (1662), Cutlerian Lector in Mechanics (1664), and Gresham Professor in Geometry (1664) – produced an influential example of experimental philosophy in *Micrographia: or Some Physiological Descriptions of Minute Bodies Made by Magnifying Glasses* (1665). In it, he studied scores of tiny specimens, peering into their crevices with his glass; he wrote about what he observed, and also oversaw engravings of the wondrous minute bodies revealed by the magnifying qualities of the microscope.

But Hooke's ant, as a specimen, refused to adhere to his protocols of scrutiny, prompting Hooke to detail his frustration and, in a powerfully revealing moment, urge readers to read a book about Barbados to learn more about ants. As we shall see, the story of Hooke's ant uncovers what Lisa Lowe calls the "intimacy" of modern, Western liberalism and the global conditions upon which it depends – in this case, early scientific practice and the institution of transatlantic chattel slavery. Taking up Lowe's encouragement that we look at "scenes of close connection in relation to global geography that one more often conceives in terms of vast spatial distances," I argue that Hooke's ant reveals the notion of scientific scrutiny, and its commensurate epistemological microscoping, to rely upon – uneasily, fitfully, yet fully – the global order of the English colonial slave economy.[1] Hooke's small ant troubles him because it moves, but this movement of an insect likewise characterizes the material and conceptual possibilities of insects more generally. As Clapperton Chakanetsa Mavhunga has recently demonstrated in the case of the tsetse fly, such an insect must be understood to exist as circulating within a system, and the insect's movements ultimately reveal that system as dynamic and fluid and made up of border crossings between

---

[1] Lisa Lowe, *The Intimacies of Four Continents* (Durham, NC and London: Duke University Press, 2015), 18.

bodies, minds, politics, and ideologies.² The story of Hooke's ant takes us into the seventeenth-century definitional work of microscopical practice, exposing the process of scientific scrutiny and its magnifying effects that in turn bring us to the shores of colonial Barbados, a place defined by sugarcane, enslaved Africans, and saltwater slavery. Small things contain the potential to reveal vast scales of geography and their networks of exploitation.

Scientific Scrutiny; or the Study of Small Things

The Preface to *Micrographia* outlines Hooke's aspirations for the minute particulars of microscopy, imagining their significance as commensurate with the great wonders of the natural world. Hooke writes, "And it is my hope ... [that] my little Objects are to be compar'd to the greater and more beautiful Works of Nature, A Flea, a Mite, a Gnat, to an Horse, an Elephant, or a Lyon."³ To elevate the flea, the mite, and the gnat to the majesty of a horse, elephant, or lion, Hooke develops the theory and praxis for microscopical scrutiny, studying objects that are beyond human perception to enlarge them in size and significance.

Hooke's microscopy imagines small things as its objects of inquiry. They are "*exceeding small Bodies, or exceeding small Pores, or exceeding small Motions,*" though not just any "exceeding small" thing will do: "there should be a *scrupulous* choice, and a *strict examination*, of the reality, constancy, and certainty of the Particulars that we admit" (preface). The range of phenomena is capacious – bodies, pores, and motions – but each is subjected to the mechanism of scrutiny whereby the microscopist determines its validity, which Hooke measures as "reality, constancy, and certainty." Small things are selected and examined, and "the most severe, and most impartial diligence, must be imployed" by the microscopist (preface). Selection, close examination, and classification are the markers of Hooke's scientific scrutiny.

I use the term "scrutiny" to characterize the process of microscopy. The *Oxford English Dictionary* reminds us that, since the eighteenth century,

---

² Clapperton Chakanetsa Mavhunga, *The Mobile Workshop: The Tsetse Fly and African Knowledge Production* (Cambridge, MA: MIT Press, 2018), 21–22.
³ Robert Hooke, *Micrographia: or Some Physiological Descriptions of Minute Bodies Made by Magnifying Glasses* (London, 1665), preface. Subsequent references will be cited parenthetically.

"scrutiny" has conveyed "the action of looking searchingly at something; a searching gaze."[4] For Samuel Johnson, it is an "enquiry; search; examination with nicety."[5] There is an older connotation that feeds into its modern meaning, identifying scrutiny as an "investigation," "a critical inquiry."[6] And the term's etymology shows us that it comes from the Latin *scrutinium*, from *scrutari*, "to search" (originally "sort rubbish," from *scruta*, "rubbish"). In scrutiny, we have a term and a concept that connote examination, critique, and method, the search for meaning and sorting through a mess. In sum, scrutiny emphasizes that microscopy is a process.[7]

From the start, Hooke uses descriptions of small things to reenact the experience of microscopical scrutiny. He famously opens *Micrographia* with an object that everyone would agree is sharp and smooth, "the Point of a sharp small Needle." Hooke draws upon his reader's ordinary visual apprehension, announcing that "the *Point of a Needle* ... is indeed, for the most part, made so sharp, that the naked eye cannot distinguish any parts of it: it very easily pierces, and makes its way through all kind of bodies softer then it self" (1). Hooke's selection deliberately plays on the needle's image and connotation, explaining that "this point [is] commonly accounted the sharpest (whence we would express the sharpness of a point the most *superlatively*, we say, As sharp as a Needle)" (2). "Sharp as a needle," in other words, is such a familiar truth that it is a colloquialism. In the course of describing the point of a needle, Hooke rhetorically inserts the microscopic view: "But if view'd with a very good *Microscope*, we find that the *top* of a Needle (though as to the sense very *sharp*) appears a *broad, blunt*, and very *irregular* end" (1–2). In language, Hooke at first paints an image of a smooth, sharp point in order to apply the scrutiny of the microscope, which reveals the needle as instead "irregular and uneven," which are "the marks of the rudeness and bungling of *Art*" (2). The closer one examines a small thing, the less recognizable it becomes.

The movement of Hooke's description of the needle – from how it looks to the naked eye to how it looks under the microscope – narratively enacts the revelatory process of microscopical scrutiny. By chronicling this contrast, Hooke initiates a narrative structure that he repeats throughout *Micrographia*, even within the same observation. After the first contrast

---

[4] *Oxford English Dictionary*, s.v. "scrutiny," 3.
[5] Samuel Johnson, *A Dictionary of the English Language* (London, 1755), s.v. "scrutiny."
[6] *Oxford English Dictionary*, s.v. "scrutiny," 2a.
[7] There is new attention to Hooke's version of microscopy as a relatively undisciplined process. See, for example, Ian Lawson, "Crafting the Microworld: How Robert Hooke Constructed Knowledge about Small Things," *Notes and Records of the Royal Society*, 70 (2016), 23–44 (26).

and disclosure, Hooke provides a second round. The needle might seem "to the naked eye very smooth," but the microscope reveals "a multitude of holes and scratches and ruggednesses" (2). The needle's surface cannot hide its imperfections from microscopic scrutiny, a formulation that imagines the process of observation as epistemological revelation. Only aided by the scientific scrutiny of microscopy can viewers apprehend the *true* material state of an object. Through its narrative structure and figuration, Observation 1 establishes scientific scrutiny as a multifaceted process.

Hooke studies many sorts of objects in *Micrographia*, but fully one-third of the observations are small insects. The first insect observation in *Micrographia* (no. 34) is the sting of a bee and, as a sharp object, formally alludes to the needle that opens the book. In the description of the bee sting, Hooke uses his usual narrative structure that moves from the ordinary to the microscopic view, assuring the reader that "what it appears to the naked eye, I need not describe, the thing being known almost to every one" (163); of significance instead is what the microscope's magnification reveals. In the case of the flea, microscopic scrutiny yields an important aesthetic insight.[8] The description of the flea, an object ordinarily associated with disgust, not only combines visualization with narration, as Cynthia Wall observes, but also asserts the insect's beauty: "adorn'd with a curiously polish'd suit of *sable* Armour" and "beset with multitudes of sharp pins, shap'd almost like … bright conical Steel-bodkins" (210).[9] Supplementing this description is the famous engraving of the flea. These engravings contributed to the success of *Micrographia*.[10] But the engraving of the flea does more than provide a revelatory image; it serves the purpose of mimicking (though imperfectly) the process of microscopical scrutiny. At the conclusion of the observation, Hooke "refer[s] the Reader to the Figure" (211). That is, rather than continue with textual exegesis, Hooke instructs the reader to move from text to image instead, a process that requires unfolding the flyleaf to reveal the flea's pictorial enlargement.

The insect observations throughout *Micrographia* feature tiny specimens that seem to yield themselves up to Hooke's microscopic scrutiny.

---

[8] As Christa Knellwolf reminds us, microscopy "had an immediate aesthetic appeal." "Robert Hooke's Micrographia and the Aesthetics of Empiricism," *The Seventeenth Century*, 16 (2001), 177–200 (196).

[9] Cynthia Sundberg Wall, *The Prose of Things: Transformations of Description in the Eighteenth Century* (Chicago: University of Chicago Press, 2014), 53.

[10] G. L'E. Turner, "Micrographia Historica: The Study of the History of the Microscope" in G. L'E. Turner (ed.), *Essays on the History of the Microscope* (Oxford: Senecio, 1980), 1–29 (20).

An exception is the ant.[11] More than other insects he examines, ants thwart Hooke's attempts to study them and, as a consequence, become the object of his descriptive frustration. The louse may be "impudent" and "proud," "intruding itself in every ones company" (211), for example, but the ant challenges Hooke's protocols of scientific scrutiny.

Hooke's frustration emerges because ants squirm, move about, and run away – in sum, they refuse to be disciplined by the scrutiny of microscopy. The blue fly is similarly difficult to pin down, as recounted in Observation 42 (204), but Observation 44, "*Of an Ant or Pismire*," opens with a complaint: "This was a creature, more troublesom to be drawn, then any of the rest, for I could not, for a good while, think of a way to make it suffer its body to ly quiet in a natural posture" (203). The word "drawn" points to the significance of seeing as a practice in *Micrographia*: such seeing not only results in thick, textual description, but also in the vivid engravings that contributed to the volume's wild success.[12] Calling on his experience with the visual arts, Hooke developed a process of synthesizing the images he observed under the microscope, which artists then engraved, an aesthetic practice Matthew C. Hunter calls "wicked intelligence."[13] Yet the ant resists Hooke's usual protocols for scrutiny. Hooke explains that trapping its legs in "Wax or Glew" results in the ant twisting about so "that I could not any ways get a good view of it" (203). Killing the ant does not solve the problem: "if I killed it, its body was so little, that I did often spoile the shape of it, before I could thoroughly view it" (203). Hooke explains that, like moss, the structural integrity of an ant's body requires moisture, which in turn requires that the ant be kept alive; otherwise, the ant's body "does almost instantly shrivel and dry, and your object shall be quite another thing, before you can half delineate it" (203). A dead ant transforms from an ant into something else altogether, rendering microscopic scrutiny futile.

---

[11] For discussions of ants' biology, social formations, and cultural meanings (many of which personify them), see Bert Hölldobler and Edward O. Wilson, *The Ants* (Cambridge, MA: Harvard University Press, 1990); Charlotte Sleigh, *Ant* (London: Reaktion Books, 2003); Laurent Keller and Élisabeth Gordon, *The Lives of Ants*, trans. James Grieve (Oxford: Oxford University Press, 2009); and Jae C. Choe, *The Secret Lives of Ants* (Baltimore, MD: Johns Hopkins University Press, 2012).

[12] Turner, "Micrographia Historica," 20.

[13] Matthew C. Hunter, *Wicked Intelligence: Visual Art and the Science of Experiment in Restoration London* (Chicago: University of Chicago Press, 2013), 28–67. For Hooke's experience with the visual arts, and his indebtedness to seventeenth-century conventions of portraiture, see Meghan C. Doherty, "Discovering the 'true form': Hooke's Micrographia and the Visual Vocabulary of Engraved Portraits," *Notes and Records of the Royal Society*, 66 (2012), 211–234.

The fact of the difficult ant is less surprising than the amount of time Hooke spends discussing its kineticism as a problem he must solve. And how does he solve it? With a "Gill of Brandy" (a quarter of a pint) or a "Spirit of Wine" (that is, distilled wine). In his own words, Hooke got an ant "dead drunk" until "it ceased to move," at which point he "put its body and legs into a natural posture" to study it under the microscope (204). But we learn that getting to the point of having the ant drunk and transformed into a specimen takes time: while the ant "struggled for a pretty while very much, till at last, certain bubbles issuing out of its mouth, it ceased to move," Hooke explains that he kept it doused in the liquor for an hour, "Because I had before found them quickly to recover again, if they were taken out presently" (204). After an hour in the spirit and an hour under the microscope, the ant "then, upon a sudden, as if it had been awaken out of a drunken sleep, it suddenly reviv'd and ran away" (204). In Hooke's observation, the ant always revives and starts scrambling again. And Hooke always needs to repeat his procedure. Over and over.

In some ways, the manipulation of the specimen accords with Hooke's methodology, in which a composite takes on the qualities of an observed particular.[14] Hooke makes clear that the microscopist discovers a specimen's "true form" or "true appearance" not through a singular observational instance but through a series of ocular examinations (preface). Scientific scrutiny requires looking again and again, with different light and with different lenses. The quest for a "true form" presupposes the stability of an object under view, of course, as well as a certainty that multiple viewings will ultimately reveal it, even though these viewings inevitably produce a synthesis. Hooke explains, "the same Object [may] seem quite differing, in one position to the Light, from what it really is, and may be discover'd in another" (preface). Faced with different images under the microscope, images that may or may not resemble each other, Hooke does not enumerate his method apart from an insistence that he performs "many examinations in several lights, and in several positions to those lights" (preface). Peering through the microscope repeatedly, Hooke explains, enables the production of experimental knowledge; thus "I had discover'd the true form" (preface). The repetition of scrutiny – always with a difference (several lights, several positions) – is methodology.

Yet in the case of the ant, Hooke encounters a specimen that impedes his observational technique because it refuses to stay still. Hooke devotes

---

[14] See my discussion in Tita Chico, *The Experimental Imagination: Literary Knowledge and Science in the British Enlightenment* (Stanford, CA: Stanford University Press, 2018), 32–35.

more than half the observation to describing the process he must go through to get the ant in a position to study it. The ant's movements and its fragile structure together demand Hooke's ingenuity, certainly, but they also prod Hooke into rhetorical excess. Not only does the troublesome ant resist being affixed, but it also refuses a simple discursive accounting. Even the engraving of the ant leaves Hooke dissatisfied; the ant, he writes, is "not so carefully graven as it ought to be" (204).

And if the singular ant thwarts Hooke's microscopic scrutiny, then its collectivity further challenges him. While describing the process of getting a single ant drunk, Hooke interrupts himself to describe the behavior of ants as a collective. The type of ant he chooses to study, he explains, is "inhabited under the Roots of a Tree, from whence they would sally out in great parties, and make most grievous havock of the Flowers and Fruits, in the ambient Garden, and return back again very expertly, by the same ways and paths they went" (203). Yet the individualized ant, both in its description and the accompanying engraving, is ultimately circumscribed within its collective identity – and *this* quality cannot be captured by microscopic scrutiny. Vermin in the early modern period, as Lucinda Cole argues, are imagined not so much in terms of their breed but in terms of their "stark collectivity," which raises political, ethical, and aesthetic anxieties.[15] Hooke's description of ants as a collective in motion presents a unit that cannot be reduced to a singular, stationary specimen. Hooke's microscopy, an experimental practice of scrutiny, insists upon the particular. The singular ant – dunked in liquor, temporarily immobilized – can be disciplined into being a subject of scientific scrutiny. But Hooke's version of microscopy cannot accommodate a specimen's movement, nor can it account for the collective.

From *Micrographia* to Barbados

Individually and collectively, the behavior of ants is outside the purview of Hooke's scientific scrutiny: the observational tools and processes Hooke develops in *Micrographia* limit what he can *see*. But the behavior of ants does not escape his curiosity. In a moment in which his own body makes an unusual appearance within the pages of *Micrographia*, Hooke details lowering his finger to induce ants to crawl up his hand and says he witnessed

---

[15] Lucinda Cole, *Imperfect Creatures: Vermin, Literature, and the Sciences of Life, 1600–1740* (Ann Arbor: University of Michigan Press, 2016), 5.

"many such other [of their] seemingly rational actions ... with much pleasure, which would be too long to be here related." Rather than drop the subject, however, Hooke points the curious reader to another text: "those that desire more of them may satisfie their curiosity in *Ligons* History of the Barbadoes" (204). That is, Hooke encourages readers to put down *Micrographia* and to take up Richard Ligon's *A True and Exact History of the Island of Barbados*, published in London in 1657. In a phrase, Hooke turns from his microscope to imagine a world beyond his myriad experiments, beyond the pages of *Micrographia*, and beyond the shores of England altogether.

For literary scholars today, Ligon's *A True and Exact History* is most familiar as the source text for the Yarico and Inkle story that came to be retold and reimagined in over sixty discrete versions throughout the long eighteenth century.[16] Richard Steele's 1711 adaptation in *The Spectator* brought the narrative to prominence, plotting out the cultural encounter between an Indigenous (though sometimes African) woman and an English man, their affective relation, and his betrayal of her when he sells her as a slave.

Perhaps less familiar is the immediate readership of Ligon's text, namely figures who founded and participated in the Royal Society, including Hooke, John Evelyn, Samuel Hartlib, and Henry Oldenburg.[17] They lauded *A True and Exact History* as a model for natural history, referring to its findings in *Philosophical Transactions*.[18] Ligon's excursus was of the sort the Royal Society imagined for its members and correspondents from abroad.[19] Thus Hooke's allusion to Ligon's *A True and Exact History* in *Micrographia* is not mere happenstance but signals an intellectual community of natural and experimental philosophers.

The placement of Hooke's allusion to Ligon is significant. It comes between two paragraphs in which he describes dunking an ant and at the conclusion of a meditation upon the communal power of ants. Hooke's

---

[16] Frank Felsenstein, "Introduction" in F. Felsenstein (ed.), *English Trader, Indian Maid: Representing Gender, Race, and Slavery in the New World. An Inkle and Yarico Reader* (Baltimore, MD: Johns Hopkins University Press, 1999), 1–51 (2).

[17] Karen Ordahl Kupperman, "Preface" and "Introduction" in K. O. Kupperman (ed.), *A True and Exact History of the Island of Barbados by Richard Ligon* (Indianapolis, IN: Hackett, 2011), vi, 1–36 (33).

[18] For example, Richard Norwood, "An account of some particulars, referring to those of Jamaica," *Philosophical Transactions*, 3.41 (1668), 824.

[19] Thomas Sprat, *The History of the Royal-Society of London*, 2nd ed. (London, 1722), 38, 76; and Abraham Cowley, *A Proposition for the Advancement of Experimental Philosophy* (London, 1661), 29–31.

decision to advise curious readers to consult Ligon to understand the behavior of ants – in the midst of an observation about a specimen that will not stay still, a specimen that is also understood through its awesome collectivity – reveals deep and fundamental connections between early scientific practice, English colonialism, and the institution of slavery in the West Indies. And it is Hooke's ant that makes these relations visible to us today.

By the time Hooke and his contemporaries were reading Ligon, Barbados had been claimed by the English for thirty years, first with a group of about twenty Englishmen and forty enslaved Africans in 1627. In 1640, Barbados was the first English colony in the West Indies to begin sugar cultivation, after a brief and unsuccessful period of growing tobacco.[20] After 1650, Cromwell had many of his political opponents "Barbadozz'd" – that is, rounded up and sent to the island.[21] The term "Barbadozz'd" circulated as shorthand for the process of imprisonment and extradition of Irish and Scots prisoners. Some were criminals; others were royalists of all ranks.

But this synopsis is radically incomplete without understanding that the largest population on the island consisted of enslaved African laborers: between 1640 and 1700, approximately 134,500 enslaved Africans were transported to Barbados.[22]

If Barbados was, "both in absolute numbers and population density, not to mention the great wealth of the sugar industry," England's "leading colony" in the seventeenth century, then it likewise was a key location of the transatlantic slave economy, where thousands of enslaved Africans labored in horrific conditions to produce the sugarcane that fed British wealth and power.[23] A 1636 political directive mandated that all Africans brought to Barbados were legally considered lifelong chattels. And in 1661, Barbados planters passed the first comprehensive slave code, legislation that distinguished between indentured servants, often Irish or Scottish, who could buy their freedom, and enslaved Africans and Indigenous peoples,

---

[20] Richard B. Sheridan suggests that sugarcane was cultivated for personal use as early as 1627, only becoming a commercial enterprise in the 1640s. *Sugar and Slavery: An Economic History of the British West Indies, 1623–1775* (Baltimore, MD: Johns Hopkins University Press, 1974), 129.

[21] John C. Appleby, "English Settlement in the Lesser Antilles" in Robert L. Paquette and Stanley L. Engerman (eds.), *The Lesser Antilles in the Age of European Expansion* (Gainesville: University Press of Florida, 1996), 101; Keith Sandiford, *The Cultural Politics of Sugar: Caribbean Slavery and Narratives of Colonialism* (Cambridge: Cambridge University Press, 2000), 26.

[22] Jerome S. Handler and Frederick W. Lange, *Plantation Slavery in Barbados: An Archaeological and Historical Investigation* (Cambridge, MA: Harvard University Press, 1978), 15.

[23] Sheridan, *Sugar and Slavery*, 132.

who could not – and whose descendants were to be enslaved in perpetuity through the maternal line.[24] Inspired by the wealth generated by enslaved African laborers in Barbados, Cromwell and his allies in the 1650s resuscitated the long-held English aspiration to surpass Spanish colonial power in the West Indies.[25]

The Barbados slave law consolidated the slave economy culture and instituted strictures for the enslavement of Africans. Africans forcibly transported to Barbados were only chattels, the result of what Stephanie E. Smallwood calls "saltwater slavery" – the physically and socially violent process by which traders transformed people into commodities.[26] Thus the planter George Downing could write to his cousin in 1645, without seeming irony, that enslaved Africans were "the life of this place," a claim that forcibly ignores saltwater slavery's violent erasure of the Africans' humanity.[27] As Hilary McD. Beckles explains, by the 1650s, Barbados was the first Black slave society: the English "discourse on trade and economic growth, wealth creation and mercantilism, sovereignty and security, and ethnic identity were tightly tied to the colony's performance as a black slave society."[28]

This is the context in which Ligon wrote and published *A True and Exact History*, the text to which Hooke turns to explain the ant. Ligon's text vividly contributed to the self-justifying colonial and imperial discourse that naturalized and justified the system of saltwater slavery, African enslavement, and the emergence of what came to be the British empire. As Keith Sandiford reminds us, *A True and Exact History* courted two audiences – slavocrats in Barbados and their financial and political allies in London.[29] Ligon was linked to both groups: a royalist who had bought a half share in a sugar plantation on Barbados in 1647, Ligon lived on the island for three

---

[24] For analysis of the Act for the Better Ordering and Governing of Negroes (1661), the slave laws, see Hilary McD. Beckles, *The First Black Slave Society: Britain's "Barbarity Time" in Barbardos, 1636–1876* (Kingston, Jamaica: The University of the West Indies Press, 2016), 19–22. Jennifer L. Morgan makes the important point that the Barbados code regulated the population "in the absence of a legal definition of who—what category of person—was enslaved." She also notes that Virginia, in 1662, was the first colony to "regulate maternal descent." "Partus sequitur ventrem: Law, Race, and Reproduction in Colonial Slavery," *Small Axe*, (55) 22.1 (2018), 1–17 (2).

[25] Kupperman, "Introduction," 29.

[26] Stephanie E. Smallwood, *Saltwater Slavery: A Middle Passage from Africa to American Diaspora* (Cambridge, MA: Harvard University Press, 2007), 33–36.

[27] Sir George Downing to John Winthrop, Jr., August 26, 1645, "Winthrop Papers," V, 43; quoted in Kupperman, "Introduction," 21.

[28] Beckles, *First Black Slave Society*, xii.

[29] Sandiford, *Cultural Politics of Sugar*, 2.

years before returning to London, his business having failed. Some scholars grapple with Ligon's easy acceptance of saltwater slavery and his apparent sympathy for enslaved Africans, while others conclude that Ligon's text is an effective, if chilling, "field manual to Caribbean colonization" that refuses Africans their humanity.[30] Regardless, Ligon's words reflect a deep belief in slavery and the extraction of labor from enslaved Africans to produce colonial wealth, resulting in a text excited about the possibilities of colonialists getting rich.[31]

The Intimacy of Hooke's Ant and Saltwater Slavery; or a Contrapuntal Reading of Sugar

When Hooke interrupts his own narrative about the difficult and uncontrollable ant on his microscope slide by advising his readers to consult Ligon's narrative about the difficult and uncontrollable ant in Barbados, the allusion is hardly neutral or innocent, for it expressly situates microscopy in relation to saltwater slavery and Barbados. With this intertextuality, Hooke lays bare the connection between the work of early English science – a project deeply invested in notions of objectivity – and the colonialist and racist ideologies of the seventeenth century. Lowe's heuristic of "intimacy" allows us to understand that transatlantic saltwater slavery did not occupy a separate ideological sphere from the developments of early English scientific practice. Intimacy, as Lowe explains, is "a means to observe the historical division of world processes." These divisions result in modernity, including modern liberal subjects, and those "that are forgotten, cast as failed or irrelevant because they do not produce 'value' legible within modern classifications."[32] Hooke's ant and saltwater slavery might seem separate – indeed, they are geographically distant – but the heuristic of intimacy reveals that their division is more accurately an enabling fiction of Western modern liberalism.

---

[30] Recent examples include Rebekah Mitsein, "Humanism and the Ingenious Machine: Richard Ligon's True and Exact History of the Island of Barbados," *Journal for Early Modern Cultural Studies*, 16.1 (2016), 95–122; and Anthony Lioi, "Delight Is a Slave to Dominion: Awakening to Empire with Richard Ligon's History" in Thomas Hallock, Ivo Kamps, and Karen L. Raber (eds.), *Early Modern Ecostudies: From the Florentine Codex to Shakespeare* (New York: Palgrave, 2008), 219–234 (219).

[31] David Chan Smith, "Useful Knowledge, Improvement, and the Logic of Capital in Richard Ligon's True and Exact History of Barbados," *Journal of the History of Ideas*, 78.4 (2017), 549–570.

[32] Lowe, *Intimacies of Four Continents*, 17–18.

In concert with Lowe's heuristic of "intimacy," I want to evoke Simon Gikandi's model of reparative reading that gives us the critical tools to apprehend the legacies of slavery in the constitution of British taste and aesthetics. With an eye on the other side of the Atlantic, Gikandi teaches us that the anglophone long eighteenth century was a world in which "the projection of an Augustan order based on politeness, good taste, and manners was at odds with the logic of economic development in the reaches of empire, which demanded total control and brutal governance—and slave labor."[33] To read this world accurately, Gikandi argues, we must perform a "contrapuntal reading of slavery and the culture of taste."[34] Doing so helps us to understand the connections between the empire and the metropole, between the business of slavery and its enabling of "the culture of taste." In what follows, I adopt Gikandi's call to imagine how the business of slavery might be understood to enable, even authorize, the early scientific culture in which Hooke played such a pivotal role. Therefore, bringing together the heuristic of intimacy and the practice of contrapuntal reading, I suggest that Hooke's turn to Ligon reveals that the small ants in *Micrographia* far exceed their status as specimens of scientific scrutiny: they instead stand as intimates of saltwater slavery.

Recall first Hooke's account of the collectivity of ants in his observation. The ants gather in "great parties," they "make most grievous havock," and they maneuver "very expertly." As a group, ants work cohesively and overwhelmingly, even threateningly. At this point, Hooke's description pivots to Ligon's, and Ligon's discussion begins with the ubiquity of ants in Barbados in a passage marked by a frenetic, panicked quality:

> If I should say, they are here or there, I should do them wrong; for they are every where, under ground, where any hollow or loose earth is, amongst the roots of trees, upon the bodies, branches, leaves, and fruit of all trees, in all places without the houses and within, upon the sides, walls, windowes, and roofes without; and on the floores, side-walls, sealings, and windowes within; tables, cupbords, beds, stooles, all are covered with them, so that they are a kind of Ubiquitaries.[35]

Ligon's description conveys the collectivity that the scientific scrutiny of microscopy cannot accommodate, redoubling Hooke's own account in *Micrographia*. Recalling Cole's insight about vermin and collectivity, Ligon's

---

[33] Simon Gikandi, *Slavery and the Culture of Taste* (Princeton, NJ: Princeton University Press, 2011), 52.
[34] Ibid., 67.
[35] Richard Ligon, *A True and Exact History of the Island of Barbados*, ed. Karen Ordahl Kupperman (Indianapolis, IN: Hackett, 2011), 63. Subsequent references will be cited parenthetically within the text.

narrative cannot separate his experience of being a white Englishman in Barbados from the experience of being surrounded by ants in all places, at all times. The number of places where ants go and are is overwhelming, and Ligon's own language slides into repetition and listing. The designations "here" and "there" are inadequate, and Ligon concludes with the term "Ubiquitaries." Ants "are, can be, or seem to be, everywhere at once."[36] And if ants are overwhelming in their numbers, then they are likewise in terms of their collective strength. When ants discover a dead cockroach, "They will divide him amongst them into Atoms; and to that purpose, they carry him home to their houses or nests," and although "his body is bigger than a hundred of them, … they will find the means to take hold of him and lift him up" (63), navigating together seamlessly. Individual ants may well be small things, but collectively they are ubiquitous and overwhelming.

Within the narrative logic of *A True and Exact History*, ants also cannot be known apart from sugar, the crop and commodity fueling the engine of saltwater slavery and the colonial economy, and the crop and commodity that required vast numbers of laborers and tracts of land to produce it.[37] For Ligon, sugar was a commodity beyond compare:

though it has but one single taste, yet, that full sweetness has such a benign faculty, as to preserve all the rest from corruption, which, without it, would taint and become rotten; and not only the fruits of this Island, but of the world, which is a special preeminence due to this Plant, above all others, that the earth or world can boast of (86).

Sugar astounds because it is sweet and it preserves, yet it likewise accrues symbolic and economic meaning well beyond these properties when Ligon announces that sugar has "now grown the soul of Trade in this Island" (87). *A True and Exact History* presents the natural history of sugarcane and its production into the consumable commodity sugar, using these descriptions to detail the extraordinary wealth the crop has generated for the slavocrats (94–96). For Sandiford, Ligon's grasp of sugar demonstrates the enabling incoherence of the concept of "sweete negotiation," a phrase based on Ligon's own language. "Sweete negotiation" tells the story of the colonial and imperial logics that attempted to justify chattel slavery

---

[36] *Oxford English Dictionary*, s.v. "ubiquitary," 2a. The *OED* defines this as "A person or thing that is, can be, or seems to be, everywhere at once; someone or something that is ubiquitous (in various senses)," noting additionally that the term is "Frequently used (chiefly humorously) of insects" and listing Ligon's sentence as an illustrative usage.

[37] Sidney W. Mintz, *Sweetness and Power: The Place of Sugar in Modern History* (New York: Penguin, 1985), 19–73.

as merely yet another form of economics.[38] *A True and Exact History* is defined by its commitment to this ideological incoherence and labors to naturalize the oppression and violence of the institution of saltwater slavery as the centerpiece of English economic imperialism.

The figuration of sugar plays a key role in the text's ideological incoherence and racism: sugar, in Ligon's words, is the colony's "soul of Trade" (87); so, too, do the ants working collectively "all have one soul" (63). Sugar also becomes an instrument to study the behavior of ants. Ligon explains that "other trials we make of their Ingenuity" consist of leaving sugar out to lure ants. Quickly dispensing with the "we" and "they" that dominate his language up to this point, Ligon adopts the personal pronoun, I, at the moment he recounts filling a shell with sugar and attaching it to a brown rope he has nailed to the ceiling, "thinking [the sugar] safe" from ants; "but when I returned, I found three quarters of my sugar gone, and the Ants in abundance, ascending and descending, like the Angels on Jacobs Ladder, as I have seen it painted, so that I found no place safe, from these more then busie Creatures" (64).

Ants may be in this moment, through simile, "like the Angels on Jacobs Ladder" and evocative of biblical space and time. But their ubiquity, collective strength, and inextricability from sugar render them a pestilence in the here and now of colonial Barbados. Antonio Benítez-Rojo explained to us nearly thirty years ago that ants, in a world of Caribbean sugar production and the slave system built to enable it, function narratively as the uncanny. In *Historia de las Indias*, Bartolomé de Las Casas (writing a century before Ligon, and in Hispanola rather than Barbadoes) narratively imagines a plague of ants and their destruction of sugarcane as divine punishment. For what? Benítez-Rojo asks. "Plagues in Hispaniola are the consequence of one transgression: slavery."[39] The comingling of ants, sugar, and pestilence reveals their intimacy, and reading these small things in Ligon's text contrapuntally discloses the ideological network of the saltwater slave economy.

To circle back to Hooke's *Micrographia*: when Hooke tells his reader to consult Ligon to learn more about ants, a command Hooke utters at a moment of his own methodological troubles, he makes the ant mean more than his own microscopic scrutiny can accommodate. Hooke's small ant refuses to be still; so, too, does his narrative, jolting the reader to Barbados

---

[38] Sandiford, *Cultural Politics of Sugar*, 24–40; esp. 33, 37.
[39] Antonio Benítez-Rojo, *The Repeating Island: The Caribbean and the Postmodern Perspective*, 2nd ed. (Durham, NC: Duke University Press, 1996), 102. I am grateful to Chad B. Infante for making this connection to Benítez-Rojo's work.

and to an intimacy between early microscopical practice and saltwater slavery. And Hooke's own language anticipates this intimacy with the title "Observation 44, *Of an Ant or Pismire*." "Pismire" signifies ant, yet it likewise mobilizes a negative connotation, for its second definition is "derogatory": a pismire is "An insignificant person; a person exhibiting behaviour or habits usually associated with the ant."[40] This supplementary, disparaging definition has been available for as long as the word's primary meaning of "ant." In other words, pismire has always been both a noun for an ant and a term of derision for a person. Of course, one of the tricks of microscopy is to convert vermin into art, base objects into valuable specimens – recall the example of the flea. But the term "pismire" refuses to allow the ant to undergo such a recuperative transformation and instead emphasizes its degraded status. The title "*Of an Ant or Pismire*" tellingly prefigures the intimacy of two forms of epistemic disciplinarity, microscopical scrutiny and saltwater slavery.

The scrutiny of microscopy here reveals itself to be expansive rather than delimiting, opening the frame rather than narrowing it. Scrutiny is a process that simultaneously examines and classifies, but it is emphatically a *process*, a dynamic of meaning making that requires, following Gikandi, a contrapuntal reading practice. Hooke's ant not only crawls about the microscope slide and refuses to be seen properly but also evokes the British slave economy. In so doing, Hooke's ant reveals that while scrutiny might well be a technology of ocular and epistemological classification, it likewise contains the potential to reveal the fundamental incoherence, inequities, and obfuscations of those same technologies of discrimination.

Scientific scrutiny, like so many of our Enlightenment legacies, seems to offer a tantalizing clarity, particularly when its focus is on small, seemingly knowable things: it enables new modes of knowledge acquisition such as Hooke and Ligon provide. Close observation of the natural world has become the cornerstone of scientific objectivity, a legacy that shoots through our own cultural moment. But the analytic of scientific scrutiny also requires our collective, critical intervention, a refusal to forget what it tries to forget and to bring forth what this intimacy reveals. To apprehend the fullness of early scientific discourse is, in this instance, to follow Hooke's ant from the rooms at Gresham College to the sugarcane slave plantations in Barbados, from the willfulness of ants as scientific specimens to – through their connections to sugar – their representational and historical intimacy with saltwater slavery. Hooke's ant contains these multitudes.

[40] *OED*, s.v. "pismire," 2.

15 Portable Patriotism

Britannia and Material Nationhood in Miniature

SERENA DYER

In 1789, Britannia rejoiced. Her king, George III, who had suffered for years from a debilitating mental health condition, appeared to have recovered. The regency bill, which parliament had passed in February of that year, was no longer required. The courtiers, politicians, and aristocrats who had spent the previous year circling and supporting the Prince of Wales now swiftly changed tack, eager to demonstrate their loyalty to the reigning monarch. Some clamored to write stanzas of loyalist verse, while others planned balls and assemblies.[1] This shift in power and politics was also displayed visually and materially, as sartorial declarations of royalist allegiance were rapidly modified. People who, mere months earlier, had brandished colors and motifs supporting the prince, now used their dress, jewelry, and accessories to convey support for the king.[2] As a figurehead of the nation, Britannia's image was readily exploited in this flash of patriotic fervor. Britannia, like her people, displayed her relief and adulation at the king's recovery. She appeared on a plethora of small, portable gewgaws – including snuffboxes and rings, fans and lockets, trinkets and brooches – at this moment of patriotic outpouring, as she did sporadically throughout the eighteenth century. These small items, as this chapter will show, held chronometric and affective significance for their owners, and were complex signals of both transient and more enduring feelings of patriotism.

As Melinda Alliker Rabb has argued, "a fad, however short-lived, encapsulates a great deal about the cultural moment of its popularity," and small things were often mobilized as material markers of these fleeting flashes of patriotic feeling.[3] The smallness of accessories allowed them to be both transferable and portable, and their ephemerality also meant that

---

[1] David Chandler, "'In sickness, despair, and in agony': Imagining the King's Illness 1788–1789" in Tristanne Connolly and Steven Clark (eds.), *Liberating Medicine, 1720–1835* (Abingdon: Routledge, 2009), 109–126 (116); Louisa Stuart, "*Gleanings from an Old Portfolio, 1785–1799*," vol. 2, ed. Mrs. Godfrey Clark (Edinburgh: D. Douglas, 1895), 133.

[2] Hannah Greig, *The Beau Monde: Fashionable Society in Georgian London* (Oxford: Oxford University Press, 2013), 127.

[3] Melinda Alliker Rabb, *Miniature and the English Imagination: Literature, Cognition, and Small-Scale Culture, 1650–1765* (Cambridge: Cambridge University Press, 2019), 122.

they could be easily discarded or replaced. As Joseph Roach has identified, accessories "make a useful sign out of a practical superfluity."[4] Sartorial smallness enabled objects to move around and between bodies, as transporters and transmitters of national sentiment. As political fads and currencies shifted, accessories provided temporal markers that were key to commemorative and patriotic practices. This chapter tackles how the concept of British nationhood was mediated by small, portable material goods in the century that followed the 1707 Acts of Union. While existing narratives of nation-making have focused on the political, religious, and military forging of Britishness, this chapter instead considers how Britain's intersecting industrial and commercial transformations offered opportunities for manufacturers and retailers to commoditize nationhood through material culture.[5] In doing so, my discussions restore the materiality of nationhood to historical narratives of patriotism to show that the commercialization of Britishness, through small things, provided a means of manufacturing and molding an affective form of British identity. This manufactured material nationhood took the form of cheap, rapidly produced paraphernalia of patriotism, alongside more robust, permanent objects that stood as memorials and timekeepers of the nation's history. My discussions focus specifically on how the figurehead of Britannia signaled a material patriotism that could be worn, carried, and displayed at moments of national importance. Her image, as warrior queen, mother of the nation, and colonial pioneer, was replicated on fans, jewelry, and other decorative objects to formulate miniature material articulations of a national rhetoric.

The iconography of Britannia had long been called upon during moments of political uncertainty, such as James I and VI's ascension to the thrones of both England and Scotland.[6] In her material form, Britannia was shaped into a mouthpiece for a mercantilist vision of British nationhood. Not only was she used to adorn trade cards, bill heads, and advertisements, but she was also molded, carved, or stitched into material

[4] Joseph Roach, *It* (Ann Arbor: University of Michigan Press, 2007), 52.
[5] For studies of the political, religious, and military formation of Britishness, see, for example, Linda Colley, *Britons: Forging the Nation, 1707–1837* (London: Yale University Press, 1992); Steven G. Ellis and Sarah Barber (eds.), *Conquest and Union: Fashioning a British State, 1485–1725* (London: Longman, 1995); Emma Major, *Madam Britannia: Women, Church, and Nation, 1712–1812* (Oxford: Oxford University Press, 2011).
[6] On Britannia's origins and development over the eighteenth century, see Major, *Madam Britannia*, 23–68. While Britannia was overshadowed by John Bull in satirical articulations of the British people, she continued to dominate commercial and material expressions of the British nation. See, for example, Tamara L. Hunt, *Defining John Bull: Political Caricature and National Identity in Late Georgian England* (London: Routledge, 2017).

objects that were held, worn, used, and displayed. Focusing on representations of Britannia on fashionable accessories, including snuffboxes, fans, and rings, this chapter considers how these small things mediated and embodied everyday material practices of nationhood. These handheld Britannias travelled between pockets and palms and attached notions of nationhood to the bodies that wore and held them. Patriotism could be performed and dynamically displayed through these small, portable, and concentrated nuggets of Britishness.

The vision of British nationhood conveyed in these small objects was neither homogeneous nor universal. Such objects were produced alongside seditious and subversive Jacobite and anti-British propaganda.[7] As condensed and concentrated articulations of political and cultural issues, they allow us to interrogate the tensions and intersections between the identities of each of the four home nations, the identities of colonized nations, and Britishness as a category. These small objects acted as crucibles for a multiplicity of patriotic consumer practices and influences, as they merged commercial enterprise, colonial expansion, military and naval power, local cultures, and international trade with sartorial, personal, and affective customs and styles. Within grand narratives of nation-making and commercial cultures, the patriotic power of these small material things has often been overlooked in favor of more overtly politicized architectural and sartorial symbolism.[8]

These small objects played with scale to shape the political and cultural capital that they encapsulated, as discussed in the first section of this chapter. Here, the monumentality of Britannia is shrunk down into handheld trinkets, which translated the expression of civic, affective patriotism into palm-sized affirmations of national loyalty. This chapter will go on to address how this pocket-sized figurehead was depicted on fans. Fans were ephemeral accessories, quickly produced and just as easily discarded. They conveyed a form of loyalty that aligned with fashionable change and the fleeting performance of patriotism at moments of national significance, such as the swift shift in support from the Prince of Wales to George III in 1789. Here, the smallness of the objects added to

---

[7] Extensive work exists on Jacobite material culture in this period. See Murray Pittock, *Material Culture and Sedition, 1688–1760: Treacherous Objects, Secret Places* (London: Palgrave, 2013); Neil Guthrie, *The Material Culture of the Jacobites* (Cambridge: Cambridge University Press, 2013); Viccy Coltman, *Art and Identity: A Cultural History from the Jacobite Rising of 1745 to Walter Scott* (Cambridge: Cambridge University Press, 2019).

[8] See, for example, Katrina Navickas, "'That Sash Will Hang You': Political Clothing and Adornment in England, 1780–1840," *Journal of British Studies*, 49.3 (2010), 540–565.

their disposability. The short lifespan of their cultural relevance means that only a few have been saved, resulting in an archival scarcity that is unrepresentative of their original ubiquity. Notably the design of fans afforded distinct opportunities for affective engagement and manipulation. These transient objects offered up interactive surfaces that permitted their owners to creatively transform and personalize them. Examples of these altered artifacts, as this chapter will show, integrated cultures of making with the performance of patriotism. Finally, this chapter will turn to exquisite patriotic jewelry, which played an interconnected but temporally opposed role in the memorialization of personal and national grief. These more permanent objects acted as chronometric memorials of moments in the nation's history, leaving a trail of material objects that attested to the British historical narrative.[9] These solid, enduring objects embodied potent concentrations of patriotism and crafted expensive emblems of Britishness through precious stones and prized materials. In examining how handheld symbols of national unification, and exquisite and costly memorials to national grief, constituted forms of monumental miniaturization, this chapter unearths Britannia's infiltration of the pockets, hearts, and minds of the British. Through these small things, little Britannias passed between hands as ambassadors for British patriotism.

From Monumental to Handheld: Britannia Miniaturized

The Britannia with which we are most familiar is not small at all. She reigns in the form of monumental statues on the façades of the imposing public buildings still dominant in British towns and cities today, and which are used to convey majesty and (usually imperial) British power.[10] Other Britannia statues stand as bitter reminders of British colonial rule

---

[9] On fashion's role in mediating historical narratives, see Timothy Campbell, *Historical Style: Fashion and the New Mode of History, 1740-1830* (Philadelphia: University of Pennsylvania Press, 2016).

[10] On monuments in the eighteenth century, see Gill Perry, "Women, Allegory and Symbolic Conventions" in Gil Perry and Michael Rossington (eds.), *Femininity and Masculinity in Eighteenth-Century Art and Culture* (Manchester: Manchester University Press, 1994), 23–30; Joan Coutu, *Persuasion and Propaganda: Monuments and the Eighteenth-Century British Empire* (Montreal and Kingston: McGill-Queen's University Press, 2006); Joan Coutu, "Sculpture and the Forming of National Tastes in the Middle of the Eighteenth Century" in Sarah Burnage and Jason Edwards (eds.), *The British School of Sculpture c. 1760-1832* (London: Routledge, 2017), 35–53.

in countries around the globe.[11] In 1728, for instance, Michael Rysbrack began work on his marble bass-relief, entitled "Britannia being presented with the riches of the East," for the court room of East India House.[12] The relief depicts Britannia, seated on a globe, with a trident grasped in one hand, and with her other hand draped over a shield adorned with the union flag. In her magisterial throne, she receives goods from female continental representatives: India presents a casket, Asia grasps at the bridle of a camel, and Africa has her arm around an exceptionally tame lion. Britannia graciously accepts these goods as gifts, the bloody realities of colonialism hidden beneath a façade of grace and trade. Seventy years later, Britannia's role as public purveyor of patriotic loyalty was further cemented in the East India Company's headquarters on Leadenhall Street in London, which were rebuilt in 1799. The building's new frontage took Britannia to her enormous extreme.[13] On top of the portico of New East India House sat a giant stone Britannia, flanked by figures of Asia to the left and Europe to the right. Britannia oversees the pediment below, in which George III is depicted protecting her with his shield, and she graciously receives the proffered produce of Asia, who kneels before her. These uncomfortably colonial and paternalistic representations of Britannia acted as public and civic symbols of monumental patriotism that would endure into the twentieth century.

The political propaganda of material culture spread beyond the grand and the civic to infiltrate the homes, clothes, pockets, and hands of the British in miniaturized form.[14] Motifs celebrating Tory-Anglican Church-and-King loyalism spread across pots, jugs, and plates, which were mass-produced and widely available to consumers across the social strata. Britannia's enduring and collective resonance was in no small part thanks to her having quite literally taken up residence in the pockets of her people. Since the reign of Charles II, Britannia had begun to appear on coinage.[15] She resided on the halfpenny throughout the eighteenth century, appeared on the penny from 1797 onwards, and was also used on tokens throughout

---

[11] Jason Edwards, "From the East India Company to the West Indies and Beyond: The World of British Sculpture, c. 1757–1947," *Visual Culture in Britain*, 11.2 (2010), 147–172.

[12] Michael Rysbrack, *Britannia being presented with the riches of the East*, marble bas-relief, 1729, British Library, G70036-76 British Library, G70036-76.

[13] James Elmes, *The East India House, Leadenhall Street*, 1803, print, British Library, WD4585.

[14] Katrina Navickas, "The 'Spirit of Loyalty': Material Culture, Space and the Construction of the English Loyalist Memory, 1790–1840" in Allan Blackstock and Frank O'Gorman (eds.), *Loyalism and the Formation of the British World 1775–1914* (Woodbridge: Boydell, 2014), 43–60.

[15] She also appeared on bank notes from 1694.

the century.[16] Cast in relief and accompanied by her familiar union shield and trident, these small coins present a numismatic reduction of the Britannia who reigned above municipal buildings or East India Company House. These Lilliputian Britannias took the essence of the patriotic commercial message broadcast and spectacularized on porticos and statues and shrunk it down into an object of exchange, from person to person. As Britannia passed from pocket to pocket, she quietly established herself as a symbol of commercial Britishness. Eighteenth-century numismatists viewed coins as affective and powerful historical agents, as Crystal B. Lake explains in this volume (Chapter 5).[17] As a miniature effigy of nationhood, Britannia's depiction on coins established her power as a symbolic figurehead of the nation, much like the monarchs she accompanied. However, she also presented a timelessness that transcended the mortality of kings and queens. While monarchs presented a sequential historical timeline for the nation's history, Britannia offered a solid and deceptively consistent national figurehead. Her smallness surreptitiously generated a bodily intimacy between the British people and the national figurehead, as she infiltrated pockets and tumbled between fingers.

The details of these pocket-sized Britannias emphasized the same salient characteristics as their architectural counterparts. Global trade, commercial cultures, and regal nationhood were emblematically intertwined. For example, the Britannia on a 1797 halfpenny is posed with her union shield on a rocky seat.[18] The rocks of Britain's shorelines are shaped into Britannia's throne. This rock encapsulated the island nation – the very geological substance of Britain becomes Britannia's station. She gazes out towards a ship in the distance, its masts just visible on the left-hand edge of the coin. By the 1790s, at the height of Nelson's fame and success, Britannia, alongside Neptune, had become associated with the nation's naval power. This coin was struck during the tumultuous year that saw the Battle of Cape St. Vincent, the blockade of Cadiz, and the Battle of Santa Cruz de Tenerife, when British naval support and symbolism were at their heights. Britain had "come to view its navy as a central icon of its self-consciousness."[19] Nautical preeminence and national pride were interlaced in the emerging British consciousness that was solidified during the latter quarter of the

---

[16] Katharine Eustace, *Britannia: Icon on the Coin* (London: Royal Mint Museum, 2016).
[17] See also Crystal B. Lake, *Artifacts: How We Think and Write about Found Objects* (Baltimore, MD: Johns Hopkins University Press, 2020).
[18] This coin is in a private collection.
[19] Nicholas Tracy, *Britannia's Palette: The Arts of Naval Victory* (Montreal: McGill-Queen's University Press, 2007), 10.

Figure 15.1 Enameled box depicting Britannia, 1789, Metropolitan Museum of Art, 26.33.4.

eighteenth century, and Britannia offered an ideal icon for this union. As Britain's global commercial and colonial powers grew, Britannia distilled these vast and distant concepts into an accessible message for the British people. A tiny ship and miniaturized Britannia, held in the hand, caused this immense global power to appear at once condensed and comfortingly comprehensible. Through Britannia, it was possible to hold the British world in the palm of one's hand.

Once within the nation's pockets, Britannia progressed from coins onto other small, handheld objects. One such trinket from 1789, an enameled box produced in Staffordshire (Figure 15.1), depicts Britannia cradling a portrait of the newly healthy king, flanked by her faithful lion and Union-Jack-emblazoned shield. Around the box, we hear Britannia's thoughts: "Proud of her GEO III Britannia rears Her Herd & hopes he will reign many Years." This patch box offered its owner a dynamic mode of material expression through which to convey royal loyalty. The box was probably used to hold the small, black circles of silk or paper known as patches. It would have sat upon its owner's dressing table, clearly displayed to visitors, and was at once a vessel for the materials of bodily beautification and an adornment for the domestic interior. The designs on similar boxes marked them as souvenirs of fashionable towns such as Bath or Cheltenham or as tokens of affection gifted between lovers.[20] Used to decorate an object that was usually reserved for personal and private meaning, Britannia's presence signals her patriotic foothold within the affective material language of the eighteenth century. These boxes memorialized sentiment and could be intensely personal. As containers for a bodily ornamentation, the patch box intensifies this sense of personal intimacy.[21] Britannia guards and provides the patches to her owner. Patriotic affiliation is transferred from the box and onto the face through the application of the patches, adding to the strata of Britannia's bodily permeation. Squeezed onto the box's small lid, Britannia's form was shrunken compared with the monumental statues that peppered civic spaces. Yet this miniaturization has not lessened her affective patriotic significance. It is, instead, intensified and condensed, as public grandiosity is transformed into personal and possessable patriotic intimacy.

Fanning the Union

Small-scale, portable items offered surfaces upon which personal and cultural meaning could be displayed and transported. As Rabb has delineated, fans were read as "miniature worlds" that contained "symbolic representations … capable of eliciting strong reactions."[22] Far more than a useful tool for cooling the body, topical fans were intensely politicized. Although the figure of Britannia herself is absent, the "Rule Britannia" fan produced in 1760 celebrates Britain's industrial and commercial affluence.[23] Like the coins, this fan leaf abridges the vastness of global trade into something handheld. The fan leaf is divided into three sections, each scene wildly out of scale with its counterparts. The content of each cartouche was scaled to match its significance within the scheme of the fan, rather than their

---

[20] Sally Holloway, *The Game of Love in Georgian England: Courtship, Emotions, and Material Culture* (Oxford: Oxford University Press, 2019), 102.
[21] Aileen Ribeiro, *Facing Beauty: Painted Women and Cosmetic Art* (London: Yale University Press, 2011), 192.
[22] Rabb, *Miniature and the English Imagination*, 122.
[23] Fan Museum: HA1575.

relative size to each other. Here, actual scale is dismissed in favor of representational purpose. On the left of the fan, a cartouche depicts the familiar maritime scene of trading vessels under full sail: British ships signal the nation's global trading networks. They are poised to set out across the ocean, perhaps to China or India, and return laden to the gunwales with goods. To the right, peaches and grapes denote the prosperity and fruitfulness of this international trade and industry. The central cartouche transports us away from docks and foreign lands, and into a draper's shop. Shelves laden with silks cover the walls, and rolls of sumptuous fabric are in the process of being unfurled on the shop counter. This scene is inhabited by three fashionably dressed women consumers and two obliging male retailers. The central consumer holds the very same fan upon which she is depicted. Such self-referentiality cements the fan as a handheld object, which is moved, transported, and displayed in the hand. The woman's friends browse the colorful and diverse assortment of fabrics that fill the shelves and spread over the counter. The connection between global trade, national prosperity, and consumer activity are made explicit through this scaled-down and out-of-scale composition. Although Britannia herself is not depicted, her spirit is very tangibly present as an agent of rescaled, portable patriotism.

The women who carried these fans proactively "turned themselves into political canvasses."[24] As Elaine Chalus has shown, the use of politically charged symbols within dress had the power to generate collective statements about identity and allegiance.[25] They could transform the parlor or ballroom into a politicized space and the individual into a beacon of protest or support.[26] Bodies – and especially women's bodies – were transmuted into billboards for the material rhetoric of politics. Occasionally, this was achieved through a complete outfit that could both unite and distinguish its wearers. The Duchess of Devonshire's infamous "blue and buff uniform," denoting support of the Whigs, and the 1789 "Windsor uniform," prescribed for a ball celebrating George III's recovery, offer rare examples of an entire women's ensemble being designated as political.[27] Far more common was the mobilization of small tokens of political or patriotic allegiance. Many

---

[24] Elaine Chalus, "Fanning the Flames: Women, Fashion, and Politics" in *Women, Popular Culture and the Eighteenth Century*, ed. Tiffany Potter (Toronto: University of Toronto Press, 2012), 92–114, 92.
[25] Ibid., 95.
[26] Greig, *The Beau Monde*, 128.
[27] *The New Annual Register* (May 1784), 39; Stuart, *Gleanings from an Old Portfolio*, vol. 2, 133. For a visual depiction of the latter, see Ann Frankland Lewis's "dress of the year" watercolor for 1789, Los Angeles County Museum of Art: AC1999.154.15.

of these, as Chalus and Navickas have demonstrated, marked out the Whig and Tory divide of 1780s London and articulated domestic politics rather than national unity.[28] Cockades and ribbons, flowers and garlands, trinkets and fans: a plethora of sartorial accessories politicized as well as beautified eighteenth-century women. Small sartorial items could be incorporated into any number of outfits, swapped as allegiances changed, and easily hidden if in unsympathetic company. The smallness of these accessories facilitated their power as political tools. Their display was impermanent but saturated with intensely significant cultural value. Their ephemerality, mass production, and (often) low economic value meant they could be discarded as tastes and trends evolved. Yet this disposability, in turn, preserved those objects as microcosms of moments of patriotic meaning. Similarly, when in use, a fan could be swiftly closed to disguise its decorative leaf or thrust deep into a concealing pocket. They were able to at once offer a portable prospectus for patriotic expression and act as agents of "secrecy and deception."[29] One example of a Jacobite fan, for instance, was floral on one side and political on the reverse. A swift switch mid-flutter ensured that the political connotations were concealed.[30] The smallness and maneuverability of fans, patch- and snuffboxes, buttons, ribbons, and jewelry gave them dynamic purpose within men's and women's wardrobes.

Britannia's presence on such accessories was part of a broader visual political vocabulary, which included Jacobite insignia, symbols of Irish nationalism, and French revolutionary emblems. Depending on their context, fans depicting Britannia could be celebratory or inflammatory, supportive of the state or disruptive. Britannia was present in both Jacobite and Hanoverian iconography, each claiming rightful ownership of her image in material culture as they did her kingdoms.[31] A 1745 Jacobite fan, for example, depicts Prince Charles Edward Stuart, the Jacobite claimant, alongside famed Jacobite supporters Flora MacDonald and Cameron of Lochiel as Bellona and Mars.[32] The Hanoverian family retreats in terror from the scene, pursued by cosmically delivered lightening, while Britannia, seated at the foreground of the fan, watches on serenely. Here, she appears as a passive character to be fought over and appeased by the two royal houses. The small canvases offered by sartorial accessories provided a venue for the complexities and nuances of Britannia's various characters to be deliberated and contested.

---

[28] Navickas, "That Sash Will Hang You"; Chalus, "Fanning the Flames."
[29] Rabb, *Miniature and the English Imagination*, 122.
[30] Victoria and Albert Museum: T.160–1970.
[31] See, for example, National Library of Scotland: 75240314.
[32] British Museum: 1891,0713.144.

Figure 15.2 Unmounted fan leaf depicting The United Sisters, 1801, 1891,0713.391. © The Trustees of the British Museum.

On other fans, however, Britannia was a symbol of idealized mercantile accord and political harmony. To mark the 1800 Act of Union with Ireland, Britannia and Hibernia swiftly became firm friends in visual and material culture, appearing not only on fans but also on the printed ephemera of trade. The figures were used to promote Irish linen, in particular. Linen had long been a source of dispute between the two nations, but with the union this once unpatriotic fabric became acceptable on both sides of the Irish Sea.[33] The *United Sisters* fan depicts Britannia alongside Hibernia and Caledonia – Cambria is, as usual, noticeably absent (Figure 15.2).[34]

[33] Louis M. Cullen, *Anglo-Irish Trade, 1660–1800* (Manchester: Manchester University Press, 1968), 62.
[34] British Museum: 1891,0713.391. Although this copy is unmounted, other mounted copies exist. For example, one was sold in the auction of the Tilley collection of antique fans on April 10, 2018, in Newbury, Berkshire. For a depiction of Cambria, see British Museum: 2010,7081.581.

The accoutrements of their nations frame the three women: a lion for Britannia, a harp for Hibernia, and a unicorn for Caledonia. The composition of this sisterly union subtly positions Britannia's Scottish and Irish siblings as subservient, despite their apparent familial unity.[35] Britannia, the central figure, grasps their hands and leads them forwards towards an imagined unified future. The caption beneath reads: "Fair sister Isles of antient [sic] fame! / In Commerce Arms & Arts ye same: / Long may sweet Union bind you three / Each blessing each and blest as free." The mention of commerce in the caption underscores the intrinsic association between these women as national figureheads and the mercantile interests of their respective nations. The economic benefits of trade bind the union more firmly than any sisterly bond. As a microcosm of national union, the fan leaf attempts to manufacture harmony and political success. Unlike municipal or monumental efforts to cement this new chapter in the British political tale, the small scale of the fan attaches the political event of the Acts of Union to bodily adornment and activity. The (presumably) female hand that twirled and wafted this fan would be aligned with the "united sisters" it depicted. The connection visualized an extended sisterhood between the allegorical "united sisters" referenced upon the fan and the fan's owner.

Britannia functioned also as a unifying figure between countries beyond the four nations, as shown by her appearance on other fans that similarly condensed the vastness of political power and connection down to the small scale of the fan. When George III married Princess Charlotte of Mecklenburg-Strelitz in 1761, for instance, Britannia blessed the union on commemorative fans that promoted national support of the marriage. On one 1761 example, Britannia and Neptune gaze across at the royal couple with approval and open, welcoming arms.[36] For a royal family still dogged by xenophobia towards their German roots, symbolically mobilizing Britannia as a supporter and champion was visually powerful. Queen Charlotte would become one of the most vocal and consistent supporters of British production and patriotic consumption, meaning the use of Britannia on a sartorial accessory was particularly prescient.[37] This symbiotic support – Queen Charlotte for British manufacture and patriotic consumption, and Britannia for the queen's legitimacy and role – joined monarch to national figurehead, cementing their mutual Britishness and patriotism.

---

[35] Major, *Madam Britannia*, 28–29.
[36] Royal Collections Trust: RCIN 25159.
[37] Jenny Lister, "Twenty-Three Samples of Silk: Silks Worn by Queen Charlotte and the Princesses at Royal Birthday Balls, 1791–1794," *Costume*, 73 (2003), 51–65 (56); Colley, *Britons*, 275.

Britannia in Mourning

Small Britannias brought the nation together in mourning as well as in triumph and celebration. The death of Frederick, Prince of Wales (1707–1751), saw the image mobilized as mother of the nation, who mourned the loss of her prince, on fans that displayed Britannia weeping at the foot of a cenotaph, the figure expressing and performing the nation's grief.[38] Madge Dresser has credited Britannia's femininity with equipping her with the ability to "express the emotions which men were expected to suppress."[39] Mourning was certainly fashioned as a feminine activity through visual and material culture.[40] However, as Thomas Dixon has shown, the act of weeping held complex emotive, moral, and cultural power.[41] Eighteenth-century medical advice recommended tears as a response to grief in order to avoid "mental derangement or death."[42] Britannia's tears were noble, healthy, and appropriate as a response to national grief. She cries in order to maintain the well-being of the nation. As a product of this cultural language of tears as curative and therapeutic, Britannia was represented as a restorative nurse who would lead the nation in their collective recovery. That she enacted this role through small things is not coincidental. Miniature objects could house immense emotional power and act as "vehicles" for the management of emotions.[43] Similarly, they could act as emotional agents, triggering and signaling appropriate emotions to those around them.

Britannia's role as chief mourner was amplified amid the naval activity of the late eighteenth and early nineteenth centuries. The death of Admiral Rodney in 1792 foreshadowed the outpouring of national grief directed towards Nelson's death thirteen years later, and Britannia played a leading role in the sorrow. An unmounted fan leaf commemorating his death displayed Britannia not in tears but as a conduit for a grateful and gracious nation (Figure 15.3). She reaches out from her shoreline seat to place a crown on the deceased naval officer's head, while Neptune floats on

---

[38] British Museum: 1891,0713.385. See also Thomas Dixon, *Weeping Britannia: Portrait of a Nation in Tears* (Oxford: Oxford University Press, 2015).

[39] Madge Dresser, "Britannia" in *Patriotism: The Making and Unmaking of British National Identity*, ed. Raphael Samuel (London: Routledge, 1989), 26–49, 37.

[40] Ariane Fennetaux, "Fashioning Death/Gendering Sentiment: Mourning Jewelry in Britain in the Eighteenth Century" in Maureen Daly Goggin and Beth Fowkes Tobin (eds.), *Women and the Material Culture of Death* (Abingdon: Ashgate, 2009), 27–50.

[41] Dixon, *Weeping Britannia*.

[42] Ibid., 135.

[43] Rabb, *Miniature and the English Imagination*, 90.

Figure 15.3 Unmounted fan leaf mourning the death of Admiral Rodney, 1792, 1891,0713.386. © The Trustees of the British Museum.

his open shell as he mimics her action. Rodney himself, posed in a heroic stance, gazes dutifully towards Britannia. The central cartouche of the fan was an uncolored mezzotint engraving, which was mass-produced and appeared on similar examples.[44] What is remarkable about this example is the hand-applied paint and additional decoration that surround the central print, including the black border, swirling foliage, and urn decorations. Unevenly and naively applied, this appears to be an amateur addition to the purchased printed fan leaf. The personalization of this patriotic memento aligns with cultures of making that saw consumers interact with the prints they purchased.[45] Coloring, embellishing, and copying printed images acted as a means of creative expression. Prints acted as "emblematic and illustrative aids to learning," and the practice of copying and coloring prints was framed as a fundamental skill within contemporary educational texts.[46] Unlike grand monuments, small sartorial items provided opportunities for these creative expressions of patriotism, even if the brief moment for commemoration was over before the fan was made up and used.[47] Once more, the transient nature of these small objects is amplified and captured in this snapshot of making. The fan leaf, half complete, speaks to a cultural moment that was at once significant enough for the owner to intimately and creatively engage with political messaging, and also so fleeting that the object was useless before it was finished. As a commercial product, the fan's nationalist imagery upholds patriotic consumption, but one that bears the traces of the purchaser's own hand in the paint and ink she has applied herself. If we accept the printed fan leaf as a commemorative national artifact, the act of personalizing and altering this surface could generate an individual attachment between the owner and the moment of national historical significance and shared feeling.

Fans were far from the only sartorial accessories upon which Britannia performed as a marker of mourning. Her wistful and mournful gaze also stared out from jewelry, including rings, lockets, and bracelets. Unlike the relative ephemerality of fans, which could be swiftly manufactured and sold with each new rapidly changing patriotic moment, these bejeweled

---

[44] Another example was sold at auction on October 8, 2019, by Lawrences, Crewkerne, Somerset.
[45] See Serena Dyer, *Material Lives: Women Makers in the 18th Century* (London: Bloomsbury, 2021), chapters 2 and 4.
[46] Ann Bermingham, *Learning to Draw: Studies in the Cultural History of a Polite and Useful Art* (London: Yale University Press, 2000), xi. See, for example, George Brookshaw, *A New Treatise on Flower Painting, or, Every Lady Her Own Drawing Master* (London: Longman, 1816).
[47] On fashion accessories as a "rapid, cheap response to current events," see Hilary Davidson, *Dress in the Age of Jane Austen: Regency Fashion* (London: Yale University Press, 2019), 257.

Britannias constituted more permanent mementos. Like coins, they acted as temporal markers, which manufactured a material timeline of British history. The brief moment of unified national feeling might be fleeting, but some of these objects were permanent. They can be read as private remembrances, as many were made to commemorate the death of naval family members.[48] Such lockets were mass-produced as mourning jewelry and included depictions of Britannia painted on ivory within an engraved gold frame. This mass production did not dilute Britannia's cultural resonance, rather it amplified it. Through these small things, her cultural permeation was immense and yet discreet. The image was familiar and standardized: Britannia on a rock, looking out to ships at sea, shoulders forlornly slumped in an affective pose, with her lion and shield beside her. She was usually monochrome, reflecting the somber mood and the practicalities of efficient mass production. Yet this culturally ubiquitous image was also personalized. Privately concealed on the reverse of an example in the Victoria and Albert Museum is an inscribed name and lock of hair, memorializing a lost loved one.[49] As Marcia Pointon has argued, the iconography of mourning in jewelry was made up of "images from a repertoire of funerary motifs," of which Britannia was a popular example.[50] The relationship between these objects and loss, memory, and ritual is well established; however, the iconography of these objects sits in an intermedial position between private sentimental memorialization and public affective patriotism.[51] It was not only the wearer who mourned this loss but Britannia, as a representative of the nation. Britannia's role thus spanned public, private, and liminal stages for patriotic expression.

Britannia was, of course, far from the only figurehead through which national loyalty or patriotism could be displayed. Portraits of members of the royal family, slogans, and oak leaf patterns were also imbued with British meaning. Even expanses of text were used to inscribe the nation's

---

[48] On other forms of private remembrance, see Malcolm Baker, "Public Fame or Private Remembrance? The Portrait Bust and Modes of Commemoration in Eighteenth-Century England" in W. Reinink and J. Stumped (eds.), *Memory & Oblivion* (Dordrecht: Springer, 1999), 527–535.

[49] Victoria and Albert Museum: 943–1888.

[50] Marcia R. Pointon, *Brilliant Effects: A Cultural History of Gem Stones and Jewellery* (London: Yale University Press, 2009), 301.

[51] For more on mourning jewelry, see Lou Taylor, *Mourning Dress: A Costume and Social History* (London: George Allen and Unwin, 1983); Marcia Pointon, "Materializing Mourning: Hair, Jewellery, and the Body" in Marius Kwint, Jeremy Aynsley, and Christopher Breward (eds.), *Material Memories* (London: Bloomsbury, 1999), 39–71; Fennetaux, "Fashioning Death/Gendering Sentiment."

history on material goods.[52] Britannia was, however, an integral figure in this broader culture of material patriotic expression and an icon that acted as a conduit for a uniquely mercantile and material vision of Britishness. Britannia's presence on these portable and wearable objects exposes how the material rhetoric of nationhood was integrated into quotidian material practices. The towering, gargantuan Britannia who reigned over public buildings was transmuted and miniaturized into a complex and diverse tool for the expression of national allegiance. Creative interventions in the patriotic narrative, such as through the amateur artistry displayed on the fan commemorating Rodney's death, transformed these artifacts of national heritage into something creative and personal. It was not simply prescribed but proactively enacted. These objects created a kind of contemporary archaeology, self-consciously constructed as the material remnants and memorialization of a united nation. Yet, simultaneously, it reflected the fluid and transitory nature of national feeling. Similar to the "God Save the King" ephemera of 1789, most of these objects were as quickly created and worn as they were discarded and forgotten. Both transient and historicizing, objects – even small ones – depicting Britannia were affective and introspective as well as public and performative.

[52] In 1793, J. Cock and J. P. Crowther published a fan printed with a written version of the nation's history, entitled "England since the conquest." Hampshire Cultural Trust: HMCMS:KD1991.60.

16 | Revolutionary Histories in Small Things

Louis XVI and Marie Antoinette on Printed Ceramics, c. 1793–1796

CAROLINE MCCAFFREY-HOWARTH

Between the years 1793 and 1796, a proliferation of small, creamware ale mugs and jugs, transfer-printed in enamel, were made by regional English ceramic factories. They depicted scaled-down images of two of the most well-publicized historical moments of the French Revolution: "The Final Farewell" of Queen Marie Antoinette and King Louis XVI with their family (Figure 16.1), and the execution of Louis XVI, "La Guillotine" (Figures 16.2–4). Produced quickly in the years following the execution of the French king, now only a few examples remain.[1] These fascinating yet largely overlooked objects form the focus of this chapter, which seeks to describe the processes involved in, and the material and historical consequences of, scaling down such monumental sociocultural events onto handheld ceramics. It pays particular attention to four scaled-down printed ceramic versions of "The Final Farewell" and "La Guillotine."

Transfer printing involved covering engraved copper plates in linseed oil. The oil was then picked up by flexible slabs covered in gelatinous glue and these were applied directly onto the ceramic body.[2] Often the printed image covered the whole ceramic surface, or was framed in an oval or circular format and accompanied by decorative pattern borders such as laurel leaf branches or foliate sprays and textual descriptions of the scene at hand. By embracing what Alden Cavanaugh and Michael E. Yonan have termed the "cultural aesthetics" of ceramics, I contextualize these objects within the broader sociocultural framework in which they were designed, produced, and consumed.[3] As I will show, these printed ceramics raise significant questions about the complex nature of counter- and pro-Revolutionary sentiment in England. By tracking the depiction of the visual iconography of the Revolution, from the "Final Farewell" to "La Guillotine," this chapter

---

[1] David Bindman, *Shadow of the Guillotine: Britain and the French Revolution* (London: British Museum Press, 1989), 9.
[2] Peter Hyland, *The Herculaneum Pottery: Liverpool's Forgotten Glory* (Liverpool: Liverpool University Press, 2005), 11.
[3] Alden Cavanaugh and Michael E. Yonan (eds.), *The Cultural Aesthetics of Eighteenth-Century Porcelain* (Farnham: Ashgate, 2010), 5.

studies how the scaling down of large-scale events made politics and the emerging histories of the French Revolution accessible to a broader public and, in doing so, created a form of political engagement and visual shorthand for users of ceramic vessels in the 1790s.

While scholars have paid attention to the visual and material phenomena of the French Revolution, few studies have centered on ceramics as historical and political agents.[4] For example, Rolf Reichardt and Hubertus Kohle have considered the Revolutionary ties of painting, sculpture, and architecture, but not ceramics; and likewise Joan Landes mentions the existence of printed mugs only in passing.[5] Ranging from 8.7 cm to 14.9 cm in height, these printed Revolutionary ceramic mugs can be identified as either half-quart or full-quart mugs for ale; the accompanying jugs would have been used for pouring ale.[6] What does it mean to reduce a complex French political event to an image printed on a quotidian material object used primarily in a British tavern or alehouse? Did such printed ceramics shape the way ordinary and everyday people saw or engaged with the French Revolution and its ideals? Did they foster radical or reactionary ideas through their imagery? As objects that were used and exchanged within the tavern space, these mugs and jugs formed part of what Jon Mee has called the "conversable world": they were made for settings that produced conversations about current cultural events.[7] By 1792, at least thirty English towns had established radical corresponding societies and reformist clubs, several of which met regularly in taverns.[8] Mee has investigated the distinct convivial sociability that emerged through radical tavern culture in the 1790s.

---

[4] Notably, Harriet Guest has dismissed such creamwares as merely "for popular edification and consumption," in *Unbounded Attachment: Sentiment and Politics in the Age of the French Revolution* (Oxford: Oxford University Press, 2013), 32. Lynn Hunt has also emphasized the disciplinary boundaries that have limited a serious engagement of the varying visual modes of the Revolution, in "The Experience of Revolution," *French Historical Studies*, 32.4 (2009), 671–678 (675).

[5] Rolf Reichardt and Hubertus Kohle, *Visualizing the Revolution: Politics and the Pictorial Arts in Late Eighteenth-Century France* (London: Reaktion Books, 2008); Joan Landes, *Visualizing the Nation: Gender, Representation, and Revolution in Eighteenth-Century France* (Ithaca, NY: Cornell University Press, 2018), 217.

[6] This was in accordance with standardized English law, as from June 1700 ale could be served only in a "full Ale Quart or Ale Pint" in order to combat immoral drunken behavior. See Charles Leadbetter, *The Royal Gauger, The Sixth Edition Now Augmented and Improved by Samuel Clark* (London, 1766), 261.

[7] Jon Mee, *Conversable Worlds: Literature, Contention, and Community 1762 to 1830* (Oxford: Oxford University Press, 2011).

[8] Towards the end of the eighteenth century, printed pottery including punch bowls, mugs, and jugs were found frequently in taverns. See Karen Harvey, "Barbarity in a Teacup? Punch, Domesticity and Gender in the Eighteenth Century," *Journal of Design History*, 21 (2008), 205–221 (207); Rachel Conroy, "Boors and Beer: English and Welsh Pottery Drinking Vessels," *English Ceramics Circle*, 21 (2010), 135–148; Danielle Thom, "'Sawney's Defence': Anti-Catholicism, Consumption and Performance in 18th-Century Britain," *V&A Online Journal*, 7 (2015), n.p.

In particular, he has emphasized the power of "print magic" within these spaces, which emerged from the "faith that print could liberate mankind simply by bringing ideas into printed circulation."[9] In this chapter, I will explore the capacity of nontextual representations of the French Revolution to generate forms of visual magic that circulated political imagery. Melinda Alliker Rabb has argued that the phenomenon of scaling objects down onto things such as teapots has a "relationship to large-scale events ... that challenge old modes of representation and interpretation and demand new ones."[10] These ceramics offered users the opportunity to hold the mugs in their hands and bring their scaled-down images closer to their eyes, providing a multisensory engagement with these objects. They invited a different kind of political engagement and representation to textual forms of print in a historical moment in which, by 1795, only 60 percent of English men were literate.[11] As functional objects, these ceramic vessels also had the potential to influence or play a part in the social practices of tavern culture, through songs, toasts, political gestures, and by provoking debate or argument.[12]

These printed mugs and jugs participated in the established genre of print culture during the French Revolution, an effective engine for the circulation of political ideologies in both France and England.[13] In Paris, at least 40,000 prints and pamphlets were produced quickly and in large quantities, with engravings featuring on large folio sheets or illustrated broadsides that were soon disseminated across Europe and made their way to England.[14] Such pictorial propaganda opened access to current

---

[9] Jon Mee, *Print, Publicity, and Popular Radicalism in the 1790s: The Laurel of Liberty* (Cambridge: Cambridge University Press, 2016), 8.

[10] Melinda Alliker Rabb, *Miniature and the English Imagination: Literature, Cognition, and Small-Scale Culture, 1650–1765* (Cambridge: Cambridge University Press, 2019), 3–4.

[11] Michael Suarez, Introduction to *The Cambridge History of the Book in Britain*, vol. 5, *1695–1830*, ed. Michael Suarez, S. J. and Michael L. Turner (Cambridge: Cambridge University Press, 2009), 1–36 (11).

[12] Archaeological investigations of taverns in England and in America have also revealed a large proportion of printed creamware from the late eighteenth century onwards. See Robert Hunter, *Ceramics in America* (Milwaukee, WI: Chipstone Foundation, 2006), 18–19; Helen Walker, "Finds from a Well behind 2 High Street, Kelvedon," *Essex Archaeology and History: The Transactions of the Essex Archaeological Society*, 3rd ser., 35 (2004), 233–239.

[13] As the printing press gained more freedom it became "an active force in history." For this and a greater discussion of the role of printing and the press during the Revolution, see Robert Darnton and Daniel Roche, *Revolution in Print: The Press in France, 1775–1800* (Los Angeles: University of California Press, 1989), xiii.

[14] Rolf Reichardt has more recently likened the print culture during the French Revolution to one of the first European media events, as it offered a "democratization of political mass communication." "The French Revolution as a European Media Event" in *European History Online (EGO)* (Mainz: Leibniz Institute of European History [IEG], 2012), www.ieg-ego.eu/reichardtr-2010-en (accessed April 9, 2020).

sociopolitical events to non- or semi-literate audiences. Although many of these printed ceramics were inspired by or directly copied from well-known French print sources, as we shall see, close visual analysis reveals that they did not merely replicate larger-scale counterpart images but often reinterpreted or created hybrid versions of the original prints. Another issue, namely constraint of space, also determined the process of scaling down, as often the image presented on the ceramic surface truncated part of the original visual source.

Printed creamware in Britain was a relatively affordable product that was aimed at the middle and laboring classes. As this chapter will show, these mass-produced ceramics acted as a form of political visual shorthand, shaping understandings of the French Revolution, especially as men, and some women, interacted with the material world in taverns. By the 1750s, transfer-printed creamware had gained significant commercial success in Britain. Its production was championed by the Liverpool firm Sadler and Green.[15] Transfer printing enabled an increased production of relatively inexpensive ceramics that were both decorative and utilitarian. For example, printed creamware punchbowls retailed at between two shillings and five shillings, and a "set [of] Blue printed teacups and saucers" from Swansea in the 1790s cost only two shillings.[16] These printed ceramics therefore not only addressed but also catered to non-elite social groups, thus underscoring how their small-scale images offered access to Revolutionary events. As Richard Taws has argued, the production of ephemeral printed objects negotiated "the historical significance of the Revolution."[17] Tavern mugs and jugs constituted forms of ephemeral printed ceramics: they were produced quickly for short-term use and were inherently fragile, especially if used in boisterous settings. Their political imagery scaled down prints and paintings, whose larger forms made them more likely to circulate among elite networks. These small Revolutionary ceramics possessed the potential to inform the political consciousness of the users who held them in their hands.

---

[15] Often manufacturers commissioned local engravers to make detailed etched copper plates or bought finished plates from Liverpool or sometimes London. Hilary Young, *English Porcelain, 1745-95* (London: Abrams Books, 1999), 204; Pat Halfpenny, *Penny Plain, Twopence Coloured* (Stafford: Stoke on Trent City Museum, 1994), 14–16.

[16] David Drakard, *Printed English Pottery: History and Humour in the Reign of George III* (London: Jonathan Horne, 1992), 29–32; Jonathan Gray, *Welsh Ceramics in Context*, part 2 (Swansea: Royal Institution of South Wales, 2005), 4.

[17] While Taws examines passports, prints, coins, and even furniture, he does not consider ceramics. See *The Politics of the Provisional: Art and Ephemera in Revolutionary France* (University Park, PA: Penn State University Press, 2013), 3.

The Final Farewell

As many scholars have addressed, the British reaction to the French Revolution was complex, with defenders and critics sometimes changing positions in response to events in Paris.[18] At its beginning many British writers and political thinkers had praised the equality of the French Revolution as the epitome of eighteenth-century Enlightenment principles.[19] Yet growing violence in France, where by August 1792 an uprising against the monarchy had overthrown Louis XVI, soon led to British anxiety.[20] Following his sentencing to death on January 20, 1793, Louis XVI visited his family for a final farewell; his priest the Abbé Edgeworth prayed with him late into the night before the king was led to the guillotine the next morning.[21] The executions of the French king and queen, and the pervading news of the Terror, led to a growing concern in England for the longevity of monarchical structures, as many feared a radical uprising in Britain. A range of publications soon appeared that attempted to capture the immediate history of the French Revolution, including John Gifford's *A narrative of the transactions personally relating to Lewis the Sixteenth, from the period of his evasion from Paris to his death* in 1793; an English translation in 1794 of Monsieur de Viette's short biography of Marie Antoinette that detailed her life, trial, and execution; and Mary Wollstonecraft's *An Historical and Moral view of the origin and progress of the French Revolution: and the effect it has produced in Europe* in 1794.

Capitalizing on rising public interest surrounding the final moments of the French royal family in Britain, factories quickly produced a range of printed ceramics depicting the "Final Farewell." According to Abbé Edgeworth, this was a traumatic event: "not only tears were shed, and sobs were heard, but piercing cries."[22] Several textual and visual versions of this scene

---

[18] Bindman, *Shadow of the Guillotine*, 12; Marilyn Butler, "Telling It Like a Story: The French Revolution as Narrative," *Studies in Romanticism*, 28.3 (1989), 345–364; Jennifer Mori, *Britain in the Age of the French Revolution: 1785–1820* (London: Routledge, 2000), vii; Peter Mandler, *The English National Character: The History of an Idea from Edmund Burke to Tony Blair* (New Haven, CT: Yale University Press, 2006), 3.

[19] R. R. Fennessy, *Burke, Paine, and the Rights of Man: A Difference of Political Opinion* (New York: Springer, 1963), 103.

[20] See, for example, F. O'Gorman, *The Whig Party and the French Revolution* (New York: St. Martin's Press, 1967).

[21] C. Sneyd Edgeworth, *Memoirs of the Abbé Edgeworth: Containing His Narrative of the Last Hours of Louis XVI* (London: Rowland Hunter, 1815), 62–74; Lynn Hunt, *Family Romance of the French Revolution* (London: Routledge, 2013), 54–55; *The Trial at Large of Louis XVI, Late King of France: Containing the Accusation, Trial, Defense, Sentence, &c. of that Unfortunate Monarch: to which is Added, His Majesty's Last Will* (London, 1793).

[22] Edgeworth, *Memoirs*, 62.

circulated in England, often coupled with a sympathetic tone as pro-monarchists sought to reinforce the idea of a loving, loyal, and paternal British king in George III.[23] One printed Staffordshire mug exemplifies how pot engravers took inspiration from a visual culture in which abundant images of the French monarchy circulated. The mug shows the French royal family in triangular composition in a simple room, resembling a cell or prison, signed by the pot printer "[Thomas] Fletcher & Co. Shelton."[24] Although it shares similarities with a hand-colored etching by Isaac Cruikshank (1764–1811) from March 1793, no exact print source has been identified.[25] The engraving on the mug has been attributed to Thomas Radford, who was also based in Shelton.[26] It is likely that Radford took inspiration from a range of existing visual material as he negotiated the aesthetic and political components of this printed ceramic, choosing first and foremost to emphasize a humble and emotional setting, perhaps to encourage sympathy for the king.

The "Final Farewell" also appears on a Liverpool creamware quart ale mug, transfer printed in black enamel (Figure 16.1), in which a rather youthful King Louis consoles his family. The image is framed within an oval border with cropped decorative laurel leaves, a motif used frequently to signify mourning. An inscription at the bottom reads "The Last Interview of LOUIS the Sixteenth with his Family." The pot engraver has based the transfer print on an engraving by John George Murray (act. 1793–1856) after an original drawing by the illustrator Henry Singleton (1766–1839). Singleton's drawings had been featured in Gifford's pro-monarchist book of 1793, which praised the French king's paternal nature. Singleton produced a rather sentimental version of *The Last Interview*. In the Singleton drawing and subsequent print, the king gestures towards a globe and a bookcase. But the pot engraver has made a small but significant change, replacing the globe with a crucifix on the wall. This change, while small, indicates the engraver's artistic agency over the mug's political message. By emphasizing the king as a religious martyr, this mug offered a counter-Revolutionary narrative. This was perhaps an attempt by the ceramics factory or by the individual pot engraver to condemn the brutality of

---

[23] Bindman, *Shadow of the Guillotine*, 23. John Barrell emphasizes the shift towards a greater sense of sentimentality in art, literature, and politics, whereby the king is shown to be a constant father and protector of his people, in *Imagining the King's Death: Figurative Treason, Fantasies of Regicide, 1793–1796* (Oxford: Oxford University Press, 2000), 49–54.

[24] Mug, Victoria & Albert Museum, London, 3638-1901.

[25] See Isaac Cruikshank, *The Last Interview between Louis XVI, king of France, and his family*, London, 8 March 1793, British Museum, 1878,0511.1411.

[26] See William Chaffers, *Marks and Monograms on Pottery and Porcelain of the Renaissance and Modern Periods*, 4th ed. (London: Bickers and Son, 1874), 713.

Figure 16.1 Mug with *The Last Interview*, c. 1793–1795, perhaps Liverpool, creamware, transfer printed in black, h. 14.9 cm. © British Museum.

the French Revolution and the treasonable nature of regicide, whilst also responding to growing consumer interest by selling pro-monarchist materials as a form of popular culture. As an ideologically charged object, this small thing gestures towards wider political strategies that sought to celebrate monarchical hegemony. Yet, as we will see, rising pro-Revolutionary feelings in cities such as Liverpool may have also enabled this piece to act as a historical agent for the laboring and middling classes, suggesting that aristocratic and established power structures could be challenged, not only in France, but also in Britain.

La Guillotine

Considered to be the most humane method of execution during the Enlightenment, the guillotine has been deemed to be "both an image and a producer of images."[27] Immediately following the king's death, many Londoners attended exhibitions of working guillotines; at 45 Oxford Street, there were even reduced entry fees for "tradesmen and servants."[28] A proliferation of visual and written texts were disseminated widely, which described in great detail the "cruel massacre of the King & Queen of France."[29] One pamphlet even noted how the king was "fastened to a Board, which reached no higher than his Breast, laid along his Belly, with his Head through the Hole in the Two boards."[30] Whilst some visual illustrations embraced a more satirical tone, including caricatures by James Gillray, others struck a gruesome line.[31] *The Wonderful Magazine*, for instance, shows blood dripping from the sharp blade of the guillotine, spurting from the king's severed body into a basket that overflows as blood seeps out over the scaffold.[32] This print was scaled down and directly translated onto a creamware mug printed in black in Staffordshire (Figure 16.2). The mug is signed by John Aynsley, a pot engraver and pot printer based at Lane End, Staffordshire.[33] Aynsley depicts visually and textually who and what was present at the execution, almost willing his illustration into a tangible record of recent political events, a handheld form of history in the making. The guillotine occupies the central point of the image; to the right the executioner brandishes Louis XVI's head and holds it up to the crowd as blood drips downwards, and to the left the commandant général, Antoine Joseph Santerre, holds a sword upright confirming that justice has been served.

---

[27] Richard Taws, "The Guillotine as Anti-Monument," *Sculpture Journal*, 19.1 (2010), 33–48; see also the catalogue of an exhibition held at Musée de la Révolution française: Valérie Rousseau-Lagarde, *La Guillotine dans la Révolution: 27 mars–24 mai 1987* (Vizille: Musée de la Révolution française, 1987); and Daniel Arasse, *La Guillotine dans la Révolution* (Florence: La Stampa, 1987).

[28] These working models were advertised in a variety of newspapers across England.

[29] Anonymous, *The cruel massacre of the King & Queen of France. With the decree of the National Convention*, (London, 1793), 40.

[30] Samuel William Fores, *Description of a correct representation of the guillotine … The martyrdom of Louis XVI* (London, 1793), 1.

[31] See, for example, James Cuno, *French Caricature and the French Revolution, 1789–1799* (Los Angeles: Grunwald Center for the Graphic Arts, 1989).

[32] "Important particulars of the Extraordinary Trial and Massacre of the late unfortunate MONARCH of FRANCE, LOUIS XVI," *The Wonderful Magazine and Marvelous Chronicle*, January 1793, 64. According to Bindman, this was "Taken from a Drawing made on the spot by that most eminent Artist M. Le Brun" (*Shadow of the Guillotine*, 115).

[33] Geoffrey Godden, *Encyclopaedia of British Pottery and Porcelain Marks* (London: Random House, 1964), 44.

Revolutionary Histories in Small Things 265

Figure 16.2 Mug with a guillotine scene, c. 1793–1795, John Aynsley, Lane End, Staffordshire, creamware, transfer printed in black, h. 12 cm. © British Museum.

Aynsley captures the immediate aftermath of the murder of the king, emphasizing those who witnessed and were responsible for his execution. Each figure is identified through a number key system directly below: "1 the Guillotine— 2 the Ax— 3 The King— 4 De Fermand [sic] His Confessor— 5 One of the Executione [sic]" and so on. In the process of scaling down the visual imagery, Aynsley has positioned the figures closer together and printed them tightly onto the bottom section of the mug. Such cramped details would have required close scrutiny by the mug's tavern users to make out the figures. As Lynn Hunt has observed, not only did the French Revolution challenge old paradigms, but it also created new ones by enabling ordinary people across Europe to reclaim and reimagine their role within current sociopolitical and cultural events.[34] Here, the user could study and handle a piece of popular culture, reveling in the gore, exploring a potentially treasonous plot of their own, or even chastising the violence of the French. Or they could interpret this detailed scene as a form of commemoration, in line with the tradition of commemorative transfer-printed ceramics, produced from the mid-eighteenth century onwards.[35] Through their subjective and haptic interactions, users accessed a range of sensory and potentially conversational ways to engage the recent history that the Revolutionary mug marked. As Leora Auslander has suggested, such "objects not only are the product of history, they are also active agents in history."[36] The Revolutionary imagery of small things simultaneously captured current political events and had the potential to shape the historical record and circulate quotidian understandings of the French Revolution.

Aynsley's mug thereby participated in the broader popular (and morbid) fascination with the guillotine, which was marked by an increase in republican and pro-Revolutionary sentiments, especially in London and other English cities. Interest in the guillotine was fueled by the growth of egalitarian moral philosophy, as championed by Mary Wollstonecraft's *Vindication of the Rights of Men* (1790) and Thomas Paine's *Rights of Man* (1791–1792). Galvanized by the radical press, these texts circulated widely: twenty thousand copies were sent to the north of Ireland as well as to Sheffield, Leeds, and Liverpool.[37] The corresponding societies, established first in Sheffield and then in London from 1791 onwards, further sought to educate the ordinary person about the egalitarian nature of parliamentary reform, often issuing cheap copies of Paine's *Rights of Man*.[38] Following the death of Louis XVI in 1793, republicans realized the British constitution could be

---

[34] Hunt, "Experience of Revolution," 671.
[35] See, for example, John May and Jennifer May, who note that "the British have long commemorated their history in pottery." *Commemorative Pottery* (London: Heinemann, 1972), 1.
[36] Leora Auslander, "Beyond Words," *American Historical Review*, 110.4 (2005), 1015–1045 (1017).
[37] Mee, *Print, Publicity, and Popular Radicalism*, 84–87; Wil Verhoeven, *Americomania and the French Revolution Debate in Britain, 1789–1802* (Cambridge: Cambridge University Press, 2013), 28–70.
[38] For further reading on the complexities of pro-Revolutionary republican radicalism, see John Dinwiddy, "Conceptions of Revolution in the English Radicalism of the 1790s" in Eckhart Hellmuth (ed.), *The Transformation of Political Culture: England and Germany in the Late Eighteenth Century* (Oxford: Oxford University Press, 1990), 535–560.

similarly reimagined.[39] Some radicals turned towards notions of regicide, energized by political pamphlets, many of which were sold at meetings of the corresponding societies, including *King Killing* by Richard "Citizen" Lee, who demanded his audience "destroy this huge Colossus."[40] Ceramic reproductions of *La Guillotine* thus formed part of a landscape of political tools that catered to non-elite audiences, conveying how ordinary drinking vessels could support challenges to monarchical power structures in Britain.

One exemplary guillotine scene appears on a pearlware cylindrical mug, juxtaposed with a decorative border of stylized flower designs on the inner rim (Figure 16.3). Here, the printed scene captures the moment before the king's execution itself has taken place. It derives from a broadside (with a woodcut engraving) by William Lane entitled *Massacre of the French King!*[41] Lane made his woodblock before the death of Louis XVI by way of illustrating the new invention. On the mug, the engraving has been scaled down and embellished with a textual inscription: "View of LA GUILLOTINE or the modern beheading machine at Paris by which LOUIS XVI late king of France suffered on the Scaffold Jan 21 1793."[42] The pot engraver and printer likely intended this mug to represent the fall of the monarchy. Such handheld ceramics could be read as forms of pro-Revolutionary propaganda, used perhaps to cement radical imaginings of the death of King George III. In fact, the laboring classes were frequently accused of uttering "treasonable expressions" about King George, such as, "I wish his head was cut off, like the French K—'s."[43] Such regicidal imaginings were taken seriously; during one court case in 1796, a Mr. Robert Thomas Crossfield was charged with "having compassed and imagined the death of the king."[44] One of the witnesses cross-examined during the case even confessed to possessing a paper "entitled the Guillotine, or George's Head in a Basket," which he admitted he had acquired from "the committee of correspondence."[45]

---

[39] Bindman, *Shadow of the Guillotine*, 14.

[40] For a more detailed account of the imaginings of the king's death, see Barrell, *Imagining the King's Death*, 101–102; Richard "Citizen" Lee, *King Killing* (A handbill, reprinted from one entitled "Tyrannicide.") Sold by Citizen Lee, at the British Tree of Liberty, No. 98, Berwick Street, Soho (London, 1797 [1795?]).

[41] See, for example, *Massacre of the French King!*, British Museum, 1856,0712.1101.

[42] This print also appeared on other small things, featuring on the lid of a colorful, painted-enamel patch box on copper, made in Staffordshire, now at the British Museum, 1987,0708.1.

[43] *A Looking-glass for a Right Honourable Mendicant* (London, 1794), 28, quoted in Barrell, *Imagining the King's Death*, 102.

[44] Old *Bailey Proceedings Online* (www.oldbaileyonline.org, version 8.0, March 2018), May 1796, trial of Robert Thomas Crossfield (t17960511-1).

[45] Ibid.

Figure 16.3 Mug with a guillotine scene, c. 1793–1796, previously thought to be Cambrian pottery, Swansea, but probably Staffordshire, transfer printed in black underglaze, h. 8.7 cm. © British Museum.

Could the act of drinking from a tankard printed with *La Guillotine* be viewed similarly as a treasonous act? Certainly such detailed and small handheld ceramics had the potential to set conversation topics within the social space of the tavern, in which politics intersected with sociability. As Ian Newman has observed, political toasts and rousing songs frequently occurred in these sociable spaces.⁴⁶ Several popular songs responded to the French Revolution: "The Permanent Guillotine" (1793) celebrated the machine's invention; and in the ballad "John Gilpin's Ghost" (1794), written by the well-known orator John Thelwall, a disembodied voice states that "all tyranny must bow."⁴⁷ As Amanda Goodrich has contended, radical toasts damning the king were also frequently made in taverns, with some supported by ceramic wares on hand. On one such occasion, Thelwall, in attendance at a London Corresponding Society meeting, supposedly "blew the head off his pot of porter and declared, 'Thus I would serve all Kings.'"⁴⁸ Here, the metaphor of blowing off the frothy foam traditionally found on porter, sometimes known as "froth-crown'd porter," evokes the imagined beheading of the king of England.⁴⁹ Through the sociable act of toasting, users may have engaged in a form of treasonous performance whereby radical ideologies emerged, furthered perhaps by the printed ceramics held in their hands.

A notable printed execution scene features on a creamware baluster-shaped ale jug that was probably produced in Liverpool (Figure 16.4).⁵⁰ Transfer printed in red enamel, the jug's color almost echoes the red blood spilling from the beheaded body and separated head in the original print. The jug's scene scales down a full-color print by Isaac Cruikshank, published by S. W. Fores only a few weeks after the death of King Louis XVI, alongside a notice stating "the MARTYR of EQUALITY, representing the Axe down, and the Body laying on the Board, the Duke of Orleans holding by the Hair, the King's Head, to the Populace, exclaiming, 'Behold the Progress of our System!'"⁵¹ Of oval form, the image is enclosed with an interlaced band of laurel leaves, tied with a ribbon. This particular decorative motif is found

---

⁴⁶ Ian Newman, *The Romantic Tavern: Literature and Conviviality in the Age of Revolution* (Cambridge: Cambridge University Press, 2019), 183–185.

⁴⁷ Barrell, *Imagining the King's Death*, 112–113.

⁴⁸ Amanda Goodrich, "Radical Popular Attitudes to the Monarchy in Britain during the French Revolution" in Andreas Gestrich and Michael Schaich (eds.), *The Hanoverian Succession: Dynastic Politics and Monarchical Culture* (Farnham: Ashgate, 2015), 261–279 (265). See also Mee, *Print, Publicity, and Popular Radicalism*, 168.

⁴⁹ For further discussion of the trope of ceramics as metaphor, see Cavanaugh and Yonan, *Cultural Aesthetics*, 1–3. The term "froth-Crown'd Porter" appears in *The Oxford Sausage; or, Select Poetical Pieces, Written by the Most Celebrated Wits of the University of Oxford* (Oxford, [1798?]), 222. Afterwards the room toasted to "The Lamp-irons in Parliament Street," which referred to the treasonous act of hanging a corpse in Parliament Street from a lamppost. John Thelwall, *The Tribune, a Periodical Publication, Consisting Chiefly of (his) Political Lectures* (London, 1795), 119, 188.

⁵⁰ A smaller printed jug in black with the same print and border pattern to the example in the Willett collection can also be found at the Musée de la Révolution française, 1990.32.

⁵¹ "Description of a correct representation of the guillotine," 1.

Figure 16.4 Jug with a guillotine scene, c. 1793–1795, perhaps Liverpool, transfer printed in red, Henry Willett esq. Collection, Royal Pavilion & Museums, Brighton & Hove.

on a variety of pieces thought to be of Liverpool production, and such laurel leaves appear frequently on political scenes found on Herculaneum pottery.[52] Once again the scene dwells on the immediate aftermath of the execution of Louis XVI. It focuses on the central figure of Philippe Egalité,

---

[52] See, for example, Jug, Metropolitan Museum of Art, New York, 14.102.428. The Herculaneum factory was based in Toxteth in Liverpool. They started production in early 1793 and produced a range of creamware pottery (Hyland, *Herculaneum Pottery*, 60–61).

the former Duke of Orléans and the king's cousin, who was also one of those responsible for condemning Louis to death. Egalité holds the severed head triumphantly. An emblazoned bannered scroll above him states "THE MARTYR OF EQUALITY, Behold the Progress of the French System."

Cruikshank's source print is often read as a form of sympathetic counter-Revolutionary propaganda, or what Reichardt and Kohle have termed a "satirical lamentation."[53] On the one hand, this print reads as a shock tactic for the British public, encouraging viewers to fear the dangers associated with equality and democracy, as if such a fate would similarly befall King George III. On the other hand, Cruikshank's print can register as a violent visual satire that could incite anti-French and anti-Revolutionary sentiment, given that the duke betrayed his own cousin and king.[54] However, the scaling down of Revolutionary iconography onto a creamware ale jug made in Liverpool, a regional city rife with radical beliefs, opens up other interpretations. Whilst the "Progress of the French System" could here refer to the guillotine itself or the triumph of the French people over the privileged aristocracy, it also gestures towards the possibility of a democratic revolution within Britain, if it too could succeed in overthrowing the monarchy.[55] A consideration of the complexities of the material, textual, and visual nature of this object requires us to understand not only the political economy of design in which it was produced but also how it might have been consumed by the non-elite classes in and around Liverpool, or in other similar cities within the social space of the tavern.

Together at Last: Final Farewell and La Guillotine

Through the process of scaling down and manipulating large-scale events, these ceramics, encoded with a multiplicity of meanings, constituted a visual shorthand for current events, acting as political and historical agents. Through a haptic interpretation, which required significant close looking and handling, the user may have gained a better understanding of the scene

---

[53] Reichardt and Kohle, *Visualizing the Revolution*, 190.
[54] Edward Bell Krumbhaar, *Isaac Cruikshank: A Catalogue Raisonné with a Sketch of his Life and Work* (Philadelphia: University of Pennsylvania Press, 1966), 110; Regina Janes, *Losing Our Heads: Beheadings in Literature and Culture* (New York: New York University Press, 2005), 72; Valerie Mainz, "The Inequalities of Infamy," *Oxford Art Journal*, 39.2 (2016), 217–227 (221).
[55] Paine would write in 1795 that "I have always considered the present Constitution of the French Republic the best *organized system* the human mind has yet produced"; see Amanda Goodrich, *Debating England's Aristocracy in the 1790s: Pamphlets, Polemics, and Political Ideas* (Woodbridge: Boydell & Brewer, 2005), 125.

at hand and the key figures who were involved in the final moments of King Louis XVI's life. Produced immediately following the death of the French king, these handheld ceramics had the capacity to shape both an individual and a collective understanding of the emerging history of the French Revolution. In fact, these ceramics would soon become collectible historicist objects during the nineteenth century, where they were taken up as a historical record of the British response to the French Revolution.[56] According to the ceramics scholar Gustave Gouellain (1836–1897), writing in 1872, the history of the French Revolution "s'est imprimé puissamment sur les choses de la céramique."[57] Similarly, as the ceramics collector Henry Willett (1823–1905) commented in 1899, "this collection has been formed with a view to develop the idea that the history of the country may to a large extent be traced on its homely pottery."[58]

As engravers tweaked and interpreted existing prints, they may have sought to encourage a sentimental, sympathetic reaction to the violent treatment of the French monarchy. Other printed ceramics perpetuated the guillotine as the pervading emblematic symbol of the French Revolution, encouraged by and perhaps even contributing to a pro-Revolutionary sentiment among the laboring and middling classes. Nonetheless, perhaps the time has come to distance ourselves from this stark binary of pro- or counter-Revolutionary political rhetoric in Britain during the mid-1790s.[59] In recent years, two printed creamware baluster ale jugs have appeared that show a pairing of these two somewhat opposing images on the one object, the scene of "The Final Farewell" paired with that of "La Guillotine."[60] Rarely have these two scenes appeared on the same vessel, suggesting this was produced with a particular agenda and cultural aesthetic in mind. The circulation of these events on one object further demonstrates their place as two of the most popular moments in the history of the French Revolution. The user of such jugs could engage in a tactile relationship with scaled-down versions of famous political events that fit easily into their hands. They may have even poured ale from one of these vessels into an accompanying mug

---

[56] *La Guillotine* (Figure 16.3) was originally in the ceramics collection of the antiquarian Sir Augustus Wollaston Franks, who donated it to the British Museum.

[57] "Has been powerfully imprinted on ceramic things." Gustave Gouellain, *Céramique révolutionnaire: l'assiette dite à la guillotine* (Paris: Manufacture de Sèvres, 1872), 10.

[58] Henry Willett, *Catalogue of a Collection of Pottery and Porcelain Illustrating Popular British History* (London: Eyre and Spottiswoode, 1899), 9. Willet owned two "La Guillotine" jugs.

[59] Taws moves towards a similar conclusion regarding the unnecessarily stark binaries in the scholarship of the history of the French Revolution (*Politics of the Provisional*, 8).

[60] Rosebery's, West Norwood, May 9, 2006, lot 46; another jug with the same paired images was sold at Cheffin's, Cambridge, June 25, 2003, lot 24.

with similar Revolutionary images. This pairing illustrates how pot manufacturers and engravers created pieces that made complex, material forms of political rhetoric accessible by scaling down larger Revolutionary narratives onto smaller printed ceramics. As relatively inexpensive vessels for ale, they were used during intimate sociable conversations and may have assumed pivotal roles in acts of toasting, the singing of songs, or treasonous gestures amid rising political unrest. Perhaps users of these mugs and jugs rejoiced in the gore and guts of French politics, whilst also fearing for their own supposedly beloved English king. Or perhaps such objects inspired a more radical response. Whatever the outcomes within the tavern's space, such examples indicate the very slipperiness of these ceramics – potentially anti-French, counter-Revolutionary, pro-Revolutionary, anti-monarchy, anti-democracy – their meaning ultimately determined by those who held them in their hands.

17 | A Box of Tea and the British Empire

ROMITA RAY

A tortoiseshell tea caddy, possibly from the Regency period or early Victorian era, unlocks to reveal two compartments nestled inside, their lids embellished with mother-of-pearl knobs (Figure 17.1).¹ It was designed to store tea, a commodity so prized that the ornamental container was kept under lock and key. Boxes such as these invited wonder, curiosity, and imagination. Opening them meant finding a leafy commodity that changed the history of taste in Britain, sparked fierce rivalry with the Dutch, and paved the way for a revolution in North America.² No other commodity in eighteenth-century Britain would trigger such radical shifts on a global scale, and no other commodity would inspire as wide an assortment of boxes as Chinese tea. From storage crates and botanical containers that transported leaves, seeds, and specimens, to chests, caddies, and canisters that drew the leafy commodity into domestic spaces, boxes of tea "provided order," as Anke Te Heesen observes, while ushering the movement of wealth and knowledge across the growing expanse of Britain's empire.³ They also introduced new design ideas and technological innovations that would revolutionize taste and aesthetic sensibility. What then do we make of these small artifacts that were entangled with the histories of commerce, culture, and science?

A ubiquitous motif in visual representations and literary narratives, the box of tea appeared regularly in correspondence, novels, poems, medical and botanical treatises, ship logs, advertisements, China trade pictures,

---

¹ For more about tea caddies like this, see Antigone Clarke and Joseph O'Kelly, *Antique Boxes, Tea Caddies, & Society 1700–1880* (Atglen, PA: Schiffer, 2018), 130–137.
² By the 1830s, tea had triggered the Opium Wars in China and paved the way for a new agricultural industry in India.
³ Anke Te Heesen, *The World in a Box: The Story of an Eighteenth-Century Picture Encyclopedia* (Chicago: University of Chicago Press, 1997), 9; Sarah Easterby-Smith, "Reputation in a Box: Objects, Communication, and Trust in Late 18th-Century Botanical Networks," *History of Science*, 53.2 (2015), 180–208. From the late 1840s until the mid-1850s, Wardian Cases, invented by the surgeon and amateur naturalist Nathaniel Bagshaw Ward, were used to transport tea seeds and live tea plants from China to India. See Luke Keogh, *The Wardian Case: How a Simple Box Moved Plants and Changed the World* (Chicago: The University of Chicago Press, 2020), 1, 89–92.

Figure 17.1 Unknown maker, Tea Caddy, wood with tortoiseshell and mother-of-pearl knobs, 1800–1840, gift of Dr. and Mrs. Eugene R. Smith, Syracuse University Art Museum, 1969.1651.

grocer's trade cards, and conversation pieces. Linked with an array of places, spaces, and imaginaries, it testified to the extent to which a "noble Leaf and Drink" had settled into the intimate rhythms of everyday life in Britain, but not without raising troubling questions about its impact on health and well-being.[4] Despite controversial claims that tea was "pernicious to Health" and capable of "obstructing Industry, and Impoverishing the Nation," while causing "low nervous diseases," the commodity

---

[4] Thomas Garway, "An Exact Description of the Growth, Quality and Vertues of the Leaf Tea," a 1660 broadside reproduced in George van Driem, *The Tale of Tea: A Comprehensive History of Tea from Prehistoric Times to the Present Day* (Leiden: Brill, 2019), 387.

continued to be in high demand, its influx into domestic spaces made visible by a staggering array of ornamental chests, canisters, and caddies that complemented porcelain and silver teaware.[5] Between 1664, around the time the first advertisement for tea was published in Britain, and 1785, when the American Revolution was still simmering, tea imports into Britain increased from just 2 pounds, 2 ounces, to an astounding 15 million pounds, the escalating demand affirming that tea was now "the most conspicuous Chinese" import from the China trade to enter eighteenth-century English households.[6]

While much has been written about tea utensils as signs of politeness and respectability – their design "tend[ing] towards refinement on a small scale rather than an expensive, conspicuous display" as Woodruff D. Smith puts it – by comparison, very little has been discussed about the box of tea, an indispensable article in the China tea trade.[7] Still less has been written about its smallness, which facilitated the movement of tea across maritime and domestic thresholds. The primary function of the box was to enclose, protect, and preserve its prized contents. Depending on their spatial contexts, boxes of tea varied in size, their smallness shrinking as they made their way into domestic interiors where caddies, canisters, and chests represented the smallest and most ornate of tea containers, their size and ornamentalism complementing the small porcelain things at the tea table. Broadly speaking, the box of tea represented the thickening influx of foreign goods into British homes, fragments of distant geographies that

---

[5] Jonas Hanway, *A Journal of Eight Days Journey from Portsmouth to Kingston upon Thames … To Which was Added, An Essay on Tea, Considered as Pernicious to Health, Obstructing Industry, and Impoverishing the Nation: With an Account of Its Growth, and Great Consumption in these Kingdoms* (London, 1756), title page; John Coakley Lettsom, *The Natural History of the Tea-Tree, with Observations on the Medical Qualities of Tea, and on the Effects of Tea-Drinking* (London, 1772), 61; see also Beth Kowaleski-Wallace, "Tea, Gender, and Domesticity in Eighteenth-Century England," *Studies in Eighteenth-Century Culture*, 23 (1994), 131–145.

[6] David Porter, "A Peculiar but Uninteresting Nation: China and the Discourse of Commerce in Eighteenth-Century England," *Eighteenth-Century Studies*, 33.2 (2000), 181–199 (182). See also Lisbet Koerner, "Purposes of Linnaean Travel: A Preliminary Research Report" in David Philip Miller and Peter Hanns Reill (eds.), *Visions of Empire: Voyages, Botany, and Representations of Nature* (Cambridge: Cambridge University Press, 1996), 117–152; Romita Ray, "Ornamental Exotica: Transplanting the Aesthetics of Tea Consumption and the Birth of a British Exotic" in Yota Batsaki, Sarah Burke Cahalan, and Anatole Tchikine (eds.), *The Botany of Empire in the Long Eighteenth Century* (Washington, DC: Dumbarton Oaks Research Library and Collections, 2016), 259–281. For more about Britain's tea trade with China, see Markman Ellis, Richard Coulton, and Matthew Mauger, *Empire of Tea: The Asian Leaf that Conquered the World* (London: Reaktion Books, 2015), 52–72.

[7] See, for instance, Ching Jung-Chen, "Tea Parties in Early Georgian Conversation Pieces," *The British Art Journal*, 10.1 (2009), 30–39; Woodruff D. Smith, "Complications of the Commonplace: Tea, Sugar, and Imperialism," *The Journal of Interdisciplinary History*, 23.2 (1992), 259–278 (277).

were now commoditized into desirable things for British consumers. And key to its transferal and dispersal was its mobility and portability, which enabled the movement of merchandise as well as the movement of wealth, capital, ideas, culture, and knowledge, whose complex, entangled trajectories were often precarious, fragile, and disruptive.

Can the scale and size of the box of tea enable us to reassess how an emergent British empire was fundamentally an empire of small things in whose smallness we find inscribed the perils and pleasures of wealth and knowledge production? While tea utensils brought the beverage out into the open (as Melanie Keene reminds us, "cups of tea ... were quite literally within everyone's grasp"), the box of tea remained sealed off, protective of its contents, and slightly mysterious.[8] As Jonathan Swift cautioned, the prized commodity must always be kept under "Lock and Key" in "small Chests and Trunks."[9] How then did smallness contribute to the growing allure of a Chinese commodity? Can smallness itself be positioned as a hallmark of a British colonial aesthetic sharpened by the commercial *and* cultural complexities of maritime trade? In order to explore these questions, I first examine boxes of tea as mobile merchandise, before turning to botanical containers and tea caddies as sites of sensory engagement. Smallness, I contend, emerged as a powerful paradigm of intimacy that embedded an article of botany and commerce into the ebb and flow of domestic life. And it is from the intimacies, shaped by the sensory, domestic, botanical, and commercial realms of tea, that a Chinese exotic emerged a favored British commodity.

Maritime Merchandise

In a ceiling painting made in 1778 for the Revenue Committee Room of the East India House in London, the little-known artist Spiridione Roma depicted a small box of tea perched on a rock by the sea as if to remind the viewer of its precariousness.[10] Unscathed and intact, its value was determined not just by its contents but also by the distances it would traverse

---

[8] Melanie Keene, "Familiar Science in Nineteenth-Century Britain," *History of Science*, 52.1 (2014), 53–71 (61).
[9] Jonathan Swift, *Directions to Servants in General* (London, 1745), 81,
[10] The East India House served as the East India Company's headquarters on Leadenhall Street; R. C. D. Baldwin, "Sir Joseph Banks and the Cultivation of Tea," *RSA Journal*, 141.5444 (1993), 813–17. Baldwin notes that the Flemish sculptor John Michael Rysbrack depicted a tea caddy in the mantelpiece of a fireplace in the East India House. Brian Allen, however, identifies the object as a "jewel casket." Allen, "From Plassey to Seringapatam: India and British History Painting c.1760–c.1800" in C. A. Bayly (ed.), *The Raj: India and the British 1600–1947* (London: National Portrait Gallery, 1990), 26–37.

and the odds against which it would survive at sea, where the prospect of shipwrecks, war, and pirate attacks rendered maritime trade a challenging, if not dangerous, enterprise. The mobility of the box was bound up with its fragility, a paradigm that might be read simultaneously as a material sign of the need for survival as well as a cultural trope for the need to grapple with "an empire richer, more populous, and larger than any in Europe," in which Britain had struggled to gain a foothold in the eighteenth century, so glaringly exposed by the failure of the 1792 Macartney embassy to forge "an intimate alliance with the [Chinese] emperor" and "a free intercourse with all parts of China."[11]

In the fragile contours of the box are imprinted the East India Company's fears that if utmost discretion were not exercised during the Macartney mission, the Chinese government might "entirely exclude [the Company] from entering their ports."[12] Fragility was thus a metonymic reminder of the imbalance of cultural and economic power in Britain's China trade. Furthermore, as David Porter observes, the very notion of fragility ascribed to Chinese tea utensils (among other porcelain things) can be read as a means of coming to terms with the "overwhelming power and history of the Chinese empire," even as prized porcelain items were stark reminders of "England's cultural backwardness, material dependency, and relatively late arrival on the world stage."[13] The box of tea might be seen as amplifying these tensions as well, its leafy contents shaping powerful imaginaries of fear that were rooted in medical and cultural anxieties about imbibing and ingesting a Chinese product.[14] Fragility now extended to the body's capacity to cope with a foreign beverage.

By the end of the eighteenth century, Chinese tea was widely recognized as the company's most lucrative import.[15] From the moment it was acquired from Hong merchants in Canton and loaded onto East Indiamen, the commodity was repositioned as a company acquisition whose

---

[11] Robert Markley, *The Far East and the English Imagination, 1600–1730* (Cambridge: Cambridge University Press, 2006), 85; Sir George Staunton, *An Historical Account of the Embassy to the Emperor of China, Undertaken by Order of the King of Great Britain; Including the Manners and Customs of the Inhabitants; and Preceded by An Account of the Causes of the Embassy and Voyage to China. Abridged Principally from the Papers of Earl Macartney* (London, 1797), 21. Staunton served as secretary to George, Lord Macartney, who led the embassy to the Chinese imperial court.

[12] Staunton, *Historical Account*, 21.

[13] David Porter, *The Chinese Taste in Eighteenth-Century England* (Cambridge: Cambridge University Press, 2010), 7.

[14] Lettsom, *Natural History of the Tea-Tree* (1772), 57–59.

[15] Ray, "Ornamental Exotica," 259. According to Staunton, tea sales in Britain increased from "fifty thousand pounds weight" at the beginning of the eighteenth century to "nearly twenty millions of pounds" by the end of the century. Staunton, *Historical Account*, 16.

commercial and cultural trajectories were articulated by a global British diaspora.[16] From Canton to Calcutta, Bombay, Madras, London, Boston, Philadelphia, and Charleston, Chinese tea traveled through and into the lives of Britons stationed at home and abroad, its global footprint testifying to the extent to which an emergent British empire was now "both Atlantic *and* Asian, commercial and conquering."[17] Shored up by the kind of fluidity and intercultural flows that we associate with today's global commodities that move between and through different cultural spaces, tea was fundamentally a mobile product that shaped a British cultural habit (tea drinking), while its implements – small and delicate Chinese porcelain utensils – spawned an entire British industry of imitation porcelainware; the imitations still seeking to "convey the taste for the original" and thereby continuing to enhance the desirability of a Chinese exotic.[18] Tea would also inspire another strand of British craftsmanship, from which emerged ornate caddies, canisters, and chests that displayed some of the most innovative design ideas of the time.

Chinese tea slid in and out of British aesthetic and cultural sensibilities. While its identity remained Chinese, its consumption asserted the evolution of a new and decidedly British domestic ritual. But such cultural slippages commenced at the very source at which tea was procured: the port of Canton where British merchants and ship captains negotiated with Hong merchants to purchase tea. A Chinese export oil painting, made between 1790–1820 by an unknown Chinese artist, highlights some of these transactions. Here, tea crates are packed and weighed under the watchful gaze of European or American ship captains (or supercargoes perhaps?), in anticipation of being ferried to company ships waiting in the distance at Whampoa, the berthing place for foreign ships (Figure 17.2).[19]

---

[16] An East India Company ship was known as an East Indiaman. Canton is modern-day Guangzhou.

[17] Maya Jasanoff, *Edge of Empire: Lives, Culture, and Conquest in the East, 1750–1850* (New York: Vintage Books, 2006), 21. Italics are Jasanoff's. Jane T. Merritt, *The Trouble with Tea: The Politics of Consumption in the Eighteenth-Century Global Economy* (Baltimore, MD: Johns Hopkins University Press, 2017), 51–91.

[18] Maxine Berg, "From Imitation to Invention: Creating Commodities in Eighteenth-Century Britain," *Economic History Review*, 55.1 (2002), 1–30 (12); Frank Trentmann, *Empire of Things: How We Became a World of Consumers, from the Fifteenth Century to the Twenty-First* (New York: HarperCollins, 2016), 89.

[19] Supercargoes were Western traders who oversaw the buying and selling of goods (cargo) in China where strict rules governed commercial transactions. Paul A. Van Dyke and Maria Kar-Wing Mok, *Images of the Canton Factories 1760–1822: Reading History in Art* (Hong Kong: Hong Kong University Press, 2015), xv–xvi; Patrick Connor, *The China Trade 1600–1860* (Brighton: Royal Pavilion, Art Gallery and Museums, published with the assistance of the J. Paul Getty Trust, 1986), 7–9.

Figure 17.2 Unknown Chinese artist, *Tea Production in China*, 1790–1820, oil on canvas, H: 143 cm, W: 205 cm, Peabody Essex Museum, M25794, Museum Purchase with funds donated anonymously, 1993.

Each handmade crate represents a geographical and cultural node, its Chinese identity marked by labels, its wooden contours bearing the imprints of Chinese craftsmanship, its contents plucked, manufactured, and packed by Chinese hands, rendering it a material reminder of the Chinese landscapes of tea cultivation and production that we see interspersed with the cascading hills, valleys, and rivers that stretch far out into the horizon.

Lined with lead and paper, these small wooden boxes convey the need to condense vast geographies of production into portable forms of wealth and capital. But they did not simply transfer a commodity from one global destination to another; rather, they carried a piece of China, its soil and climate in which tea was grown, to different parts of the world.[20] Once loaded onto ships, they were stored in the hull, deep in the lower deck, often with crates of porcelain.[21] "Keep the tea in the coolest place of the Ship," advised the merchant Charles Lockyer, "what is put in the Hold, open the Hatches in fair Weather to give it Air, as often as you have the Opportunity."[22] Lockyer also recommended enclosing tea in "Tutanague" (a type of zinc) and wrapping it in "leaves" before placing the entire package in "Tubs of dry, well season'd," and "unscented" wood.[23] Smallness can therefore be conceptualized as a paradigm of protection and security, the size of the box making it easy to pack the container with materials that would shield the expensive merchandise from salty air and stormy weather.

Chinoiserie

Ushered through the maritime corridors of transnational commerce, the box of tea emerged a global commodity. Containers carrying Hyson, Bohea, Singlo, Gunpowder, Souchong, Pekoe, and Congou teas arrived

---

[20] Li Tana and Paul A. Van Dyke, "Canton, Cancao, and Cochinchina: New Data and New Light on Eighteenth-Century Canton and the Nanyang," *Chinese Southern Diaspora Studies*, 1 (2007), 10–28; Lettsom, *Natural History of the Tea-Tree* (1772), 24. Lettsom describes "square wooden boxes" lined with lead, paper, and dried leaves for transporting tea overseas.

[21] John R. Haddad, *America's First Adventure in China: Trade, Treaties, Opium, and Salvation* (Philadelphia, PA: Temple University Press, 2013), 59–60.

[22] Charles Lockyer, *An Account of the Trade in India: Containing Rules for Good Government in Trade, Price Courants, and Tables: With Descriptions of Fort St. George, Acheen, Malacca, Condore, Canton, Anjengo, Muskat, Gombroon, Surat, Goa, Carwar, Telichery, Panola, Calicut, the Cape of Good-Hope, and St. Helena* (London, 1711), 119.

[23] Ibid., 118.

regularly in Calcutta, Bombay, and Madras from Canton, together with Chinese porcelain, textiles, and lacquer furniture – all advertised in local English newspapers as "China goods."[24] For ships sailing towards Africa, tea was "commonly sold at the Cape [of Good Hope]" where the East India Companies' trade in tea and textiles converged.[25] Philadelphia, Boston, and Charlestown too saw a steady influx of Hyson and Bohea tea, and Chinese export porcelain, throughout the eighteenth century.[26] In London, tea grocers and dealers formed a tea dealers' association and promoted their goods with the help of ornate trade cards, as seen, for instance, in a card published by Timbrell and Harding for "Arnaud & Green Late Blakistons Grocers & Tea Dealers," featuring an open box of dried tea leaves next to canisters of coffee, green tea, and other goods; the card is topped with the shop sign of a "Chinaman's head" in a medallion with decorative scrolls dangling above (Figure 17.3).[27] To partake of a cup of Chinese tea now meant embracing the very fantasy of Chineseness constructed for European taste. It also gestured at an "invented tradition" (borrowing from Benedict Anderson) that centered on a drink, signaling the burgeoning sense of modernity cemented by a wide array of colonial products ranging from tobacco to tea, sugar to spices, and textiles to dyes (among many others). In a sense, the small box of tea pried open the seams of both British taste *and* imagination, enabling its consumers to experience and imagine a modern – and very global – sense of Britishness that relied, sometimes

---

[24] See for instance, "Advertisement," the *Madras Courier*, January 5, 1791; "China Goods, per General Elliott Captain Lloyd, For Sale, at Price's Warehouse," the *Calcutta Gazette; or Oriental Advertiser*, March 3, 1791; "China Goods, for Sale, at Pope, Fairlie, & Campbell's," the *Calcutta Gazette; or Oriental Advertiser*, September 6, 1787; "China Goods," *Bombay Courier*, March 3, 1798.

[25] Lockyer, *Trade in India*, 303. Chris Nierstratz, *Rivalry for Trade in Tea and Textiles: The English and Dutch East India Companies (1700–1800)* (New York: Palgrave Macmillan, 2015), 3.

[26] Bohea tea was advertised regularly in the *American Weekly Mercury* in Philadelphia and the *Boston News-Letter* in the opening decades of the eighteenth century, whereas sales of Hyson tea featured in the *Boston Evening Post* and *Boston Gazette* throughout the 1750s and 1760s. See, for instance, an advertisement for Bohea tea in the *Boston News-Letter*, May 4, 1719, 4; advertisement for Hyson tea in the *Boston Evening Post*, March 11, 1751, 3; advertisement for Bohea tea in the *American Weekly Mercury*, January 26, 1720, 2. On Chinese porcelain, see Robert A. Leath, "'After the Chinese Taste': Chinese Export Porcelain and Chinoiserie Design in Eighteenth-Century Charleston," *Historical Archaeology*, 33.3 (1999), 48–61; Caroline Frank, *Objectifying China, Imagining America: Chinese Commodities in Early America* (Chicago: University of Chicago Press, 2011), 143–173.

[27] The Association of London Tea Dealers counted prominent tea dealers among its leaders, including Richard Twining, who became the chairman of the association in 1784. Hoh-Cheung and Lorna H. Mui, "Smuggling and the British Tea Trade before 1784," *The American Historical Review*, 74.1 (1968), 44–73; *The Twinings in Three Centuries: The Annals of a Great London Tea House 1710–1910* (London: R. Twining, 1910?), 25.

Figure 17.3 Trade card, "Arnaud & Green Late Blakistons, Grocers & Tea Dealers No. 29. Strand," etching, 1792–1799. © The Trustees of the British Museum, Heal, 68.4.

uncomfortably, on foreign things that inevitably raised questions about authenticity.

Labelled "Tea from the East," the Chinese lettering on the box in the trade card – however flawed – advertises the contents of the box as genuine at a time when the practice of adulterating tea was rampant.[28] Between 1724 and 1776, a series of laws threatened steep penalties for harming "the health of His Majesty's subjects," diminishing "Revenue,"

---

[28] I am grateful to Tammy Hong, Andrew W. Mellon Research Assistant in Modern Materials at the National Gallery of Art in Washington DC, for translating the label. Hong notes that the strokes of the Chinese characters are incorrect, thus indicating that they were most

and ruining the "fair trader" by contaminating tea with dyes, drugs, and other additives.[29] If, by proclaiming its "eastern origins," the box of tea pushes back against the possibility of adulteration, it does so by also tapping into what Adam Geczy calls the "decorative armature" of Chinoiserie so fashionable at the time, the motif of a "Chinaman's head" inserting a recognizable visual "cliché" of the Chinese-inspired European aesthetic into the picture space.[30] Positioned as both a cultural *and* commercial fragment whose associations with Chinoiserie lift it out of the realm of commerce and profit, and realign it instead with the aristocratic taste for Chinoiserie, the box crystallizes into a site of tension between the desire for a Chinese commodity and the paradoxical need to flatten out the very idea of "Chineseness" – a tension that further underscored "a cultural displacement from aristocratic property to a commercial order of things."[31]

If anything, the merchandise we see before us is an unmistakable sign of the birth of a new consumer society built upon the cosmopolitan strands of imperial commerce, its Chineseness appealing precisely because it mirrored the growing *British* taste for things Chinese, while simultaneously claiming a space for colonial commodities "dispersed by modern commerce into 'everyday' English life" across the British empire.[32] Boxes and canisters of tea were tangible signs of this expanding space of British domesticity, their smallness representing the influx of modern commerce into the intimate spaces of life where colonial commodities were recalibrating the very registers of British taste. Yet they also asserted the fragmentary nature of this influx, for commodities

---

probably made by a British or European hand that tried to imitate Chinese letters. Email correspondence with Tammy Hong, July 9, 2019.

[29] Thomas Herbert, *The Law on Adulteration, Being the Sale of Food and Drugs Acts, 1875 and 1879* (London, 1884), 8–9, 12; F. Leslie Hart, "A History of the Adulteration of Food Before 1906," *Food, Drug, Cosmetic Law Journal*, 7.1 (1952), 5–22; Judith L. Fisher, "Tea and Food Adulteration, 1834–75," *BRANCH: Britain, Representation and Nineteenth-Century History*, ed. Dino Franco Felluga, extension of *Romanticism and Victorianism on the Net*, www.branchcollective.org/?ps_articles=judith-l-fisher-tea-and-food-adulteration-1834-75 (2012, accessed September 16, 2020).

[30] Adam Geczy, *Fashion and Orientalism: Dress, Textiles and Culture from the 17th to the 21st Century* (New York: Bloomsbury Academic, 2013), 59.

[31] David Porter, *Ideographia: The Chinese Cipher in Early Modern Europe* (Stanford, CA: Stanford University Press, 2001), 138; Eugenia Zuroski Jenkins, *A Taste for China: English Subjectivity and the Prehistory of Orientalism* (New York: Oxford University Press, 2013), 163.

[32] Jenkins, *Taste for China*, 163.

fundamentally embodied bits and pieces of global commerce that trickled into British homes. To be more specific, smallness can be tied to the very idea of a fragment whose mutability and mobility is captured by the tea boxes, canisters, and the "Chinaman's head" – cultural and commercial fragments in and of themselves – that were brought together in the trade card. Broadly speaking, if the fragmentary characterizes the very modernity of imperial commerce, then smallness, by extension, emerges as a metaphor of modernity.

And it was precisely the dialectic between culture and commerce mediated by smallness that was brutally destroyed in the Atlantic Ocean, when the American Sons of Liberty dumped £10,000 worth of Bohea, Congou, Singlo, Souchong, and Hyson teas into Boston Harbor on a wintery night in 1773, stripping away any associations with cultural refinement to reduce the commodity to exactly what it was – a commercial article that created wealth for the East India Company and the British government.[33] As they "hack[ed] away" at the chests, which had fallen into the water, to "ensure their final destruction," tea was mobilized as a powerful political tool to destabilize networks of wealth and power.[34] Quite simply, a Chinese exotic had crystallized into a contested *British* commodity. The morning after the protest, a small lacquered wooden box measuring 25.4 cm high, 33.2 cm wide, and 30.2 cm deep was discovered along the coast at Dorchester Heights, a few miles south of Boston Harbor.[35] One of only two tea chests to have survived today, its empty interior evokes the controversial contents that once stirred Bostonians to violent action and changed the course of a nation's history.[36] None of this would have been feasible without the smallness of the box that made it possible to destroy 340 containers of tea in a single night, producing in the process a spectacle of destruction that dismantled the very material and semiotic thresholds that linked the American colony with British trade and governance.[37]

---

[33] Benjamin L. Carp, *Defiance of the Patriots: The Boston Tea Party & The Making of America* (New Haven, CT: Yale University Press, 2010), 128–129.

[34] Jennifer L. Roberts, *Transporting Visions: The Movement of Images in Early America* (Berkeley: University of California Press, 2014), 58.

[35] The chest is displayed at the Boston Tea Party Ships and Museum. "A Box Worth Keeping," Boston Tea Party Ships and Museum, www.bostonteapartyship.com/partners/a-box-worth-keeping, (accessed November 3, 2016).

[36] A second surviving chest can be seen at the Daughters of the American Revolution Museum, Washington, DC. Lon Schleining, *Treasure Chests: The Legacy of Extraordinary Boxes* (Newtown, CT: Taunton Press, 2003), 28.

[37] Carp, *Defiance of the Patriots*, 129. Roberts, *Transporting Visions*, 59.

Containers and Caddies

At a purely practical level, the Boston Tea Party demonstrated the precariousness of the box of tea. Yet fragility applied not only to boxes of merchandise but also to botanical containers designed to shield seeds and live plants from the physical challenges of maritime travel. With botanical matter traveling more frequently between different ports dotting the expanse of imperial trade, the safety and security of transporting prized plants such as tea became more imperative than ever. But shipping live plants was a tricky business. "Sea spray," insects, and "shipboard animals" posed perennial problems.[38] As a protective measure, the naturalist John Ellis recommended using portable containers that could be housed in one of the ship's cabins and moved to the deck in the right conditions.[39] A cluster of boxes illustrated in Ellis's influential 1770 volume on shipping seeds and plants from the "East-Indies" (Figure 17.4) demonstrates how these containers were fashioned to enclose botanical fragments, each box making visible the need to organize, record, and preserve empirical knowledge (the illustration was later reproduced in John Coakley Lettsom's 1799 edition of his volume on the tea tree).[40] Particularly striking is the box with multiple compartments for carrying "different seeds in earth and cut moss," its interior resembling a small cabinet of curiosities where the thingness of botanical matter, seeds in this instance, was singled out.[41] Boxes could be 0.9 meters long, 38.1 cm wide, and 48.3 cm deep, making them "most convenient for stowing them on board merchant-ships" where there was "very little room to spare."[42]

Just as we saw with the boxes of merchandise, here too the box functions as a container for fragments of tea-growing landscapes; however, it does so not by sealing off its contents but, rather, by opening up plants and seeds to an empirical gaze such that their condition could be carefully monitored during the long and arduous voyage by sea. Smallness therefore facilitated scientific practice, with the size of the box calibrated for

---

[38] Jordan Goodman, "After Cook: Joseph Banks and His Travelling Plants, 1787–1810," *The Historian* (Winter 2016/17), 10–14 (11).

[39] Ibid., 11–12.

[40] John Ellis, *Directions for Bringing over Seeds and Plants, from the East-Indies and Other Distant Countries, in A State of Vegetation* (London, 1770), frontispiece; John Coakley Lettsom, *Natural History of the Tea-Tree with Observations on the Medical Qualities of Tea, and on the Effects of Tea Drinking* (London, 1799), n.p.

[41] Ellis, *Directions*, 8. Luke Keogh points out that tea seeds were very fragile and therefore difficult to transport (*Wardian Case*, 89).

[42] Ellis, *Directions*, 9.

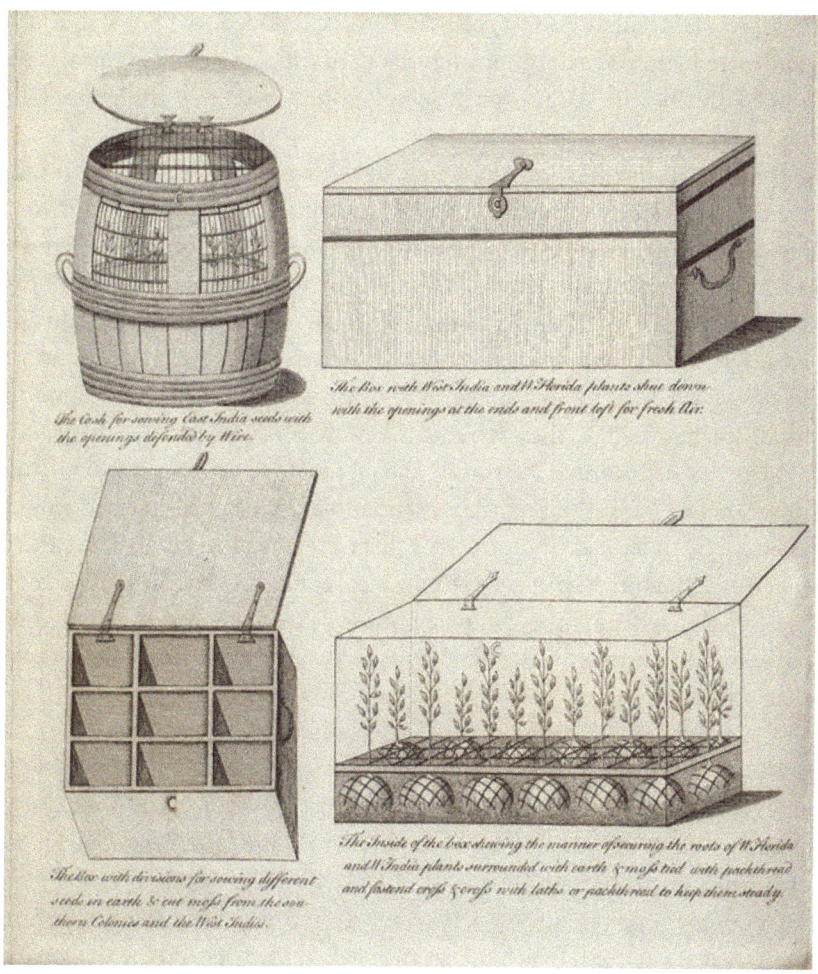

Figure 17.4 Frontispiece, John Ellis, *Directions for Bringing over Seeds and Plants, from the East-Indies and Other Distant Countries, in A State of Vegetation: Together with a Catalogue of Such Foreign Plants as are Worthy of being Encouraged in our American Colonies, for the Purposes of Medicine, Agriculture, and Commerce, to Which is Added the Figure and Botanical Description of a New Sensitive Plant, called Dionæa Muscipula: or, Venus's Fly-Trap* (London, 1770). © Dumbarton Oaks Research Library and Collection, Rare Book Collection, Trustees for Harvard University, Washington, DC.

transporting small saplings and seeds whose survival depended both on the robustness of the tea plant from which they had been extracted and on the conscientiousness of the ship's captain who had agreed to transport them. Their survival also relied on their size, for as Ellis observes, the "smallest" of the "young trees" were "the most likely to succeed, provided they are well rooted."⁴³ Even so, as Lettsom cautioned, the box could not guarantee foolproof safety, for even the hardiest of tea plants might grow "sickly" during the voyage (only one plant had "survived the passage to England" from China).⁴⁴

Botanizing relied on manual contact with plants. Cutting, plucking, pruning, encasing the seeds in wax, embedding the live saplings in soil and digging them out, and lining the seed boxes with "silk paper" were all tasks that relied on the haptic thresholds of scientific study.⁴⁵ Smallness helped engage the senses on an intimate level by drawing the materiality of small botanical fragments into a close dialogue with the human body. And if sensory experiences were integral to the production and codification of botanical knowledge, they were also key to consuming tea, with small caddies and canisters orchestrating the pleasures of tea consumption. The "fragrant leaf" that the English writer Samuel Johnson so relished would be boxed up in tea caddies and chests that were often locked to secure their expensive contents.⁴⁶ In effect, the botanical container and the tea caddy or chest performed similar functions: both were portable boxes designed to safeguard prized plant matter, and both invited the intimacies of corporeal engagement.

The eighteenth-century poet laureate Nahum Tate noted that the "Tea-Leaf, tho' never so good when you Buy, will lose it self (being of a very volatile Spirit,) unless carefully preserv'd in Silver, Pewter, or Tin Boxes, shut close from the Air; and above All, kept from Damps, and Neighbourhood of strong Scents, whether Sweet or Offensive."⁴⁷ The desire to protect tea from competing aromatics was in part driven by the need to preserve the fragrance of tea itself, which brings me back to the tea caddy with which I began this chapter, an artifact whose interior compartments ensured that the "fragrant leaf" was sealed off from any interfering particulate matter. Inserted into a tea party, its size and luxury materials complemented the porcelain and silver surfaces of the small and delicate utensils that shaped the aesthetics of tea drinking, its diminished scale further drawing out the sensory potential of the body. Picking up on this relationship between smallness and corporeal encounters, artists such as Josef Van Aken and William Hogarth translated the ornamentalism of the tea ceremony into

⁴³ Ibid., 9.
⁴⁴ Lettsom, *Natural History of the Tea-Tree* (1772), vi.
⁴⁵ Ellis, *Directions*, 4–6, 9–10.
⁴⁶ James Boswell, *The Life of Samuel Johnson*, 3rd ed., vol. 1 (London, 1799), 363.
⁴⁷ Nahum Tate, *A Poem Upon Tea: With A Discourse on its Sov'rain Virtues; and Directions in the Use of it for Health* (London, 1702), 44.

the ornamentalism of the body. By this I mean that artists frequently drew attention to how their sitters grasped their small and delicate tea utensils, occasionally even exaggerating their gestures to emphasize the conviviality of tea drinking, as we see, for instance, in Hogarth's conversation piece depicting the Strode family (1738), in which hands holding teacups and teapots or touching someone are deployed to convey the chitter-chatter of a tea party.[48]

Unsettling the serenity of the gathering in Hogarth's painting, however, is the tea caddy positioned on the floor, its smallness accentuated by the two dogs seated at opposite ends, each "warily" eying the other as if to guard its territory, each heightening the possibility of the box being accidentally destroyed in a scuffle.[49] With its fragility exposed in the face of a hostile exchange, Hogarth suggests that the caddy is a luxury item worth guarding. As significantly, its proximity to Lady Anne Cecil, the only woman seated at the table, indicates that it is she, rather than the men in the portrait, including her new husband – the wealthy William Strode standing next to her – who is in charge of the tea ceremony. Smallness is therefore bound up with the expectation that a newly married couple will continue the polite tradition of tea drinking to nurture the social bonds of family and friendship. Yet the caddy's precariousness serves as a stark reminder that these bonds could just as easily be broken.

Social bonds often relied on the spatial and temporal flows of objects within households, the mobilities of domestic things shaping and reshaping relationships between employers, servants, friends, and visitors who occupied different domestic spaces at different times. Seen from this perspective, the caddy can be read as a portable object that dispersed the "fragrant leaf" within the domestic interior, its mobility facilitated most probably by a servant who had delivered it to the mistress at the tea table.[50] Locked and opened only when necessary, it emphasized the careful management of tea in wealthy homes, the pleasures of drinking the commodity

---

[48] William Hogarth, *The Strode Family*, c. 1738, Tate, N01153. See Romita Ray, "Storm in a Teacup? Visualising Tea Consumption in the British Empire" in Tim Barringer, Geoff Quilley, and Douglas Fordham (eds.), *Art and the British Empire* (Manchester: Manchester University Press, 2007), 205–222.

[49] Piers Beirne, "Hogarth's Animals," *Journal of Animal Ethics*, 3.2 (2013), 133–162 (148).

[50] By the 1860s, different types of tea were consumed in different spaces of a stately home. For instance, an 1863 household tea inventory from Stowe reveals that souchong was consumed in the parlor and dining room, whereas green tea was consumed throughout the house (including the kitchen). This domestic custom most likely began in the eighteenth century. "Stowe-Store Room 1863–73," Stowe Inventories and Lists, Stowe Papers, ST 259, Huntington Library, San Marino, California.

now mediated by the complex network of social relations that defined an elite household.[51] As such, the smallness of the tea caddy coaxes us to reflect upon the thresholds at which intimacy was forged and possibly even dismantled within these social networks. In small things lie both the pleasures and perils of lived experience.

To conclude, the box of tea emerged a border crosser of sorts whose smallness enabled it to slide in and out of different social spaces and cultural contexts, its diminished scale and size ushering in an expanded sense of the world constructed by the global flows of commerce. And it was this interconnectedness that helped shape the vectors of modernity in eighteenth-century Britain, producing new ways of engaging with – and thinking about – Britain's place in the world, while entrenching the body of the British consumer at the heart of debates and discussions about the moral and physical impact of foreign luxuries such as tea. From this complex orbit of commerce, culture, and science emerged the Industrial Revolution and a Victorian empire that would displace, transplant, and rebrand tea as an imperial commodity cultivated under British supervision in India and Africa.[52] Boxes of tea would continue to grow smaller, paving the way for the small ornamental tins and plastic-wrapped cardboard containers we encounter in today's specialty shops and grocery stores.[53] Smallness therefore lingers on as a tangible sign of modern-day consumption, its reduced scale extending the very forces of modernity put into motion in the eighteenth-century British empire into our contemporary lives.

---

[51] Servants might ask for a few grams of tea in addition to their pay. Trentmann, *Empire of Things*, 90.

[52] Erika Rappaport, *A Thirst for Empire: How Tea Shaped the Modern World* (Princeton, NJ: Princeton University Press, 2017), 85–119.

[53] Large tea chests used to ship out tea from plantations are an exception to the ever-shrinking box of tea.

Afterword

A Thing's Perspective

HANNEKE GROOTENBOER

The Foundling Museum in London contains a remarkable collection of eighteenth-century tokens, small pieces made of metal or textile often carrying inscriptions, that are meant to be worn on the body as jewelry. One of these tokens is a hazelnut that has been pierced with a hole so that it can be worn on a string as a necklace.[1] The token is small in all aspects: it is modest in size; insofar as it serves as a piece of jewelry, it is without any monetary value; and it could be called an artifact, but on the basis of a bare minimum of craftsmanship. Yet despite the fact that it is so ordinary, it is priceless. Like the other tokens in the collection, this hazelnut was left with a foundling by its mother as a gesture of love at a heartbreaking moment of separation. It might well have been the only connection of the child to its family.

As the chapters in this volume demonstrate, in the eighteenth century, small things were often characterized by the contradiction between significance and diminutive size. The emphasis on *things* is essential. Studies on miniatures in the (English) imagination have often focused on literary texts or consider the notion of downsizing more broadly so as to include puppet theaters, architectural models, or the microcosm of curiosity cabinets.[2] The contributors to this volume have gone beyond the notion of the miniature, which always has a properly sized original, by looking at all things small, a category for which the hand has been used as a standard measurement. Small things, and especially the even smaller marks on them, get quickly overlooked.[3] It is easy to disregard the hole in the hazelnut, but when interpreted as a sign, the nut transforms into a fascinating thing with a life story.

---

[1] Token, hazelnut, pierced for a string or cord, eighteenth century, The Foundling Museum, London.

[2] Melinda Alliker Rabb, *Miniature and the English Imagination: Literature, Cognition, and Small-Scale Culture, 1650–1765* (Cambridge: Cambridge University Press, 2019); Susan Stewart, *On Longing: Narratives of the Miniature, the Gigantic, the Souvenir, the Collection* (Durham, NC: Duke University Press, 1993).

[3] For the significance of small marks, see Cynthia Wall's and Chloe Wigston Smith's contributions to this volume (Chapter 3 and Chapter 4 respectively).

Like other small things, the hazelnut has a great impact on our perception. In order to be seen, it demands from us, as beholders, to shift positions, to bend forward or lift it up for closer inspection. When peeping in a doll's house, for instance, the world around us seems to shrink once we visually "enter" its miniaturized domestic space. We start to look not *at* small things but *alongside* them, thereby changing our perspective on the world and our position in it.

Like other trinkets discussed in this volume, the hazelnut-token might have been meaningless to the eyes of the world, but it was an immensely valuable object to the mother who might have hoped to be eventually reunited with her child through this humble yet unique piece of identification. The potential of such unpretentious tokens resonated widely in British novels of the time. Reunions of family members through things – for instance by means of unifying two halves of a coin or through possession of a portrait miniature – was a recurrent motif. Usually, such treasured objects drive the narrative, as protagonists take great pains to protect them with their lives or go to great lengths to find them.

Indeed, in the eighteenth century, small things were on the move. In the wake of the birth of consumerism, people started not only to collect things but carry them around. This was the age of the portable, miniaturized items such as the pocketbook, the pocket watch, and the snuffbox. Even rather unneeded items as pocket globes were produced in great numbers, along with various types of cases in which they were kept. Tie-on pockets worn underneath skirts enabled women to hide their belongings by keeping them close to their bodies.[4] For lower-class women, such as servants, these pockets served as their only form of private space. Men's sewn-in pockets also grew deeper, and in addition they sported watch fobs showing entire collections of dangling trinkets.[5]

Attached to bodies visibly or invisibly, small things had started a life of their own, quite literally: through the popular it-narratives, things were given a voice and were even provided with a kind of (auto)biography, as these narratives present adventures from the perspective of a tiny object, such as a coin, thimble, or pin cushion that, traveling from pocket to pocket, would spy on people's private interactions without them noticing.[6]

---

[4] Barbara Burman and Ariane Fennetaux, *The Pocket: A Hidden History of Women's Lives, 1660–1900* (New Haven, CT and London: Yale University Press, 2019).
[5] For porcelain toys, see Chapter 12 by Patricia F. Ferguson in this volume.
[6] Mark Blackwell (ed.), *The Secret Life of Things: Animals, Objects, and It-Narratives in Eighteenth-Century England* (Lewisburg, PA: Bucknell University Press, 2007).

Part of the attraction of it-narratives is that they allowed readers access to the inside spaces of containers in which these objects were usually kept. The visual equivalent of it-narratives are eye miniatures, tiny portraits of an individual's eye that were mounted on brooches or rings and exchanged as gifts among lovers and family members. Like the protagonists in it-narratives, these eye pictures were not meant to be looked at, but instead served as a kind of camera, following the dealings of their owners through an intensely private form of surveillance.[7]

In his *Philosophical Enquiry* (1757), Edmund Burke compares our experience of the vastness and greatness of the sublime with the perception of little things.[8] He wonders why small things are generally perceived as delightful and finds the answer in power relations inherent in scale. In case of things sublime, Burke explains, we submit to what we admire, but we tend to love small things because they submit to *us*. Burke was only partly right. We may delight in small things because they are tiny, but as the chapters in this volume have shown, they do not quite submit to us. Diminutive things are distinctly slippery, sliding through our fingers as easily as falling outside our field of vision. When our fingers play with small things, small things also play with us, undermining our perception: they are bewildering, such as the miniature guillotines, or witty, in the case of a tape measure nestled inside the shell of a nutmeg that seems to want to determine its own minuteness.[9] Others are downright disobedient, such as miniature books that are illegible, defying our senses even when we squint and try our hardest.[10]

Their charming smallness is deceptive, even manipulative. By perceiving these articles as enchanting, we have unwittingly started to give in to their demands. It is perhaps precisely the way in which they destabilize the traditional separation between subject and object that evokes the sense of delight in us, an awareness that size is not only relative but also fluid,

---

[7] Hanneke Grootenboer, *Treasuring the Gaze: Intimate Vision in Late-Eighteenth-Century Eye Miniatures* (Chicago: University of Chicago Press, 2014).

[8] Edmund Burke, *A Philosophical Enquiry into the Origin of our Ideas of the Sublime and Beautiful* (Cambridge: Cambridge University Press, 2014), section 13, "Beautiful Objects Small," 212.

[9] For the guillotine, see Chapter 9 by Anna McKay in this volume. The nutmeg tape measure is from the seventeenth century: the parchment tape measure, wound around a wire, sits inside the shell of a nutmeg, which is decorated with needlepoint in silk and metal threads; the piece measures 9 × 7 × 2 cm (WA1947.191.325, Ashmolean Museum, Oxford, WA1947.191.325). See Ben Wilkinson-Turnbull, "Measuring Metre: The Sociability of Versified Embroidered Tape Measures" (paper presented at the Small Things in the Eighteenth Century conference, University of York, June 6, 2019).

[10] For illegible miniature books, see Chapter 1 by Abigail Williams in this volume.

and that there is an in-between realm where subject and object overlap. One of the most profound insights that this volume has provided is that the understanding of small things requires "concrete knowledge," to use Claude Levi-Strauss's term, provided to us by our senses through the materiality of things.[11]

---

[11] Claude Lévi-Strauss, *The Savage Mind* (Oxford: Oxford University Press, 1996), chapter 2. A related, more recent term that has been used in the Humanities is "embodied cognition."

Select Bibliography

Abbott, Don Paul. *Rhetoric in the New World*. Columbia: University of South Carolina Press, 1996.

Addams, Chris. "Counterfeiting on the Bermuda Convict Hulk Dromedary." *Journal of the Numismatic Association of Australia*, 18.1 (2007), 3–17.

Allen, Brian. "From Plassey to Seringapatam: India and British History Painting c.1760–c.1800." In Christopher Alan Bayly, ed., *The Raj: India and the British 1600-1947*. London: National Portrait Gallery, 1990, 26–37.

Anderson, Jennifer L. *Mahogany: The Costs of Luxury in Early America*. Cambridge: Cambridge University Press, 2012.

Appadurai, Arjun, ed. *The Social Life of Things*. Cambridge: Cambridge University Press, 1986.

Arnold, Ken. *Cabinets for the Curious: Looking Back at Early English Museums*. New York: Routledge, 2006.

Auslander, Leora. "Beyond Words." *American Historical Review*, 110.4 (2005), 1015–1045.

Bachelard, Gaston. *The Poetics of Space*. 1958. Boston: Beacon Press, 1994.

Baker, Nicholson. *The Size of Thoughts*. 1982. New York: Vintage Books, 1997.

Baldwin, R. C. D. "Sir Joseph Banks and the Cultivation of Tea." *RSA Journal*, 141.5444 (1993), 813–817.

Barnett, Teresa. *Sacred Relics: Pieces of the Past in Nineteenth-Century America*. Chicago: University of Chicago Press, 2013.

Barrell, John. *Imagining the King's Death: Figurative Treason, Fantasies of Regicide, 1793-1796*. Oxford: Oxford University Press, 2000.

Batchelor, Robert. "On the Movement of Porcelains: Rethinking the Birth of Consumer Society as Interactions of Exchange Networks, 1600–1750." In Frank Trentmann and John Brewer, eds., *Consuming Cultures, Global Perspectives: Historical Trajectories, Transnational Exchanges*. Oxford and New York: Berg, 2006, 95–122.

Beaudry, Mary C. *Findings: The Material Culture of Needlework and Sewing*. New Haven, CT: Yale University Press, 2006.

Beckles, Hilary McD. *The First Black Slave Society: Britain's "Barbarity Time" in Barbardos, 1636-1876*. Kingston: The University of the West Indies Press, 2016.

Beirne, Piers. "Hogarth's Animals." *Journal of Animal Ethics*, 3.2 (2013), 133–162.

Benedict, Barbara. "The Moral in the Material: Numismatics and Identity in Evelyn, Addison, and Pope." In Cedric D. Reverend, ed., *Queen Anne and the Arts*. Lewisburg, PA: Bucknell University Press, 2015, 65–83.

Benítez-Rojo, Antonio. *The Repeating Island: The Caribbean and the Postmodern Perspective*. 2nd ed. Durham, NC: Duke University Press, 1996.

Bennett, Jane. "Systems and Things: A Response to Graham Harman and Timothy Morton." *New Literary History*, 43.2 (2012), 225–233.

Berg, Maxine. "From Imitation to Invention: Creating Commodities in Eighteenth-Century Britain." *Economic History Review*, 55.1 (2002), 1–30.

Berg, Maxine. "Women's Consumption and the Industrial Classes of Eighteenth-Century England." *Journal of Social History*, 30.2 (1996), 415–434.

Bermingham, Ann. *Learning to Draw: Studies in the Cultural History of a Polite and Useful Art*. New Haven, CT and London: Yale University Press, 2000.

Bien, David D. "The Army in the French Enlightenment: Reform, Reaction and Revolution." *Past & Present*, 85.1 (1979), 68–98.

Bindman, David. *Shadow of the Guillotine: Britain and the French Revolution*. London: British Museum Press, 1989.

Bingeman, John M. and Arthur T. Mack. "The Dating of Military Buttons: Second Interim Report based on Artefacts Recovered from the 18th-Century Wreck *Invincible*, between 1979 and 1990." *International Journal of Nautical Archaeology*, 26.1 (1997), 39–50.

Blackwell, Mark, ed. *The Secret Life of Things: Animals, Objects, and It-Narratives in Eighteenth-Century England*. Lewisburg, PA: Bucknell University Press, 2007.

Blair, Ann. *Too Much to Know: Managing Scholarly Information before the Modern Age*. New Haven, CT: Yale University Press, 2010.

Bondy, Louis W. *Miniature Books: Their History from the Beginnings to the Present Day*. London: Richard Joseph, 1981.

Bonneuil, Christophe and Jean-Baptiste Fressoz. *The Shock of the Anthropocene*. London and New York: Verso Books, 2016.

Bromer, Anne and Julian Edison. *Miniature Books: 4,000 Years of Tiny Treasures*. New York: Grolier Club, 2007.

Brown, Bill. "Thing Theory." *Critical Inquiry*, 28.1 (2001), 1–22.

Brown, Gillian. "The Metamorphic Book: Children's Print Culture in the Eighteenth Century." *Eighteenth-Century Studies*, 39.3 (2006), 351–362.

Brown, Laura. *Fables of Modernity: Literature and Culture in the English Eighteenth Century*. Ithaca, NY and London: Cornell University Press, 2001.

Buckridge, Steeve O. *The Language of Dress: Resistance and Accommodation in Jamaica, 1760–1890*. Kingston: University of the West Indies Press, 2004.

Buettner, Brigitte. "Past Presents: New Year's Gifts at the Valois Courts, ca. 1400." *The Art Bulletin*, 83.4 (2001), 598–625.

Burman, Barbara and Ariane Fennetaux. *The Pocket: A Hidden History of Women's Lives, 1660–1900*. New Haven, CT and London: Yale University Press, 2019.

Campbell, Timothy. *Historical Style: Fashion and the New Mode of History, 1740–1830*. Philadelphia: University of Pennsylvania Press, 2016.

Candlin, Fiona and Raiford Guins, eds. *The Object Reader*. New York: Routledge, 2009.

Carr, Gilly and Harold Mytum, eds. *Cultural Heritage and Prisoners of War: Creativity behind Barbed Wire*. London: Routledge, 2012.

Casid, Jill. *Sowing Empire: Landscape and Colonization*. Minneapolis: University of Minnesota Press, 2004.

Cavanaugh, Alden and Michael E. Yonan, eds. *The Cultural Aesthetics of Eighteenth-Century Porcelain*. Farnham: Ashgate, 2010.

Chalus, Elaine. "Fanning the Flames: Women, Fashion, and Politics." In Tiffany Potter, ed., *Women, Popular Culture and the Eighteenth Century*. Toronto: University of Toronto Press, 2012, 92–114.

Chandler, David. "'In Sickness, Despair, and in Agony': Imagining the King's Illness 1788–1789." In Tristanne Connolly and Steven Clark, eds., *Liberating Medicine, 1720–1835*. Abingdon: Routledge, 2009, 109–126.

Chico, Tita. *The Experimental Imagination: Literary Knowledge and Science in the British Enlightenment*. Stanford, CA: Stanford University Press, 2018.

Childs, Adrienne L. "Sugar Boxes and Blackamoors: Ornamental Blackness in Early Meissen Porcelain." In Alden Cavanaugh and Michael E. Yonan, eds., *The Cultural Aesthetics of Eighteenth-Century Porcelain*. Farnham, Surrey, and Burlington, VT: Ashgate, 2010, 159–178.

Clery, E. J. "Introduction." In W. S. Lewis, ed., *The Castle of Otranto*, by Horace Walpole. Oxford: Oxford University Press, 1996, vii–xxxiii.

Cohen, Margaret. *The Novel and the Sea*. Princeton, NJ: Princeton University Press, 2010.

Cohen, Margaret. *The Sentimental Education of the Novel*. Princeton, NJ: Princeton University Press, 1999.

Cole, Lucinda. *Imperfect Creatures: Vermin, Literature, and the Sciences of Life, 1600–1740*. Ann Arbor: University of Michigan Press, 2016.

Czisnik, Marianne. "Nelson, Navy, and National Identity." In Quintin Colville and James Davey, eds., *Nelson, Navy & Nation: The Royal Navy & the British People 1688–1815*. London: Conway, 2013, 188–207.

Daly, Gavin. "Napoleon's Lost Legions: French Prisoners of War in Britain, 1803–1814." *History*, 89.295 (2004), 361–380.

Davidson, Hilary. *Dress in the Age of Jane Austen: Regency Fashion*. London: Yale University Press, 2019.

Deetz, James. *Small Things Forgotten: An Archaeology of Early American Life*. 1977. New York: Doubleday, 1996.

Drakard, David. *Printed English Pottery: History and Humour in the Reign of George III*. London: Jonathan Horne, 1992.

Dresser, Madge. "Britannia." In Raphael Samuel, ed., *Patriotism: The Making and Making of British National Identity*. London: Routledge, 1989, 26–49.

Dyer, Serena. *Material Lives: Women Makers in the 18th Century*. London: Bloomsbury, 2021.

Dyer, Serena and Chloe Wigston Smith. "Introduction." In Serena Dyer and Chloe Wigston Smith, eds., *Material Literacy in Eighteenth-Century Britain: A Nation of Makers*. London and New York: Bloomsbury Academic, 2020, 1–15.

Easterby-Smith, Sarah. "Reputation in a Box: Objects, Communication, and Trust in Late 18th-Century Botanical Networks." *History of Science*, 53.2 (2015), 180–208.

Ellis, Markman, Richard Coulton, and Matthew Mauger. *Empire of Tea: The Asian Leaf that Conquered the World*. London: Reaktion, 2015.

Engelbrecht, William. *Iroquoia: The Development of a Native World*. Syracuse, NY: Syracuse University Press, 2005.

Felsenstein, Frank, ed. *English Trader, Indian Maid: Representing Gender, Race, and Slavery in the New World. An Inkle and Yarico Reader*. Baltimore, MD: Johns Hopkins University Press, 1999.

Fennetaux, Ariane. "Female Crafts: Women and Bricolage in Late Georgian Britain." In Maureen Daly Goggin and Beth Fowkes Tobin, eds., *Women & Things, 1750–1950: Gendered Material Strategies*. Farnham: Ashgate, 2009, 91–108.

Fennetaux, Ariane. "Toying with Novelty: Toys, Consumption, and Novelty in Eighteenth-Century Europe." In Bruno Blondé, Natacha Coquery, Jon Stobart, and Ilja Van Damme, eds., *Fashioning Old and New: Changing Consumer Patterns in Western Europe (1650–1900)*. Antwerp: Brepols, 2009, 17–28.

Fennetaux, Ariane. "'Work'd Pocketts to My Intire Sattisfaction': Women and the Multiple Literacies of Making." In Serena Dyer and Chloe Wigston Smith, eds., *Material Literacy in Eighteenth-Century Britain: A Nation of Makers*. London: Bloomsbury, 2020, 18–34.

Festa, Lynn. *Fiction Without Humanity: Person, Animal, Thing in Early Enlightenment Literature and Culture*. Philadelphia: University of Pennsylvania Press, 2019.

Festa, Lynn. "Personal Effects: Wigs and Possessive Individualism in the Long Eighteenth Century." *Eighteenth-Century Life*, 29.2 (2005), 47–90.

Field, Michele and Timothy Millett, eds. *Convict Love Tokens: The Leaden Hearts the Convicts Left Behind*. Kent Town, Australia: Wakefield Press, 1998.

Forsberg, Laura. "Multum in Parvo: The Nineteenth-Century Miniature Book." *Papers of the Bibliographic Society of America*, 110.4 (2016), 403–432.

Galinou, Mireille, ed. *City Merchants and the Arts*. London: Oblong Creative for the Corporation of London, 2004.

Gerritsen, Anne and Giorgio Riello, eds. *The Global Lives of Things: The Material Culture of Connections in the Early Modern World*. New York: Routledge, 2016.

Gerritsen, Anne and Stephen McDowall. "Global China: Material Culture and Connections in World History." *Journal of World History*, 23.1 (2012), 3–8.

Gibson, James J. *The Ecological Approach to Visual Perception*. Boston, MA: Houghton Mifflin, 1979.

Gikandi, Simon. *Slavery and the Culture of Taste*. Princeton, NJ and Oxford: Princeton University Press, 2011.

Girouard, Mark. *Life in the English Country House: A Social and Architectural History*. New Haven, CT and London: Yale University Press, 1978.

Goodman, Jordan. "After Cook: Joseph Banks and His Travelling Plants, 1787–1810." *The Historian* (Winter 2016/17), 10–14.

Goodrich, Amanda. "Radical Popular Attitudes to the Monarchy in Britain during the French Revolution." In Andreas Gestrich and Michael Schaich, eds., *The Hanoverian Succession: Dynastic Politics and Monarchical Culture*. Farnham: Ashgate, 2015, 261–279.

Gowrley, Freya. "Craft(ing) Narratives: Specimens, Souvenirs, and 'Morsels' in A la Ronde's Specimen Table." *Eighteenth-Century Fiction*, 31.1 (2018), 77–97.

Graeber, David. *Toward an Anthropological Theory of Value*. New York: Palgrave Macmillan, 2001.

Greig, Hannah. *The Beau Monde: Fashionable Society in Georgian London*. Oxford: Oxford University Press, 2013.

Grenby, M. O. *The Child Reader, 1700–1840*. Cambridge: Cambridge University Press, 2011.

Groom, Nick. "A Note on the Text." In Horace Walpole, ed., *The Castle of Otranto*. Groom: Oxford University Press, 2014, xxxiv.

Grootenboer, Hanneke. *Treasuring the Gaze: Intimate Vision in Late-Eighteenth-Century Eye Miniatures*. Chicago: University of Chicago Press, 2014.

Grundy, Isobel. "'Slip-Shod Measure' and 'Language of Gods': Barbauld's Stylistic Range." In William McCarthy and Olivia Murphy, eds., *Anna Letitia Barbauld: New Perspectives*. Lewisburg, PA: Bucknell University Press, 2014, 23–36.

Guest, Harriet. *Unbounded Attachment: Sentiment and Politics in the Age of the French Revolution*. Oxford: Oxford University Press, 2013.

Guichard, Charlotte. *Les Amateurs d'art à Paris Au XVIIIe Siècle*. Seyssel: Champ Vallon, 2008.

Guyatt, Mary. "The Wedgwood Slave Medallion." *Journal of Design History*, 13.2 (2000), 93–105.

Haas, Angela M. "Wampum as Hypertext: An American Indian Intellectual Tradition of Multimedia Theory and Practice." *Studies in American Indian Literatures*, 19.4 (2007), 77–100.

Haggerty, John and Sheryllynne Haggerty. "Networking with a Network: The Liverpool African Committee 1750–1810." *Enterprise and Society*, 18.3 (2017), 566–590.

Haggerty, Sheryllyne. "Risk, Risk Networks and Privateering in Liverpool during the Seven Years War, 1756–1763." *International Journal of Maritime History*, 30.1 (2017), 30–51.

Hallett, C. F. E. Hollis. *Forty Years of Convict Labour: Bermuda 1823–1863*. Bermuda: Juniperhill Press, 1999.

Hathaway, Jane. *The Chief Eunuch of the Ottoman Harem: From African Slave to Power-Broker*. Cambridge: Cambridge University Press, 2018.

Hamann, Byron Ellsworth. "How Maya Hieroglyphs Got Their Name: Egypt, Mexico, and China in Western Grammatology since the Fifteenth Century." *Proceedings of the American Philosophical Society*, 152.1 (2008), 1–69.

Hamlett, Jane, Hannah Greig, and Leonie Hannan, eds. *Gender and Material Culture in Britain since 1600*. London: Palgrave, 2015.

Hancock, David. *Citizens of the World: London Merchants and the Integration of the British Atlantic Community, 1735–1785*. Cambridge: Cambridge University Press, 1995.

Harter, Deborah. *Bodies in Pieces: Fantastic Narrative and the Poetics of the Fragment*. Redwood City, CA: Stanford University Press, 1994.

Heesen, Anke te. *The Newspaper Clipping: A Modern Paper Object*. Manchester: Manchester University Press, 2014.

Heesen, Anke te. *The World in a Box: The Story of an Eighteenth-Century Picture Encyclopedia*. Chicago: University of Chicago Press, 1997.

Hellman, Mimi. "Scents and Sensibilities." In Rachel Gotlieb and Karine Tsoumis, eds., *30 Objects 30 Insights: Gardiner Museum*. London: Black Dog, 2014, 104–111.

Holloway, Sally. *The Game of Love in Georgian England: Courtship, Emotions, and Material Culture*. Oxford: Oxford University Press, 2018.

Holm, Christian. "Sentimental Cuts: Eighteenth-Century Mourning Jewelry with Hair." *Eighteenth-Century Studies*, 38.1 (2004), 139–143.

Horowitz, Sarah. *Friendship and Politics in Post-Revolutionary France*. University Park, PN: Penn State University Press, 2013.

Hume, Ivor Noël. *A Passion for the Past: The Odyssey of a Transatlantic Archaeologist*. Charlottesville: University of Virginia Press, 2010.

Hunt, Lynn. "The Experience of Revolution." *French Historical Studies*, 32.4 (2009), 671–678.

Hunt, Tamara L. *Defining John Bull: Political Caricature and National Identity in Late Georgian England*. London: Routledge, 2017.

Hunter, Matthew C. *Wicked Intelligence: Visual Art and the Science of Experiment in Restoration London*. Chicago: University of Chicago Press, 2013.

Hyland, Peter. *The Herculaneum Pottery: Liverpool's Forgotten Glory*. Liverpool: Liverpool University Press, 2005.

Ingold, Tim. *Making: Anthropology, Archaeology, Art and Architecture*. Abingdon: Routledge, 2013.

Irving, Sarah. *Natural Science and the Origins of the British Empire*. London: Pickering & Chatto, 2008.

Jasanoff, Maya. *Edge of Empire: Lives, Culture, and Conquest in the East, 1750–1850*. New York: Vintage Books, 2006.

Jenkins, Eugenia Zuroski. *A Taste for China: English Subjectivity and the Prehistory of Orientalism*. Oxford: Oxford University Press, 2013.

Jung-Chen, Ching. "Tea Parties in Early Georgian Conversation Pieces." *The British Art Journal*, 10.1 (2009), 30–39.

Keene, Melanie. "Familiar Science in Nineteenth-Century Britain." *History of Science*, 52.1 (2014), 53–71.

Kelsey, Penelope Myrtle. *Reading the Wampum: Essays on Hodinöhsö:ni' Visual Code and Epistemological Recovery*. Syracuse, NY: Syracuse University Press, 2014.

Keogh, Luke. *The Wardian Case: How a Simple Box Moved Plants and Changed the World*. Chicago: University of Chicago Press, 2020.

Kitson, Peter J. *Forging Romantic China: Sino-British Cultural Exchange 1760–1840*. Cambridge: Cambridge University Press, 2013.

Klemann, Heather. "The Matter of Moral Education: Locke, Newbery, and the Didactic Book–Toy Hybrid." *Eighteenth-Century Studies*, 44.2 (2011), 223–244.

Kowaleski-Wallace, Elizabeth. *Consuming Subjects: British Women and Consuming Cultures in the Eighteenth Century*. New York: Columbia University Press, 1997.

Knellwolf, Christa. "Robert Hooke's *Micrographia* and the Aesthetics of Empiricism." *The Seventeenth Century*, 16.1 (2001), 177–200.

Kurlansky, Mark. *Salt: A World History*. London: Vintage, 2003.

Lake, Crystal B. *Artifacts: How We Think and Write about Found Objects*. Baltimore, MD: Johns Hopkins University Press, 2020.

Lamb, Jonathan. "The Crying of Lost Things." *English Literary History*, 71.4 (2004), 949–967.

Lamb, Jonathan. *The Things Things Say*. Princeton, NJ: Princeton University Press, 2016.

Landes, Joan. *Visualizing the Nation: Gender, Representation, and Revolution in Eighteenth-Century France*. Ithaca, NY: Cornell University Press, 2018.

Latour, Bruno. "Factures/Fractures: From the Concept of Network to the Concept of Attachment." *Res: Anthropology and Aesthetics*, 36 (1999), 20–32.

Latour, Bruno. "On Using ANT for Studying Information Systems: A Somewhat (Socratic) Dialogue." In Chrisanthi Avgerou, Claudio Ciborra, and Frank Land, eds., *The Social Study of Information and Communication Technology: Innovation, Actors, and Contexts*. Oxford: Oxford University Press, 2004, 62–76.

Latour, Bruno. *Reassembling the Social: An Introduction to Actor-Network-Theory*. Oxford: Oxford University Press, 2007.

Lawson, Ian. "Crafting the Microworld: How Robert Hooke Constructed Knowledge about Small Things." *Notes and Records of the Royal Society*, 70 (2016), 23–44.

Lennard, John. "In/visible Punctuation." *Visible Language*, 45.1/2 (2011), 121–138.

Lévi-Strauss, Claude. *The Savage Mind*. Oxford: Oxford University Press, 1996.

Lewis, Wilmarth Sheldon. *Rescuing Horace Walpole*. New Haven, CT: Yale University Press, 1978.

Liebersohn, Harry. *The Return of the Gift: European History of a Global Idea*. Cambridge and New York: Cambridge University Press, 2011.

Lioi, Anthony. "Delight Is a Slave to Dominion: Awakening to Empire with Richard Ligon's History." In Thomas Hallock, Ivo Kamps, and Karen L. Raber, eds., *Early Modern Ecostudies: From the Florentine Codex to Shakespeare*. New York: Palgrave, 2008, 219–234.

Lloyd, Clive. *Arts and Crafts of Napoleonic and American Prisoners of War, 1756–1816*. Woodbridge: Antique Collectors' Club, 2007.

Lopenzina, Drew. *Red Ink: Native Americans Picking Up the Pen in the Colonial Period*. Albany, NY: SUNY Press, 2012.

Lowe, Lisa. *The Intimacies of Four Continents*. Durham, NC and London: Duke University Press, 2015.

Lugo-Ortiz, Agnes I. and Angela Rosenthal. *Slave Portraiture in the Atlantic World*. New York: Cambridge University Press, 2013.

Lutz, Deborah. "The Dead Still among Us: Victorian Secular Relics, Hair Jewelry, and Death Culture." *Victorian Literature and Culture*, 39.1 (2011), 127–142.

Lynch, Deidre Shauna. "Money and Character in Defoe's Fiction." In John Richetti, ed., *The Cambridge Companion to Daniel Defoe*. Cambridge: Cambridge University Press, 2009, 84–101.

MacGregor, Arthur. "The Cabinet of Curiosities in Seventeenth-Century Britain." In Oliver Impey and Arthur MacGregor, eds. *The Origins of Museums: The Cabinet of Curiosities in Sixteenth- and Seventeenth-Century Europe*. London: House of Stratus, 2001, 201–215.

Mack, A. T., D. R. Houghton, and William Y. Carman. "'Invincible' Buttons." *Journal of the Society for Army Historical Research*, 69.279 (1991), 192–196.

Mack, John. *The Art of Small Things*. London: British Museum, 2007.

Major, Emma. *Madam Britannia: Women, Church, and Nation, 1712–1812*. Oxford: Oxford University Press, 2011.

Markley, Robert. *The Far East and the English Imagination, 1600–1730*. Cambridge: Cambridge University Press, 2006.

Marsh, Ben. *Unravelled Dreams: Silk and the Atlantic World, 1500–1840*. Cambridge: Cambridge University Press, 2020.

Matthew, Patricia A. "A Taste of Slavery: Sugar Bowls, Abolition, and the Politics of Gender." *Eighteenth-Century Fiction*, forthcoming 2022.

Mauss, Marcel. *The Gift: The Form and Reason for Exchange in Archaic Societies*, translator W. D. Halls. New York and London: Routledge, 2002.

Mavhunga, Clapperton Chakanetsa. *The Mobile Workshop: The Tsetse Fly and African Knowledge Production*. Cambridge, MA: MIT Press, 2018.

McGurl, Mark. "Gigantic Realism: The Rise of the Novel and the Comedy of Scale." *Critical Inquiry*, 43.2 (2017), 403–430.

McNeil, Peter. *Pretty Gentlemen: Macaroni Men and the Eighteenth-Century Fashion World*. New Haven, CT: Yale University Press, 2018.

Mee, Jon. *Conversable Worlds: Literature, Contention, and Community 1762 to 1830*. Oxford: Oxford University Press, 2011.

Mee, Jon. *Print, Publicity, and Popular Radicalism in the 1790s: The Laurel of Liberty*. Cambridge: Cambridge University Press, 2016.

Merritt, Jane T. *The Trouble with Tea: The Politics of Consumption in the Eighteenth-Century Global Economy*. Baltimore, MD: Johns Hopkins University Press, 2017.

Mignolo, Walter. *The Darker Side of the Renaissance: Literacy, Territoriality, & Colonization*. Ann Arbor: University of Michigan Press, 1995.

Mintz, Sidney W. *Sweetness and Power: The Place of Sugar in Modern History*. New York: Penguin, 1985.

Mitchell, W. J. T. "Romanticism and the Life of Things: Fossils, Totems and Images." *Critical Inquiry*, 28.1 (2001), 167–184.

Mitsein, Rebekah. "Humanism and the Ingenious Machine: Richard Ligon's *True and Exact History of the Island of Barbados*." *Journal for Early Modern Cultural Studies*, 16.1 (2016), 95–122.

Morgan, Jennifer L. "*Partus sequitur ventrem*: Law, Race, and Reproduction in Colonial Slavery." *Small Axe*, 22.1(55) (2018), 1–17.

Morgan, Kenneth. "Liverpool's Dominance in the British Slave Trade, 1740–1807." In David Richardson, Suzanne Schwarz, and Anthony Tibbles, eds., *Liverpool and Transatlantic Slavery*. Liverpool: Liverpool University Press, 2007, 14–42.

Najmi, Samina. "Naomi Shihab Nye's Aesthetic of Smallness and the Military Sublime." *MELUS*, 35.2 (2010), 151–171.

Navickas, Katrina. "'That Sash Will Hang You': Political Clothing and Adornment in England, 1780–1840." *Journal of British Studies*, 49.3 (2010), 540–565.

Neis, Cordula. "European Conceptions of 'Exotic' Writing Systems in the Seventeenth and Eighteenth Centuries." *Language & History*, 61.1–2 (2018), 39–51.

New, Elisa. "'Both Great and Small': Adult Proportion and Divine Scale in Edward Taylor's 'Preface' and *The New-England Primer*." *Early American Literature*, 28.2 (1993), 120–132.

Newman, Ian. *The Romantic Tavern: Literature and Conviviality in the Age of Revolution*. Cambridge: Cambridge University Press, 2019.

Nierstratz, Chris. *Rivalry for Trade in Tea and Textiles: The English and Dutch East India Companies (1700–1800)*. New York: Palgrave Macmillan, 2015.

Norman, Donald. *The Design of Everyday Things*. Rev. ed. 1990. Cambridge, MA: MIT Press, 2013.

Otto, Paul. "'This is that which … they call Wampum': Europeans Coming to Terms with Native Shell Beads." *Early American Studies: An Interdisciplinary Journal*, 15.1 (2017), 1–36.

Otto, Paul. "Wampum: The Transfer and Creation of Rituals on the Early American Frontier" In Axel Michaels, ed., *Ritual Dynamics and the Science of Ritual*, 5 vols. *Transfer and Spaces*, editors Gita Dharampal-Frick, Robert Langer, and Niles Holger Peterson. Wiesbaden: Harrassowitz Books, 2010, vol. 5, 171–188.

Parker, Rozsika and Griselda Pollock. *Old Mistresses: Women, Art & Ideology*. New York and London: Bloomsbury Academic, 2013.

Parkes, Malcolm B. *Pause and Effect: An Introduction to the History of Punctuation in the West*. Aldershot: Scolar Press, 1992.

Pasanek, Brad. *Metaphors of Mind: An Eighteenth-Century Dictionary*. Baltimore, MD: Johns Hopkins University Press, 2015.

Pastoureau, Michel. *The Devil's Cloth: A History of Stripes and Striped Fabric*, translator Jody Gladding. New York: Columbia University Press, 1991.

Pennell, Sara. "Mundane Materiality, or Should Small Things Still Be Forgotten? Material Culture, Micro-Histories and the Problem of Scale." In Karen Harvey, ed., *History and Material Culture: A Student's Guide to Approaching Alternative Sources*. London: Routledge, 2009, 173–191.

Petroski, Henry. *The Toothpick: Technology and Culture*. New York: Vintage Books, 2008.

Pichichero, Christy. "Le Soldat Sensible: Military Psychology and Social Egalitarianism in the Enlightenment French Army." *French Historical Studies*, 31.4 (2008), 553–580.

Pierson, Stacey. "The Movement of Chinese Ceramics: Appropriation in Global History." *Journal of World History*, 23.1 (2012), 9–39.

Pointon, Marcia. *Brilliant Effects: A Cultural History of Gem Stones and Jewellery*. London: Yale University Press, 2009.

Pointon, Marcia. "'Surrounded with Brilliants': Miniature Portraits in Eighteenth-Century England." *The Art Bulletin*, 83.1 (2001), 48–71.

Porter, David. *The Chinese Taste in Eighteenth-Century England*. Cambridge: Cambridge University Press, 2010.

Porter, David. "A Peculiar but Uninteresting Nation: China and the Discourse of Commerce in Eighteenth-Century England." *Eighteenth-Century Studies*, 33.2 (2000), 181–199.

Porter, Roy. *The Making of Geology: Earth Science in Britain, 1660–1815*. Cambridge: Cambridge University Press, 1977.

Pratt, Stephanie. "The Four Indian Kings." In Jocelyn Hackworth-Jones, ed., *Between Worlds: Voyagers to Britain 1700–1850*. London: National Portrait Gallery, 2007, 22–35.

Prown, Jules David. "The Truth of Material Culture: History or Fiction?" In Jules David Prown and Kenneth Haltman, eds., *American Artifacts: Essays in Material Culture*. East Lansing: Michigan State University Press, 2000, 11–29.

Rabb, Melinda Alliker. *Miniature and the English Imagination: Literature, Cognition, and Small-Scale Culture, 1650–1765*. Cambridge: Cambridge University Press, 2019.

Rappaport, Rhoda. *When Geologists Were Historians, 1665–1750*. Ithaca, NY and London: Cornell University Press, 1997.

Rauser, Amelia. *The Age of Undress: Art, Fashion, and the Classical Ideal in the 1790s*. New Haven, CT: Yale University Press, 2020.

Ray, Romita. "Ornamental Exotica: Transplanting the Aesthetics of Tea Consumption and the Birth of a British Exotic." In Yota Batsaki, Sarah Burke Cahalan, and Anatole Tchikine, eds., *The Botany of Empire in the Long Eighteenth Century*. Washington: Dumbarton Oaks Research Library and Collections, 2016, 259–281.

Ray, Romita. "Storm in a Teacup? Visualising Tea Consumption in the British Empire." In Tim Barringer, Geoff Quilley, and Douglas Fordham, eds., *Art and the British Empire*. Manchester: Manchester University Press, 2007, 205–222.

Reichardt, Rolf. "The French Revolution as a European Media Event." In *European History Online (EGO)*. Mainz: Leibniz Institute of European History [IEG], 2012.

Reichardt, Rolf and Hubertus Kohle. *Visualizing the Revolution: Politics and the Pictorial Arts in Late Eighteenth-Century France*. London: Reaktion Books, 2008.

Ribeiro, Aileen. *Facing Beauty: Painted Women and Cosmetic Art*. London: Yale University Press, 2011.

Richardson, Robbie. *The Savage and Modern Self: North American Indians in Eighteenth-Century British Literature and Culture*. Toronto: University of Toronto Press, 2018.

Riello, Giorgio. *Cotton: The Fabric that Made the Modern World*. Cambridge: Cambridge University Press, 2013.

Rivett, Sarah. *The Science of the Soul in Colonial New England*. Chapel Hill: University of North Carolina Press, 2011.

Roach, Joseph. *It*. Ann Arbor: University of Michigan Press, 2007.

Roberts, Jennifer L. *Transporting Visions: The Movement of Images in Early America*. Berkeley: University of California Press, 2014.

Rogers, Rebecca. *From the Salon to the Schoolroom: Educating Bourgeois Girls in Nineteenth-Century France*. University Park, PA: Penn State University Press, 2010.

Schmidt, Mario. "Wampum as Maussian *objet social totalitaire*." In Hans P. Hahn and Hadas Weiss, eds., *Mobility, Meaning and Transformation of Things*. Oxford: Oxbow Books, 2013, 133–146.

Sedgwick, Eve Kosofsky. "The Character in the Veil: Imagery of the Surface in the Gothic Novel." *Publications of the Modern Language Association of America*, 96.2 (1981), 255–270.

Sennett, Richard. *The Craftsman*. London: Yale University Press, 2008.

Sharp, Katherine. "Women's Creativity and Display in the Eighteenth-Century British Domestic Interior." In Susie McKellar and Penny Sparke, eds., *Interior Design and Identity*. Manchester: Manchester University Press, 2004, 10–26.

Sheridan, Richard B. *Sugar and Slavery: An Economic History of the British West Indies, 1623–1775*. Baltimore, MD: Johns Hopkins University Press, 1974.

Silver, Sean. *The Mind Is a Collection: Case Studies in Eighteenth-Century Thought*. Philadelphia: University of Pennsylvania Press, 2015.

Sloboda, Stacey. "Displaying Materials: Porcelain and Natural History in the Duchess of Portland's Museum." *Eighteenth-Century Studies*, 43.4 (2010), 455–472.

Smallwood, Stephanie E. *Saltwater Slavery: A Middle Passage from Africa to American Diaspora.* Cambridge, MA: Harvard University Press, 2007.

Smith, Chloe Wigston. "Bodkin Aesthetics: Small Things in the Eighteenth Century." *Eighteenth-Century Fiction*, 31.2 (2019), 271–294.

Smith, Chloe Wigston. *Women, Work, and Clothes in the Eighteenth-Century Novel.* Cambridge: Cambridge University Press, 2013.

Smith, David Chan. "Useful Knowledge, Improvement, and the Logic of Capital in Richard Ligon's True and Exact History of Barbados." *Journal of the History of Ideas*, 78.4 (2017), 549–570.

Smith, Kate. *Material Goods, Moving Hands: Perceiving Production in England, 1700–1830.* Manchester: Manchester University Press, 2014.

Smith, Maya Wassell. "'The fancy work what sailors make': Material and Emotional Creative Practice in Masculine Seafaring Communities." *Nineteenth-Century Gender Studies*, 14.2 (2018).

Smith, Pamela H. *From Lived Experience to the Written Word: Reconstructing Practical Knowledge in Early Modern Europe.* Chicago: University of Chicago Press, forthcoming.

Smith, Pamela H., Amy R. W. Meyers, and Harold J. Cook, eds. *Ways of Making and Knowing: The Material Culture of Empirical Knowledge.* New York and Ann Arbor: Bard Graduate Center/University of Michigan Press, 2014.

Somers, Tim. "Micrography in Later Stuart Britain: Curious Spectacles and Political Emblems." In Rosamund Oates and Jessica Purdy, eds., *Communities of Print: Readers and Their Books in Early Modern Europe.* Leiden: Brill, 2021, 215–237.

Spitta, Sylvia. *Misplaced Objects: Migrating Collections and Recollections in Europe and the Americas.* Austin: University of Texas Press, 2009.

Stafford, Barbara Maria. *Body Criticism: Imaging the Unseen in Enlightenment Art and Medicine.* Cambridge, MA: MIT Press, 1990.

Stallybrass, Peter and Ann Rosalind Jones. "Fetishizing the Glove in Renaissance Europe." *Critical Inquiry*, 28.1 (2001), 114–132.

Starr, Fiona. "An Archaeology of Improvisation: Convict Artefacts from Hyde Park Barracks, Sydney, 1819–1848." *Australasian Historical Archaeology*, 33 (2015), 37–54.

Stewart, Susan. *On Longing: Narratives of the Miniature, the Gigantic, the Souvenir, the Collection.* Durham, NC: Duke University Press, 1993.

Styles, John. *The Dress of the People: Everyday Fashion in Eighteenth-Century England.* New Haven, CT: Yale University Press, 2007.

Styles, John. "Georgian Britain 1714–1837: Introduction." In Michael Snodin and John Styles, eds., *Design and the Decorative Arts: Britain 1500–1900.* London: V&A Publishing, 2001, 154–185.

Styles, John. *Threads of Feeling: The London Foundling Hospital's Textile Tokens, 1740–1770.* London: Foundling Museum, 2010.

Styles, John and Amanda Vickery. *Gender, Taste, and Material Culture in Britain and North America, 1700–1830.* New Haven, CT and London: Yale University Press, 2007.

Sweet, Rosemary. *Antiquaries: The Discovery of the Past in Eighteenth-Century Britain*. London: Hambledon Continuum, 2006.

Taws, Richard. "The Guillotine as Anti-Monument." *Sculpture Journal*, 19.1 (2010), 33–48.

Taws, Richard. *The Politics of the Provisional: Art and Ephemera in Revolutionary France*. University Park, PN: Penn State University Press, 2013.

Thoen, Irma. *Strategic Affection? Gift Exchange in Seventeenth-Century Holland*. Amsterdam: Amsterdam University Press, 2007.

Tilly, Chris, ed. *The Handbook of Material Culture*. London: Sage, 2006.

Trentmann, Frank. *Empire of Things: How We Became a World of Consumers, from the Fifteenth Century to the Twenty-First*. New York: HarperCollins, 2016.

Vallone, Lynne. *Big & Small: A Cultural History of Extraordinary Bodies*. New Haven, CT: Yale University Press, 2017.

Van Horn, Jennifer. *The Power of Objects in Eighteenth-Century British America*. Chapel Hill: University of North Carolina Press, 2017.

Verhoeven, Wil. *Americomania and the French Revolution Debate in Britain, 1789–1802*. Cambridge: Cambridge University Press, 2013.

Vickery, Amanda. *Behind Closed Doors: At Home in Georgian England*. New Haven, CT and London: Yale University Press, 2009.

Vickery, Amanda. *The Gentleman's Daughter: Women's Lives in Georgian England*. New Haven, CT and London: Yale University Press, 1998.

Vizenor, Gerald. *Manifest Manners: Narratives on Postindian Survivance*. 1994. London: University of Nebraska Press, 1999.

Wahrman, Dror. *Mr. Collier's Letter Racks: A Tale of Art & Illusion at the Threshold of the Modern Information Age*. Oxford: Oxford University Press, 2012.

Wakely-Mulroney, Katherine. "Riddling the Catechism in Early Children's Literature." *The Review of English Studies*, 70.294 (2018), 272–290.

Wall, Cynthia Sundberg. *The Prose of Things: Transformations of Descriptions in the Eighteenth Century*. Chicago: University of Chicago Press, 2006.

Walvin, James. *Slavery in Small Things: Slavery and Modern Cultural Habits*. Chichester: Wiley Blackwell, 2017.

Warkentin, Germaine. "In Search of 'The Word of the Other': Aboriginal Sign Systems and the History of the Book in Canada." *Book History*, 2 (1999), 1–27.

Welsh, Doris V. *A Bibliography of Miniature Books, 1470–1965*, Francis J. Weber, ed. Cobleskill, NY: K. I. Rickard, 1989.

Welsh, Doris V. *The History of Miniature Books*. Albany, NY: Fort Orange Press, 1987.

White, Daniel E. "The 'Joineriana': Anna Barbauld, the Aikin Family Circle, and the Dissenting Public Sphere." *Eighteenth-Century Studies*, 32.4 (1999), 510–533.

Wile, Aaron. *Watteau's Soldiers: Scenes of Military Life in Eighteenth-Century France*. New York: Frick Collection, 2016.

Yang, Chi-ming. *Performing China: Virtue, Commerce and Orientalism in Eighteenth-Century England, 1660–1760*. Baltimore, MD: Johns Hopkins University Press, 2014.

Yonan, Michael. "Toward a Fusion of Art History and Material Culture Studies." *West 86th: A Journal of Decorative Arts, Design History, and Material Culture*, 18.2 (2011), 232–248.

Yonan, Michael and Eugenia Zuroski, eds. "Material Fictions." *Eighteenth-Century Fiction*, 31/32.1 (2018/19), 1–18.

Index

Page numbers for illustrations are in *italics*.

A la Ronde (house, Exmouth, Devon, UK), 110, 117–120, *118*
abridgement, 22, 29, 44
accessibility
  concealment and, 27
  effortful, 27–28
  limited, 29
accessories, 240–242
  boxes, 246–247, *246*
  fans, 242, 243, 247–251
    commemorative, 251
    mourning, 252–254, *254*
    United Sisters, 250–251, *250*
  handkerchiefs, 69, 74
  mobility of, 249
  political allegiances, displayed by, 248–249
  toothpick cases, 9, 204, 205
  see also letter cases.
accumulation, 80, 91
Ackermann, Rudolph, 113
Act for the Better Ordering and Governing of Negroes (1661), 233–234
Act of Union (1800), 250
Addison, Joseph, 104
  Dialogues upon the Usefulness of Ancient Medals, 82–83
Ades, Dawn, 110
adulteration, 283
advertisements, 190, 192, 282, *283*
Aesop, 42, 44
affordability, 260
affordance, 65–66, 69, 70, 76
Africa, 282
agency, 2, 5, 107, 266, 293
  of punctuation, 53
  women's, 116
Aglaé Auguié Ney, Duchess of Elchingen and Princess of the Moskova, 207–208, 211–213
Aken, Josef Van, 288
albums, 113

Alders, Brian, 42
Alexander I of Russia, 210
almanacs, 21
ambiguity
  of fictional characters, 55–57, 60–61
  of categorization, 99–100
America
  American Revolutionary War, 166–167
  Boston Tea Party, 285
  buttons, military, 166–167
  Mesoamerica, 130
  tea trade in, 282
  see also Indigenous people.
amusement, 9
Anacreon, 24, *25*
Anderson, Benedict, 282
animacy, 107
animals, 195
  see also insects.
Anne, Queen of Great Britain, 133–135
antiquarianism, 81
  see also numismatism.
ants, 9, 225, 229–232, 236–239
Appadurai, Arjun, 140
Arnaud & Green (tea dealers), 282–284, *283*
Arnold, Ken, 128
art
  amateur, *206*, 211–217, *218*, 254
  calligraphy, miniaturized, 28–29
  collage, 110, 111, 117–120
  collections, 214
  decoupage, 119
  drawings, 209, 217, *218*
  engravings, 228, 229, 231
  painting, 192–193, 204–206
  sailor-made, 146
  see also assemblage.
Ashmole, Elias, 127, 129
Ashmolean Museum (Oxford, UK), 127, 129
assemblage, 8, 111, 112
  équipages/ châtelaines, 189, 190, *191*

assemblage (cont.)
  joineriana, 8, 109–124
    biographical meaning of, 116, 119–120
    herbaria (*hortus siccus*), 113–114
    stained-glass windows, 114–116, *115*
    textiles, 120–124
associations, 91–92
attention, 34, 44, 209
  to detail, 69, 213
  duration of, 86
  excessive, 89
  scale and, 3
Augusta of Bavaria, 215
Auslander, Leora, 266
Australia, 144, 150
authority
  centralized, 166, 168
  failures of, 170
  military, 160, 162–164
  monarchical, 163
  organization and, 159
  rejection of, 156
  structures of, 168
Aynsley, John, 264, *265*

Bacon, Sir Francis, 106
Baker, Nicholson, 50, 52
banknotes, forgery of, 156
Barbados, 9, 99, 225, 233–238
Barbauld, Anna Letitia, 109, 111, 112
  Lessons for Children, 32, 36–43, 46
Barbosa, Duarte, 106
Barrell, John, 262
Bath (UK), 189
Beattie, James, *The theory of language*, 139
Beauharnais, Eugène de *see* Eugène de Beauharnais.
Beauharnais, Hortense de *see* Hortense de Beauharnais.
Beauharnais, Joséphine de *see* Joséphine de Beauharnais.
Beauharnais, Stéphanie de *see* Stéphanie de Beauharnais.
beauty, 4, 228
Beck, Cave, 130
Beckles, Hilary McD., 234
Benedict, Barbara, 81
Benítez-Rojo, Antonio, 238
Bennett, Jane, 2, 3
Bentley, Thomas, 102
Berg, Maxine, 120, 279
Bermuda, 152–154, 156
Berquin, Arnaud, *L'Ami des Enfants*, 208

Bible in Miniature, 23, 24
bibles, miniature, 16, 23–24, 153
biography
  in assemblage, 112, 119–120
  in joineriana, 116
  memoirs, 218–219
  of things, 292
Birmingham (UK), 179, 180
Black figures, 198–203
Blair, Ann, 22
Blount, Thomas, 49
bodies, 2
  child, 38
  dialogue with, 288
  faces, 93
  fingers, 2, 6
  hands, 2, 8, 107, 188
  of animals, 99–100
  potential harms to, 278
  smallness, relationship with, 288
  things, wearing of, 22, 25, 256, 292
  see also accessories; clothing.
Bonaparte, Joséphine (de Beauharnais) *see* Joséphine de Beauharnais.
Bonaparte, Louis *see* Louis Bonaparte.
Bonaparte, Napoleon *see* Napoleon Bonaparte.
bone-work, 143, 146–149, *147*, 152
books
  albums, 113
  bibles, miniature, 16, 23–24, 153
  children's, 7, 21, 31–46
    compendiums, 42
    content of, 34, 36–42
    graduated, 36–37
    miniature, 34–35
    physical size of, 33–35
    religious, 32
    scale in, 38–41
    spiritual urgency of, 32, 35
    subscriptions to, 34
    syntax of, 36–37
    tactility of, 33, 35
    titles of, 32
    toys, seen as, 35
    typography of, 32, 35–38, 42
  colonization and, 130
  commonplace, 113
  craftsmanship of, 20
  feared proliferation of, 22
  microminiature, 16
  miniature, 15–30
    almanacs, 21

bibliography, 20
children's, 23-24, 34-35
collections of, 16, 17
dedications, 17
definitions of, 16, 33
digitization of, 17
for children, 19
haptic challenge of, 24
high cost of, 27
histories, 20, 21
legibility, 7, 17, 25-30
marginalia in, 15, 24
materiality of, 19-20
micrography, 28-29
omissions in, 16, 22-24, 29
paratexts in, 19
readerly trust in, 16, 29
religious, 18, 22-24
scale and, 20-22
scholarship on, 16-17
secular, 19
text in, 24
typography in, 16, 17-18
virtuosity in, 25-30
museum catalogues, 127, 128
small, 6
dexterity, challenge to, 7, 15
legibility, 7
magnifying effect of, 34
Boreman, Thomas
A Description of Three Hundred Animals, 42
Gigantick Histories, 21, 33, 41
Boreman, Zachariah, 193
botany, 113-114, 286-288
Boucher, François, 197
Boyer, Robert, 193
Bradford, William, 132
Brailsford, John, 181
bricolage, 111, 113
Bridge, James, 176, 177, 179
Bridge, John, 174-181, 183
Bristol (UK), 183-185
Britannia (personification of Britain), 10, 240-256, *247*
coins, shown on, 244-246
fans, shown on, 247-251, *250*, *253*
femininity of, 252
material patriotism and, 241-242
miniaturization, 243-247
mourning, symbol of, 252-255, *253*
national, 250-251
political allegiances and, 249
unity, symbol of, *250*

British Museum (London, UK), 129
Britishness, 241-242, 256, 283-285
Bromer, Anne, 16
Brown, Gillian, 33
Brown, Laura, 196
Browne, Thomas, 129
Bryant, Gilbert Ernest, *Chelsea Porcelain Toys*, 194-197, *195*
Buchanan, James, 61, 62
Buckridge, Steeve O., 202
Buffon, Comte de, *Les Époques de la Nature*, 103
Bunyan, John, 48
  The Pilgrim's Progress, 50-51
burial, 105-106
Burke, Edmund, *Philosophical Enquiry*, 293
Burman, Barbara, 70
Butler, Lady Eleanor, 110, 114-116
buttons, 9, 70
  functional, 164
  manufacture of, 166
buttons, military, 158-171
  archaeological discovery of, 167-168
  archaeological value of, 169-170
  British, 164-166, *165*
  classifying function of, 169-170
  decorative, 161
  French, 161-164
  marked with insignia, 158-159
  North American, 166-167
  numbered, 163, 164-166, 168
  patterned, 160
  variation in, 164

cabinets of curiosity, 99
calcite-cave flowstone, 153-154
calligraphy, miniaturized, 28-29
Callot, Jacques, 197
Campan, Henriette, 211, 217
Canton (Guangzhou, China), 279-281, *280*
carnelians, 189, 190
Cartwright, William, 26-27
categorization, 73-74, 99-100, 163
Cavanaugh, Alden, 257
Cecil, Lady Anne, 289
celebrity, 197
centralization, 163, 166
ceramics, 257-273
  Chinese, 105-106
  color, use on, 101
  decoration of, 104, 106
  durability, 97, 194
  enamelled, 246-247, *246*

ceramics (cont.)
　ephemeral, 260
　factories, 102, 190–193, 261, 270
　fragility of, 103–104
　jugs, 269–271, *270*, 272
　Liverpool, 262, 269–271
　miniature figures, 192, 196–197, *199*
　mugs, 262–267, *263*, *265*, *268*
　plaques, 119
　porcelain, 104–106, 192, 279
　　Chinese, 281, 282
　　factories, 190–193
　　seal trinkets, 9, 187–188, *191*
　prices of, 260
　printed, 10, 257–260
　　"The Final Farewell", 257, 262–263, *263*, 272
　　"La Guillotine", 257, 264–273, *263*, *268*, *270*
　　historiographic, 261, 266, 272
　slip-casting, 192
　Staffordshire, 96, *97*, 100, *105*, 262, 264, *265*
　tactility of, 107
　tea accessories, 10, 279
　see also teapots.
Chalus, Elaine, 248
Charles Edward Stuart, Prince, 249
Charlotte of Mecklenburg-Strelitz, Queen of Great Britain, 251
châtelaines/équipages, 189, 190
Chatsworth House (UK), 106
Chelsea porcelain factory (London, UK), 187, 190–193, 200
Chico, Tita, 67
Chieux, Jacques-Louis, 146
childhood, temporality of, 35–36
children, 6, 121–123
　death of, 36
　development of, 36, 38
　labor of, 193
　miniature figures of, 196
　see also books, children's.
China, 105–106, 278–281, *280*
china see ceramics.
Chineseness, 282, 284
chinoiserie, 197–198, *199*, 281–285
Chipstone Foundation (Milwaukee, USA), 100, 104, 107
Choiseul, César, Duc de (comte du Plessis-Praslin), 161
class see social class.
classification, 113, 114, 226, 235, 239
Cleland, John, *Dictionary of Love*, 193

Clery, E. J., 47, 62
closeness, 260, 266, 271
　of observation, 67, 117
clothing
　men's, 172, 292
　patriotism, expressed through, 240
　pockets, 292
　political allegiances, displayed by, 248–249
　slavery, associated with, 201, 202
　see also uniforms, military.
clumsiness, 24, 30
coats of arms, 115, 189
Cochelet, Louise, 209, 214
coins, 7, 80–94
　accumulation of, 80
　affordability of, 81
　as biographical objects, 90–91
　Britannia on, 244–246
　commemorative, 85
　damage to, 91
　definition of, 84
　diffusion of, 84–85
　durability of, 81–82, 85
　engraved, as love tokens, 151
　forgery of, 155
　historical value of, 84
　materiality of, 81–82, 88–89
　melting down of, 87–88
　patriotic images on, 244–246
　perception of, 86–87
　plenitude of, 85–87
　portability of, 85
　recognizability of, 69–70
　remarkableness, 70
　smallness, celebration of, 80
Colden, Cadwallader, *The History of the Five Nations*, 137
Cole, Lucinda, 231, 236
collage, 110, 111, 117–120
collections, 7, 8
　art, 214
　ceramics, 272
　of fossils, 99
　herbaria (*hortus siccus*), 113–114
　Indigenous material culture in, 125, 127–129
　libraries, miniature, 34–35
　literary, 109
　of miniature books, 16
　Tradescant, 127, 129
　wampum in, 125, 127–129
collectivity, 231, 236–237
　of making, 147, 152

colonialism, 6, 76, 130, 188, 233–238
  aesthetics of, 277
  Britannia, on monuments to, 244
  commodities of, 284–285
  imagery of, 9
  power of, 168, 243
  Roman, 85–87
color
  buttons, use on, 163
  ceramics, use on, 101
  leather, use on, 174, 178, 183
  paper, 174, 178, 179
  uniforms, use in, 160, 161, 163
commemoration, 241, 243, 266
  on coins/medals, 85
  on fans, 251
  private, 255
commerce *see* trade.
commodification
  of nationhood, 241
  of wampum, 132, 140
commodities, 6
  colonial, 284
  sugar, 95, 185, 233, 237–239
  tea, 274–276, 278–279, 281–283
commonplaceness, 4–5, 64, 68, 76, 196, 258–259
communication, 6
  emotional, 114
  historical, 90–92
  wampum and, 128–132, 136, 138–140
compendiums, 42
comprehension, 8, 23, 32, 131
compression, 15
  formal, 44
  in miniature histories, 21
  temporal, 22
  totality through, 15, 22–25, 29
concealment, 27, 151, 152, 249
Concise Epitome of the History of England, A
  (miniature book), 16
conflict *see* prisoners of war; wars.
connection, emotional, 110
connoisseurship, 16
consumption, 112, 284, 290
  patriotic, 251, 254
  women's, 248
content
  in children's books, 34, 36–42
  vs. form, 19, 20
  scale of, 20, 21
control, 163, 166
convicts, 8, 144
  crafts by, 143, 144, 150–154, *154*

calcite-cave flowstone, 153–154
  erotica, 152
  skeleton keys, 152
earnings of, 155
forgery by, 156
gambling goods, making of, 155
tourist visits to, 151
Corresponding Societies, 258, 266, 267, 269
Cortés, Hernán, 126
costs, 27, 189, 260
country houses, 106–109
crafts, 143–157
  by convicts, 143, 144, 150–154, *154*
    calcite-cave flowstone, 153–154
    erotica, 152
    skeleton keys, 152
  by prisoners of war, 143–150, *147*
  by women, 110–113, 117–121
craftsmanship, 19, 20, 28, 120–121, 279
  transmission of, 146
  virtuosity in, 25–30, 28
craftspeople *see* makers.
crime
  forgery, 155–156
  murder, 182
  theft, 7, 64–76
    dexterity and, 95
    in *The Beggar's Opera*, 72–76
    of letter cases, 182
    of patchwork, 121
    pilfering, 151–152, 155
    vulnerability to, 66
  treason, 267–269
  trials for, 66
crinoidal limestone, 96, 98, 106–107
Cromwell, Oliver, 233, 234
Cruikshank, Isaac, 262, 269–271
cryptography, 131
Cupid, 196, *199*
Cuvier, Georges, 103

damage, 5, 91
Dassier, Jean, *Concise Epitome of the History of England*, 21
Davenport, Thomas, 179
death, 119
  children's, 36
  executions, 156, 257, 261, 264–271, *265*, *270*
  murder, 182
  suicide, 156
  see also mourning.

decay, 80
  of coins/medals, 82–83
  historical, 92
  moral, 83, 88, 89
  perceptual, 79
  through remaking, 88
  resistance of, 81–82
decoration, 4, 120
  ceramic, 104, 106
  interior, 117–120
  ornamental stonework, 106–107
  on seal trinkets, 192–193
decoupage, 119
Deetz, James, 4, 64
defamiliarization, 19
Defoe, Daniel, 48
  Moll Flanders, 51
  The Life of Colonel Jack, 181–182
Derby porcelain factory (UK), 193, 196
description, 3, 229
details
  in joineriana, 117
  loss of, 194
  recall of, 67
  scrutiny of, 266, 271
dexterity, 2, 107
  children's, 35
  in joineriana, 117
  lack of, 24, 30
  small books' challenge to, 15
  and theft, 72
Diaconoff, Suèllen, 219
differentiation, 76
  excessive, 75
  loss of, 74
  in military uniforms, 160–161
  by owners, 7, 64, 66, 68–72
difficulty
  as spiritual exercise, 27–28
  in making, 27
  of use, 7, 15, 24, 107
digital media, and scale, 17
diplomacy, 135, 137–139, 278
disposability, 243
distinctions/distinctiveness
  excessive, 75
  loss of, 74
  to owners, 7, 64, 66, 68–72, 76
divinity, 15, 22, 28–29
Dixon, Thomas, 252
dockyards, 151–153
Dove, John, *An essay on Inspiration*, 139, 140
Downing, George, 234

drawings, 209, 217, *218*
Dresser, Madge, 252
du Radier, J. F. Dreux, *Dictionnaire d'amour*, 193
ductility, 81
Duesbury, William, 193
Dugaw, Dianne, 73
durability, 107, 108
  of coins/medals, 81–82, 85
  of ceramics, 97, 194
  of stone/rock, 96, 97
Dürer, Albrecht, 126
dwarfs, 196–197, *199*
Dyer, Serena, 120

East India Companies, 282
  British, 189, 278
  Dutch, 190
East India House (London, UK), 244, 277
Edgeworth, Abbé (Henry Essex Edgeworth), 261
Edison, Julian, 16
egalitarianism, 266–267
Eginton, Francis, 115
Ellis, John, 99–101, 286, 287
embossing of names, 174, 176, 178, 180, 181, 183
embroidery, 122–123
emotions, 122, 252
  communication of, 114
  connection and, 110
  frustration, 2, 225, 229
  weeping, 252, 261
empire, 6, 10, 76, 188, 236–238
  aesthetics of, 277
  Britannia, on monuments to, 244
  Chinese, 278
  commodities of, 284
  imagery of, 9
  Indigenous languages and, 130
  and metropole, 236
  military organization in, 168–169
  power of, 243
  representations of, 197–203, *199*
  Roman, 85–87
Empson, William, 73
encapsulation, 32
encrinus (fossilized marine animal), 98–101
engravings, 228, 229, 231
Enlightenment, 67, 81, 82
enslaved people, 9, 188, 233–234
ephemerality, 8, 240, 242, 249, 254, 260
équipages/ châtelaines, 189, 190, *191*

erotica, 152, 196, 202
Etruria (Stoke-on-Trent, UK), 102
Eugène de Beauharnais, Duke of Leuchtenberg, 205, 206, 213, 214, 219
Evelyn, John, 232
  Numismata, 83–94
everyday activities, 2, 275
everyday things, 4, 64, 68, 76, 196, 258–259
exchange
  of gifts, 9, 135, 137, 207, 208, 213
  social, 6
executions, 156, 257, 261, 264–271, *265, 270*
exoticism, 188, 197–203, 284

fables, 32, 41, 42, 44
fame, 197
familiarity, 7, 64, 76, 188
fans, 242, 243, 247–251
  commemorative, 251
  mourning, 252–254, *253*
  United Sisters, 250–251, *250*
fashion, 240
fastenings, 174, 178–180, 183
  see also buttons.
feathers, 117
femininity, 188, 212, 252
Fenn, Ellenor, 32, 37
  Cobwebs to Catch Flies, 32, 37–38
  Fables in Monosyllables, 32, 37
  Lilliputian Spectacle de la Nature, 40
Fennetaux, Ariane, 70, 72, 111, 113
Festa, Lynn, 5
Fielding, Henry, 48
  Joseph Andrews, 48, 53–54
  Tom Jones, 48
fingers, 2, 6
First Peoples *see* Indigenous people.
Flahaut, Charles de, 218
Fletcher & Co. (pot printers, Shelton, UK), 262
fob seals *see* seal trinkets.
foreignness, 157, 188, 276, 278, 283
  fears of, 284
  representations of, 197–203
Fores, S. W., 269
form
  vs. content, 19, 20
  and function, 122
Forsberg, Laura, 33, 35
Fort Ticonderoga (USA), 158, 167
fossils, 7, 96, 98–103
Foucault, Michel, 103, 113
found objects, 113, 117, 118

Foundling Museum (London, UK), 121–123, *123*, 291
fragility, 194, 278
  and mobility, 278
  of ceramics, 103–104
  of tea boxes, 278, 289
  of tea plants, 287
  women's, 104
fragments, 109–114, 121–123, 284–286
France, 9, 149–150, 210–212
  army uniforms of, 161–164
  in children's books, 39
Frederick, Prince of Wales, 252
Fremantle, Elizabeth Wynne, 143, 149
French language, 193, 207
French Revolution, 10, 163, 210
  British response to, 258–273
  "Final Farewell" of Louis XVI, 261–263
  historiography, 261, 266, 272
  print culture of, 259–260, 264
  on printed ceramics, 257
  visual culture of, 258
friendships, 9, 210–211
  maintenance of, 207–209, 213
frustration, 2, 225, 229
function, 8
  form and, 122
  of buttons, 164, 169–170
fungibility, 76
furniture, 118–120, *118*
futility, 24

Galley, William, 182
gambling, 153, 155
Garneray, Louis, 148
Garway, Thomas, 275
Gay, John, *The Beggar's Opera*, 7, 66, 72–76
Geczy, Adam, 284
gemstones, 189, 190, 192, 243
gender
  and chinoiserie, 198
  femininity, 188, 212, 252
  syntactical subversion of, 62
Genlis, Stéphanie de, *La Duchesse de la Vallière*, 217–220
geology, 8, 96, 98, 108
  see also stone/rock.
George III of Great Britain, 240, 244, 251, 262
Georgiana Cavendish, Duchess of Devonshire, 248
gestures, 289
  graceful, 103, 107, 188
  typographical, 52

giants, 21, 40–41
Gibson, James J., 65, 67
Gifford, John, *A narrative of the transactions personally relating to Lewis the Sixteenth*, 261
gifts, 9, 115, 116, 204–221
    amateur artworks as, 212–214
    criticism of, 209–210
    economy of, 207–209
    hair in, 215, *216*
    patriotic images on, 247
    portrait miniatures, 214–215, *216*
    reciprocity, 207, 208, 213
    seal trinkets as, 187
    self, sign of, 214–220
    small things as, 206–208
    value of, 207, 208, 212
        financial, 213
        modest, 213–214
        sentimental, 213–214
    wampum, 135, 137
Gikandi, Simon, 200, 236, 239
Gillray, James, 264
Girouard, Mark, 106
glass, 114–116, *115*
Goldsmith, Oliver, *The Vicar of Wakefield*, 181
Goodrich, Amanda, 269
gothic syntax, 7, 47–62
    absence of punctuation and, 54–63
    ambiguous, 54, 58–60
    architecture of, 61–62
    direct speech, representation of, 50–61
    paragraphs, 48, 51, 54, 57, 58, 62
    parentheticals, 51, 52, 53
    quotation marks, 48–54
    sentences, 61–62
    speech-prefixes, 51
Gouellain, Gustave, 272
Gouyn, Charles, 191–192
Graeber, David, 132
Great Britain
    buttons, military, 164–166, *165*
    nationhood of, 241–242, 245, 256
    nations, unity of, 250–251
    naval power of, 245
    see also empire.
Greece, 84
greed, 83, 85, 86
Grenby, M. O., 33
Grew, Nehemiah, 128
Groom, Nick, 54–55
growth, 40–41, 44–45
Grundy, Isobel, 45

Guangzhou (Canton, China), 279–281, *280*
Guérin, Jean Urbain, *Portrait of Queen Hortense*, 215, 216
Guest, Harriet, 258
guillotines
    on printed ceramics, 257, 264–272, *265*, *268*, *270*
    prisoners of war, made by, 143, 149

Haase, H., 194
Haggerty, John, 177
Haggerty, Sheryllyne, 177
hair, 215, *216*
handkerchiefs, 69, 74
handling, 260, 266, 271
hands, 2, 8, 107, 188
Hanway, Jonas, 275
Harman, Graham, 3
Harter, Deborah, 111
Hartlib, Samuel, 232
Haudenosaunee/Iroquois people, 132, 133–37, *134*, 138
Haywood, Eliza
    Fantomina, 51–52
    Love in Excess, 60
Heesen, Anke te, 111, 274
Hellman, Mimi, 188
heraldry, 115, 128
herbaria (*hortus siccus*), 113–114
Hesketh, Anne (later Yarburgh), 183
hierarchies
    material, 5, 172
    social, 208–209
hieroglyphs, 138
Hillam, Harold, 178–179, 181, 183
Hillam, Thomas, 179
historicity, 103
historiography, 261, 266, 272
history
    communication of, 90–92
    knowledge and, 79
    numismatism and, 80, 81, 83, 84, 89, 90–92
    patriotic accessories, told through, 243
Hobbes, Thomas, 83, 93, 94
    Leviathan, 79–80, 82, 87
Hogarth, William, 202, 288
    The Strode Family, 289
Holloway, Sally, 193
Hooke, Robert, 9, 225, 232
    Micrographia, 28–29, 225, 226–233, 236, 238–239
Horowitz, Sarah, 210

Hortense de Beauharnais, Duchess of
    Saint-Leu, Queen Consort
    of Holland, 9, 204–221
  amateur art of, 211–212
  friendships of, 211
  gift giving by, 206–208, 214–215
  gifts given to, 209
  Madame de la Vallière Carmélite,
    miniature copy of, 204–206, *206*,
    213–214, 217, 220–221
  memoirs, 218–219
  political position of, 210–212, 217
  View of Lake Geneva at Prégny, 217, *218*
hugeness *see* largeness.
humor, 195
Hunt, Lynn, 258, 266
Hunter, Matthew C., 229

identification, 163, 167, 168
identity
  ambiguous, 60–61
  collective, 231
  in miniature figures, 197
  national, 279–281, 282
  possessions, evidence of, 182, 189
  typography and, 54, 55–57
  women's, 75
imagination, models of, 79–80
imitation, 279
imperialism, 6, 76, 84, 188, 236–238
  aesthetics of, 277
  Britannia, on monuments to, 243
  commodities of, 284–285
  imagery of, 9
  power of, 168, 243
  Roman, 85–87
impracticality, 7, 15, 24
indentured servants, 233
indexicality, of gift-giving, 215–217
Indigenous languages, 129–131
Indigenous people, 8, 125
  Cherokee, 137, 138
  cultures of
    destruction, 126, 130
    survivance, 126
  England, visits to, 133–137, *134*
  Great Law of Peace, 132
  Haudenosaunee/Iroquois, 132–138,
    134
  Iroquois Confederacy, 133
  literary representations of, 137–138
individualism, 72, 74
  erasure of, 73

information
  children's processing of, 38
  delayed processing of, 82
  management, 22
  perception and, 67
  totality of, 22
inscriptions *see* ownership; marks of.
insects, 225, 228–230
  ants, 9, 225, 229–232, 236–239
  bees, 228
  fleas, 228
insignificance, 4, 112
integrity, material, 104
interchangeability, 76
interior decoration, 117–120
interiority, 16
intersubjectivity, 60
intimacy, 188, 277
  with patritiotic symbols, 245, 247
  and personalization, 254
  science/slavery, 235–236
inversions, of size, 39–40
Ireland, 250–251
Iroquois/Haudenosaunee people, 132,
    133–138, *134*
Isola Bella, Lake Maggiore (Italy), 118

J. G. (author), *A Play-Book for Children*, 37
Jacobitism, 249
Janeway, James, *Token for Children*, 36
Jasanoff, Maya, 279
Jenkins, Eugenia Zuroski, 198
Jerningham, Lady, 148, 152
jewelry, 74, 201
  hair, use in, 215, *216*, 255
  lockets, 255
  mourning, 254–255
  patriotic, 240, 243
  rings, 242
Johnson, Richard, *Lilliputian Library*, 40
Johnson, Samuel, 227
joineriana, 8, 109–124
  biographical meaning of, 116, 119–120
  collage, 110, 111, 117–120
  herbaria (*hortus siccus*), 113–114
  stained-glass windows, 114–116, *115*
  textiles, 120–124
joining, 109, 111, 116, 122
Jones, Ann Rosalind, 2
Joséphine de Beauharnais (Bonaparte), 214
Journal des Dames et des Modes,
    209–210
jugs, 269–272, *270*

juxtapositions, 96, 104, 107
    of fragments, 111
    large/small, 20–22
    meaning, complicated by, 116

Keene, Melanie, 277
Kent, William, 197
Kilner, Dorothy, 37
    Little Stories for Little Folks, 38
knowledge
    accessibility of, 26–28
    historical, 89
    organization of, 113, 114
    production, 6
    scale of, 21
    sensory, 294
    unreliability of, 22
Kohle, Hubertus, 258, 271

labor
    amateur art, 211–217, *218*, 254
    of children, 193
    of prisoners, 155
    spiritual value of, 27–28
    see also crafts; slavery.
Lake, Crystal B., 245
Lamb, Jonathan, 73, 76
Landes, Joan, 258
Lane, William, *Massacre of the French King!*, 267
language
    French, 193, 207
    hieroglyphs, 129
    Indigenous North American, 129–131
    speech circumvented by, 130
    symbolic, 129–131
    universal, 131–132
Laporte, Jean De, 147
largeness, 21, 83
    of fossilized bones, 102
    giants, 21, 40–41
    growth, 40–41, 44–45
    monumentality, 243–244
    production of sense of, 34
    smallness, juxtaposed with, 20–22
    vastness, 98
Latour, Bruno, 2, 3
leather, *175*, 179, 204, 213
    color, use on, 174, 178, 183
    status of, 5, 172
Leclerc, Georges-Louis, 103
Lee, Richard "Citizen", *King Killing*, 267
legibility, 7, 17, 25–30

Lennard, John, 50
letter cases, 9, 172–186, *175*, *184*
    clasps, 174, 178–180, 183
    manufacture of, 179–180
    provenance of, 182
    purchase of, 183
    sale of, 180–181
    slave trade and, 174–179
    social status and, 181–185
Lettsom, John Coakley, 275, 286, 288
Leuchtenberg, Duke of see Eugène de Beauharnais.
Levi-Strauss, Claude, 294
Lewis, W. S., 47, 54, 55
liberalism, 209, 225, 235
libraries, miniature, 34–35
Ligon, Richard, *A True and Exact History of the Island of Barbados*, 9–10, 232–238
Lioi, Anthony, 235
literacy
    aids to, 36, 38, 45
    colonization and, 130
    cultural, 125
    material, 120
    visual, 259, 260
    wampum as form of, 140
Liverpool (UK), 174–179
Locke, John
    Essay Concerning Human Understanding, 131
    Second Treatise, 127
Lockyer, Charles, 281
London Almanacks, 21
longevity, 107, 108
    of coins/medals, 81–82, 85
    of ceramics, 97, 194
Lopenzina, Drew, 130
loss, 5
    see also theft.
Louis Bonaparte, 217
Louis XVI of France, 257, 261–271, *263*, *265*, *268*, *270*
love
    interracial, 232
    language of, 193
    tokens, 150–151, 196, 201, 202
Lowe, Lisa, 225, 235
Lupton, Ellen, 49
luxury, 27, 198, 203, 288, 289
Lynch, Deidre Shauna, 70

Macartney, George, 1st Earl Macartney, 278
Macie, John, 185

Mack, John, 35
Mackenzie, Henry, *The Man of the World*, 138
magnification, 9, 29, 34, 225–231, 238–239
makers
  amateur art by, 211–217, *218*, 254
  artists, 214
  decorators, 192–193
  gift-givers as, 215–217
  jewelers, 192, 214
  of letter-cases, 180–181
  owners as, 243
  seal engravers, 189
  women, 110–113, 117–121
  see also convicts; prisoners of war.
making, 112
  collective, 147, 152
  foregrounding of, 19
  individualizing effect of, 72, 74
  by owners, 254
Marie Antoinette, 257, 261–263, *263*
Markley, Robert, 278
marks of ownership *see* ownership.
marriage, 75–76
Marshall, John, *The Infant's Library*, 34–35, 41, 42
mass production, 192, 194, 198, 244, 249, 255
materialism, 79–80, 82
materiality, 5, 35
  metallic, 80–82, 87, 88–89
materials
  bone-work, 143, 146–149, *147*, 152
  calcite-cave flowstone, 153–154
  convicts, used by, 151–152
  crinoidal limestone, 96, 98, 106–107
  feathers, 117
  gemstones, 189, 190, 192, 243
  hierarchy of, 5, 172
  leather, *175*, 179, 204, 213
    color, use on, 174, 178, 183
    status of, 5, 172
  luxury, 288
  manipulation of, 8
  paper, 117–119, 156
    marbled ('Dutch'), 174, 178, 179
  pilfering of, 151–152, 155
  prisoners, used by, 144
  shells, 113, 117–118, 133
  straw-work, 147–148, *147*
  see also ceramics; jewelry; metals; textiles.
Mauss, Marcel, 207, 214
Mavhunga, Clapperton Chakanetsa, 225
Maximilian I Joseph of Bavaria, 213
Mazuyer, Valérie, 215

McGurl, Mark, 40
McKenzie, D. F., 52
meaning
  biographical, 116, 119–120
  double, 239
  emotional, 122
  of fragments, 111, 112
  juxtaposition and, 116
  symbolic representation of, 129–131
  unstable, 8
  of wampum, 125, 126
medals, 7, 80–94
  accumulation of, 80
  affordability of, 81
  as biographical objects, 89–91
  commemorative, 85
  definition of, 84
  diffusion of, 84–85
  durability of, 81–82, 85
  historical value of, 84
  materiality of, 81–82, 87–89
  melting down of, 87–88
  perception of, 86–87
  plenitude of, 85, 87
  portability, 85
  rust/decay of, 82–83
  smallness, celebration of, 80, 83–84
Mee, Jon, 258
Meissen porcelain factory (Germany), 187, 192, 194, 196
mementos, 150–151, 255
memorials *see* commemoration.
memory, 69, 91–92
  coins/medals, preserved by, 84–85
  cultural, 125
  Indigenous, colonization of, 130
  materialist models of, 79–80
  of travel, 118
men
  clothing of, 172, 292
  personal possessions, 173
mercantile elite, 182–185
mercantilism
  Britishness and, 256
  class and, 176, 181–185
merchants, 177, 178, 179, 181, 182, 185, 279
  see also slave trade.
Mesoamerica, 130
metals
  clasps, 174, 179–180
  copper, 185
  gold, 189
  greed for, 83, 86

metals (cont.)
  lead, 156
  materiality of, 80–82
  pinchbeck, 189
  rust/decay of, 82–83
  seal trinket mounts, 189, 192
  silver, 174, 179, 189
  steel, 179
metaphors
  coins/medals as, 81
  of perception, 82
  treasonous, 269
Metropolitan Museum of Art (New York, USA), 100
micrography, 28–29
microscopy, 9, 28, 225, 226–231, 238–239
Mignolo, Walter, 130
Millar, Andrew, 53
Milton, John, *Paradise Lost*, 19
mimicry, 18
miniatures and miniaturization, 4, 194, 260, 291
  calligraphic, 28–29
  celebration of craft through, 20
  defamiliarization through, 19
  and divinity, 22
  as mimicry, 18
  of Britannia, 243–247
  painting, 204–206
  reliability of, 29–30
  vs. smallness, 92–93
  see also books, miniature.
Mitchell, W. J. T., 102
Mitsein, Rebekah, 235
mobility, 6, 9–10, 241, 284–285, 292
  of domestic objects, 289
  exile, 211, 213, 214, 217, 220
  fragility and, 278
  of gifts, 215
  of accessories, 249
  of ants, 225, 229
  of tea, 276–281
  transport
    of tea, 277–281
    of tea plants, 286–288, *287*
  transportation (punishment), 150–152, 233
  travel, 39–40, 118, 119, 277–281
modernity, 196, 198, 235, 282, 284–285
monarchism, 261–263
monarchy, 163, 166
money
  earnings, 149, 151, 155
  lending of, 176

value, expressed through, 68, 172, 213
  low, 187, 207, 249, 291
  wampum, as currency, 127–128, 137
  wealth, 177, 178, 237
monumentality, 243–244
Moodie, William, *Old English, Scots and Irish Songs with Music*, 18, *18*
morality
  decay of, 83, 88, 89
  lack of, 36
  smallness, enhanced by, 86
Morgan, Jennifer L., 234
Morny, Charles de, 218
mortality, 97
  child, 32, 36
  human, 103, 108
Morton, Timothy, 3
Motraye, Aubry de la, *Travels through Europe*, 201
mourning, 119, 149, 150
  femininity of, 252
  motifs of, 262
  public/private boundaries of, 255
  symbols of, 252–255
mugs, 262–267, *263*, *265*, *268*
multum in parvo, 29, 42, 44
Murray, John George, 262
museum catalogues, 127, 128
museums, 172
mutability, 39–40, 43, 86, 284–285

Najmi, Samina, 187
Napoleon Bonaparte, 149, 150, 204, 210–211
narrative, 227
  it-narratives, 292
  joineriana as form of, 116, 119
  voices, 55–57, 60–61
national identity, 279–282
National Maritime Museum (Greenwich, UK), 146
nationhood, 10, 241–242, 245, 256
natural history, 99–100, 108, 113–114, 232
Navickas, Katrina, 249
Nebrija, Antonio de, 130
needles, 227
needlework, 71–72, 74, 120–123, *123*, 179
Neis, Cordula, 131
Nelson Atkins Museum of Art (Kansas City, USA), 100
Nelson, Horatio, Lord, 149, 150, 245
Newbery, John, 32, 33, 45
  A Little Pretty Pocket-Book, 35
  Nurse Truelove's Gift, 42

The Lilliputian Magazine, 31, 40
Tom Thumb's Folio, 42–45
New-England Primer (children's book), 36
Newman, Ian, 268
Newry (Northern Ireland), 178
Norman, Donald A., 65
numismatism, 7, 79–94
  Addison on, 82–83
  Evelyn on, 83–94
  greed in, 83
  and history, 80, 81, 83, 84, 89–92
  Pope on, 86–87
  and rust/decay, 82–83
  and scale, 87
  smallness, celebration of, 80, 83–84, 89–90

Oakleaf, David, 60
objectivity, 235, 239
objects
  vs. subjects, 293
  vs. things, 2
observation, 113, 227, 239
  in children's books, 38
  close, 67, 117
  see also scrutiny.
Old Bailey court trials, 7, 66
  letter cases, theft of, 182
  patchwork, theft of, 121
  recognition of ownership in, 66–72
Oldenburg, Henry, 232
ontology
  object-oriented, 3
  profusion of, 32
  of smallness, 15
organization, 114
  authority and, 159
  of knowledge, 113
  military, 161, 163, 164, 166–169
ornament, 4, 117–120
  ceramic, 104, 106
  on seal trinkets, 192–193
  stonework, 106–107
ornamentalism, 288
otherness, 97, 108
ownership, 19
  claims of, 67
  evidence of, 64
  of information, 22
  marks of, 23, 65, 68–72
    coins, 69–70
    embossed, 174, 176, 178, 180, 181, 183
    embroidered, 72
    erased, 73–74

  form, 189
  initials, 68, 69
  shop goods, 69
  social status, indicated by, 177, 179, 181–185
  women's, 72, 203
Oyens, Felix de Marez, 42

Paine, Thomas, *Rights of Man*, 266
painting
  miniature, 204–206
  on seal trinkets, 192–193
paper, 117–119, 156
  marbled ('Dutch'), 174, 178, 179
paradoxes
  of accessibility, 27
  of scale, 34, 43
paratexts, 55, 62
Parkes, M. B., 52
Parminter, Elizabeth, 119
Parminter, Jane and Mary, 110, 117–120, 119
part, and whole, 112, 114, 116, 119
  dialogue between, 109
  fragments and, 111–112
  meaning and, 111
  relationship of, 110, 120
Pasanek, Brad, 82
passivity, 2, 249
patchwork, 110, 120–124
Paterson, Samuel, *Joineriana: Or, the Book of Scraps*, 109
patriotism, 10, 149, 240
  coins, images on, 244–246
  fans, shown on, 247–251
  jewelry, expressed through, 243
  material, 241–242
  monumental, 243–244
  mourning and, 252–255
patterns
  on military buttons, 160, 164
  straw-work, 148
  of wampum, 128–129, 132, 136
perception, 67, 65, 292, 293
  of coins/medals, 86–87
  information and, 67
  materialist models of, 79–80, 82
  temporality of, 70, 82
Percivall, Joseph, 185
permanence, 81, 83, 97, 104–106, 108
personalization, 243, 254, 255
  see also ownership, marks of.
perspective, 39, 43–44, 86
Philippe Egalité (Duke of Orléans), 271

Philosophical Transactions of the Royal Society, 99, 101, 232
physiognomy, 93
Pinchbeck, Christopher, 189
Piroux, Lorraine, 140
plants
 herbaria (*hortus siccus*), 113–114
 tea, 286–288, *287*
Plas Newydd (Llangollen, Wales, UK), 110, 114–116, *115*
play, 35
playthings *see* toys.
pleasure, 198
 gifts and, 208, 210
 scale and, 40
 tactile, 188
 of tea consumption, 288, 290
 visual, 89, 193
plenitude, 92, 94
 of coins/medals, 83–87
Plessis-Praslin, César, comte du (Duc de Choiseul), 161
pockets, 292
Pointon, Marcia, 255
politeness, 95, 103, 236, 276, 289
Ponsonby, Sarah, 110, 114–116
Pope, Alexander, 83, 86–87, 104
Pope, David, 177
porcelain, 104–106, 187, 192
 Chinese, 281, 282
 factories, 102–193, 190–193
 seal trinkets, 9, 187–188, *190*
portability, 6, 10, 64, 76, 241
 of coins/medals, 85
 of miniature books, 22
 of tea, 227, 289
 and vulnerability to theft, 66
Portchester Castle (Hampshire, UK), 143, 149
Porter, David, 278
Porter, Roy, 104
portraits, miniature, 2, 214–215, *215*
possessions
 identity and, 182, 189
 personal, 173
 social class and, 177, 179, 184–185, 189
 see also ownership.
posterity, 91–92
Potteries Museum & Art Gallery (Stoke-on-Trent, UK), 101
power, 106, 171
 cultural, 252
 emotional, 252

 feudal, 159
 imbalances of, 278
 imperial, 168, 244
 military, 168
 miniaturization and, 246
 naval, 245
 scale and, 293
 structures of, 263, 267, 285
 symbolic, 245
precision, 15, 24, 27, 30, 168
preservation, 11, 205
 of memory, 84–85
prices, 27, 189, 260
print culture, 20, 254
 advertisements, 190, 192, 282, *284*
 French Revolution, 259
 radical, 259, 267
 trade cards, 282–283, *283*
 see also books.
prison hulk ships, 8, 143, 144
 convicts on, 150–154
 Dromedary, 144, 152–154
 Portland, 152, 255
 prisoners of war on, 145–146
 Prothee, 147
 religion on, 153
prisoners of war, 8
 crafts by, 143–145, *148*
 depots, 143, 156
 earnings of, 155
 forgery by, 155–156
 French, 149
 gambling goods, making of, 155
 increase in numbers of, 145
 markets of work, 149
 materials used by, 144
 as tourist attraction, 148–149
privateering, 177
production
 knowledge, 6
 mass, 192, 194, 198, 244, 249, 255
 tea, *281*
 see also making.
profusion, 92, 94
 of coins/medals, 84, 85, 88
 ontological, 32
propaganda, 260
proportion, 20–22, 24
 see also scale.
prosperity, 9
Protestantism, 153
proverbs, 94
Prown, Jules David, 5

proximity, 260, 266, 271
punctuation, 7
  colon, 51, 54, 61
  commas, 55
  dashes, 52, 54, 55, 57
  diples, 49, 52–53, 55
  exclamation points, 52
  full stops/periods, 62
  inverted commas, 48, 49–50, 52–55
  invisibility of, 50
  quotation marks, 48–55, 57, 58
  reciprocal quality of, 50
  semicolon, 54, 62
  silence, indicated by, 49, 53, 54
puppets, 197
putti, 198, *199*

quilting, 110, 117, 120–124
quipu (Peruvian knot-writing), 131, 138–139

Rabb, Melinda Alliker, 4, 92–93, 240, 249, 259
racism, 200, 238
Radford, Thomas, 262
rarity, 64, 84, 119, 128, 172, 198
reading
  children's, 34, 35
  confusion in, 55, 60–61
  reparative, 235–236
reciprocity
  of gift-giving, 207, 208, 213
  of punctuation, 50
recognizability, 7, 66, 68–72, 76
  of coins, 69–70
  excessive, 75
  loss of, 74, 227
  of patchwork, 121
Recueil de diverses figures chinoise
  (engravings), 197
reform
  age of, 159–160
  military, 163
  of military uniforms, 161
Reichardt, Rolf, 258, 260, 271
relationality, 3
  friendships, 9, 207–211, 213
  personal, 116, 121
relationships, material, 111
relics, 102, 205
religion
  Christianity, 135
  conversion, 201
  devotional objects, 153
  labor and, 27–28

on prison hulk ships, 153
  representation of, 262
  sin, 36
remaking, 87–88
remarkableness, 67, 70–72, 74
repetition, 23
Repository of the Arts (shop, Strand, London, UK), 113
republicanism, 266–269
respectability, 276
Restriction Period, 156
reunion, 122, 292
Revolution, 149
Rich, Jeremiah, *The Whole Book of Psalms in Meter*, 26–28, *26*
Richard, Fleury, 204–205, 214
  Madame de la Vallière Carmélite, 204, 207, 214, 220
Richardson, Dorothy (b. 1748), 113
Richardson, Samuel, 48
  Clarissa, 54, 181
  Pamela, 65, 181, 197
Richardson, William, *The Indians*, 138
ritual
  gift-giving, 207, 208, 213
  tea drinking, 279, 289
  wampum and, 133, 135, 137
  see also mourning.
Rivett, Sarah, 131
Roach, Joseph, 24
Robertson, Joseph, 50
rock *see* stone.
Rodney, Admiral George Brydges, 1st Baron Rodney, 252–254, *254*
Roma, Spiridione, 277
Roman Catholicism, 153
Rome, 84–87
Rossi, Henri, 219
Royal Society, 99, 128, 232
rust, 82–83
Rysbrack, Michael, 244

Sadler and Green (ceramics firm), 260
sailors/mariners, 279
  captains, 279
  slave-ship captains, 176, 185
Saint-Leu, Duchess of *see* Hortense de Beauharnais.
Sandiford, Keith, 234
Santerre, Antoine Joseph, 234
Sappho, 24, *25*
satire, 271
Saunders, Edmund, 185

Saxe, Comte de (Maurice de Saxe), *Reveries*, 162
scale, 2, 3, 96, 108
  assemblage, essential to, 112
  in children's books, 38–41
  of content, 20, 21
  contrast in, 98
  digital media, absence in, 17
  disruption of, 247
  divine, 15
  divinity, metaphor for, 28–29
  dynamic, 33
  ephemerality and, 8
  human, 15, 97, 108
  mutability of, 39–40
  numismatism and, 87
  paradoxes of, 34, 43
  pleasure and, 40
  power and, 293
  of prehistoric animals, 102
  reduction in, 258–260, 271
  reversals of, 242–247
  in small books, 20–22
  temporal, 20, 98
Scaliger, Justus Caesar, 106
Scheemakers, Peter, 197
Schmidt, Mario, 133
science
  botany, 113–114, 286–288
  natural history, 99–100, 108, 232
  practice of, 286, 288
  scrutiny in, 225
  slavery and, 225, 235
  see also geology.
Scotland, 250–251
scrutiny, 9, 67, 76, 239
  definitions of, 226–227
  detail, required by, 265, 271
  repetition of, 230
  scientific, 225
  truth through, 230
seal trinkets (fob seals), 9, 187–203, *191*, *195*
  animals on, 195
  Black figures on, 198–203
  chinoiserie, 197–198, *199*
  consumers of, 194
  decoration, 192–193
  designs of, 194–197
  empire, representations of, 197–203, *199*
  global market for, 190
  making of, 188–193
  metal mounts of, 189
  miniature figures on, 196–197, *199*
  mottos, 190, 193, 200, 201
  size, 190
seals, 71
secrecy, 131, 151, 152, 249
secularization, 18–19
security, 277, 281, 288, 289
Sedgwick, Eve Kosofsky, 60
selection, 111, 114, 180, 226
selfhood, 214–220
self-referentiality, 248
senses, 82, 259
  smell, 288
  see also perception; sight; touch.
sensibility, 208–209, 215
sentimentalism, 217, 219–220
separation, 114, 122, 291, 293
sewing, 72, 74, 120–123, *123*, 179
sexuality, 196, 202, 217
Shakespeare, William, 197
shapes
  of clasps, 180
  of wampum, 128–132, 136
Shebbeare, John, *Lydia*, 137
shells and shellwork, 113, 117–118, 133
Sheridan, Richard B., 233
Sheringham, H. T., 23
ships
  representations of, 345, 248
  slave, 176
shops, 248
Short Account of the First Rise and Progress of Printing, A (miniature book), 20
Sichterman, Jan Albert, 190
Sichterman, Johanna Maria, 190
sight, 67
  affordance through, 65–66, 69, 70, 76
  see also observation; scrutiny.
significance, 43, 114, 240, 291
  of fragments, 121–123
signification, 130, 132
Silver, Sean, 91
sin, 36
Singleton, Henry, 262
skills, 15, 19–20, 28, 279
  needlework, 120–121
  transmission of, 146
  virtuosity in, 25–30, 28
slave trade, 184–185, 188
  letter cases and, 174–179
  representations of, 200–202
  science, reliance on, 225
slavery, 9, 233–239
  justification of, 234, 237

legislation on, 233–234
reparative reading and, 236
saltwater, 234
science, intimacy with, 225, 235
smallness, 4, 5, 187, 240
celebration of, 80, 83–84, 89–90
children's, 24, 38, 41, 43
colonial aesthetics of, 277
consumption and, 290
disposability of, 243
intimacy and, 284
metaphor for children's literature, 32
vs. miniatures, 92–93
morality, connected to, 86
ontological implications of, 15, 23
sensory engagement through, 288
Smallwood, Stephanie E., 234
smell, 288
Smith, Chloe Wigston, 120
Smith, David Chan, 235
Smith, John (fl. 1755), 49, 53
Smith, Pamela H., 5
Smith, Woodruff D., 276
sociability, 207–209, 212, 289
friendships, 9, 210–211, 213
of tavern culture, 258, 259, 268–269
women's, 95, 116, 121
social class, 9, 120, 173, 179
elite, 188, 195
gentry, 181, 183–185
hierarchies of, 208–209
laboring, 120–123, 267
mercantile elite, 176, 181–182
middling, 120
mobility in, 179
non-elite, 260
plebeian, 66
possessions, indicated by, 177, 179, 181–185, 189
on prison hulk ships, 146
Society of Merchant Venturers (Bristol, UK), 184
solidity, 97, 104, 105, 106–107
songs, 269
souvenirs, 118, 119, 247
see also guillotines.
spareness, stylistic, 32
Spectator, The (journal), 232
Spitta, Sylvia, 126
Spofforth, Robert, *Lord's Prayer*, 28
Sprimont, Nicholas, 190–192, 193
St. James's porcelain factory (London, UK), 187, *191*, 191–192, 201–202

stained-glass windows, 110, 114–116, *115*
Stallybrass, Peter, 2
Steele, Richard, 232
Stéphanie de Beauharnais, Grand Duchess of Baden, 212
Stewart, Susan, 4, 16, 20, 213
stone/rock
assemblages of, 119
calcite-cave flowstone, 153
crinoidal limestone, 96, 98, 106–107
durability of, 96, 97
gemstones, 192, 243
Stower, Caleb, 50
straw-work, 146, *147*–148
Styles, John, 66, 95, 122
subjects, 2, 60, 293
sublime, 293
sugar, 95, 185, 233, 237–239
supercargoes, 279
Sweet, Rosemary, 81
Swift, Jonathan, 277
Gulliver's Travels, 19, 40, 131
symbolism
cross-cultural, 128
of language, 129–131
mourning, 252–255
national, 249–251
patriotic, 245, 247
power and, 245
smallness, enhanced by, 213–214
syntax
in children's books, 36–37
gothic, 7, 47–62
absence of punctuation and, 54–63
ambiguous, 55, 58–60
architecture of, 61–62
direct speech, representation of, 50–61
paragraphs, 48, 51, 54, 57, 58, 62
parentheticals, 51–53
quotation marks, 48–54
sentences, 61–62
speech-prefixes, 51

tables, 118–120, *118*
tactility, 188
and children's books, 33, 35
of ceramics, 107
pleasure of, 2, 188
Tassart, Olive Florence, 194
taste, 198, 236
Tate, Nahum, 288
Taws, Richard, 260, 272

Taylor, Jane and Ann, *Signor Topsy Turvey*, 40–41
Taylor, John, *Verbum Sempiternum*, 15, 22
tea
    accessories, 10, 276, 279
    as commodity, 274–276, 278–279, 281–283
    demand for, 276
    drinking, in Britain, 95–96
    fragrance of, 288
    global trade in, 276, 279, 281–283
    mobility of, 276–281
    plants, 286–288, *287*
    portability of, 277
    production, *280*
tea boxes, 274–290
    Boston Tea Party, survivors from, 285
    botanical containers, 286–288, *286*
    caddies, 274, *275*, 288–290
    fragility of, 278, 289
    representation of, 277, 282–284
    smallness of, 276, 285
teapots, 8, 95–108, *107*
    crinoidal limestone, represented on, 96–98, *97*, 100–101, *101*, 104–108, *105*
tears, 252, 261
temporality, 3
    of childhood, 35–36
    compression of, 21
    deep time, 96, 98, 102–104, 108
    disruption of, 88–89
    geological, 8
    historical, 87, 92
    past time, 7–8
    of perception, 79, 82
    and scale, 98
    scale of, 20
textiles
    Foundling Hospital tokens, 121–123, *123*, 291, 292
    patchwork, 110, 120–124
theft, 7, 64, 67–76
    dexterity and, 72
    of letter cases, 182
    of patchwork, 121
    pilfering, 151, 155
    in *The Beggar's Opera*, 72–76
    vulnerability to, 66
Thelwall, John, 269
Theyanoguin (Hendrick), 135, *136*, 139
things, 284, 284
    agency of, 2, 5, 107, 266, 293
    definition of, 2–3
    everyday, 4–5, 64, 68, 76, 196, 258–259

functions of, 8
historicity of, 103
stolen, 64, 67–76
Thomas, Bronwen, 50, 60
thumb bibles, 16, 23–24
Timbrell and Harding (printers), 282–284
time, 3
    childhood and, 35–36
    compression of, 21
    deep, 96, 98, 102–104, 108
    disruption of, 88–89
    geological, 8
    historical, 87, 92
    past, 7–8
    perception and, 67, 79
    and scale, 98
    scale of, 20
timelessness, 245
toasts, political, 269
tokens
    Foundling Hospital, 121–123, *123*, 291, 292
    love, 150–151, 196, 201, 202
Tom Thumb (character), 43–44
toothpick cases, 9, 13, 205
totality
    compression and, 15, 22–24, 25, 29
    of information, 22
touch, 188
    affordance through, 65
    of ceramics, 107
    and children's books, 33, 35
    pleasure of, 2, 188
toys, 146, *147*, 153
    books as, 35
    porcelain, 187–188
    trade in, 189
trade
    cultural meaning of, 284
    earnings from, 149, 151, 155
    global, 9, 95, 188
        representations of, 197–203, 245, 247
        tea, 276, 279, 281–283
    illicit, in prison crafts, 144, 146, 148–149, 151–152
    in letter cases, 180–181
    maritime, 277–281
    in stolen goods, 73–75
    see also slave trade.
trade cards, 282–284, *284*
Tradescant, John (junior), 127
Tradescant, John (senior), 127
transport
    of tea, 277–281

of tea plants, 286–288, *287*
transportation (punishment), 150–152, 233
travel, 39–40, 118, 119, 277–281
truth, 228, 230
types, 73–74, 99–100, 163
typography, 7, 61
    in children's books, 32, 35–37, 42
    direct speech, representation of, 50–61
    identity and, 54–57
    italics, 51, 52, 57
    miniature books, 16–18
    paragraphs, 48, 51, 54, 57, 58

ubiquity, 4, 236–237
Uffenbach, Zacharias Conrad von, 129
Underhill, John, *News from America*, 127
unification, 116, 131
uniformity, 73, 76
uniforms, military, 9, 159–160, 168, 169
    British, 164–166
    differentiation in, 160–161
    French, 161–164
    North American, 166–167
    procurement, 169
    variation in, 169
United States of America
    American Revolutionary War, 166–167
    Boston Tea Party, 285
    buttons, military, 166–167
    tea trade in, 282
    see also Indigenous people.
unity, symbolism of, 250–251
Universal Magazine, 100
use, difficulty of, 7, 15, 24, 107
utility, 4
    lack of, 15, 18, 24

Valle Crucis Abbey (Llangollen, Wales, UK), 115
Vallone, Lynne, 42
value, 64
    archaeological, 169–170
    cultural, 249
    determination of, 277
    of gifts, 207, 208, 212–214
    historical, 84
    monetary, 68, 172, 213
        low, 187, 207, 249, 291
    sentimental, 64, 213–214
    of stolen goods, 73
    of wampum, 128, 138
Vanmour, Jean-Baptiste, 202
variety, 7, 68, 93, 110, 111

Vasco da Gama, 105
vastness, 98
Verelst, Jan (Johannes), 135, *136*
vermin, 231, 237, 239
vices, 36, 83, 86, 88–89
Vickery, Amanda, 95
Vico, Giambattista, 130
Viette, Monsier de, 261
viewing
    close, 67, 117
    parts and whole, 112
    see also observation; scrutiny.
virtuosity, 25–30, *28*
Vizenor, Gerald, 126
voices, narrative, 55–57, 60–61
vulnerability, 30, 66, 188, 194

Wall, Cynthia, 228
Walpole, Horace, 138
    The Castle of Otranto, 7, 47–48, 54–63, *56*
wampum, 8, 125–140, *134*, *136*
    in British collections, 125, 127–129, 135
    color of, 128, 129
    commodification of, 132, 140
    functions of, 125
        adornment, 127, 128, 138, 139
        ceremonial, 133
        currency, 127–128, 137
        diplomacy, 135, 137–139
        linguistic/communicative, 128–132, 136, 138–140
    gifts of, 135, 137
    Great Law of Peace and, 132
    literary representations of, 137–138
    manufacture of, 132, 133
    meanings of, 125
        cross-cultural, 132–140
        kinship/friendship, 138
    shapes and patterns in, 128–129, 132, 136
Warburton, William, *The Divine Legation of Moses*, 138, 140
Ward, Ned, 126
Warkentin, Germaine, 140
Warmstry, Thomas, *A Box of Spikenard*, 17
wars, 8, 149, 169, 252
    American Revolutionary War, 166–167
    French Revolutionary, 245
    Seven Years' War, 158, 161, 177
    see also prisoners of war.
Washington, George, 166
watches, 71, 190
wealth, 177, 178, 237
wear, 5

wearability, 22, 25, 256, 292
Wedgwood, Josiah, 102, 200
weeping, 252, 261
Weever, John, *An Agnus Dei*, 23
Wentworth, Darcy, 71
White, Daniel E., 109
White, Thomas, *A Little Book for Little Children*, 35
whole, and part, 114, 116, 119
   dialogue between, 109
   fragments and, 111–112
   meaning and, 111
   relationship of, 110, 120
wholeness, 105
Wicksteed, James, 189
Wild, Jonathan, 73
Wilkins, John, *Mercury: or the secret and swift Messenger*, 131
Willems, Joseph, 193
Willett, Henry, 272
Williams, Roger, *A Key into the Language of America*, 129
Wilson, Joseph, 185
Winterthur Museum (Delaware, USA), 100
Wollstonecraft, Mary
   An Historical and Moral view of the origin and progress of the French Revolution, 261
   Vindication of the Rights of Men, 266

women
   agency of, 116
   amateur art by, 211–217, *218*, 254
   Black, 202
   consumers, represented as, 248
   fragility of, 104
   identity of, 75
   laboring classes, 120–123
   makers/craftswomen, 110–113, 117–121
   mothers, 121–123, 252, 291
   ownership by, 72, 203, 292
   political allegiances of, 248–249
   sociability of, 95, 116, 121
   wives, 75
   see also Britannia; femininity.
Wonderful Magazine, The, 264
Wordsworth, William, 103, 108
work *see* labor.
writing, 130, 131, 138–140
   micrography, 28–29

xenophobia, vs. exoticism, 284

Yang, Chi-ming, 198
Yarburgh, Henry, 183, 185
Yarburgh, Hesketh, 183–185
Yarburgh, Sir James, 183
Yonan, Michael E., 5, 257

For EU product safety concerns, contact us at Calle de José Abascal, 56–1º, 28003 Madrid, Spain or eugpsr@cambridge.org.

www.ingramcontent.com/pod-product-compliance
Lightning Source LLC
LaVergne TN
LVHW080304260326
834688LV00039B/1134